PRODUCT LIABILITY LAW IN TRANSITION

Markets and the Law

Series Editor:
Geraint Howells, Lancaster University, UK

Markets and the Law is concerned with the way the law interacts with the market through regulation, self-regulation and the impact of private law regimes. It looks at the impact of regional and international organizations (e.g. EC and WTO) and many of the works adopt a comparative approach and/or appeal to an international audience. Examples of subjects covered include trade laws, intellectual property, sales law, insurance, consumer law, banking, financial markets, labour law, environmental law and social regulation affecting the market as well as competition law. The series includes texts covering a broad area, monographs on focused issues, and collections of essays dealing with particular themes.

Other titles in the series

The Yearbook of Consumer Law 2009
Edited by Deborah Parry, Annette Nordhausen, Geraint Howells, and Christian Twigg-Flesner
ISBN 978 0 7546 7574 7

Statutory Priorities in Corporate Insolvency Law
An Analysis of Preferred Creditor Status
Christopher F. Symes
ISBN 978 0 7546 7519 8

The Future of Consumer Credit Regulation
Creative Approaches to Emerging Problems
Edited by Michelle Kelly-Louw, James P. Nehf, and Peter Rott
ISBN 978 0 7546 7417 7

For more information on this series, visit www.ashgate.com

Product Liability Law in Transition

A Central European Perspective

MAGDALENA TULIBACKA
Oxford University, UK

ASHGATE

Published by
Ashgate Publishing Limited
Wey Court East
Union Road
Farnham
Surrey, GU9 7PT
England

Ashgate Publishing Company
Suite 420
101 Cherry Street
Burlington
VT 05401-4405
USA

www.ashgate.com

British Library Cataloguing in Publication Data
Tulibacka, Magdalena
Product liability law in transition : a Central European perspective. - (Markets and the law)
1. Products liability - Europe, Central
I. Title
346.4'37038

Library of Congress Cataloging-in-Publication Data
Tulibacka, Magdalena.
Product liability law in transition : a Central European perspective / by Magdalena Tulibacka.
p. cm. -- (Series:markets and the law)
Includes index.
ISBN 978-0-7546-4710-2
1. Products liability--Europe. 2. Products liability--Europe, Central. 3. Products liability--European Union countries. 4. Consumer protection--Law and legislation--Europe. 5. Consumer protection--Law and legislation--Europe, Central. 6. Consumer protection--Law and legislation--European Union countries. 7. Law--Europe--International unification. I. Title.

KJC1688.T85 2008
346.2403'8--dc22

2008029507

ISBN 978-0-7546-4710-2
e-ISBN 978-0-7546-8925-6

Mixed Sources
Product group from well-managed forests and other controlled sources
www.fsc.org Cert no. SGS-COC-2482
© 1996 Forest Stewardship Council
FSC

Printed and bound in Great Britain by
TJ International Ltd, Padstow, Cornwall

Contents

Acknowledgements

The process of writing this book spanned over six years. During this time I was inspired and encouraged to continue by the generous support of a great number of people, all of whom I owe the deepest debt of gratitude. Thanks are due to Professor Penny Green, Dr John Paterson and Professor John Flood of the University of Westminster Law School, to Professor Geraint Howells of Lancaster University, to Professor Stephen Weatherill of Oxford University, and to Professor Mirosław Nesterowicz of Nicolas Copernicus University in Poland. Civil servants of Ministries responsible for the implementation of the Product Liability Directive in the Czech Republic, Hungary and Poland, representatives of Central European consumer organizations, as well as academics and practitioners from various Central European universities and law firms assisted me in gathering data for the project. These were in particular: the Czech Ministry of Trade and Industry (Monika Dobiasova), the Hungarian Ministry of Justice and Law Enforcement (Dr Péter Gárdos), the Polish Consumer Federation (especially its President – Małgorzata Niepokulczycka), as well as Cameron McKenna in Budapest. Frequent major changes within civil laws of the Czech Republic, Hungary and Poland needed to be traced regularly, and I wish to thank the following people for their patience and help with keeping me updated on these: Dr Jiri Hradek and Professor Lúbos Tichy (of Charles University, Prague) who provided the translation and the commentary of the draft Czech Civil Code; Monika Dobiasova (of the Czech Ministry of Trade and Industry) who provided the translation of the up-to-date version of the Czech Civil Code; Dr Péter Gárdos (of the Hungarian Ministry of Justice and Law Enforcement) who referred me to the commentary and the translated version of the Hungarian Civil Code; and Aneta Wiewiórska (of the Polish Civil Law Codification Commission) who kindly enabled me to obtain a copy of the 'Green Book' for the Polish draft Civil Code. Dr Christopher Hodges, my colleague at the Centre for Socio-Legal Studies of the University of Oxford, has been an invariable source of inspiration. His enthusiasm for interdisciplinary research is contagious; his open-minded view of consumer law and practice indeed motivated me to significantly widen the focus of the book.

While a considerable number of people assisted in the process of writing the book, any mistakes and omissions are mine only.

List of Abbreviations

ABGB – *Allgemeines Bürgerliches Gesetzbuch* – Austrian General Civil Code of 1811.

Commission of the European Communities Background Brief (1992) – Report by the European Commission *Association Agreements with Poland, Czechoslovakia and Hungary, Background Brief* (Brussels, February 1992).

'The Conception' – Official Commentary to the draft Hungarian Civil Code – *The Conception and Regulatory Syllabus of the New Civil Code*, Codification Committee, Hungarian Ministry of Justice.

The European Community and its Eastern Neighbours Study 1990 – study by the European Commission, DG Information, Communication and Culture, Luxembourg: Office for Official Publications of the European Communities.

Europe and the Challenge of Enlargement Report 1992 – Report by the European Commission, Bulletin of the European Communities, Supplement 3/92.

The Fondazione Rosselli Report – report by Fondazione Rosselli (2004) *Analysis of the Economic Impact of the Development Risk Clause as provided by Directive 85/374/EEC on Liability for Defective Products*, Study for the European Commission.

'The Green Book' – Official Commentary to the Polish Civil Code Reform (2006) – *Optimal vision of the Civil Code in the Republic of Poland* (*Zielona Księga. Optymalna Wizja Kodeksu cywilnego w Rzeczypospolitej Polskiej*), Codification Commission for Polish Civil Law.

The Lovells Report – Report by Lovells (2003) *Product Liability in the European Union. A Report for the European Commission*, February 2003 MARKT 2001/11/D.

The Product Liability Database – British Institute of International and Comparative Law *Product Liability Database* – only available to members of the Product Liability Forum at the Institute <www.biicl.org>; (several reports written for the database were used in this book, with the permission of the authors).

The Third Commission Report on the Product Liability Directive – Report from the Commission to the Council, the European Parliament and the European Economic and Social Committee, *Third report on the application of Council Directive on the approximation of laws, regulations and administrative provisions of the Member States concerning liability for defective products (85/374/EEC of 25 July 1985, amended by Directive 1999/34/EC of the European Parliament and of the Council of 10 May 1999)*. Brussels, 14 September 2006 COM(2006) 496 final.

ZGB – *Zivilgesetzbuch* – Swiss Civil Code of 1907.

Dla mojej rodziny, za odwagę i siłę ducha.

Chapter 1
Introduction

The dynamics of developments in Central European[1] laws, markets and societies are extraordinary. Product liability illustrates them particularly strongly. This initially judge-made area of law, which constituted a response to transformations within contemporary markets, ties together the political, the legal and the socio-economic. As part of 'the laws of the market', although originating in the rules and philosophy of civil liability, it has specific roles, aims and effects. With the use of risk-benefit analysis or social/consumer expectations tests it apportions product risks, compensates damage, and also shapes market behaviour. The book focuses on the process of evolution of product liability (*odpovědnost za výrobek, termékfelelõsség, odpowiedzialność za product*) systems in the Czech Republic, Hungary and Poland. It observes changes within substantive law, developments in court judgements, and doctrinal writings following or sometimes anticipating these developments. However, it also reaches beyond this doctrinal view of product liability law into other legal and non-legal domains, presenting a more contextual inquest into the topic. Particular focus is on effects of the shift from socialism and centrally planned economy to democracy and free market economy. This shift encouraged a very dynamic evolution within the Central European product liability systems. It is shown that the process of transformation of these systems is a multi-disciplinary, multi-level, multi-layer, comprehensive process of change triggered by voluntary convergence with the 'West' (consequence of political and socio-economic changes described here) and further enforced by the obligations of the membership of the European Union. With regard to the latter, the book also illustrates the impact of the Product Liability Directive[2] (which the Central European states implemented). It concludes that, although constituting a crucial milestone for the Central European product liability systems, the implementation of the Directive did not result in a dramatic alteration of the pre-existing position. Nevertheless, ultimately the enquiry sheds some light on the implications of changes taking place in Central Europe for the harmonized European product liability system governed by the Directive.

---

1 Whenever relevant, the Czech Republic (the inquiry here focuses on Czechoslovakia and after its division in 1993 – on the Czech Republic), Hungary and Poland are referred to by common terms 'Central European countries', or 'Central Europe'. See below for a further explanation of the focus on Central Europe.

2 The Council Directive of 25 May 1985 on the approximation of laws, regulations and administrative provisions of the Member States concerning liability for defective products, hereinafter referred to as 'The Directive', or 'Product Liability Directive'.

The legal systems of Central Europe remain in a stage of transition. Although there is no doubt as to their political, legal and socio-economic identity, and links with other Western European civil law systems, the book refers to them as 'post-socialist' in order to reflect the nature and origin of transformations which they are undergoing. The 'transition' referred to in the title of the book consists in the process of return to the civil law roots,[3] return to democracies and free market economies, accession to the European Union, adoption of new consumer protection policies and laws, and establishment of new regulatory and institutional frameworks able to withstand the challenges posed by these developments. The full understanding of the transition requires a comprehensive, interdisciplinary analysis. Such an analysis is impossible in a single monograph, but this book introduces and maps out certain crucial issues. It illustrates the fate of a complex legal mechanism in this transitional turmoil. Product liability can be presented in various contextual arrangements, and the main arrangements are assessed. The analysis focuses on the links of product liability with markets and market laws, and in particular with consumer protection laws. The value of the book, therefore, is on the one hand in the presentation of the development of law and practice of product liability in this often misunderstood region of Europe, and on the other hand in providing a map and some analysis of contextual issues which affect the development of this area of law.

As Central European legal systems started taking part in the process of building the European Union legal system, the transition they are undergoing has gained much wider implications. Product liability law and its practice are excellent examples of the depth of these implications. Although the Product Liability Directive has been implemented as part of the *acquis communautaire*[4] before the countries joined the European Union, the nature and legal force of this legal instrument entail the continuing importance of national laws, practices and legal cultures – thus the continuing importance of the state of transition in Central Europe. Essentially, the 'European product liability law' is the law applied by national courts, and it is argued that such law is the product of these various influences.

In a wider perspective, using product liability law the book offers some insight into the necessary features and requirements of the wider process of legal harmonization between the European Union and the post-socialist Europe. Furthermore, product liability can be seen as the trendsetter within the philosophy and practice of civil liability more universally. Thus, the book may be of some value in presenting the patterns of development within civil liability in the newly enlarged European Union. In the face of the efforts to harmonize European contract

3 This statement links the analysis to the concept of 'legal families'. See Chapter 2 of Part I for the explanation of the place of Central Europe on the map of European legal families.

4 For a further description of this term as well as more details regarding the process of association preceding the enlargement of the EU in 2004 see below (Chapter 3 of Part I).

and tort laws in general, the process of harmonizing European product liability laws can demonstrate the challenges which lie ahead.

THE STARTING POINT – ADDRESSING THE SPECIFICITY OF CENTRAL EUROPEAN PRODUCT LIABILITY LAW

One encounters a surprising phenomenon when starting the enquiry into the topic: it is surprising because one expects an area of Central European law which developed during the times of socialism, especially an area as complex and as 'market-focused' as product liability, to be very different from the law of the 'West'. In fact, the general tendencies in the development of product liability systems in Central Europe were similar to the tendencies which could be observed earlier in the United States of America and in Western Europe. Lack of written provisions concerning product liability was accompanied by attempts of courts to deal with cases of damages caused by defective products. Contractual liability in many respects gave way to tortious liability, the standards of which became more objective, even strict. However, a different picture transpires upon a closer look at the manner and the context in which the product liability systems functioned. At this point one sees noteworthy peculiarities in Central Europe. In fact, regardless of the recent developments – the end of socialism, implementation of the Product Liability Directive, and accession to the European Union (in this exact chronological order) – Central European law of product liability still retains certain idiosyncrasies.[5] The book describes these idiosyncrasies and traces their roots.

The analysis of Central European product liability law is placed within the wider framework of these legal systems in general – as conceptually, historically and politically independent legal units exhibiting quite distinctive features. These features lie at the roots of the idiosyncrasies of Central European product liability law, but other reasons for them should be sought in the essence of the product liability law itself.

THE NATURE OF PRODUCT LIABILITY

Various elements of political, legal and socio-economic nature interact in affecting the way product liability law is shaped, the roles it is supposed to play, and the

5 It is clear that differences can also be observed in the product liability laws and practice of Western European states, even in the laws implementing the Product Liability Directive (see in particular: Lovells Report of 2003; or the Third Commission Report on Product Liability Directive). However, the book emphasizes the specificity of the differences between the 'East' (indicating the 'post-socialist' legal systems) and the 'West' (mostly the countries of Western Europe, as well as the United States of America).

way it operates in practice. History has shown that a number of developments are necessary for a product liability system to emerge. With a large dosage of simplification one may offer the following exegesis. Certain elements of market economy – a market equipped with mechanisms allowing competition between businesses, and the resulting strive for technological progress – are required. This on the one hand strengthens the position of consumers by giving them a greater choice of products, but on the other presents problems for them because of growing powers of businesses and dangers inherent in products. While competition in the market is capable of securing certain standards of conduct and standards of quality and safety of products, such pressures are not always sufficient to safeguard the interests of those who come in contact with those products. Emerging market policies (also involving regulatory market intervention) are additionally supported by the pressures of the legal profession, academics, as well as consumers. State intervention in markets may translate itself into various types of output, of which product liability law is an example.[6] Product liability is meant to provide compensation for those who have been injured or who suffered losses as a result of coming in contact with defective products (Howells 2005b: 202). Based on ideas of fairness it is said to place the burden of compensating on those who caused the damage (following Aristotle's ideas of corrective justice). On the other hand, according to economic analyses it is supposed to realize other postulates: such as the one of risk allocation in the hands of the cheapest cost avoider (Calabresi's strict liability theory and Posner's arguments for negligence liability) (Stapleton 1994).[7] The legal basis and the conceptual framework of product liability law differ depending upon the strength and political context of the developments described above in a particular country. The prevailing factor in building the foundations and determining the scope of product liability law has, however, always been consumer protection.

Normally product liability law accompanies a whole array of other laws protecting consumers. What the contents of these laws are and how they balance the interests of consumers and businesses depends upon the shape and the perception of the market within a particular legal system: how strong the businesses are, how strong and free the competition between them is, what the position of consumers is, why in the mind of those shaping and applying the law they should be protected, from what dangers, and to what extent. Consumer law can take a form of various measures of private law: substantive rules of contract and tort on the one hand

6 Part I contains a brief account of the mechanics and the rationales of state intervention in markets. These issues, and in particular various regulatory theories, are not explored in detail in this book. For a review of some fundamental issues underlying the need for and the scope of regulation, the concept of responsive regulation and the "diffuse sources of power" in the contemporary society – see Ayres and Braithwaite (1992: 3–18); and for an excellent attempt to merge the postulates of responsive regulation and restorative justice see Braithwaite (2002).

7 See Chapter 3 of Part I for an analysis of the roles of product liability.

and the rules of civil procedure on the other; public regulation: quality and safety standards, regulating professions, informational duties of traders; as well as self-regulation mechanisms or codes of practice (Howells and Weatherill 2005: 9–76). Product liability law is a private law measure contained within the laws of contract and, more so, tort. It is to perform very specific functions and thus has been endowed with specific features, but its operation and development are linked to other laws aimed at protecting consumers and indeed to other laws regulating markets.

The phenomena described above have had a crucial impact, which this book explores, on the development of product liability in Central Europe. Recently, a further factor – the 'European product liability law' – has also become material in shaping Central European product liability law.

A FURTHER TIER OF ANALYSIS – THE 'EUROPEAN PRODUCT LIABILITY LAW'

The picture of product liability law within Europe, including Central Europe, becomes much more complex when one takes into account the influences of the European Community law.[8] The relationship between national product liability law and the 'European product liability law' is one of mutual interaction and interdependence. The European Community is determined to harmonize the product liability laws of its Member States, and the Product Liability Directive set out the framework for this harmonized system. Again, here the link of product laws with markets triggered the need for a legislative intervention. However, it also entailed very specific problems in achieving the appropriate balance between consumer interests and business interests. In the European 'internal market',[9] consumers and businesses are encouraged to buy or offer products across the European Union, beyond their home state.[10] Differences in national laws concerning such fundamental issues as product liability may constitute a challenge for consumers as well as a burden on businesses.[11] Yet, in spite of the very clear presence of the Product

8 The European Community (previously European Economic Community) is one of the three Communities establishing the first pillar of the European Union. The law analysed in the book is that of the European Community, not of the European Union as a whole, unless otherwise mentioned. For the nature and history of the European Community see for instance: Weatherill (2000), Craig and de Búrca (2000, 1998), Sandholtz and Stone Sweet (1998), Rhodes and Mazey (1995), Nelsen and Stubb (1994), and the literature referred to there.

9 Chapter 3 of Part I explores the meaning of this notion.

10 See in particular the Consumer Policy Strategy 2007–2013; and A Single Market for Citizens Interim Report 2007 for the emphasis on empowering consumers as well as retailers to explore the benefits of the internal market.

11 This contention has not been universally approved in policy and academic circles. On the one hand one sees the Preamble to the Product Liability Directive using the

Liability Directive aiming to reconcile these differences, harmonization of product liability law within the European Union is far from complete (Sengayen 2007).[12] The European Commission Reports, the Lovells and Fondazione Rosselli Reports, the recent jurisprudence of the European Court of Justice, and jurisprudence of some Member State courts, all mentioned in the book, indicate elements of the complex picture of the 'European product liability law'. The Product Liability Directive is an example of a fragmented, selective harmonization mechanism (von Bar and Drobnig 2002: 42). The Directive completely harmonizes the issues which it covers,[13] while retaining links with national general civil liability rules which have not been harmonized, and allowing for a continuing application of "the rules of contractual and non-contractual liability or a special liability system" which operated when it was notified.[14] Among the Member States of the European Union, significant divergences are clearly noticeable in those pre-existing general and specific liability rules, and even in the interpretation and application of the harmonized rules. Crucial elements of the product liability system which the Directive established but did not clearly define continue to leave scope for differing interpretation by the national legislatures and courts. The manner in which the Directive is enforced and interpreted throughout the European Union is essentially based on cooperation between the European Court of Justice and national legislatures and, more importantly, national courts.[15] The essence of product liability law introduced above entails that the law of each Member State

differences as the rationale for harmonization of product liability laws of the Member States. On the other hand, some very prominent scholars oppose this view. Stapleton expressed doubts regarding the motives for the introduction of the Product Liability Directive, and in particular whether differences in product liability rules truly disrupt trade (1994). Wagner elaborated on this issue in the context of his inquiry into harmonization of European tort law, and concluded that the economic costs of legal diversity and the resulting "uncomfortable situation of the insurance industry" were the most convincing reason for harmonization (2005: 1272–5). See also Howells (2005b: 203–7) who considers how much harmonization with regard to product liability is indeed necessary in the European Union.

12 For a more general perspective on the harmonization of European consumer law, see Wilhelmsson who argues convincingly that if one looks beyond the surface level, substantially there is no 'European consumer law' either (2000: 1–3).

13 Chapter 2 of Part I explores the effect of the Directive, and in particular the notion of 'maximum harmonization'. See the jurisprudence of the European Court of Justice: C-52/00 *Commission of the European Communities v French Republic* 25 April 2002; Case 177/04 *Commission of the European Communities v French Republic* 14 March 2006; Case C-154/00 *Commission of the European Communities v Hellenic Republic*; Case C- 183/00 *Gonzalez Sanchez v Medicina Asturiana*; Case C-203/99 *Veedfald*; Case C-402/03 *Skov AEg v Bilka LavprisvarehuscA/S and Bilka Lavprisvarehus A/S v Jette Mikkelsen, Michael Due Nielsen* 10 January 2006; Case C-127/04 *Declan O'Byrne v Sanofi Pasteur MSD Ltd, Sanofi Pasteur SA* 9 February 2006.

14 Article 13 of the Directive.

15 See Chapter 2 of Part I for an explanation of this relationship and its implications for Central European judicial activity, judicial methodology and legal culture.

of the European Union retains the influences of national laws of obligations, other areas of consumer and market law, and other related legal and non-legal phenomena (such as civil procedures, judicial practice, legal cultures, the shape of private insurance markets, the generosity of social insurance or the shape of health systems). The transition taking place in Central Europe reaches into all these phenomena – and thus this transition has now also become an element of the 'European product liability law'.

THE SCOPE OF ENQUIRY

The law of product liability in Central Europe is observed from the point of view of its historical development in the changing political, economic and social conditions. These are contrasted with the developments within 'Western' laws and markets. The comparative-historical approach is essential because "(o)nly by understanding the 'socialist' past of contemporary Eastern European societies can we properly grasp the current processes of systemic transformation that these societies are now undergoing" (Puchalska-Tych and Salter 1996: 163).

The doctrinal analysis of product liability law in Central Europe is presented as an account of the historical development of this liability system originating in a branch of civil law – the law of obligations. Although its boundaries are delimited by some specific concepts such as product, defect, introduction into circulation, development risk defence, specific approach to the standard of liability (fault or strict liability?) or specific understanding of damage, product liability should not be understood as being entirely separate from "the general organization of civil obligations" (Stapleton 1994: 3). These links can be seen throughout the book, where concepts such as fault, causation or damage are analysed. Product liability law is said to follow, but also sometimes to inspire, changes within the contract and tort philosophy in general. The book contains a jurisprudential look at the developments within fundamental legal constructs of law of obligations, contrasting the Western and Central European approaches, as well as a more detailed elaboration of the law of obligations and its role in product liability, in Chapter 3 of Part I. Central European civil laws are changing with astonishing dynamics. After numerous amendments of the civil codes triggered by the transformation to market democracies, Central European states are presently working on entirely new civil codes. The influence of European Community law can be felt throughout these legal systems. Fundamentally, also for product liability, civil law concepts such as fault, strict liability, causation or damages have already been transformed and further changes are forthcoming. They are examined as far as they are significant in the product liability context.

As explored above, the development of product liability law into what it is today has been influenced by the inception of new ideas about markets and the role of the state in regulating and monitoring markets. In particular, product liability is seen as a crucial part of consumer protection law. The legal thought concerned with product liability law and its harmonization within Europe also focuses on the links between product liability and markets.[16] It is, therefore, paramount that the evolution of Central European product liability law is considered in a similar context. Developments in Czech, Hungarian and Polish market policies and laws, consumer protection policies and laws, and the role of product liability law within these, are contrasted with the Western European developments. When observing changes taking place on the pan-European level, the book focuses on market laws and policies, and specifically consumer laws and policies, of the European Community, and on the place of product liability law within this framework. It briefly assesses the Community activities in the area of consumer protection, and emphasizes the role, features and effects of the Product Liability Directive.

POSSIBLE ALTERNATIVE APPROACHES

The specific aims of the book necessitate the historical-comparative assessment of the manner in which product liability rules developed in Central Europe. For reasons of space and consistency the book cannot contemplate other crucial phenomena which have been highlighted in the contemporary literature on product liability or on the law of obligations.

The widely acknowledged dichotomy of functions of product liability – deterrence and compensation – implies its interactions with other mechanisms fulfilling similar aims. In this context, changes within legal and economic systems which took place in the twentieth century entail the correlation of product liability with such other mechanisms aimed at compensation or wealth redistribution as insurance (first and third party insurance – of contractual and obligatory nature, as well as social security) (Perram 1992: 257), or various compensation schemes (such as no-fault compensation schemes).[17] The operation, the role, and indeed the popularity of product liability as a remedy depends among other factors upon the existence, role, and popularity of insurance (Perram 1992)[18] or other compensatory mechanisms (Hodges 2006). Looking even wider, product liability can be seen as part of a regime which aims at securing safety of products (deterrence). Thus, it may be deemed to constitute a part of a regulatory regime aimed at establishing and enforcing safety standards. The latter is a contentious postulate, yet it has the potential to stand its ground in the light of the contemporary 'tort as regulation'

16 This link of product liability with the area of consumer protection law is much more clearly visible in Europe (Pasa and Benacchio 2005: 111–12) than in the United States (see Owen [2005: 7, 1993] on the "moral foundations" of 'products liability' in the US).

17 For an introduction to these issues see Cane (2006, 1999). On the interaction between tort law and insurance see also Baker (2005). On no-fault compensation schemes in the Nordic countries where they are particularly prominent see Hodges (2006).

18 See Perram's paper for very interesting insights into the reasons for lack of tort litigation in socialist countries. These are also analysed in Part I of the book.

train of academic thought.[19] Notwithstanding the importance of these issues, for reasons of scope and clarity the book does not explore them. It also does not follow the path of seeking even wider 'patterns of liability' recommended by Whittaker (2005)[20] and reflected in the contemporary research papers devoted to harmonization of European civil laws. Indeed, there is an observable recognition of the need for a much wider look at the laws of civil liability and at civil procedure. This comprehensive approach allows one to see grander systems of liability, compensation and justice on the one hand, and on the other enables a greater understanding and an informed approach to the process of European harmonization of laws. More recent reviews of civil liability in general follow this broader look – recognizing the interactions of civil liability with other types of liability (von Bar and Drobnig 2002), as well as with the procedure involved in obtaining redress – including civil procedure (Whittaker 2005) and the widely understood access to justice.[21] Again, the aims of the book do not allow the author to follow this path. The political and academic climate in Europe is changing towards recognition of the need to see product liability law, and the Product Liability Directive, as a component of wider 'patterns of liability'.[22] It has been acknowledged that the Directive itself is unable to harmonize product liability law in Europe because of other areas of law and procedural issues which directly or indirectly affect product liability law and practice. On the substantive law side – the existence of unharmonized systems of contractual and tortious liability may well distort the effect of the Directive. On the procedural side, issues such as access to justice, funding of litigation, existence or non-existence of class actions and other collective enforcement mechanisms may produce different effects of even the most precisely harmonized rules of substantive law. As indicated in the Lovells Report, procedural matters, access to justice and 'litigation culture' may well constitute a barrier to trade of a much greater strength than any differences in substantial laws of liability among the Member States of the European Union. Various academic networks and

19 Academic writings on this issue appeared both in the United States and in Europe. See in particular: Betlem (2005), Cane (2002), Pontin (2000), Teubner (1998b, 1986b), Ogus (1994), Landes and Posner (1984), and Wittman (1977).

20 Whittaker (2005) takes a much wider approach to product liability which is reflected in the fact that he refers to 'liability for products' instead of 'product liability'. He covers civil liability, but also assesses the role of criminal and administrative liability in the area of 'liability for products'.

21 This issue has recently come to the fore within the European Union – see for instance the Reports for the Commission DG XXIV: Feldtman, von Freyhold, Vial (1998), von Freyhold, Gessner, Vial, Wagner (1996). See Part I of the book for a further elaboration of the EU-level initiatives in the area of civil procedure, and consumer redress in particular. For some recent commentaries on access to justice in Central European countries see: Bukovská (2002), Kádár, Pardavi, Zádori (2002), Bojarski (2002).

22 For some initial indications of such concerns see Stapleton's arguments on whether product liability ought to be distinguished from general tortious liability regime at all (1994); with regard to tort liability in general: Cane (1999).

projects throughout Europe are researching national laws and seeking the ways in which they could be harmonized. The complexity of the task of harmonization of tort or contract law is increasingly emphasized. The book does not follow these developments, nor does it observe the measures of private international law of the European Community origin which influence the practice of product liability in Europe: the Brussels Convention,[23] replaced by the Brussels Regulation,[24] the Regulation creating a European Order for Payment Procedure,[25] or the Rome Convention,[26] the proposed Rome I Regulation[27] and Rome II Regulation.[28]

WHY CENTRAL EUROPE?

Central European states offer excellent examples of systems in transition. Admittedly, the notion 'Central Europe', as used in this book, might by some be perceived as geographically or even historically imprecise. However, it is considered that common trends in the political, historical, legal and economic development of these countries justify placing them in a distinct group or category, distinguishing them from other post-socialist states.[29] Although remaining under a strong socialist influence until 1989, Central Europe has had a long and relatively close relationship with the 'West'. This relationship placed it in a position described by Alan Mayhew as "floating dangerously between East and West" (1998: viii). David and Brierley, in 1985, classified Czechoslovakia, Hungary and Poland, together with Slovenia and Croatia, as the 'countries of western tradition' (1985: 167) among the socialist jurisdictions. They pointed to the common elements of the history of the 'western tradition' with Germany, Austria and France, the tradition of Romano-Germanic law (ibid.).[30] Central European laws and economies were too highly developed for a direct implementation of communist ideas from Soviet Russia. They were the first nations to break free from the socialist grip,

23 Convention of 27 September 1968 on jurisdiction and the enforcement of judgements in civil and commercial matters.

24 Council Regulation (EC) No 44/2001 of 22 December 2000 (Brussels I).

25 Regulation (EC) No 1896/2006 of the European Parliament and the Council of 12 December 2006.

26 Rome Convention on the law applicable to contractual obligations 80/934/EEC.

27 See Proposal for a Regulation of the European Parliament and the Council *on the law applicable to contractual obligations (Rome I)*.

28 See Regulation (EC) 864/2007 of the European Parliament and of the Council of 11 July 2007 *on the law applicable to non-contractual obligations (Rome II)* – it will be directly applicable in the EU from 11 January 2009. The Regulation will apply to events which occurred after this date. It will apply to cases brought under the Product Liability Directive.

29 For a review of rationales behind such 'regionalization' in this part of Europe see: Janowski, Iordachi and Trencsényi (2005).

30 See Chapter 2 of Part I for the exploration of the theory of 'legal families'.

and the first post-socialist nations to have concluded Association Agreements with the European Union. Izdebski noted how after the demise of socialism Poland, Hungary and the Czech Republic rejected the approach of other Eastern European states seeking the 'third way' of building more democratic and market-oriented systems (rejecting both real socialism and capitalism) (1996: 4). He stressed that they focused on building "overt capitalist institutions in both politics and the economy" (1996: 6). Thus, he referred to them as the "vanguard in the process of democratization and the introduction of a market economy" (1996: 8).

The three countries formed the 'Visegrad Three' in 1990, when their presidents met in Visegrad, Hungary, and agreed to cooperate in the field of foreign policy (in particular – foreign economic policy), aiming at the membership of the European Community (Rupp 1999: 89). The 'Visegrad Three' subsequently became 'Visegrad Four' when the division of Czechoslovakia took place in 1993. The book does not extend its scope onto Slovakia, and continues observing the Czech Republic after the division. Therefore, depending on the historical period referred to, it refers to Czechoslovakia or the Czech Republic.

While the book encourages a wider outlook on the issue of transformations in the post-socialist countries, the reader ought to bear in mind that there are crucial divergences between them. On the other hand, some general truths about the post-socialist transformations are presented here. Although the book does not contain an answer to the present struggle of a large number of academic writers concerning the true nature of these transformations (Dupré 2003a: 4, 5), it is only by exploring examples of the ongoing change that such answers can be formulated in future.

A NOTE ON THE SOURCES OF CENTRAL EUROPEAN CIVIL LAW – THE FORTHCOMING CHANGES IN THE CIVIL CODES

A short note concerning the sources of civil law used in the book is necessary at this point. All the substantive, written law, and case law are analysed as they developed until the latest possible moment before the publication of the book, not later than June 2008. The analysis presented in the book takes account of the drafts of civil codes of Hungary and the Czech Republic, which at the time of completing the manuscript have not been finalized (Ronovska 2008, Gárdos 2007). These drafts are examined in the course of the book whenever they are proposing to change the existing law which directly affects product liability. How exactly they will be phrased and indeed how they will affect product liability is obviously still uncertain. The main body responsible for reforming civil law in Poland – the Civil Law Codification Commission[31] – is at present considering whether there is a need for a new civil code, or whether a comprehensive

31 The Civil Law Codification Commission is an independent body assigned to inform and assist the work of the Ministry of Justice in reforming civil law, and in opining legislative proposals presented by other Ministries and governmental and non-governmental

amendment of the existing code would suffice. In order to stimulate public debate on this issue, the Commission published 'The Green Book', which specifies the underlying ideas and main directions of reform. These are also included in the analysis, whenever appropriate, but the reader ought to be aware of their preliminary nature.

The changes regarding contractual and tortious liability within the draft codes in the Czech Republic and Hungary, as well as the proposed changes of the Polish Civil Code, are assessed in Part II of the book alongside the analysis of the developments within the product liability regimes. Although the book demonstrates the most significant changes which are under way in the Czech Republic, Hungary and Poland, it concentrates upon the law currently in action.

STRUCTURE OF THE BOOK

Part I of the book introduces the reader to the complexities of the subject matter. It starts with the main characteristics of Central European legal systems. These are presented in the context of the doctrine of 'legal families'. Central European legal systems are observed as they evolved within the socialist to now post-socialist political, legal, philosophical, social and economic context. The analysis then turns to the characteristics and scope of product liability and deals with its development in Western and Central Europe. It presents the way product liability is recognized and categorized in academic literature, and thus sets the limits of the focus of research. The analysis deals briefly with the questions of delimitation of boundaries and nature of liability for defective products, as well as its historical development in the World – pinpointing the contrast between the 'West' and the 'East'. As mentioned above, the book proceeds on the assumption that it is crucial to establish the position of product liability law within wider contextual arrangements which affect its evolution and operation. This is done through two main contextual arrangements. First of all, the development of the roots of product liability – the law of obligations – is presented, and disparities between Western and Central Europe are highlighted. Further, product liability is observed as part of a wider group of laws and policies of the market, and consumer protection laws in particular. Again, differences between Western and Central Europe are emphasized. The Western European position is observed through the development of market laws and consumer laws on the European Union level, including the role and effect of the Product Liability Directive, and the Central European position through developments during and after socialism, and the current efforts to harmonize the laws and policies with those of the European Union.

In Part II attention turns to the evolution of Central European substantive laws of product liability. The examination commences with contractual liability (Chapter

bodies. It is presided by Professor Zbigniew Radwański – one of the most prominent civil law scholars in Poland.

4), and follows with the tortious liability rules: before the implementation of the Directive (Chapter 5), and subsequently after the implementation (Chapter 6).

As heralded above, ultimately the book aims to present a case study of some of the challenges for the process of harmonizing European product liability law. The conclusions contain some modest predictions concerning the future of this process in the light of the issues discussed here.

PART I
Setting the Scene: Product Liability Law 'In Transition'

Introduction

Part I of the book constitutes the backbone for the analysis of Central European substantive product liability law in Part II. The quintessence of this Part is the answer to the question: what is unique about product liability systems in the Czech Republic, Hungary and Poland? The rationale for peculiarities of the product liability regimes is sought in a variety of phenomena and through various means. First of all, the very specific developments within Central European legal systems are a source of some such peculiar features. These are explored in Chapter 2 using the concept of 'legal families', and the book elaborates on the systemic, historical, political, legal and economic reasons for the continued distinctiveness of Central European legal systems. Further, the peculiarities of Central European product liability systems have their source in the nature of product liability law itself. Chapter 3 explores the origins and the essence of product liability as a distinct area of law. It assesses what product liability is, seeks its place within legal systems, considers various caveats inherent in the area of law of this kind and explores doctrinal responses to them. The differences in the approach to these key phenomena in Western Europe (especially the European Union) and in Central Europe are stressed. The chapter focuses on the developments in the law of obligations, and in consumer protection policy and law. When assessing the Western European position, it emphasizes the policies and laws of the European Union – as the triggers of the process of harmonization of the European product liability laws and as the phenomena which now very strongly influence Central Europe.

Part I observes product liability law through the lens of various contextual arrangements in which it exists. By depicting the specific context within which product liability law developed and operated in the Czech Republic, Hungary and Poland, the book traces the peculiarities in the evolution of product liability in these countries. Transition which takes place in Central European legal and socio-economic arrangements is emphasized throughout the enquiry.

Chapter 2

Legal Systems of Poland, Hungary and the Czech Republic

INTRODUCTION

Although the roots of Central European legal systems can be traced to the civil law systems of Western Europe, their law and practice were, and to some extent still remain, quite distinct from those in the 'West'. At the time when the Civil Codes[1] – the main sources of civil law in Central Europe – were drafted, the region was under the influence of socialist political and philosophical ideas.[2] The spirit of socialism permeated the provisions of the Codes, including the law of obligations, and the practice of law. At present the Codes are being subjected to numerous amendments, and draft new Codes also appeared in Central Europe.[3] The development of law of obligations is increasingly inspired by Western European legal systems[4] and is affected by the harmonization of law conducted by the European Union. The combined influences of these phenomena contribute to the distinctiveness of Central European legal systems, which the comparative law doctrine of 'legal families' is able to throw some light upon. The doctrine is a non-normative taxonomic device which emphasizes commonalities between various legal systems. The book uses it with some caution. The contemporary comparative law treatises emphasize that the doctrine, useful as a "product of its times" of "radical legal nationalism", is now outdated (Glenn 2006: 422). It is incapable of sufficiently accounting for singularities in legal systems, as well as for various forms of non-state (especially supranational) law (such as the Product Liability Directive) emerging at present, for "multiplication of sources of law in a given territory", and for convergence of legal systems (Glenn 2006: 437, 438). While comparative lawyers still debate over the plausibility of introducing other

1 Civil Code of the Hungarian People's Republic, Act IV of 1959; 'Kodeks Cywilny' (Civil Code) (Poland), of 23 IV 1964; 'Občanský zákoník' (Czechoslovakia) No. 40/1964 Coll.

2 For the introduction of the main features and the background of the Polish and the Hungarian Civil Codes see Grzybowski (1961).

3 See the analysis of the draft Czech and Hungarian Civil Codes, and the 'Green Book' of the Polish Codification Commission – below.

4 In fact, there is a long tradition in Central Europe of drawing upon Western models for building their own legal systems and drafting codes – see Kühn (2006a: 217–19). This issue is explored further below.

devices (such as 'legal traditions' – Glenn 2006) or the rationales of taxonomic devices in general (Glenn 2006, Feger 2001: 1972), the use of the doctrine retains some utility in an analysis such as this. The criteria used for the assignment of a particular legal system to a particular legal family are comprehensive enough to encapsulate the key features of Central European legal systems which need to be accounted for here.

The analysis below starts building a conceptual basis for the portrayal of product liability law. It refers to the manner in which its evolution is affected by the general trends of evolution of a legal system.

THE COMPLEX NATURE OF CENTRAL EUROPEAN LEGAL SYSTEMS

The book uses notions 'socialist', 'post-socialist', 'hybrid', and on occasion also 'communist' and 'post-communist' to describe Central European states (the two latter terms are only used when quoting other authors). The reader should not be misled by the term 'post-communist', as none of those countries was ever a communist entity (communism assumes the abolishment of the state). As David and Brierley pointed out, Central and Eastern European countries were merely "on their way" to communism (1985: 156). 'Socialist' is a much more precise notion, widely used by comparative law.

While it is a fact that Central European legal systems are on their way back to the civil law family, the case study of product liability in Central Europe in this book and the writings of other authors (in particular Kühn) clearly demonstrate that this is a complex process. The features which entailed a distinct legal tradition for the socialist legal systems were profound and they permanently marked their law, its practice, as well as their legal cultures. In fact, Central European systems are very likely to remain distinct from other civil law systems; just like the Romanistic legal systems (France, Belgium, Luxembourg) are distinct from the Germanic ones (Germany, Austria). They are also distinct from one another. Their heritage remains material in shaping the manner in which they are now transforming.

The scope of this book does not permit one to engage in these issues in depth, but the crucial point in understanding the Central European legal systems is to continue emphasizing their remaining internal (as between these systems themselves) and external (in relation to other legal systems) distinctiveness. The key features of this distinctiveness are elaborated below with the help of the methodology of 'legal families', while its more practical implications appear throughout the book. To stress the external distinctiveness, the term 'post-socialist' is used for the Central and Eastern European legal systems as they have been since the end of socialism.[5] Due attention is also given to the internal distinctiveness. Thus, the notions 'socialist' and 'post-socialist' ought not to be understood as implying uniformity. Izdebski stresses that the Eastern European countries which are in the process of establishing market economies and democratic systems "display marked divergences" (1996: 4). Even Central Europe, which over time was brought closer together politically, economically and legally, has not been a homogenous legal environment. On the other hand, the existing commonalities motivated Izdebski to formulate a view that "there is ... such a thing as a common Central European legal tradition" (Izdebski 1996: 3, 1991).

EXTERNAL AND INTERNAL DISTINCTIVENESS OF CENTRAL EUROPEAN LEGAL SYSTEMS

Below is an inquest into the most significant factors which characterized Central European states as representatives of the socialist legal family and those which contribute to their 'post-socialist' nature at present (external distinctiveness). For this purpose the book uses Zweigert and Kotz's ideas determining the inclusion of a legal system into a particular legal family (1998: 68). The criteria suggested by them include history, ideology, mode of thought in legal matters and sources of law. They cover the positive, normative 'law', as well as aspects of legal cultures and extra-legal phenomena which affected the development of the Central European legal systems. The analysis of the commonalities in these legal systems is accompanied by an account of their individual specificities (internal distinctiveness).

The focus of the analysis remains on civil law,[6] in particular the law of obligations, and the possible impact of the presented developments on product liability systems.

HISTORY

Introductory remarks

History is a crucial determinant of the fate of legal systems.[7] While the similar broad historical context in which legal systems evolve often determines their inclusion into the same legal family, history also contributes to the existing divergences

5 Although this term can be applied also to other former socialist Eastern European systems, Central European legal systems are presented in the book as specific examples of post-socialist systems (see Introduction to the book).

6 Here the notion is not used in the context of the doctrine of legal families, but to indicate the area of private law which is the subject of attention of this book.

7 In this respect, according to Zweigert and Kotz, the division between European legal systems, and especially the civil law systems, can be seen very clearly. They distinguish

between them. A more detailed analysis of the development of Central European civil laws follows in Chapter 3. Here the focus is on how history contributed to the evolution of their legal systems in general.

Before the Second World War – legal heterogeneity and building national legal identities

Until the end of the Second World War, Central European states remained within the civil law family.[8] However, while civil law systems of Western Europe "achieved their national legal unity through codes in the nineteenth century", Central European legal systems emerged from the domination of the Ottoman, Austro-Hungarian, German and Russian empires as a complex blend of legal systems and cultures (Kühn 2006a: 217). They built their own legal frameworks on the basis of the old customary law as well as the influences of foreign laws which already permeated their legal practice and legal culture.

Czechoslovakia gained national autonomy in 1918. Its legal system was a mixture of Austrian and German influences (Zweigert and Kotz 1998: 154). The Act No. 11 of 1918 transposed all the existing Austrian written laws, including the Austrian General Civil Code of 1811 (ABGB), into the Czechoslovak law (Tichy 2002a: 106). The ABGB was applicable in the current territory of the Czech Republic, and Hungarian law was applicable in Slovakia (ibid.). Although in 1920 work commenced on drafting a Civil Code, it did not produce substantive results (ibid.). Interestingly, in 1938 Czechoslovakia was ranked the ninth industrial nation in the world and the third largest European economy; it was indeed the only European country with a strong industrial base after the Second World War (Kozminski 1992: 356).

Hungary gained a relative level of independence within the Austro-Hungarian Empire in the nineteenth century. The ABGB was repealed in 1861.[9] Although the Austrian influences did not diminish completely, Hungarian courts also applied the old Hungarian customary law and German law. In fact, until the adoption of the Civil Code of 1959 Hungarian civil law developed to a large extent through judicial practice (Grzybowski 1961: 253). The enacted statutes which did exist (for instance on commercial law and on civil procedure, or the drafts of the Hungarian Civil Code[10]) were relying heavily on German law principles (Zweigert and Kotz

Romanistic, Germanic and Nordic families (1998: 90) among what others (de Cruz) consider as one – civil law family.

8 The civil law family is the oldest one, existing since 450 BC (publication of the XII Tables of Rome) (Merryman 1969: 3).

9 It was imposed on Hungary after the Revolution of 1848 – Grzybowski 1961: 253.

10 Codification efforts were significant, with two 'partial drafts' between 1871 and 1892, a comprehensive draft in 1900, a revised version of the draft presented to Parliament as a bill in 1913 and again in 1915, and the Private Law Bill of 1928. These were significant

1998: 154). Some commentators concluded that the nineteenth century civil and commercial law of Hungary was at a similar level of development as in most other European countries (Harmathy 1998: 15).

Poland, having regained its independence in 1918 became a true 'legal Tower of Babel' (Lasok 1973: 2). It inherited the influences of five legal systems and found itself in great need of legal unification (ibid.). The enactment of the Code of Obligations in 1933[11] and the Code of Commercial Law in 1934[12] (both inspired by the French *Code Civil*) brought some stability into civil law, but other areas of civil law (such as family law or property law) were not unified. The role of jurisprudence was therefore significant, and so was the value of legal writings (Lasok 1973: 2). Doctrinal writers sought consistency even among the rules which were not yet harmonized (ibid.). It needs to be said that the high quality of statutes and codes enacted before the Second World War was renowned. Many contemporary pieces of Polish legislation were modelled upon the legislation of this time. In fact, Polish written law, its doctrinal analysis and practice were quite refined, and the relative sophistication endured even the socialist period of legal stagnation (Kühn 2004: 542).

After the Second World War – imposition of socialist legality on central european legal systems

After the Second World War, Poland, Hungary and Czechoslovakia found themselves under the influence of Soviet Russia. They formed part of what was known as the 'socialist law family' which originated in the October Revolution of 1917. The civil codes were adopted, still under the influence of Austrian, German or French law, but with serious socialist connotations (the Hungarian Civil Code in 1959, and the Czechoslovak and Polish Civil Codes in 1964). Interestingly, Czechoslovakia had also enacted a Civil Code in 1950,[13] which was supposed to prepare the transition of the legal system into the socialist reality (Tichy 2002a: 109). The Czechoslovak Civil Code of 1964, adopted after the new Constitution declared that "socialism has won", was referred to by Tichy as a "third-way law" (2002a: 114, 115) because it had more provisions characteristic of a socialist legal system than the previous one (Tichy 2002a: 116, 117). Both the Czechoslovak and the Hungarian laws of obligations have been modelled on the Austrian ABGB. The most crucial similarity with the latter is lack of a clear distinction between contractual and non-contractual liability which are essentially regulated by the same provisions. The Polish Civil Code of 1964 was modelled on the Code of Obligations of 1934, which in turn was inspired by the French Civil Code of 1804.

because, although not enacted by Parliament as a Civil Code, they were used in judicial practice. *The Conception of the New Civil Code* 2002 ('the Conception').

11 The Code of Obligations entered into force on 1 July 1934.

12 The Commercial Code came into effect on 1 July 1934.

13 Act No. 141 Coll. of 25 October 1950.

Before the enactment of the 1964 Code, the general principles of civil law were already modified in the spirit of socialism in 1950 (Czachórski 2002: 137).[14]

The contents of the Central European Civil Codes evidence close ties with the civil law tradition, essentially unaffected by Marxist philosophy (Wagner 1974: 2, Lasok 1973: 9). These ties became even stronger in the last twenty to thirty years of socialism. While socialism was a dominant political force within Central Europe until 1989, it was increasingly under pressure from a more market-oriented, democratically focused approach. In Hungary this phenomenon appeared in the late 1950s, in the Czech Republic in the 1960s, in Poland it could be seen for a brief period in the 1960s but it was not as significant as in the other two countries and reverted to a more firm socialist approach in the 1970s. These pressures of a political and economic nature resulted in changes in the law, also the Civil Codes.[15] The most comprehensive reform of the Civil Code took place in Hungary, where provisions aimed at protecting consumers, for instance rules on unfair terms in contracts, appeared. Czechoslovakia also amended the Civil Code in a more market-oriented spirit. These amendments are analysed in greater detail below.

Following the Velvet Revolution – rebuilding national legal identities, legal borrowing and European integration

A rapid and far-reaching change in the political, economic and of course legal framework of the Central European states followed the peaceful revolutions which brought an end to socialism in the late 1980s. Reforms prompted by the transformation into democracy and capitalism were reinforced by the association and later by the membership in the European Union. Changes within the Civil Codes were influenced by German, Swiss, French, Dutch and English law (Zweigert and Kotz 1998: 155), and by the increased influence of the European Community law. In fact, the Czech legislators decided on an enactment of an entirely new Civil Code – drafts of 1996 and 2001, analysed by Tichy and by Hrádek, are now being considered (2002a: 118–20, 2003: 123–7). Similar developments are taking place in Hungary. The 1959 Hungarian Civil Code was already amended over 150 times since 1980s. It was decided that in spite of its "outstanding technical quality" and capability to survive even fundamental social changes, the Code needed to be replaced with a new one for reasons of legal coherence.[16] The work on the new Civil Code which was meant to reflect the change of regimes and provide law

14 The key changes included the restrictions in the principle of freedom of contract – amending Article 56 of the Code of Obligations of 1934. See Chapter 3 of Part I.

15 See Kulcsár (1984) for an elaboration of the rationale for these developments using the example of Hungary. Kulcsár stressed the overwhelming power of political thought and political theories in triggering legal change. This idea is further explored below, together with the ideology of socialist countries.

16 'The Conception'.

more suited to the new, democratic legal system began in the 1990s. Within the last year of completing the manuscript for the book, another draft Hungarian Civil Code appeared.[17] Also the Polish Codification Commission commenced work on transformation of civil law, considering the possibility of the new Civil Code. The 'Green Book' which was published by the Commission in 2006 specifies the main purposes and the possible directions of the reform. These issues are presently being discussed in working groups and in expert meetings.

Central European legal systems have undergone some very turbulent changes, and further changes are underway. The following element of analysis illustrates how these transformed the essence of the legal systems.

MODE OF THOUGHT IN LEGAL MATTERS

Introductory remarks

The historical events described above affected the way in which law was shaped, understood, analysed, commented upon and applied in Central Europe. Central European states are now transforming their mode of legal thought, which changed considerably during socialism, in accordance with the civil law approach. This does not mean building an entirely new mode of thought, but rather returning to their pre-1939 position. Before the Second World War, Central European legal thought was progressing very much in line with that of Western Europe. The process of rebuilding the civil-style mode of legal thought is, however, fraught with difficulties. It is beyond the scope of this book to analyse these issues in detail, and thus only a brief description of the most pertinent aspects of legal thought in as far as they impact the development of product liability law is conducted here. The analysis includes an account of the development of Central European legal, political and judicial rhetoric, as well as the 'legal cultures'. The latter are considered a core element, determinant, and source of mode of legal thought. In this context the influence of socialist legality could be seen particularly clearly, and the impact of these phenomena on the development of product liability law is significant. In fact, Central European 'legal cultures', and legal and judicial methodology still remain distinct from civil law systems.

Towards the civil-law-style mode of thought: a moving goal?

What is the model towards which the Central European legal systems are heading? While common law systems develop their legal thought on a case-by-case basis, civil law systems are based on general principles and rules. Chloros pointed out, with some reservations about the dangers of generalizing, that common law philosophy is "in favour of rights rather than of duties, of emancipation rather than

17 Provided by Dr. Gárdos Péter, Hungarian Ministry of Justice, Department for the Codification of Civil Law.

of control, of responsibility rather than paternalism" (1992: 86), and the civil law philosophy stresses order and authority (1992: 89). The mode of legal thought in Europe is now transforming, and the differences between common and civil law systems are becoming less clear-cut. Whether it is a result of a voluntary process of convergence[18] or the formalized programme of positive harmonization of law conducted by the European Community,[19] civil law is becoming less formalistic and increasingly focused on "more open, substantive, policy evaluating and argumentative" (Kühn 2004: 537) analysis and judicial application of law, while common law is becoming somewhat more formalized and needs to accommodate certain general principles such as 'good faith' (Teubner 1998a).[20] Both in civil and in common law systems, the presence of law is increasingly felt in society – legislation and regulation are now more omnipotent than ever, and courts are entrusted with much wider powers to apply and interpret this growing number of rules (Koopmans 2003: 270). Without becoming involved in a debate on the precise rationale, proceedings and implications of this process, a number of key issues need to be noted.

In the second half of the twentieth century, legislative, regulatory and judicial activity in Western European states experienced a significant quantitative leap. This 'juridification' and 'judicialization' of society was related to the birth and development of the welfare state. The "penetration of legal rules and procedure in all walks of life" (Teubner 1986a: 3) also led to an increase in "litigiousness within contemporary societies" (Vogel 1979). With the greater legislative coverage of everyday life, the role and power of judges significantly increased (Kühn 2004) – while in common law systems this was a natural process, in civil law systems it meant an adjustment of the traditional setting. Continental judges started using a much greater discretion and flexibility in interpreting law. The methodology of what has been referred to as "bound judicial decision-making" (Kühn 2004, 2006b) was largely abandoned in favour of more open, creative, dynamic, purposive and contextual methods. Areas such as product liability owe a great deal to this approach. While at present the legislative and regulatory activity is considerable and the sources of legislative and regulatory power became 'diffused' – decentralized on the one hand (subsidiarity) and centralized on the other (international law, European Community law) – judicial power and discretion is growing in significance. The European Court of Justice and its dynamic, teleological approach to interpreting the European Community law to some extent sets the standards for the boundaries of judicial power across the European Union. Its 'dialogue' with national courts

18 The theory of convergence developed by comparative lawyers was mentioned in the Introduction. For a further elaboration of this theory see for instance: Zweigert and Kotz (1998) and various contributions to Reimann and Zimmermann's *The Oxford Handbook of Comparative Law* (2006).

19 For a further description of this process see Chapter 3 of Part I.

20 This process of convergence was even observed by Central European comparatists – for instance by a Hungarian comparative scholar – Eörsi (1979b: 542).

– the gist of the practice of European Community law (examined below) – empowers these national courts by making them 'Community courts'. Thus it is not only their own national law but also the European Community law (sources of which are explored below) that they need to apply and interpret. With this new source of interpretative responsibility comes new political, economic and social thought. It creates a common platform for all courts, whether those operating in a common law or a civil law system. The Product Liability Directive is a product of the developments delineated above – bringing in relatively new concepts of strict liability, product, defect or development risk defence, as well as the philosophy of balancing market interests within the new internal market. Although it cannot be denied that national implementing measures as well as the practical application and interpretation of these measures show considerable divergences among Member States of the European Union, the philosophy and specific role of product liability law underpinning the Directive exerts an increasing influence over European practice of product liability. The judgements of the European Court of Justice concerning the Directive (Sengayen 2007) induce the contingency of common thought in the matters of product liability covered by the Directive.

As the nature and the balance of powers within the legal sphere are transforming, so are academic theories. These regulatory, legislative and judicial developments are assessed and commented upon by academic scholars, whose writings often impact the legal and judicial process. In the continental legal systems the influence of such doctrinal writings is significant indeed.

The goal towards which Central European legal systems are heading has been transformed, and there are serious difficulties in adjusting Central European legal thought to these changes. The tendency within the civil law European legal systems is to detract from the traditional formalistic, positivist and "static" approach to law, especially in its application by courts (Kühn 2004). There is a wider, more inclusive outlook on sources of law, and a more open attitude to applying these in judicial practice. Central European legal thought has to some extent faced an exactly opposite situation – that of return to such formalistic, positive approach and "bound judicial decision-making" (Kühn 2004, 2006b). What are the sources of this discrepancy?

Socialist legal thought

In spite of some similarities, the differences between the civil and the socialist mode of legal thought were very significant. Both the civil and the socialist legal families are rooted in Roman law; they use similar terminology and classifications (de Cruz 1999: 38, Zweigert and Kotz 1998: 69). However, while the civil law emphasis on order, authority and the rule of law is reinforced by the use of various general clauses (such as good faith), the formalistic, normative approach of socialist legal systems entailed a rather different focus of law and its practice (Kühn 2004: 541). Socialist legal systems were functioning on the basis of a peculiar legal philosophy, terminology and general concepts (such as central planning, administrative contracts, 'normative acts' or 'principles of community life', also referred to as the 'principles of socialist cooperation') which exerted major influence on the practice of civil law. This phenomenon was a result of the political pressures of socialism and the related peculiar ideological bias of these legal systems, and according to many comparative writers earned them "a category of their own" (Chloros 1992: 93). It also resulted from the widely accepted instrumental role of law – using law as a means of realizing socialist postulates (Kulcsár 1984: 205–6). This instrumentalist outlook manifested itself with various levels of strength in different Central and East European states (Kulcsár 1984: 199, Eörsi 1977: 67).

Links with the "good old law" and 'parallel' socialist laws

Hungary and Poland appear in academic writings of the time to have been least affected by the socialist influences (Izdebski, Kulcsár, David). What could be observed in those two states, and to a lesser extent also in other socialist states like Czechoslovakia, was the urge to retain the continuity of the "good old law" of the past – the laws, doctrine and customs of before the Second World War (Kulcsár 1984: 200). Kulcsár wrote of this dichotomy of influences within socialist legal systems – the historical-legal thinking of a "self-defensive nature augmented by politico-historical circumstances" on the one hand, and the reception of the instrumentalist outlook of socialism (perceived as an external force) on the other (1984: 199).[21] Chloros argued that law in socialist systems was created "outside the traditional structures" – thus although Civil Codes (retaining or incorporating legal principles which existed previously and resembling Austrian, German or French civil liability rules) were adopted, it was the law parallel to the Codes which was of much more practical importance (Chloros 1992: 91, Kühn 2006b: 574–5). Chloros gave examples of contract law and tort law – present in the Codes but in practice dealt with often by rules existing outside their scope (1992: 91). These parallel laws and regulations – "normative acts" – were particularly common in Poland, where ten thousand (sic!) of them were reported by 1956 (Grzybowski 1961: 257).[22] They were principally used in the area of contract law. In the spirit of central planning, some of them directly resulted in a creation of an obligation relationship; others introduced duties to conclude contracts (Czachórski 2002: 137–8). Their existence was a result of the specific needs of socialist market relations. Their main role was

21 Kulcsár wrote in 1984 of this emphasis on "old law" in Hungary and Poland with regard to family law and inheritance, but he also stressed the general importance of such thinking – where the "old law" was perceived as an internal defence against the efforts of the external powers (1984: 200).

22 Grzybowski defines "normative acts" as the "regulation of various aspects of public life by administrative decisions, directives, instructions, and the like, quite frequently issued by institutions not formally a part of the administrative apparatus of the country" (such as trade unions), thus creating a regulatory chaos in the socialist countries (1961: 256–7).

to regulate relations between 'socialist organizations' – the most common form of economic presence in socialist markets (Grzybowski 1961: 256–7).[23] Special rules were created only for them, including product liability rules of which below. Apart from Hungary, disputes arising from these relations were subjected to arbitration (Arbitrazh) and not to jurisdiction of civil courts (Chloros 1992: 91, Grzybowski 1961: 265). This approach reflected the general priority given to state enterprises and their interests, over the interests of individuals. It was the result of the socialist ideology which affected the general structure of legal systems as well as each specific legislative or administrative mechanism. Although socialist states formally – in the provisions of the Civil Codes – maintained the "unity of civil law",[24] the rules of Civil Codes were rarely, if ever (Czechoslovakia)[25] applicable to relations between socialist organizations. Individual or consumer interests were certainly not at the forefront of priorities for legislative activities, and the multiplicity and general complexity of rules did not benefit them either. The complexity, coupled with the instrumental role of law, was also reflected in the existence of the general concept of 'principles of socialist cooperation'. This general clause was designed to enable the courts to fulfil their role in achieving the aims of the socialist state.[26] Socialist courts were nonetheless incapable of consistently applying this clause to concrete situations before them – the rationale for this phenomenon is explored below.

Central European Civil Codes, including provisions on the law of obligations, enacted at the time of socialism were much shorter than many Western European Codes.[27] Maczonkai found the reason for such a laconic regulation in the Marxist doctrine, predominant at the time the Codes were drafted (1996: 109). As the principal role of law was to serve the needs of society, the law had to be flexible and accommodating enough to be changed together with these needs (ibid.). Socialist codifications were merely designed to provide framework rules, to be filled in with the particulars by the secondary legislation, 'normative acts' and courts' decisions (ibid.).

As mentioned above, the legal complexity caused by the presence of the 'normative acts' was particularly visible in contract law. This may have provided the background for quite a prevalent view presented by Wagner that the law of

23 'Socialist organizations' were state-owned undertakings and cooperatives (Wagner 1974: 43, 69, Lasok 1973: 7).

24 The "unity of civil law" concerns situations where Civil Codes cover all the main types of social relations – those between individuals, between undertakings, and between individuals and undertakings (Grzybowski 1961: 156).

25 They were regulated by the Commercial Code of 1964, now replaced by the Commercial Code – Act No. 513/1998 Coll. (Hrádek 2006: 187).

26 See below for a further description of this concept, its role and transformation at present.

27 The Hungarian Civil Code has 685 Articles, and the Czech Civil Code, 880 Sections, the Polish Code was the longest, with 1088 Articles.

tort, in contrast to contract law, has had an "essentially non-political character" and socialist ideology did not affect it as it affected contract (1974: 139). While the relative independence of tort from political factors could indeed be observed in the black-letter content of many legal provisions, it could not be observed in the operation of these provisions in practice. Here, in the manner in which the law has been applied and also in the way in which it was perceived by society, the influence of socialism can be clearly seen, whether in the law of tort or in the law of contract. The latter statement can be supported by the writings of Weir, who in an attempt to seek factors prompting and shaping the features of the development of tortious liability suggested the question whether the economy of a country was a market economy or whether it was centrally planned (1983: ch. 5, p. 3). Wagner acknowledged this necessity by introducing those particular characteristics of the Polish legal system which were conditioned by the existence of socialism before he commenced the detailed observation of the law of obligations (1974: 1–41).

'Legal cultures' and legal methodology of socialist systems – 'legal decay' and poor judicial reasoning

Socialist legal systems exhibited a particularly striking alienation of the legal and judicial profession and intellectual impoverishment of legal thought. Again, this phenomenon appeared with varying levels of intensity in various Central European states. The Czechoslovak legal thought and legal culture is a patent example. Consequently, Czechoslovak product liability case law and scholarly writings presented in the book are not very impressive, both in terms of quantity and quality. The deficiencies of Czech legal thought appear to be so significant that Luboš Tichỳ – a prominent Czech scholar – claims they deprive Czech law of the qualities possessed by most European, also socialist, legal systems: "stability and continual, evolutionary development of its legal arrangement" (2002a: 106). This statement seems to unnecessarily diminish the importance of similar phenomena in other socialist countries. However, the reforms taking place in the Czech legal system do not resemble law reforms in other countries, claims Tichy (ibid.). The Czech 'new' entirely replaces 'the old', and hence even the case law and doctrine of law established under the operation of 'the old' lose their utility. For the reason of lack of valuable sources of reference in case law and doctrinal writings, the legal profession have been forced to have recourse to written law only. Courts refuse to follow jurisprudence of other courts as precedents (Tichy 2002b: 76). The positivism and formalism so fashioned have manifested themselves through lack of creativity of the legal profession and this, in the opinion of Tichy, has led almost to the denial of law (denegation justitiae) (ibid.). Tichy refers directly to the regime of liability for defective products as the area suffering from the passive attitude of the legal profession and the judiciary, not willing to interpret the available legal provisions creatively (2002a, 2002b). Tichy criticizes both sides of the Czech legal profession – the lawmakers for the unavailability of a stable basis for forming opinions and judgements, and the judges, lawyers and legal writers for lack of thorough research and lack of any inspirational conceptions (2002a: 106).[28] He goes so far as to refer to the "impotence of the Czech legal community" (ibid.). Although Tichy writes of these phenomena as if they have not changed from the times of socialism until the present times, it must be said that the legal thought and method are gradually transforming in the Czech Republic (see below).

Although the other two Central European states did not seem to suffer from such a serious condition, certain tendencies common to all socialist systems were clearly observable there as well. In his excellent comparison between the 'Western' and the Central European "judicial culture", Kühn draws upon these tendencies among the socialist judiciary. Alienated from the process of shaping public policy and indeed shaping legal practice, which was dominated entirely by the ruling party, the judiciary "did not merit complex legal theories" and relied on an "extreme version of cognitivism based on the ideology of bound judicial decision-making" (Kühn 2004: 538).[29] What could be observed was the contrast between the officially pronounced self-perception and even the official external perception of judges, and the actual situation (Kühn 2004: 539, Sadurski 1984: 187). The role of judges was widely perceived to be to teach "the masses to live a proper socialist life", solving societal problems, and not simply to apply the law (Kühn 2004: 539). While this could have entailed a de-formalized, dynamic and creative approach to interpretation and application of law, nothing could be further from the truth. Based on some "Marxist clichés, intellectual impotency and ideological emphasis on centralized law-making authority" socialist judges almost exclusively relied on written law, disregarding such crucial matters as "efficacy of rules, their impact, the policy surrounding them, judicial decisions, customary practices, established conventions" (Kühn 2004: 540). This issue is further explored below when the sources of law in socialist systems are analysed.

The positivist approach to law also extended upon other members of the legal profession, thus creating the specific 'internal legal culture' within the socialist legal systems.[30] Coupled with the relative simplicity, even triviality of legal issues, disputes and case law during socialism,[31] the ideology of "bound judicial decision-making" meant a lack of inspiring, comprehensive elaboration of the law as well as, perhaps with the exception of Poland (of which below), inspiring doctrinal

28 The Czechoslovak Supreme Court recognized the poor quality of judicial interpretation of the law conducted by lower courts – Kühn 2004: 545, Statement of the Czechoslovak Supreme Court of 23 November 1967, Prz 36/67.

29 Varga described the situation in the socialist legal systems as a duality of the "rule of brute facts" of the party freely enforcing their interests through unlawful interference or by silencing the law on the one hand, and the "petty-minded rule of regulations" in "neutral areas of mass application" (2001: 191).

30 Friedman (1986, 1997) developed the concept of an 'internal legal culture' which could be described as the legal culture existing among members of the legal profession.

31 As documented in: Kühn (2004), Markovits (1986: 720) and Kulcsár (1983: 85, 89–90).

writings (Kühn 2004: 542, 544). Important and comprehensive court decisions, also those in the field of product liability, were few and far between.

Specificities of legal thought in post-socialist systems – formalism and lack of judicial activism

With time, when strict socialist ideals collapsed, the laws and regulations parallel to the Civil Codes were being abandoned. The 'principles of socialist cooperation' were no longer solely used to further socialist ideals, and the rule of law became more pronounced (Pistor 2002: 2). Laws permitting creation of private undertakings appeared, and the distinct treatment of relations between state enterprises diminished. The Civil Codes restated the principle of 'unity of civil law', the key message being that civil law ought to regulate relations between all physical and legal persons. On the other hand, a trend which appeared within the Codes was the distinct treatment of business-to-consumer transactions. The latter movement was motivated by the transformation of socialist markets into capitalist markets, and soon reinforced by influences of European Community laws and consumer protection policies (examined below). The flood of norms accompanying the new political, market and social reality, and especially the laws implementing the laws of the European Union, is only very gradually taking ground across the post-socialist states. The legal and judicial methodology did not yet reach the stage in which the contemporary Western European methodologies can be found. As documented by Galligan and Matczak (2006), Kühn (2004) and Tichy (2002b: 76), post-socialist judges still to a considerable extent retain the methodology of "bound judicial decision-making" and often refuse to go beyond literal legal interpretation. Kühn mentioned a worrying tendency among Czech judges who would refuse to consider key legal issues in cases before them and instead dismiss the cases on a technicality, merely to avoid having to deal with issues they are not accustomed to or have not dealt with before. Łętowska indicated that Polish judges often refuse to settle even the least complex matters in cases before them without having them confirmed by an expert. These observations demonstrate the difficult phase of transition with which post-socialist legal systems are grappling. Judges, entrusted with the task of interpreting and applying the plethora of new legal provisions and even the old provisions in an entirely new political and economic reality, have not so far been able to shrug off the tendency to keep faithfully to the letter of the law, the method which sustained their relatively trouble-free existence in socialist systems. Although some notable examples of dynamic, flexible and creative application of the law (including the European Community law) can be observed throughout Central Europe (especially in the Polish Supreme Court and some appeal courts, the Hungarian and Czech Constitutional and Supreme Courts), the adjustment to Western European standards of legal thought is bound to take a while longer. Application of product liability rules in the new market environment, which requires a large dosage of judicial sophistication, flexibility and creativity, especially in setting the balance between the interests of businesses and consumers, may to some extent remain unsatisfactory for some time. It may seem underdeveloped from the point of view of a sophisticated legal scholar or legal professional. At present the number of higher court judgements interpreting the provisions implementing the Product Liability Directive is negligible, and the issues considered in these judgements are relatively mundane and undemanding. It is, however, uncertain whether this is due to lack of difficult issues coming before these higher courts or the lower instance courts, or perhaps due to the fact that most product liability cases are settled. Various elements of product liability regimes are certainly being considered by the representatives of legal doctrine in an increasing number of research papers and monographs on the topic. A mature product liability regime requires such authoritative, well-documented statements concerning the role of the law, its meaning and effects on markets. These are appearing within Central Europe gradually. Their appearance is prompted, among other factors, by influences of other political and legal systems, as well as the rediscovery of 'old law' and legal thought before the socialist era.

Socialist legal thought in transition – outside influences and rediscovery of 'old law'

A number of key developments influence changes in Central European mode of legal thought at present: these are the increased emphasis on turning to the 'old law' for guidance and the increased presence of European Community law and legal philosophy. The influences of the 'old law' and emphasis on legal continuity can indeed be seen on a much wider scale. The presence of such thinking enables an easier transition from socialist law back to civil law. Again, the exact proceedings and the speed of this transition depend upon the different approaches to law before the Velvet Revolution. Central and Eastern European states use their 'old law', supplemented by the influences of the contemporary legal systems of Germany, Austria, France or the Netherlands, to build the 'new' private and public laws. The influences of the 'old law' can be seen not only in the written legislation, but also in doctrinal writings and in court judgements interpreting the 'new' law. A good example of how courts turn to the 'old law' for guidance in interpretation of the contemporary Civil Code provisions is the jurisprudence of the Polish Supreme Court (Sąd Najwyższy), for instance the recent judgement concerning the limitation period for bringing claims in tort, assessed in Part II. In the judgement of 17 February 2006, where the Court was called upon by the Ombudsman to clarify the legal position as regards commencement of the limitation period for bringing claims, express references were made to the Code of Obligations of 1934 and the Supreme Court judgements based upon its provisions.[32] While this approach can

32 The Code of Obligations contained a provision which did not significantly differ from the provision of the Civil Code. The Supreme Court referred to the Code of Obligations as well as the judgements of the Supreme Court based upon it – such as the judgement of 7 August 1967 (II PR 268/67).

be beneficial for the development of legal thought in some cases, in others it is unable to fulfil this purpose. Areas of law such as product liability need a more contemporary, refined approach, involving economic and social thought which appeared in Western Europe after the Second World War.

The influences of the European Community law can be felt throughout the Central European legal systems. The very dynamic development of Central European law, academics and representatives of the legal profession being involved in various pan-European projects concerning the harmonization of tort or contract law, and good quality doctrinal analyses of law of obligations – including Tichy, Svestka and Knappová in the Czech Republic, Nesterowicz, Bagińska in Poland, Harmathy in Hungary – indicate the birth of mature, fully-fledged legal systems. Unfortunately, the results of these changes are not always seen in areas such as consumer protection law, and in particular product liability. It is difficult to determine the full effects of the process of convergence of European laws and harmonization of laws in the European Union on the mode of legal thought in Central Europe. There is no doubt that, as mentioned previously, the transformation of the political, economic and social conditions prompted the process of return to the civil law roots by these legal systems. This included mode of legal thought, legal methodology and legal cultures. The attitudes of the legal profession to new market relations, and in particular to the position of consumers, gradually starts resembling such attitudes in Western Europe. This issue is further explored below, where the developments in Central European consumer policies and laws are assessed.

SOURCES OF LAW

Another crucial element mentioned by Zweigert and Kotz are sources of law, although the writers did stress the 'minor importance' of this element for distinguishing which legal family a system belongs to (1998: 71), especially at present. The general perception of the prominence of jurisprudence in common law systems, and the civil and socialist systems' preference for written law[33] are being transformed, influenced by the processes of legal convergence and harmonization within Europe.[34] Below is the account of the impact of these developments on the sources of law in Central Europe. The focal point remains civil law, and sources of criminal and administrative law are not analysed. Further, the theme

33 In the nineteenth and the beginning of the twentieth century, "continental law was completely identified with the written law of the nation state, i.e. national codes and statutes" (Kühn 2004: 533).

34 The process of voluntary convergence of European laws was mentioned in the Introduction – it is distinguished here from the more or less formalized and legalized process of harmonization (approximation) of laws by the European Union – see below (Chapter 3) for a further description of this process in general and with regard to the law of product liability.

of product liability entails particular focus of analysis on specific sources of rules – jurisprudence and doctrinal opinions.

The process of legal convergence observed by comparative lawyers, reinforced and formalized by the operation of the European Communities, was mentioned in the Introduction to the book. The effect of these phenomena on the mode of thought in legal matters in Europe was assessed above. Their impact on the sources of law in Europe is even clearer. Legislative and regulatory penetration of European societies throughout Europe is significant. Written law covers previously unregulated areas of human life, and expands its influence over both the civil and the common law systems. Although the content of written law is increasingly affected by the new aim of "better regulation" (Löfstedt 2004), the 'juridification' is a plainly visible phenomenon. The sources of the rules are national and regional, but increasingly also international lawmaking bodies, some with supranational powers. With regard to the latter, the European Community is a source of rules of general application and of direct effect in all the Member States.[35] The Community established itself as a 'new legal order', with new types of written law and a specific approach to jurisprudence, which are now affecting the structure of legal systems of the Member States. Regulations and especially directives are becoming a source of new, harmonized European legal rules.

This penetration of social life by legal rules is said to increase the importance of litigation and court decisions (Kühn 2004, Teubner 1986a: 3). The result of this phenomenon is that the long-established stark contrast with regard to legal force of jurisprudence in common and civil law systems is no longer so clear. Traditionally, in civil law systems such as the French system judgements of courts were seen as "authorities" (Carbonnier 1974: 91)[36] or "persuasive sources of law" (Yiannopoulos 1974: 69). They did not create binding legal rules but rather constituted elements which were "taken into consideration in the interpretation of legal rules and, when the latter are silent or insufficient, the solution to a legal problem must be found" (Carbonnier 1974: 91). Lack of formal binding effect of court judgements within the civil law systems can be traced back to their main constitutional principles – in particular the separation of powers (the role of the judges being to interpret and not to make law) and the concept of *res judicata* which denotes the binding effect of court judgements only between the parties involved in a dispute (Carbonnier 1974: 96). Carbonnier compared the role of decided cases in the English and the French legal systems. He stressed that while in the English system a court's decision had a status of an obligatory rule for the court which gave it and for "courts of coordinate jurisdiction" (*Stare Decisis*); in France it was only

35 The history, aims and methods of operation of this complex structure are explored in Chapter 3 of Part I.

36 De Cruz (1999: 68) elaborates the value of judicial decisions in French law to conclude that it has been noted practice for courts to follow precedents, especially those of higher courts. Zweigert and Kotz also noted some experience of courts following precedents in Germany (1998: 91).

to inspire judges (1974: 103). Instead of stability in respecting older judgements (English approach), French jurisprudence is to achieve flexibility – thus the latest decisions have the greatest authority (1974: 103). Carbonnier pointed out that French courts did refer to specific judgements of the *Cour de Cassation* as reasons for their decisions. This would not always be the case, because at times a court would consider a single decision of the *Cour* as too isolated to establish a general principle. Such references are however most common with regard to the *Cour de Cassation* and not lower courts (Carbonnier 1974: 97). One of the reasons for the latter fact is that judgements of lower courts are not always published in civil law systems. While formally this is still the official position of most civil law systems in Western Europe, the role and legal force of jurisprudence have grown considerably. Courts are faced with new legal rules, sometimes deriving from outside their own legal system, and also with new situations to which the existing rules do not necessarily fit well. They are finding themselves in a position where they need to be more creative and flexible than ever (Kühn 2004), especially in the face of the fact that they have also become European Community courts. The substance and effect of judgements of the European Court of Justice reach far beyond what would be considered the normal substance and effect of court judgements in the understanding of the civil law systems. The judgements of the European Court of Justice interpreting the provisions of European Community law are binding upon all national courts of the Member States. Following these key judgements, national courts are obliged to follow the provisions of the European Community law in cases before them. National courts are a key element of the enforcement mechanism within the European Union – the European Court of Justice stressed their obligation to follow EC law, not least in spite of the existence of contrary provisions of national law (Sengayen 2007).[37] A further step in the process of building greater importance of courts and jurisprudence has been the emergence of constitutional democracies across Europe, with the exception of the United Kingdom (parliamentary system). This entailed the establishment of constitutional review of legislation by constitutional courts (Koopmans 2003: 35–62). Political and democratic legitimacy crises led to the increased opportunity for judicial review of political and administrative activities of the state apparatus (Koopmans 2003: 63–97).

The new legal, economic and social phenomena also increase the need for doctrinal analyses. Scholarly writings often assess, analyse and even inform the processes of transformation taking place in Europe. Doctrine of law is a very important factor in establishing, developing and influencing the application and

37 Case C-106/89 *Marleasing SA v La Comercial Internacional de Alimentacion SA* (doctrine of indirect effect), Case 6/64 *Costa v ENEL*, Case 11/70 *Internationale Handelsgesellschaft*, Case C-48/93 *R v Secretary of State for Transport, ex parte Factortame (Factortame III)* (supremacy of EC law). For a further analysis of the issue see for instance: Weatherill (2003: 159–66), Maher (1994).

interpretation of legal concepts – both in civil[38] and in socialist legal systems. This is so especially in case of modern legal writings, which are increasingly critical of legislation and jurisprudence (Carbonnier 1974: 106). It has some value also in common law systems – English courts use doctrinal writings in their decisions (*A v National Blood Authority*).[39] The value of doctrinal writings is particularly significant in areas where no established jurisprudence exists.

The value of jurisprudence[40] and legal doctrine is growing even in legal systems where they are not formally sources of binding rules. In civil law systems jurisprudence and doctrinal opinions traditionally constituted "persuasive sources of law" (Yiannopoulos 1974: 69). The main role of such persuasive, subsidiary sources was said to enable application of law to be flexible enough to accommodate changing circumstances and social conditions in which law functions and thus to prevent denial of justice and "judicial capriciousness" to which mere adherence to the letter of written law may lead (Kühn 2004, Yiannopoulos 1974: 70).[41] Product liability is instrumental in demonstrating the implications of the operation of such sources of law – almost universally it has been the creation of jurisprudence assisted by doctrinal suggestions. Its formation was therefore dependent upon the emergence of relative strength of these "persuasive sources of law". Of course, the most important source of product liability rules in contemporary Europe is a piece of written law – the Product Liability Directive and the laws implementing it into the national legal systems. The jurisprudence of courts and doctrinal views now took over the role of interpreting these provisions and applying them to the complicated market reality which they find themselves in.

The developments described above are taking ground in Central Europe, but a certain distinctiveness and lack of maturity of the legal systems still lingers. There is no doubt that Central European legal systems have common characteristics with civil law systems as regards sources of law, in particular the emphasis on written law. The socialist period in their history did not fundamentally disrupt this approach, although the importance of 'normative acts' temporarily transformed the general legislative framework. As a result of the conversion from socialism, 'normative acts' were repealed, and the Civil Codes regained their key role. With the aim to reintroduce the rule of law, Central European legislators also enacted

38 See Dainow (1974), especially pp. 91–132 (Carbonnier, David) on the authorities (jurisprudence and doctrine) and 'supereminent principles' in French law; and pp. 134–62 (Larenz) on the 'open legal development' through doctrine in Germany.

39 [2001] 3All ER 289.

40 Here the term 'jurisprudence' is used to denote judgements of courts and not, as it often appears, as the theory and philosophy of law.

41 In socialist systems, the role of modifiers and adjusters of written law to social and economic requirements was played by the 'normative acts' mentioned above. Courts often employed the methodology of 'bound judicial decision-making' (analysed above), which effectively prevented any flexibility or creativity. Academic writings of the era also lacked solid legal analysis and sophistication.

complex statutory instruments introducing protection of private property and an entirely new outlook on social welfare, pensions and unemployment benefits (Pistor 2002: 1, 2). They also introduced new Constitutions. The magnitude of legislative effort in Central Europe is impressive. The number of amendments to the existing Civil Codes reached hundreds. Acts introducing provisions of civil law separate from the Civil Codes (for instance in consumer transactions and in the area of product liability law in Hungary and the Czech Republic) also continue appearing.[42] Further, Central Europeans are in the process of establishing new Civil Codes. Both Hungary[43] and the Czech Republic (Tichy 2002a: 117–20)[44] are quite advanced in the preparation of the new Codes. The Polish Codification Commission – an independent body assisting the Minister of Justice in reforming civil law – has been working since 2004 on the general framework of the civil law. In accordance with the spirit of unity of civil law, the Polish legislators attempted to insert as many new rules, especially those deriving from the need to implement various European Community directives, into the Civil Code. This complex picture of civil law prompted the Codification Commission to conclude that a new Civil Code ought to be enacted (the 'Green Book').

The influence of the European Union can increasingly be seen in the area of civil law, with some EC directives implemented directly into the Civil Codes and others into separate legislative instruments. The full impact of the new laws is, however, thwarted by significant problems which could be attributed to the continuing stage of transformation of the respective legal systems.[45] Regrettably, while implementation of EC directives is progressing steadily and all new EC laws are published in the Official Journal of the European Communities in the languages of Central European states, serious problems with translation of older Community laws have been noted, especially in Poland.[46] As many pieces of Community legislation have not been translated into Polish, some courts refuse to apply them

42 In Poland the Product Liability Directive was implemented into the Civil Code; in Hungary and the Czech Republic separate acts were adopted. At present there are plans to incorporate the latter into the draft Civil Codes (see below for a further assessment of the implementation of the Directive in Central Europe).

43 The work on the Hungarian draft code is in its advanced stages at the time of writing this book – see 'the Conception' and Gárdos 2007.

44 As mentioned above, during the final stages of the preparation of the manuscript of the book, the author received the most recent version of the Czech Draft Civil Code from Jiri Hradek who, together with Professor Tichy, translated the part of the Draft of the Code concerning tort liability into English.

45 See Dupré (2003b) for an assessment of this legislative effort and its possible implications – especially her considerations on "legal fatigue and complexity" created by the new laws, and the problems with appropriation of the new laws and establishing a new legal culture.

46 Interview with the Supreme Court Judge Andrzej Wróbel, 'Sądy odmawiają stosowania prawa wspólnotowego' [Courts Refuse to Apply Community law] 246 *Gazeta Prawna* 19 December 2006.

in cases they hear. The opinion on this issue is divided. According to a prominent Supreme Court Judge the lack of translation of an act into Polish does not release the court from the obligation to apply it in Poland. The reasoning of the courts, however, is that the rule of law and the related need for certainty and accessibility of law do not allow for application of legislation of the existence of which citizens could not be aware if they did not speak English, French or German.[47]

The detailed elaboration of these issues exceeds the scope of this book. The crucial issue to note is the lingering state of transition in the written law of Central Europe, only gradually starting to resemble the law of Western European states. The remaining problems concern the official presence of the new sources of legal rules as well as the exposure of ordinary members of society to these sources. Their impact on the legal culture of Central European states is therefore still limited. Thus, another piece of evidence of the continued distinctiveness of Central European legal systems from Western European legal systems presents itself.

Formally the legal force of jurisprudence in Central Europe has been similar to the civil law approach, although there was some tradition of judicial rule making and even following precedents before the socialist times. The jurisprudence of Hungarian courts created certain general rules and theories by interpreting available law.[48] Hungarian courts were known to follow previous judgements, although they would refer to them in a generalized, vague manner, "not tracing back the judgements to defined precedents" (Eörsi 1970: 31). In common with other Central European systems, jurisprudence rather referred to general "theses of law" than a concrete court judgement (ibid.). Judgements of lower courts were and still are rarely published in Central Europe, which makes it difficult to assess the development of 'judge-made' areas of law such as product liability. Of course, the notion of separation of powers gained an entirely different dimension in socialist legal systems – with the state monopoly of power in order to achieve its purposes, with the judges obliged to seek the objective truth (to support the state in achieving these purposes) and to educate citizens rather than settle disputes between them (Chloros 1992: 92). Further, it is clear that the methodology employed by judges during socialism was not conducive to the strengthening of the role of judicial decisions in socialist legal systems and the society as a whole. Increasingly in line with the developments in civil law systems of Western Europe, the role of jurisprudence in post-socialist systems is becoming more and more significant so that they are gradually achieving the status of 'persuasive sources of law'. Again, here the Central Europeans are dealing with a moving target – the role of jurisprudence in Western Europe is being transformed as mentioned above. Nevertheless, the policy-shaping and law-shaping role of courts is not an entirely new notion in the Central European legal systems. The importance of jurisprudence is growing, assisted by the ambitious and sophisticated judgements given by the

47 Wróbel, ibid.

48 The Hungarian civil law before the enactment of the Civil Code of 1959 was largely based on judicial decisions (Grzybowski 1961: 253).

highest courts – the Supreme Courts and the Constitutional Courts. The latter often find themselves confronted with abuses of power or other unconstitutional activities of the legislators and governments. The role of Supreme Courts, apart from considering cassations from the judgements of lower courts, is to ensure uniform and proper application of law by all other courts. Thus the Supreme Courts have the power to issue decisions which clarify the meaning of legal concepts – these decisions have the power of 'legal principles'.[49] They are referred to as 'legal principles' in other Supreme Court judgements and in decisions of other courts.[50] Their particular importance can be seen in areas of law such as product liability – a great majority of decisions analysed in this book were given by Central European Supreme Courts.

Indeed, particular value of court judgements can be noted in areas such as product liability law. Product liability started developing in Central Europe at the time when economic, social and political changes prompted the transformation in the socialist legal system itself, when written law was found inadequate to reflect the emerging reality. Courts followed the tendencies established by previous jurisprudence (such as a shift from contractual to tort liability, objectivization of liability, using presumptions of fault and other developments described in Part II) but often did not refer to specific court judgements as legal bases for their decisions.

The role of courts in the times of transformations, albeit pivotal, is by no means straightforward. The political environment in which they function changed dramatically. The influx of new laws, a great many of which derive from the European Union, challenge the consistency of legal frameworks in which they were so far operating. Their role was transformed from being purely national courts to being European Community courts, with obligations to follow the letter and spirit of the European Community law very clearly articulated by the European Court of Justice.

The Central European doctrine of law gradually grows in importance by writing about new social and economic phenomena as well as about the newly introduced sources of law, particularly those deriving from the European Community. Doctrinal opinions are omnipresent throughout this book – they follow, explain

49 In Poland: Constitution of the Republic of Poland of 2 April 1997, Article 183; Act of 23 November 2002 *on the Supreme Court*, Article 1 para. 1b. In Hungary: Act No. 66 of 1997 *on the Organization and Administration of Courts*, Section 25c (adopting "obligatory uniformity decisions applicable to the courts"). In the Czech Republic: Constitution (Act No. 1/1993), the Act *on Courts and Judges* (Act No. 6/2002) ("in the interest of the uniformity of courts' decision-making adopts standpoints on the courts' decision-making in the matters of particular kind" – <http://www.nsoud.cz/en/index.html>).

50 See for instance the already mentioned Judgement of the Polish Supreme Court of 17 February 2006 on limitation periods for bringing tort claims. The Supreme Court referred to a previous decision of 12 February 1969, III PZP 43/68 (OSNCP 1969, No. 9, poz. 150) "having the power of a 'legal principle'" (at page 4).

and sometimes also drive the developments within the product liability regimes and the law of obligations in general.

IDEOLOGY

According to Zweigert and Kotz who define it as a "religious or political conception of how social or economic life should be organised" (1998: 72), ideology cannot serve the purpose of distinguishing Western European legal systems from one another. Nevertheless, they also stress the importance of ideology for the existence of the socialist legal family (1998: 72). Marxism was the basic doctrine of the socialist legal systems; so crucial in fact that it was the only official ideology, all the others being "erroneous" and a "subversive threat to the social order" (David and Brierley 1985: 169, Chloros 1992: 95). The law in such systems "[wa]s just a 'superstructure' on the foundation of economic relations of the society in which it [wa]s in force, and it ha[d] to promote the ideas represented by those who [we]re governing the country" (Pistor 2002: 1, Chloros 1992: 92, 93, Wagner 1974: 2, 3). This phenomenon is not exclusive to socialist jurisdictions, although it was obviously more pronounced and clearly visible there.[51] It shaped the process of law creation and interpretation.[52] Lack of separation of powers (Wagner 1974: 2), particularly clear in the lack of judicial independence (Chloros 1992: 92), was an expression of this ideology.[53] More precisely, it was not merely the role of law as a 'tool' (Wagner 1974: 2, 3) but also the policy which the law was designed to realize and the reality surrounding this policy which were peculiar to socialist societies.[54]

So far, the book contains numerous remarks on the impact of socialism on the development of market laws, consumer laws and product liability laws. The analysis below builds upon these remarks and adds a theoretical framework to them. It does not explore in great detail how the socialist ideology affected development of legal, economic and political discourses in the context of product

51 According to Article 1 of the Constitution of the Peoples' Republic of Poland of 1952, the laws of the Republic were "the expression of the interests and will of the working people" (translated by Lasok 1973: 3). Constitutions of other Central and Eastern European countries contained similar provisions. Civil Codes of Central European states contained provisions limiting protection of individual rights to situations where they were not inconsistent with the progress of socialist societies (Articles 4 and 5 of the Hungarian Code of 1959, Articles 4 and 5 of the Polish Code of 1964 and Articles 6 and 7 of the Czechoslovak Civil Code of 1964 – see Chloros 1992: 92).

52 On the problems of law creation and application in the socialist Poland see: Suchańska (1979: 47–60), and in the socialist Hungary: Eörsi (1970).

53 As explained above, this independence was growing towards the end of the socialist rule (Wagner 1974: 3). The role of courts in socialist legal systems was to fulfil the aims of the state and educate citizens (Chloros 1992: 92).

54 Wagner pointed out that "the legal rules of every country under a communist regime ha[d] to follow the outstanding tenets of communism" (1974: 3).

liability in Central Europe (this is done in the following chapter – exploring the political, economic and legal environment which traditionally contributes to the development of product liability laws and assessing it against the environment evolving in Western Europe). Below is a more general, systemic approach to the ideological developments and their effects on the legal systems as a whole.

Historical developments described above contributed to discrepancies in the power of socialist ideology and its effect on law and its practice among the Central European states. The overarching ideological influence of socialism was, however, present throughout the region. Without engaging in a detailed assessment of socialist ideology, suffice it to remind the reader that the Marxist utopia, involving a centrally controlled social and economic system, aimed at full satisfaction of the needs of the society (Kozminski 1992: 351). This was the basis of the socialist philosophy of 'holism' – seeing the interests of individuals as subservient to the interest of the system, the state. Laws, also laws of the market, were shaped so as to conform to this philosophy. Shortly before the demise of socialism, although socialist ideology was still very potent, it came under an increasing pressure of worsening economic conditions and the discontent of citizens. Socialist governments attempted to introduce some elements of the rule of law, and market-oriented policies and laws appeared. Hungary was the pioneer reformer, with the first reforms appearing during the 1960s. Czechoslovakia and other socialist states followed in the 1970s and the 1980s. Poland was rather late with introducing reforms – most appeared during the 1980s. The reforms are scrutinized more closely in the following chapter. They brought the socialist legal systems more ideologically in line with the Western European legal systems – the emphasis on the rule of law meant the introduction of some level of accountability and control over the state. This translated into greater separation of powers, new institutional structures, and even the creation of constitutional courts. The 'holist' philosophy of socialism was quickly disappearing.

The final demise of socialism in 1989 obviously meant the demise of socialist ideology. Its effect upon substantive law, legal and institutional systems, markets and economy has gradually diminished, although the process of eradicating the influences of socialism has been much more complex than initially thought (Pistor 2002: 1). The use of law as "an instrument of power in the hands of the ruling party" has been replaced with the rule of law (ibid.). What this meant in practice was the introduction of greater political accountability and control over the state – separation of powers, new constitutions, new institutional structures and increased powers of the constitutional courts. Democracy and free market economy brought in a new approach to markets: the view of the role of the state in markets changed dramatically. The impact of these ideological changes upon product liability can be seen in the later parts of the book.

CONCLUSIONS

Certain systemic, fundamental features of a legal system are conducive to the development of the law of product liability. The analysis above indicated broadly the specificity of Central European legal systems, which is built upon below to explore the trajectories of the evolution of their product liability laws. It is clear that these legal systems remain in the stage of transition. Struggling to eliminate the reminders of the previous period produced a curious state of affairs – Central European legal systems are referred to by some comparative lawyers as 'hybrid systems' (Zweigert and Kotz 1998) and by this book as 'post-socialist' systems. The impact of the phenomenon of transition on product liability – both as it develops on the national level of Central European states and on the EU level – is significant.

Chapter 3
Product Liability – Spirit and Context – Developments in the World and Peculiarities in Central Europe

INTRODUCTION

Product liability is a grand tool for demonstrating transformations within laws, societies and markets. It combines the influences of written law and judicial activism. It attempts to exert control over markets, apportion risks, and reconcile the interests of market participants. Now the analysis turns to the fundamental characteristics of product liability as a legal category, thus determining the scope and conceptual framework of the book. Chapter 3 investigates the evolution of the underlying key ideas which affected the nature of product liability law and its practical application in Western Europe and in Central Europe. It assesses the implications of differences and similarities in approach to these key ideas between the 'West' and Central Europe.

SCOPING THE STUDY

Product liability remains a complex area of law, both in the 'West' and in Central Europe. The 'product liability system' (including the system introduced by the Product Liability Directive) is not a sufficiently coherent field of legal organization. Its intricacy and at some level also lack of internal consistence have an immense significance for the scope and structure of this book.

DEFINITIONS OF PRODUCT LIABILITY

For many European academics and legal practitioners, product liability is a new and "still rather alien" legal category (Whittaker 2005: 5). Product liability was described as liability in respect of personal injury, damage to property or loss caused by a defective product (Reich and Micklitz 1980: 93). It was also defined as liability for injury, damage, or loss caused by a shoddy or defective product to its buyer, a third person or their property, but not for the damage to the product itself (Howells and Weatherill 2005: 213, Jagielska 1999: 13, Howells 1993: 1, 2), and as "civil liability of manufacturers and others where damage or loss is caused by products which fail to meet the standards claimed expressly or impliedly for them or which are dangerous or otherwise defective" (Miller and Goldberg 2004: 1). Link and Sumbuc defined it as: "liability of the producer, seller, supplier, or quasi-producer for consequential damage resulting from the use of a defective product" (1997: 163). Stapleton (1994a: 9) identified it as: "the responsibility which the law places on those who supply products for the losses caused by their condition" (1994a: 3).[1] According to her 'product liability' denotes tortious liability for commercially supplied products (1994a: 9, also Gnela 2000: 13).[2] In perhaps the most comprehensive definition, Łętowska[3] describes it as "liability of an objective character, hence … independent, or on its way to independence, from fault for causing damage, and not conditional upon the existence of a contract, where the causes are the features of a product, whether those existing *per se* (such as the toxicity of poisons), or those related to bad construction, production, supervision, instructions for use, or neglect in the later monitoring of the product" (1999: 78).[4]

No material difference may be observed in the manner in which product liability is defined by the Western European and Central European writers. The definitions quoted above illustrate the main features of product liability which evolved both in the 'West' and in the 'East'. They portray its links with the laws of obligations on the one hand, and its specificity – emphasis on 'products', professional character of the activity of liable persons, and specific type of damage – on the other. The links of product liability with the laws of obligations have been widely commented upon (Whittaker 2005: 5, Miller and Goldberg 2004: 3, Łętowska 1999).[5] Both in the 'West' and in the 'East', the contemporary product liability laws originated in the contract law of the nineteenth century. Although later the focus shifted onto tort law, contract law did not wholly lose importance (Miller and Goldberg 2004: 3). It is true that along with the better understanding of the context of the products market the trust in the traditional principles of contract law, such as privity, largely diminished. The same, nonetheless, can be said about the trust in the traditional

1 Stapleton does not attempt to propose this definition as the ultimate one. She simply seems to be suggesting it as a guideline of the character of the legal category she discusses.

2 According to Stapleton, history and substance of contract and tort have been closely "intertwined" (1994a: 9). However, she does not hesitate to claim that at the moment "in Britain and the rest of Europe the term tends not to include liabilities in contract" (ibid.).

3 Ewa Łętowska is one of the most prominent legal scholars and consumer lawyers in Poland. She was the first Ombudsman of Poland, and at present she sits as a judge in the Polish Constitutional Court.

4 Translated by the author.

5 Whittaker compares the French and the English 'liability for products'. Importantly, he notes a much greater emancipation of the US product liability rules (section 402A of the *Second Restatement of Torts*) from the general law of obligations (2005: 5).

principles of tort: such as liability contingent on fault of the defendant. Product liability brought both these fields under sharp scrutiny.[6]

It is crucial to note that, as Stapleton observed, product liability is considerably narrower than a mere "liability arising out of product-related injury" (1994a: 9). The specificity of product liability, which is the result of its unique role and of the situations it applies to, was catered for by both the Western and the Central European legal systems in the efforts to establish distinct product liability regimes. This specificity is linked to the complex interrelations of this area of law with other laws and policies, and various socio-economic phenomena, of which below.

PRODUCT LIABILITY IN 'CONTEXT'

Product liability is a very specific type of a civil liability regime. It is the reaction of law attempting to cope with modern phenomena such as "large distant enterprises, mass marketing and a dramatic increase in scientific and economic understanding of interdependence of much human activity" (Stapleton 1994a: 8). It is crucial to recognize the complex blend of factors which affected the development of product liability law into what it is today, and its role in society. Such approach aids the readers' understanding of the nature of transition taking place in Central European product liability systems.

While it remains embedded within the doctrinal and philosophical bases of the law of obligations, product liability has specific aims – these give it a specific position within various economic, legal and social arrangements. Product liability is a market law measure, a consumer law measure; it is a compensation mechanism;[7] it is a mechanism ensuring safety of products.[8] The conceptual framework and practical application of product liability regimes are determined by the position of product liability law within these arrangements. This chapter does not map out in detail all the contextual arrangements in which product liability could be assessed; rather it focuses on these social, economic and legal phenomena which exert the most significant influence upon the development of product liability law in the context of its harmonization in Europe, now also including Central Europe.

6 "(T)he post-war developments in the area of product liability in both the EC and the US can be seen as part of a larger, albeit uncoordinated, movement within the law this century to come to terms with modern circumstances. These include the phenomena of large distant enterprises, mass marketing and a dramatic increase in scientific and economic understanding of interdependence of much human activity. In this environment the contract/tort polarity of individual free contracts and injuries between strangers is no longer adequate to deal with much of the experience of the community" (Stapleton 1994a: 8).

7 Its key function is to ensure that compensation is provided to victims of defective products.

8 This statement refers to the deterrence effect of product liability which is not analysed in detail in the book. It was briefly mentioned in the Introduction, where references to works of scholars who explored this issue can be found.

The chapter offers a mixture of theoretical considerations, setting out the aims and the key concepts inherent in product liability, and practical economic, social and legal observations which assess the tangible effects of the law. It starts with a review of the civil liability regime within which product liability evolved – the law of obligations. The place of product liability law within the wider system of obligations and the changes taking place within this system on the national and the pan-European level are introduced. The analysis deals with differences in the philosophical-jurisprudential approaches to the law of obligations and product liability in the 'West' and in the 'East'. The main tendencies in the development of obligations in Central Europe are assessed and weighed against the trends in Western Europe. The key legal constructs intrinsic to the law of obligations are examined with particular emphasis on their impact in the product liability context.

The next element of analysis is the assessment of product liability as part of a market law system. In the context of harmonization of law within the European Union, the relationship of product liability with markets – businesses and consumers, and in particular with the policies and laws of consumer protection – is critical. A large part of this chapter is devoted to the history of this relationship in academic thought and in the policies and laws of Western Europe and the European Union on the one hand, and of the Central European states on the other. It is in the links with consumer protection that the book seeks the rationale and the theoretical basis for the establishment of product liability as a distinct liability regime, separate from the general law of obligations. The chapter traces the expansion of consumer protection laws and policies in the European Union. It touches upon crucial features of this process, its implications for product liability, and its role in the transformation of Central European law. It culminates with a review of the rationale and main features of the Product Liability Directive. It assesses its effects across Europe, and evaluates the harmonized product liability system which the Directive has established so far. The continued importance of national laws, market policies and legal cultures for this harmonized system is emphasized. Further, the chapter focuses on the evolution of Central European consumer protection law from its humble beginnings in the times of socialism until today. This enquiry provides the background to Part II, where the focus shifts onto substantive product liability law of Central Europe.

PRODUCT LIABILITY AND THE LAW OF OBLIGATIONS – CONTRASTING THE 'WEST' WITH CENTRAL EUROPE

INTRODUCTORY REMARKS

There is no doubt that product liability retains very strong ties with the law of obligations. Fundamental concepts inherent in the law of obligations such as fault, causal link or damages play a significant role in product liability. Below the book maps out the developments within contract and tort law – both on the national and the pan-European level – and seeks their impact on product liability. Special attention is paid to the differences between the 'West' and Central Europe. The analysis is structured as follows: it starts with the theoretical framework of the law of obligations, observing very significant changes there; subsequently it portrays how the theories affected the changes in the law and practice of obligations.

CONCEPTS AND TERMINOLOGY

First, a short explanation concerning the conceptual framework and terminology. In order to avoid confusion among the English-speaking readers, the terminological conventions used across the English-speaking world have been adopted, with some caveats.

The book uses the notion 'law of obligations' to denote collectively the laws of contract and tort. The 'law of obligations' concerns civil liability; it is an area of private law. It offers rights to individuals which can be enforced by them directly (Howells and Weatherill 2005: 8), as opposed to rights which are enforced through public regulation and public enforcement measures. While civil law scholars, and also the socialist law scholars in the past, have commonly referred to the 'law of obligations',[9] common law legal scholars rather stress the distinct nature of contract and tort law.[10] Seeing contract and tort as parts of the wider category of 'law of obligations' entails a greater commonality of roles and characteristics. In the spirit of the Austrian ABGB, Hungarian and Czech civil laws do not establish a clear separation between obligations arising out of contracts and torts (contractual and tortious liability are for the most part regulated by the same provisions of the civil codes). The Polish Civil Code introduced such a separation, although it contains a general part which, unless otherwise specified, applies to all obligations. Following this general conceptual approach, Central European legal systems established common principles applicable to all obligation relationships (Wagner 1974: 5).[11] These principles were not always written down (in Hungary

9 For instance in the French system: see Flour, Albert and Savaux (2003). The scope of the 'law of obligations' extends also upon 'unjustified enrichment' (see for instance Visser [2006]), but this area goes beyond the topic of this book.

10 The general approach to the 'law of obligations' is reflected in the Draft Common Frame of Reference of 2008. See below for a short elaboration of harmonization of the law of obligations in Europe.

11 For doctrinal writings on the issue see Wagner (1974: 6, 7), Harmathy (1998: 95), Czachórski (2002: 45–69), and the literature referred to there. Section 489 of the Czech Civil Code reads: "Obligations arise from legal acts, in particular from agreements, as well as from caused damages, unjustified enrichment and from other acts mentioned in law" (translation provided by Dobiasova of the Czech Ministry of Trade and Industry). According to Article 353.1 of the Polish Civil Code: "An obligation consists in the obligee's right to demand performance and the obligor's obligation to perform." Paragraph 2 of the same Article adds: "Performance may consist either in a commission or in an omission." (Translated by Wagner 1974: 6).

no general part on the law of obligations existed in the Civil Code of 1959).[12] They were developed by doctrinal writings, although the extent, scope and the level of sophistication of these writings differed throughout Central Europe. While in Hungary and Poland the doctrinal analyses of the fundamental principles of the law of obligations were quite ample and thorough, the work of the Czech scholarly writers was not very comprehensive (this has improved significantly in recent times). The conceptual approach adopted in Central Europe entails common rules in both types of liability, but the practice of civil liability and doctrinal writings still clearly separates cases of contractual and tortious liability. They recognize different socio-economic roles and different legal and factual circumstances: clearly observable in the context of product liability systems. Thus, irrespective of the general conceptual approach to 'law of obligations', differences between contract and tort liability rules remain significant, and are reflected in the structure of the book which deals with contractual and tortious product liability separately.

Further conceptual and terminological choices follow. The terminology related to the Central European law of obligations has been chosen carefully in order to adequately reflect the language used by Central European legal scholarship. On the other hand, the language of obligations is often replaced by the language peculiar to product liability (for instance: consumer instead of creditor, trader instead of debtor,[13] product instead of 'thing', etc.) – this phenomenon gradually started appearing in Central European jurisprudence and doctrinal writings.

Czech and Hungarian legal scholars analyse obligations established by contracts and torts under the common umbrella of 'breach of duty'. In the case of a contract this duty is created by the parties and in the case of a tort it is created by law. Polish doctrinal writers, following the language of the Civil Code modelled on French law, refer to the general clause of 'damage caused to another' in tort liability (Article 415 of the Civil Code) and to a 'breach of duty' in cases of contractual liability. The impact of this dichotomy on product liability has been

12 There is a general part concerning the law of contracts. A short general part on the law of obligations can be found in the draft Civil Code (Part I of Book V – Gárdos 2007: 716). 'The Conception' refers to the drafts originating in the early twentieth century, based upon German law: it was assumed that the presence of a very complex and abstract general part unnecessarily complicated the adjudication process.

13 In the context of obligations, the notions of 'debtor' and 'creditor' have great significance in Central Europe. An 'obligation' is considered by Central European scholarly writers as consisting in: the creditor's right to demand performance and the debtor's obligation to perform (Wagner 1974: 6). Performance is understood as "the conduct of the (debtor) which conforms to the obligation, consists in the satisfying of an interest of the (creditor), and deserves protection" (Czachórski 1962: 48). These notions are not used in the book, which focuses on the specificity of product liability and refers to 'victims of defective products', 'consumers' or 'claimants' on the one hand (counterparts of the notion of 'creditor') and 'businesses', 'manufacturers', 'producers', 'suppliers' or 'defendants' on the other (counterparts of the 'debtor').

limited. Both these approaches utilize clauses the general nature of which must be adapted to the specific needs of product liability cases.

As regards liability arising outside of contractual relationships, the book uses the notion 'tort'.[14] This notion is not uniformly understood and accepted throughout Europe. Various concepts emerge in academic literature – such as the French *responsabilité extracontractuelle* (also used in Spain, Italy and the Czech Republic), the German *underlaubte Handlung*, the Dutch *onrechtmatige daad*, the typical for civil law jurisdictions "delict law", or the more widely described "law of compensation for damage" or "accident law" – to reflect the complex nature of this liability (Cousy 2002: 23, 24). Referring to 'tort' follows the tendency among those writing about Central European laws in English language. Wagner translated the concept '*czyn niedozwolony*' used by the Polish Civil Code (literally: 'prohibited act' or 'illicit act') into 'tort' (1974: 139), although the representatives of the Polish doctrine of law do tend to use the notion 'delict' (*delikt*) or 'liability *ex delicto*' (for instance Czachórski 2002: 197). Also Harmathy and Maczonkai use the notion 'tort' in their English-language writings on Hungarian law (1998: 115, 1996: 109), although at the same time Harmathy refers to 'delictual liability' (1998: 115). Vondracek mentioned 'torts' and 'delictual capability' when analysing the Czechoslovak Civil Code (1988: 376). The choice of 'tort' over 'delict' may also indicate more than simply a terminological preference. According to Czachórski, the notion of 'prohibited act' (tort) in the terminology of the Polish Civil Code, similar to the French *acte illicite* and the German *underlaubte Handlung*, is broader than the traditional concept of 'delict' (2002: 197). 'Delict' requires a human act committed with the necessary element of culpability. 'Prohibited acts' are also human acts committed without the existence of fault or even events not related to human conduct, provided these events have caused damage for which law renders someone responsible (Czachórski 2002: 197).

Czech and Polish laws of obligations are based on the concept of 'legal acts' (which could be defined as all acts aimed at generating legal consequences – Brouwer and Haage 2007: 11), resembling the German *Rechtsgeschäft* (Gárdos 2007: 717). This notion is used in the book, especially when quoting Central European legal scholars, but conceptually it does not affect the approach to product liability laws which require special forms of legal acts. The consequence of a universal, 'all-purpose' regulation of 'legal acts' in civil codes is that their legal effects, the requirements for their validity, and other issues such as limitation periods could also be generally regulated for greater consistency of civil law (with exceptions introduced for particular forms of legal acts, such as contracts, whenever necessary). The book refers to these general rules whenever they apply in the product liability context (which does not happen often, as there are normally special rules which take over). The Polish Civil Code devoted the entire Title IV of Book I to legal acts and their consequences. The Czech Civil Code recognizes the concept of 'legal acts' in Chapter IV, Sections 34–51. It defines a 'legal act'

14 See Goldberg (2003: 21, 22) for an analysis of the historical roots of this notion.

as "an expression of will directed in particular to emergence, change or extinction of rights and duties connected with such expression by legal regulations".[15] The Hungarian Civil Code did not recognize the utility of this general approach, and, following the Swiss Civil Code (ZGB – *Zivilgesetzbuch*) of 1907, used contracts – the main form of 'legal acts' – as the main conceptual legal category. Although the Hungarian Code did not define 'legal acts' (*jogi tény*), the concept was used in doctrinal writings: they have been classified into 'lawful acts' (for instance contracts – *szerzödés*, which are acts concluded in order to produce a legal effect) and 'unlawful acts' (torts) (Harmathy 1998: 96). The draft Civil Code intends to change this approach to some extent, separating general regulation of contracts from other provisions concerning obligations more generally (Gárdos 2007: 718).

PHILOSOPHIES OF OBLIGATIONS AND THEIR IMPORTANCE FOR PRODUCT LIABILITY

The philosophies of obligations have some significance for product liability, although they are unable to ultimately draw a firm conceptual skeleton for this area of law. Stapleton stressed that theories ought to provide an explanation for the existence and exact position of the boundaries of substantive law (1994a: 96). According to her, "perhaps the rule of law itself requires not just that we have rules but that they are based on purposes which are open to public debate" (1994a: 90). Stapleton contended that identifying the purposes of law enables one to assess their consistency, correctness, as well as the extent to which the law in fact achieves them (1994a: 90). While, "whether intentionally or not, law serves the interests of some at the expense of the interests of others", theory explains who the favoured ones are and where to set the boundaries of what is and what is not allowed at the expense of other groups (Stapleton 1994a: 98). In the context of product liability, theories should explain the 'two-party nature of the claim' – why the defendant is liable, why the claimant must be compensated and to what extent; they should make clear why only certain invasions into the claimants' interests may be actionable and others may not (Stapleton 1994a: 96). The theories ought to explain how to reconcile the causal link element, how to provide justification for limitation of rules to products, or to products supplied in the course of a business, or to special types of damage only (Stapleton 1994a: 96); they ought also to provide justification for the existence of a particular standard of liability (strict liability or fault?). Stapleton pointed out that theoretical foundations of product liability law should be sought among those inherent in civil liability in general, "based on balancing standards and causal requirements",[16] and those specific for product liability (1994a: 7). This chapter introduces both these theoretical dimensions,

15 Section 34 (translation of the Code provided by Dobiasova).

16 Owen (1985) stresses the value of the general theories of contract (Llewellyn) and tort (Prosser) for the development of product liability theories. See also Steiner (1982)

and investigates their influence on substantive rules of liability. It emphasizes their development in Central Europe and contrasts it with the development in the 'West'. While the philosophical foundations of civil liability are explored below, the later part of this chapter is an inquiry into the specificity of product liability. The latter is mainly the result of the specificity of the position of product liability within markets. Philosophical bases of product liability are linked to the theoretical considerations concerning consumer protection and market regulation.

The relationship between liability philosophy and liability rules has two facets: one of an explanatory nature and one of a normative nature. On the one hand theory explains why the rules are established, interpreted and applied in a particular manner, and on the other hand it influences the process of establishing and applying the rules.[17] Theories impact the manner in which civil liability laws are formulated by legislators as well as upon the directions the courts take in interpreting these civil liability laws. And it is through such judicial interpretation that product liability regimes were initially created – both in the 'West' and in Central Europe.

While the theoretical background of product liability in the United States is impressive, the situation is different in Europe, including Central and Eastern Europe. The focus here seems to be on substantive rules of law and their application (Jagielska 1999, Howells 1993, Geddes 1992, Kelly and Attree 1992). Both in the United States and in Europe, however, product liability thought draws heavily on the philosophies of obligations, and these are still subject to academic debate and controversy.

THE DEVELOPMENT OF THEORETICAL FOUNDATIONS OF OBLIGATIONS IN THE 'WEST' AND IN CENTRAL EUROPE, AND THEIR TRANSLATION INTO SUBSTANTIVE RULES OF LIABILITY

Introductory remarks

The key role of civil liability is protecting interests (Geistfeld 2006: 4–6) and allocating losses. The perception of which interests are to be prioritized and where the losses should lie, and thus what roles the civil liability laws are to fulfil, changed within the last century. The development of mature, stable market economies and democracies based upon the ideas of a welfare state (encompassing consumer protection postulates) combined with free market and fair competition entailed the recognition of complexity of goals of civil liability in the United States and in

---

for postulates of uniform "moral foundations" of product liability with the general law of negligence.

17 See Owen (1985) for a critique of liability theories of his contemporaries. Owen claims that rather than the product liability doctrine it was a "solid social consensus" which contributed to the development of the modern "products liability" rules in the United States.

Western Europe. Eastern and Central Europe followed a different trajectory here, of which below, but at present the liability theories there are evolving towards the Western models. Below is a brief description of academic discourses concerning the functions of the laws of obligations.

The functions of the laws of obligations – evolution

The consensus among academics, policymakers and legislators (both in the 'West' and in the 'East') as to which functions of civil liability laws ought to be emphasized stronger has not yet been reached.[18] Particularly dramatic discourses have accompanied the development of tort liability.

The evolution of academic thought in this area has been remarkable. Based on the ideas of commutative, distributive and corrective justice developed by Aristotle and other scholars exploring his thoughts (Ritchie 1894), contemporary theories of obligations draw a complex picture of roles which civil liability rules play in a modern society. The long-established approach to civil liability, stressing three objectives – compensation of victims, deterrence of injuries (behaviour modification) and risk-spreading (the approach is still to a large extent prevalent in Central Europe, of which below) – has begun to evolve to reflect developments in modern legal systems and markets. Traditionally, the roles of the law of obligations were defined and delimited very clearly. While contractual liability preserved and enforced expectations created by bargaining ("contract law concerns broken promises" – Cooter 1991: 11), tortious liability rules created relationships between people who might not have been in contact before, with a specified tortious act of one party as the basis of the relationship ("tort law concerns accidental or intentional harm of people or property" – Cooter ibid.).[19] This general description still remains correct, but it has recently been supplemented by much more intricate considerations. Cousy summarizes the functions of tort as: "punishment, vindication, redress of the social order, implementation of legal rules, protection of citizens' rights, recognition and creation of new rights and interests, appeasement of the victim ..., compensation or indemnification of

18 On the philosophical bases of tort see: for the English approach – Cane (1999); for the US approach and the introduction to the dichotomy between the law and economics movement and the traditional tort philosophies – the founders of the economic approach to tort law: normative approach – Guido Calabresi (1970) and positive approach – Posner (1972), or Landes and Posner (1983); also Cooter (1991), Stapleton (1994a), Green (1997), Schwartz (1997). On the theory of contract: Atiyah (1995), Benson (2001), Gordley (2003).

19 In spite of these clearly distinct characteristics, one could always observe certain commonalities in discourses concerning aims of contract and tort liability: in civil law countries and in socialist law countries, where these two types of liability constitute two aspects of the wider category of the law of obligations, these commonalities have indeed been quite prominent. See above for a further explanation of this phenomenon and its implications for the book.

losses, loss spreading, loss shifting, allocation of losses, deterrence …, prevention, precaution, reduction of accident costs, justice (compensatory justice, retributive justice, corrective justice)" (2002: 23).[20] According to van Dam, "[t]ort law is not just a system. It is about balancing the interests of individuals, private and public bodies. It distributes rights, duties, and money" (2006: 609-1). Contract law, which according to Kronman is a "tangled mass of legal rules that regulate the process of legal exchange" traditionally had three major functions: to specify which agreements are legally binding, to define rights and obligations established by ambiguous but enforceable agreements, and to provide the consequences of an "unexcused breach" (1980: 472). Kronman argues that contract law ought to have another function: distributing wealth among the members of society (1980: 474). Traditionally, contract law is said not to be focused on penalizing conduct, although in some contemporary writings it has been argued that contract liability ought to enable an award of punitive damages (US literature in particular).[21]

What were the triggers for these transformations in the philosophical foundations of the law of obligations? Since the beginning of the twentieth century, throughout Europe and in the United States, new socio-economic, political and legal phenomena challenged the internal coherence of liability theories. Market considerations seem to play a greater than ever role in civil liability. In the 'West' the welfare state and consumer protection, and in the 'East' the socialist political ideals and centrally planned market philosophy, were most influential. Since the 1980s the 'East' of Europe is gradually absorbing the welfarist and consumerist approach. In the United States and also increasingly in Europe the growing complexity and interdependence of civil liability rules, and their effects on economy and society, are widely acknowledged. In the spirit of improving competitiveness and increasing economic productivity, civil liability rules are to meet the goals of compensation and resource allocation (more widely recognized, traditional role of civil liability), as well as the postulates of cost reduction and efficiency. The goal of Better Regulation, so widely pronounced currently at the

20 Here Cousy refers to the classification of types of 'particular justice' as conducted by Aristotle, and later developed by thinkers ranging from Thomas Aquinas to Ritchie (1894).

21 See for instance: Lee (2007) and the US literature referred to there.

European Union level[22] and at the national level,[23] forces legislators to consider the most efficient solutions in shaping laws. This aim extends far beyond civil liability rules, into the growing body of laws and regulations covering various aspects of markets. One can observe a stronger need for civil liability rules to fulfil the goals of economic efficiency in the light of the fact that these rules are now surrounded by, and compete with, a whole array of solutions, starting with substantive law and regulation, procedural rules ensuring access to courts, operation of various means of out-of-court settlement of disputes, insurance – including social security and private insurance – and even self-regulation by industry. Accompanying these developments, the strand of economic thought dealing with civil liability initiated in the United States by Calabresi and Posner is spreading throughout Europe. It encapsulated a more generalized, systemic and contextual approach to liability rules and their aims. Their intention was to stress the role of civil liability in minimizing social costs of accidents (Grady 1983: 799). Calabresi and Posner represented two distinct strands in the economic theory of liability law: a normative theory which focused on its reform towards greater economic efficiency (Calabresi), and a positive theory which attempted to better understand the existing rules (those formulated by legislators and those used by courts) (Posner) (Grady 1983: 799–800). Although both the traditional compensation and the economic efficiency strands of thought remain relevant at the moment, the prevailing opinion seems to be that no single principle or theory is able to provide sufficient basis for civil liability. The debate between the economic theories of efficient incentives and costs reduction and the traditional tort theories of compensation still continues, albeit a strong tendency to reconcile them can be noticed in the current academic thought.[24] A more multi-dimensional, multi-disciplinary, multi-level approach transpires from contemporary writings – especially in the United States (Geistfeld 2006, 2004, Goldberg and Zipursky 2006). It started spreading in Western Europe (Widmer 2005a) and also recently in Central Europe (Nowakowski 2004, Czachórski 2002). The complexity of roles which contract and tort laws are to play is increasingly reflected in Central European scholarly writings. Czachórski – a representative

22 Analysed below. See for instance: Communication from the Commission, Second Strategic Review of Better Regulation in the European Union of 2008, Communication from the Commission, Common Actions for Growth and Employment: the Community Lisbon Programme of 2005; also <http://ec.europa.eu/growthandjobs/areas/fiche03_en.htm>. The Lisbon European Council adopted a 10-year action plan, the aim of which was initially to "make the European Union the most competitive and dynamic economy in the World" (Special Eurobarometer No. 215 Lisbon European Commission 2005). See also: Extracts from Presidency Conclusions on The Lisbon Strategy by Theme. European Councils: Lisbon (March 2000) to Brussels (June 2004).

23 Particularly visible in the United Kingdom – see the Better Regulation Executive website: <http://www.betterregulation.gov.uk/>.

24 US: see Geistfeld (2006, 2004), also Madden (ed.) (2005); in Europe: see indications of this thinking in some national contributions to Widmer's *Unification of Tort Law: Fault* (2005a: 334–5).

of the Polish legal doctrine – describes their role as regulating and preserving market relations in society, as well as protecting pecuniary and non-pecuniary interests of persons (2002: 19–21). He defines the role of tortious liability to be of a compensational, preventive and educational nature (2002: 198).

As the analysis below illustrates, the complexity and interdependence mentioned above is starting to appear throughout Central Europe, although the traditional approach to civil liability laws as mechanisms of compensation and prevention remains relevant (Czachórski 2002: 95, Perram 1992).

Central European specificities

The specificities of Central European philosophies of the law of obligations are the product of the phenomena described in Chapter 2 above (the systemic qualities of their legal systems).

First, a short note explaining the fundamentals of Central European laws of obligations. As mentioned above, they were modelled upon Western European laws – in particular those of Austria and Germany (the Czech Republic and Hungary), and France (Poland). Their expansion gained impetus in the nineteenth and the beginning of the twentieth century, although the directions in which they developed were not identical. After the Second World War, Central European civil laws gained some very peculiar qualities – the results of socialism and its ideology. At present they exhibit further peculiar features indicating the lingering state of transition. However, the main principles of the law of obligations have always been those common to all civil law jurisdictions. Referring to the Polish Civil Code at the times of socialism, Lasok wrote: "whilst the philosophy of the Code is Marxist throughout, the content of the Code reflects the present state of Poland still, it seems, in the process of transition from the capitalist to the socialist stage" (1973: 9). This position remained, not only in Poland but also throughout Central Europe, until the end of the socialist domination. It is now being built upon when laws of obligations are constructed to reflect the changing reality.

A remarkable feature of the socialist ideology was its overwhelming influence on market relations, and thus on the rules governing those relations. The implications of this feature for the framework of Central European legal systems were explored in Chapter 2. Socialist civil laws were alienated from the reality of social and economic life. Most legal relationships (in particular – those between businesses) were governed by rules deriving from sources not related to or deriving from the code-based law of obligations: by the acts of central planning ('normative acts'). The tasks which in market economies are performed by laws of obligations and legal and economic mechanisms surrounding them, in socialist systems were to be performed by these acts of central planning. The latter were meant to affect market behaviour, apportion risks, compensate failed expectations and wrongs, and also to punish undesirable conduct. The code-based law of obligations was performing quite marginal functions in these circumstances. As a consequence, there was no regulatory or judicial drive for introducing such innovative, market-related legal mechanisms grounded in the law of obligations as product liability.

The policy shift away from strict socialism and towards a more market-focused approach which took place in Central Europe in the late 1970s and early 1980s was mentioned in Chapter 2. The outcome of the reforms was a blend of market philosophy, limited consumerism and a peculiar approach to welfare policies,[25] as well as the remaining elements of socialist central planning. These market-driven reforms also resulted in legislative changes (amendments to civil codes, mostly reflecting the need for protection of consumers),[26] and generally in a much greater prominence of the rules of civil liability. It was recognized that 'normative acts', and generally the policy of central planning, were unable to perform the functions they were meant to perform.[27] The role of the law of obligations was growing, especially in relations between businesses and consumers. The establishment of product liability laws was to some extent the reflection of this transformation. The conceptual foundations of product liability systems were being built in jurisprudence and doctrinal writings during this time.

The market philosophy and consumerism obviously achieved much greater prominence after the demise of socialism. The gradual changes explained above, leading to the reintroduction of market economy, entailed re-learning of the traditional philosophies and roles of the laws of obligations. Thus the doctrinal analyses of obligations keeping in line with the 'old law' typical of a civil law system became increasingly prominent. The traditional functions of tort and contract law were emphasized (Czachórski 2002: 19–21). The number of amendments of the existing civil codes, introducing greater emphasis on private property, freedom of contract, or protection of consumers in various transactions, often reached more than one hundred.[28] Although civil codes are normally framed in general terms, and therefore are able to withstand significant transformations, the sheer number of the changes and imports within the codes causes serious difficulties for legislators wishing to retain their internal coherence and clarity. It is not surprising that legislators contemplate the possibility of introduction of completely new civil codes (Ronovska 2008, Gárdos 2007, Łętowska, Jagielska, Lis et al. 2007). The reforms introduced so far have been linked to the increasing emphasis upon market economy and democracy (Tichy 2002a: 117–20, Menyhard 2003: 252). While socialist civil codes often separated regulation of relations

25 See a further part of this chapter for a more detailed analysis of these changes and their implications for markets and consumers.

26 Again, these are analysed in more detail below.

27 The socio-economic background and implications of these transformations are further explored in the following section of this chapter dealing with consumer laws of Central European states.

28 The Codification Committee for the Draft Hungarian Civil Code noted the need to amend the existing Civil Code of 1959 more than 150 times, "despite its outstanding technical quality" (<www.im.hu>).

between businesses (which were largely state-owned) from other relations (Poland and Hungary), or even refrained from regulating them altogether (Czechoslovakia), the new approach is rather to regulate business-to-business, business-to-consumer or consumer-to-consumer relations together[29] (Ronovska 2008: 115, Gárdos 2007: 714).[30] On the other hand, the influence of the European Community law determines special treatment of business-to-consumer transactions. Various directives enacted by the Community with the aim of protecting consumers have largely been incorporated, or are about to be incorporated, into the civil codes (Gárdos 2007: 713, 714, Łętowska, Jagielska, Lis et al. 2007). These systemic changes affected the philosophies of the laws of obligations. While the traditional understanding of the role of the laws of obligations remains prominent, they have gained a more market-focused dimension. Contract liability is understood to be particularly vital in business relationships, where speedy and cost-efficient solution, speedy recovery of losses or an injunctive relief are vital. Specific forms of contracts (especially consumer contracts covered by the measures implementing EC consumer protection directives) have been given special treatment, resulting from the understanding that certain contractual parties require a greater level of protection to the one provided by general rules of contractual liability. Tortious liability is growing in scope and complexity. Central European civil codes contain general clauses which apply in cases of tortious liability, as well as some specific types of torts which are regulated separately (often because a stricter liability standard is deemed necessary). Obviously, product liability has recently joined the list of these specific torts, first of all due to the judicial interpretation of the general provisions of the civil codes, and subsequently as a result of the implementation of the Product Liability Directive. Both the general and the specific provisions are applied in the context of the transforming economic and social reality. At present, Central European civil liability rules are being reconsidered, and on the other hand they are being surrounded by a plethora of other legal mechanisms aimed at providing compensation, deterring undesirable market behaviour, or insuring risks and liability. While the role of obligations in shaping behaviour and compensating losses is becoming more grounded, the next step for Central Europe is the recognition of complexity of market economies and interrelationships between the law of obligations and other mechanisms fulfilling similar roles. As mentioned above, this view is more and more common in academic writings throughout the region.[31]

29 The Czech Civil Code of 1964 still does not regulate business relationships – they are covered by the Commercial Code of 1991. The draft civil code does not contemplate abandoning this approach (Ronovska 2008: 115).

30 As to the Hungarian draft – see remarks concerning "a code built on the monist principle" – 'the Conception' at page 7.

31 See the further part of this chapter which explores these developments in more detail with regard to methods of regulating markets and protecting consumers – it observes

The key elements of the law of obligations – East-West comparison and impact on product liability

The debate concerning the philosophical foundations and the roles of the law of obligations reflected and informed the transformations within the substantive rules of liability. And these changes affected the evolution of product liability regimes on the theoretical and practical level.[32] The gist of the analysis below is introducing product liability through the lens of the main trends of development in the substantive law of obligations.

Freedom and privity of contract are key concepts in the development of contractual liability which had a significant impact on product liability law. The remaining fundamentals reflect what is referred to throughout the book as the 'requisites of liability' – the necessary elements which need to be established for liability to arise: breach of contract, tortious/delictual behaviour (including detailed elaboration on the role of fault and the 'fault discourse'[33] in establishing a breach of contract or a tort), damage and causal link. Other issues which also warrant a note here are limitation periods and the procedural aspects of civil liability.

The analysis below contrasts the approach in Western Europe (including the Product Liability Directive) and the United States with the approach of the Central European states.

Freedom of contract

While freedom of contract is still the foundation of this area of law in Western Europe,[34] it is gradually being eroded by legislative interventions motivated by various reasons including the requirements of welfare state and consumer protection.[35] One can, therefore, observe the emergence of contractual duties which were not negotiated by the parties and which the parties cannot modify or

---

the growth in the importance of civil liability and litigation on the one hand, and of public regulation and enforcement on the other.

32 On the other hand, one cannot help noticing that it may be the specific needs of areas such as product liability that prompted the internal changes within civil liability in general. This thought is explored to some extent below.

33 The book argues that although in the evolution of product liability laws the requirement of 'fault' (the notion is chosen instead of 'negligence' for a number of reasons – see below) may gradually have disappeared, the elements of discourse typical of 'fault' – reasonability, foreseeability, avoidability and other considerations – continue to play a part in establishing liability.

34 For a further analysis of the concept of freedom of contract and its impact see Atiyah (1979).

35 See an elaboration of this issue in the context of the EC Directive on Unfair Terms in Consumer Contracts – Brownswood, Howells and Wilhelmsson (1996). The essays in Willett (ed.) (1996) elaborate on the development of the concept of fairness in European private law. This concept erodes freedom of contract – as a result fairness provides "a benefit

exclude. These duties are imposed, implied by law into some contracts (Hondius 2004: 2, Gordley 2003: 8–11). The result of the transformation is that, instead of the sole focus on enforcing bargains and protecting expectations through providing sanctions, contract law is now also aimed at controlling the contents of bargains and ensuring their fairness. This change from the "voluntaristic", positivistic and conceptualistic premises was referred to as the "breakdown of 'classical' contract law" (Gordley 2003: 3). It is important in the product liability context – it entails certain duties concerning quality and safety of products for sellers (and even for manufacturers, of which below), which cannot be excluded or limited in consumer transactions. In the United States and in Western Europe these duties were gradually built by substantive law and by courts during the first half of the twentieth century.[36] They accompanied the acknowledgement of a weaker position of consumers in market transactions. They intensified in the second half of the twentieth century with the emergence of the consumer movement, consumer protection policies and first mature consumer protection laws. In Central Europe and other socialist states this transformation appeared later – with the materialization of market ideas within socialist market philosophies and legal doctrines – in the late 1970s (Hungary and Czechoslovakia) and early 1980s (Poland). How these ideas surfaced and what they meant in the product liability context is analysed in further detail below. Before their appearance, contract law and its practice were under the influence of socialist political and economic ideas, the fundamental elements of which were explored in Chapter 2. As mentioned there, the socialist approach to markets led to the wide use of acts of planning ('normative acts' – Wagner 1974: 7, Wiszniewski 1964: 219, Czachórski 1962: 169, Grzybowski 1961: 256), which had various forms and effects. Their impact on contractual freedom was very significant. The use of the general clause referred to as 'principles of socialist cooperation' or 'principles of community life' (Eörsi 1979a: 153) could be noticed in interpreting and enforcing contractual provisions. Overall, freedom of contract was severely limited in socialist Central Europe, albeit by quite different means and with different motives than in the West.[37]

At present, welfare state ideas and the increasingly potent consumer protection policies impact the application of the principle of contractual freedom, with both the West and the East of Europe remaining under the influence of European Community consumer protection law explored below. These developments

for parties who have not bargained for this benefit" (Willett 1996: 11). On the effect of the welfare state upon transformations within law in general – see Teubner (1986a: 3–10).

36 See for instance: Stapleton's 'aclassical warranties' in the United States (1994a: 21), cases: *Mazetti v. Armour & Co* (1913), *Baxter v. Ford Motor Co* (1934); Vincy's analysis of the French *vices caches* (1986: 76, 77) and Zweigert and Kotz's elaboration on *action directe* (1998: 464); Link and Sumbuc's assessment of German developments (1997: 172); on the latter also Simitis (1986: 102).

37 See Chapter 4 of Part II for a more detailed analysis of freedom of contract in Central Europe.

create a climate where it is understood that the specific position of consumers in contemporary markets requires significant limits on the traditional approach to freedom of contract.

Privity of contract

Privity is one of the most fundamental principles of contract law (McKendrick 1994: 108–32).[38] It is, therefore, interesting to see how it was challenged by new phenomena such as insurance (during the nineteenth century – Farnsworth 2006: 933) or indeed product liability. The context of this process is explored below, where the book investigates the position of consumers in the contemporary markets. Privity of contract entails boundaries to claiming compensation for damage caused by products – both in a horizontal and vertical dimension (Stapleton 1994a: 37). Here it is sufficient to note that various methods of overcoming the boundaries of privity were used by American and European courts and academic writers (Salewski 2005). Following the example of the US judgements in the cases *Mazetti v. Armour & Co* and *Baxter v. Ford Motor Co*,[39] European courts built mechanisms such as *action directe* in France[40] or a transformed *ius negotiorum gestio* in Germany (Zweigert and Kotz 1998: 464, Simitis 1986: 102). Central European courts and doctrine of law also attempted to combat the horizontal and vertical obstacles of privity: through the concept of 'assistant in performance' in Hungary (Maczonkai 1996: 111) and various philosophical concepts such as a 'guarantee promise' (Sołtysiński 1970: 173) or a *quasi contractus* (Żuławska 1983a: 279) in Poland. The Czech approach was quite unique: it involved using contractual liability whenever there was a contract, and tortious liability when there was no contractual relationship, with no significant negative implications for victims of defective products irrespective of the basis of liability. A more detailed analysis of privity of contract in Central Europe and the mechanisms adopted to overcome its limitations can be found in Chapter 4 of Part II. In spite of these developments, privity remains an essential feature of contractual liability and one of the main factors contributing to the greater popularity of tort in areas such as product liability.

38 For more detailed analyses of privity and its evolution see: Borrie and Diamond (1981: 19), Stapleton (1994a: 10), Viney (1986: 73), Courreges (1997: 139) (France), Harvey and Parry (1996: 13) and Atiyah (1995) (UK), Zweigert and Kotz (1998: 331) (comparative context, France and Germany).

39 Buyers suing non-privy manufacturers.

40 France ought to be seen in a different light here – because of the *non cumul* rule (Courreges 1997: 141).

Breach of contract and a range of concepts of tort/delict – from liability for 'fault' to 'strict' liability focused on the source of harm (defect)

*Introduction – breach of contract and tort/*delict

The notions of breach of contract and tort/*delict* have gradually been adapted to new socio-economic and legal interactions and their undesirable consequences. Product liability systems are excellent examples of the challenges involved in this process. Here liability for a breach of contract and liability for a tort/*delict* became liability for introducing defective products into the market. 'Introduction into the market' (into circulation) is a notion which is linked to the specific economic context of product liability law, and thus it is further developed in the following part of the book (devoted to market law and consumer law). The analysis below follows the development of 'standard of liability' and its impact on product liability law and practice. The very notions of breach of contract and tort rest upon the concept of 'standard of liability': an enquiry into the conduct of the defendant, particularly with a view to delimiting the importance of his 'fault'.[41] In product liability this enquiry has been entirely dominated by the specific nature of this area of law.

Some see 'standard of liability' as a distinct feature of civil liability, others as a component part of a more general category – the breach of contract or the tort/*delict*.[42] In the course of analysis of the Central European product liability laws the book does not necessarily follow the doctrinal preferences in these states and adopts the latter approach. Why such a conceptual choice? It appears that with the evolution of product liability into an independent civil liability regime the considerations of fault were transformed into considerations concerning products and their condition. This process is a counterpart of the general transformation of liability standards in Europe and beyond: a shift of focus from conduct to its results, or in other words from "reproach for misbehaviour" to "objective dangers" (Koch and Koziol 2002: 395). In the product liability context it would be translated into the shift from reproach for not exercising due care in designing, manufacturing, or in any other way handling a product, to focusing on the defect in the product and largely dismissing the defendant's conduct as irrelevant. On the other hand, perhaps unsurprisingly for product liability, this transformation did not universally entail a substantial change in the contents of the analysis. What it did entail is portrayed below.

The concept of 'breach of contract' has presently gained a new dimension. The doctrinal approach to contractual liability has been increasingly influenced by what Gordley referred to as the "breaking down" of the 'classical contract law'

41 The book refers to concepts of 'fault', 'objective liability' or 'strict liability', the meaning of which is not to be taken for granted, especially in a comparative analysis. In order to stress the distinctiveness of these concepts in a particular context, whenever relevant the single quotation mark is used.

42 Such varied approaches can be observed in Central Europe – see below.

(2003: 4).[43] One of the key elements in this process was the appearance of implied contractual terms, which meant that a 'breach of contract' has gained a new, wider meaning and scope. In the context of product liability, various quality and safety warranties/terms were implied by courts or doctrine of law in sale and supply contracts. Thus, supply of a product which caused damage entailed liability for a 'breach of contract'. Although traditionally focused on a warranty-style recovery of the value of a product which did not comply with the contract, compensation of physical injuries or property damage reaching beyond the product was also being awarded. On the other hand, contractual liability rules are quite limited in scope as regards the persons, the products and the damage covered.[44]

Very soon after product liability started featuring as an area requiring distinct treatment, therefore, the attention shifted away from contract to tort law as a more suitable liability system. Here the courts had to accommodate the new tort/*delict* within the traditional framework of tortious liability. Across Europe one observes a dichotomy between the unitary concept of *delict* in civil law systems and the pluralistic, fact-driven law of torts in common law systems[45] (Wagner 2006: 1005). This dichotomy does not have significant implications for product liability practice (Wagner 2006: 1009) and therefore it is not assessed in detail here. Whether based on a general rule of non-contractual liability (*delict*) or a specific rule of tort, product liability does require a certain level of specificity and distinctiveness to cater for its particular needs.

It is by no means the purpose here to present a comprehensive comparative review of various approaches to these issues in Europe and beyond. The analysis draws on the main tendencies, contrasts the position in the 'West' and the one in Central Europe, and traces the position of product liability law in these developments. One important observation to be made at this point is that no significant 'West/East' discrepancy exists with regard to liability standards and their implications for product liability. Central European states may have been delayed in experiencing the evolution of civil liability standards which occurred in the 'West' because of the historical factors described in Chapter 1, but essentially the substance of the transformations was similar to Western European developments.

---

43 Already referred to above – see changes in 'freedom of contract'.

44 The book explores these limitations of contract law in various contexts: from the doctrinal/philosophical standpoint of roles and aims of contractual liability directly above (privity of contract); in a further part of this chapter in the context of consumer law and policy, while Chapter 4 of Part II explores their implications in Central Europe. In the latter section of the book it is shown that the shift from contract to tort did not take place in Czechoslovakia. (See Chapter 4 of Part II for the rationale.)

45 This dichotomy can be linked back to the style and mode of legal thought in a particular legal system: in case-law based common law systems the tendency is to formulate case-specific rules, and in principle-based civil law systems the tendency is rather to formulate general rules: see for instance Wagner (2006: 1005–7).

The discrepancies which do exist across the world are related to a deeper civil (also post-socialist) law/common law division, explored below.

The standard of liability in contract and tort – changing roles, changing contents and changing context

The notion of 'standard of liability' (referred to by most representatives of Central European doctrine of law as 'principle of liability' – Czachórski 2002: 199) is related to the standard of behaviour expected of contractual parties (contract) or reaching wider into the general public (tort). It is a multifaceted and ever-changing element of both civil liability in general and product liability (Stapleton 1994a: 96). Czachórski explains that it determines the social sense and mechanism of operation of laws by virtue of which liability is borne by the particular person and no other (2002: 199).[46] Because it particularly clearly demonstrates policy goals pursued by legislators and courts, observation of the evolution of civil liability standards provides a very interesting background for the analysis of the development of product liability.

Several types of possible classifications of liability standards were singled out in academic literature. The most rudimentary classification sets out two key opposites – fault liability and strict liability (also referred to as a no-fault liability, or liability based on risk[47] (Czachórski 2002: 199, Jagielska 1999: 68, Palmer 1989: 158).[48] The problem with classifications of liability standards, even as sophisticated as the one developed by Stapleton (1994a: 97),[49] is, however, that complex liability regimes such as product liability do not fit easily within the established categories. A closer look at the fundamental types helps one to see the true challenges involved.

'Fault' is a complex notion, sometimes referred to as 'carelessness', placed between two other liability standards: strict liability and intentional wrongdoing

46 Translated from Polish by the author of the book.

47 The latter more often in Central Europe.

48 Apart from these two most basic categories, some other types of liability standards were mentioned by academic writers: absolute liability (irrespective of fault and not limited by any other factors [Coleman 1982: 371], exceptionally used, for instance in insurance liability – Czachórski 2002: 200, Jagielska 1999: 68), and moral strict liability (used where other standards do not provide the possibility of placing liability on the desired person, but some moral determinants render liability of this person necessary [Czachórski 2002: 199, Stapleton 1994a: 97]).

49 Stapleton developed the basic fault/strict liability dichotomy into a four-component classification (1994a: 97). Her classification bears great significance for product regimes, as it stems from two premises: foreseeability of risk and the "utility of running that risk" (ibid.). While fault liability is limited by obvious considerations described below, full strict liability covers all risks – foreseeable and unforeseeable ones; limited hindsight strict liability, while covering foreseeable and unforeseeable risks, is limited for instance by the 'defect' requirement; and foresight strict liability covers all foreseeable risks (Stapleton 1994a: 97).

(Goldberg 2003: 27, Widmer 2005b). Here a word of caution: the book uses the concept of 'fault' rather than 'negligence'. This is for a number of reasons: the main one being that continental legal systems, including the French system (Whittaker 2005: 42) and the Central European systems which are to some extent inspired by the latter, use it to describe their main civil liability standard. It is also clear that 'fault' and 'negligence' are not identical concepts (Miller and Goldberg 2004: 210). Their roles and context are not always uniform, and they entail different focus in terms of legislative and judicial assessment of the required standard of conduct, different legal and factual issues, different political and socio-economic considerations, and different procedural, especially evidentiary implications (Whittaker 2005: 200–205).[50] They are linked to the methods of legal thought in civil and common law systems (analysed in Chapter 2). Whittaker exemplified this phenomenon for the French and the English legal systems: where the French system relies on the "global judicial assessment" and the English one exhibits "concern to structure its judicial assessment and thereby to create a more complex and specifically *legal* understanding of the concept of negligence" (2005: 201). This entails greater judicial flexibility coupled with the much broader concept of 'fault' in civil law systems, which is undoubtedly also true in Central European systems.[51] Another interesting point concerns the links between the fault/negligence considerations and the causal link examined below. It may be that the broader concept of 'fault' in civil law systems entails much less emphasis on the various aspects of causal link in civil liability cases. It is a clearly observable fact that Central European courts and doctrinal writers do not devote as much attention to the issue of causation as English courts and writers.[52] These issues are examined in more detail in Part II.

Another word of caution before the analysis commences: the notion of 'fault' is used to denote a liability standard which in many legal systems (including Central Europe, of which below) actually contains within it two sub-elements. One of these is 'unlawfulness' or 'wrongfulness' (the objective element), and the other is the subjective 'fault proper'. Whenever applicable, the two notions – 'fault' and 'fault proper' – will be used below to indicate these, linked but conceptually distinct, concepts.

'Fault' still remains the principal standard of tortious liability, both in Western and in Central Europe (Widmer 2005b: 332), although its understanding ranges from Holmesian ideas of a regulatory/objective paradigm based on certain

50 See Widmer (2005a) for an elaboration of some similarities between 'negligence' and 'fault'.

51 These divergences may also find their roots in the fact that French judges to a much lesser extent than their English counterparts are obliged to provide detailed justifications for their decisions. Again, the same is true of Central European judges – see Chapter 2 for a further explanation of the judicial culture of the Czech Republic, Hungary and Poland.

52 See Petr (2004) for a comparison of the Czech and the English approaches to causation in criminal medical care cases.

policy choices (this in Europe) (Holmes 1881)[53] to economic considerations of risks and benefits of a particular conduct (in the United States – commencing with Prosser representing the utilitarian approach [1966] and Posner advocating a macroeconomics-focused approach [1972]). In civil and post-socialist law systems it formally prevails also in contractual liability (Czachórski 2002: 199, Winiger 2002: 2).[54] Without becoming involved in a debate on the requisites or meaning of fault (conducted in Part II with regard to Central European liability systems) it is sufficient to state at this point that fault enables placing liability on the person responsible for an injury or damage because his or her conduct failed to conform to the required standard of behaviour (Widmer 2005a: 334, Jagielska 1999: 69). Its boundaries are to a large extent delimited by the notion of 'reasonableness' (Stapleton 1994a: 97). This follows the Aristotelian concept of *iustitia commutativa* (Widmer 2005a: 334), and satisfies the postulates of deterrence (Widmer 2005a: 335, Faure 2005: 312, 313) and retribution (Coleman 1982: 373–5). With new liability rules introduced throughout the world in response to the increasingly complex market and social relationships (see below) comes a more intricate view of liability standards tailored to these relationships. The concept of 'fault' has been transformed by these developments, both within systems which distinguish 'unlawfulness' from the subjective notion of 'fault proper' (Austria, Spain, Switzerland and all Central European states)[55] and those which do not make this distinction (France, Belgium and, arguably, England) (Widmer 2005a: 336–7). Subjective considerations are often giving way to objective factors, although the manner in which they are conceptualized and applied in practice differs widely.

'Strict liability' is independent of the existence or non-existence of fault, although it can be limited by other considerations (Koch and Koziol 2002, Stapleton 1994a: 97). As shown by experience, contemporary strict liability is often established by legislative mechanisms, or at least requires some active, creative input by courts in shifting the liability standard from the traditional fault basis (Koch and Koziol 2002: 395–6). In many ways a strict liability standard (apart from full strict liability which does not occur often) allows legislators or courts to directly input policy considerations into liability rules. Such input may sometimes be more clearly pronounced than it would be in regimes based on fault. Thus, the introduction of 'strict liability' reflects the emphasis placed on the compensatory function of liability rules, although it has also been argued that it plays a behaviour modification function. The limiting factors of 'strict liability', on the other hand, reflect the policy choices and the compromises pursued by legislators and courts. In product liability law for instance, such limitations are the

53 Holmes refers to the 'reasonability' standard of an ordinary person rather than the subjective standard of a particular person (see also Goldberg 2003: 23). The current fault liability regimes in Europe seem largely to follow this approach – see Widmer 2005a.

54 There are tendencies to limit or even entirely eliminate the requirement of fault in contractual liability in Central Europe (especially in the draft civil codes) – see below.

55 See Part II for an analysis of these two elements of 'fault'.

specific requirements concerning the defect and the damage recoverable, and the Product Liability Directive additionally enacted a list of defences which illustrate the need to balance various policy objectives.

Developments in liability standards in Europe and beyond – contrasting the 'West' with Central Europe

Let us now observe in more detail the evolution of civil liability standards in Western and Central Europe and their impact on product liability law.

Winiger elaborated on the 'sickness' of contemporary fault liability, which is "overcharged by tasks for which it had not been conceived" (2002: 2). He stressed the fact that fault liability was applied to new forms of risks "typical for industrial societies", risks which "come up without the fault of anybody" (2002: 2). One can no doubt see the effect of complex areas such as product liability on this shift in approach to liability standards. 'Strict liability', or at least a more objective liability, is becoming more common in response to these challenges. According to Koch and Koziol's suggestions, there are in fact a range of factors which may trigger introduction of 'strict liability': those focused on causes of harm (dangerousness and inability to avoid harm, or the general desire to prevent harm), those focused on the harm itself (desire to prevent and compensate harm considered particularly serious), those focused on availability of compensation and the ability to compensate (victims' weaker position, deep pockets arguments), and those focused on the interests involved (sharing of risks) (2002: 408–13).

Whilst the libertarian philosophy of contract indicates that the liability standard ought to be determined by contractual parties, the transformations leading to the establishment of welfare states entailed a stronger influence of law and courts upon the standard of contractual liability. In common law systems contractual liability has been strict; in civil law systems including Central Europe it was and still remains liability based on fault. The appearance of consumer protection laws, also those originating from the European Community, contributed to changes in liability standards in certain consumer contracts.[56] On the other hand, a growing realization of importance of general contract liability rules for business relations entailed a shift in view of the liability standard which would best meet the expectations of business partners. Thus, because the aim of contractual liability in business dealings is risk distribution and not penalizing faulty conduct, strict liability became more prominent even in civil law countries. This tendency can be observed in Central Europe – especially in the proposed changes in liability standards in draft Civil Codes.[57] In spite of these phenomena peculiar to contractual liability, conceptually

56 See for instance Directive 99/44 (Consumer Sales Directive) and its approach to sellers' liability if the goods do not 'correspond with the contract' (although this Directive does not extend to injuries and damages caused by products).

57 See: 'the Conception' in Hungary, and Hradek (2006: 188) – explanation of the Czech draft Code (Section 2416 – only *force majeure* will exonerate the defendant). These issues are further analysed in Chapter 4 of Part II.

at least the concept of 'fault' (if indeed it is applied in contractual liability) does not differ significantly from its understanding in tort law.

Contemporary developments in tort law led to 'fault' gradually losing its principal position (Goldberg 2003: 22–27). Two processes can be observed in Europe: the objectivization of the concept of 'fault' – shifting of focus onto the objective element – 'unlawfulness' ('wrongfulness'), and the objectivization of liability – abandoning the requirement of 'fault' altogether. These processes are not conceptually equivalent. While the objective element of 'fault' still requires consideration of the defendant's conduct (unlawful/wrongful conduct), objectivization of liability shifts the focus from conduct to its results, or even makes liability independent of any conduct. Traditionally throughout Europe and beyond one could observe a dichotomy with regard to approach to liability standards between civil law states, including the post-socialist Central Europe on the one hand, and England and the United States on the other (van Dam 2006: 609, Widmer 2005a: 334, 335).[58] While civil law countries such as France approach tort law as a compensatory mechanism (prioritizing the distributive justice postulate), English, and more generally, common law sees it as a behaviour modification measure (corrective justice) (van Dam 2006: 609-2 0 609-3).[59] Van Dam argued that the "approach in France and Germany [wa]s determined by a mix of free market and social policy with a strong emphasis on victim protection, whereas the English approach [wa]s predominantly free market oriented with an emphasis on the protection of freedom" (2006: 609-3). Consequently, it was easier for the French legislators and courts to modify tortious liability rules towards stricter liability standards (ibid.).[60] This dichotomy is becoming less and less clear, also as a result of the influences of the European Union in the areas such as product liability. The general attitude towards the role and the features of liability standards in tort law is gradually changing within the civil and common law countries.[61]

As hinted above, the position in Central Europe has not been very different from the developments in the 'West'. Once the Civil Codes were in force, tortious liability was based on two distinct provisions: the general liability provision containing the requirement of 'fault' and a specific 'strict liability' provision

58 Van Dam presents an example of France and Germany on the one hand and England on the other (2006: 609-2–609-3). The remark on Central Europe – own observation.

59 The US approach is more complex and will not be analysed here.

60 This view, although ultimately stressing the main tendencies within tort law, may be seen as overly generalizing the approach of civil and common law states. It is clear from comparative reports concerning European tort law that only Greek and Italian law focus mainly on the compensatory function of tort law (Magnus 2001b: 185). Other European states, including France, England and Germany, indicate both "punitive" and "distributive" – functions of tort law with equal strength (ibid., at page 186). Further, post-socialist states such as Poland did not find it straightforward to modify their liability standard to create strict liability, and remain committed to retaining the requirement of fault (at least until today).

61 The common law approach is illustrated in Stapleton's writings (1994a, 2003a).

pertaining to dangerous activities and to some other causes (the latter had a relatively limited scope of application). These are analysed in detail in Part II of the book. With growing exposure to market economies, starting from the late 1970s and early 1980s, significant changes took place in Central European contract and tort laws and practice. As Central Europe is catching up with the rest of the world in regulating markets,[62] the laws of obligations must endure much more stringent tests than ever before. In contemporary markets the need for strict liability or even absolute liability is more widespread. The world trend towards a more objective concept of liability, or at the minimum a more objective concept of 'fault' (Winiger 2002: 2–17, Nesterowicz 1979: 4–8) found a great number of followers in Central Europe. In Poland traditionally the requirement of 'fault' was said to follow the ethical assumption that a person who by his action or omission caused damage to another must repair the damage (Radwański 1986: 68, 69). Gnela considered the question whether in business relations this concept of justice had a standing, and concluded that it was impossible to place a 'fault' upon the undertaking as such (an employee? the company itself?) (2000: 125). Therefore she postulated the benefits of strict liability in such relations – a person who gains profits from a thing or an act which caused damage to another, ought to repair the damage (*eius damnum cuius commodum*) (ibid.).[63] This approach could also be seen in courts' jurisprudence, although not always in written law. Czech law exhibits a growing preference for an objective liability standard – this can be seen in the Civil Code provisions after the 1991 amendment, analysed below (Tichy 2005: 53). The forthcoming changes in the law of obligations heralded in the draft Civil Code indicate a further movement towards an objective concept of contractual liability (Hradek 2006: 188).[64] The Hungarian draft Code introduces a very specific kind of strict contractual liability,[65] and 'the Conception' justifying such a change points to the key role of contract law in business transactions and thus the main role of contractual liability being compensatory rather than punitive. Tort liability continues to be based on fault in both drafts. The Polish Codification Commission has not so far declared any change in liability standards of the draft Civil Code.

62 See below for a more detailed examination of methods of market regulation in Central Europe.

63 Also Radwański (1986: 205) and Dybowski (1981).

64 In the previous versions of the draft Civil Code, contractual liability continued to be based on 'fault', but the concept of fault was an objective one (Hradek 2006: 188). The most recent version (2008) provided by Professor Tichy provides that contractual parties can only defend themselves by claiming *force majeure* (Section 2416 of the draft).

65 This is a type of liability which can only be avoided by the defendant upon proving that the non-performance was due to an obstacle beyond his or her control and that he or she could not "reasonably have been expected to take the impediment into account at the time of the conclusion of the contract" ('the Conception' at page 15). On the other hand, the recovery of damages is limited by the 'foreseeability clause', analysed in Part II.

Product liability is obviously an excellent example of how general civil liability rules based on the requirement of 'fault' needed to be adapted and interpreted very creatively in order to accommodate the new market conditions. How can one position the development and role of product liability law within the changes portrayed above?

Liability standards in product liability cases – introduction

The essence of product liability and the *raison d'être* of its separation from the general law of obligations is the fact that it involves defective products which cause injury or damage.

The notion of 'defect' has always dominated the product liability discourse, but the focus of this discourse shifted quite significantly when mature product liability systems were being built. Initially, in systems based on the requirement of 'fault' (both in Western and Central Europe) the emphasis of courts and doctrine was not upon the product or its condition but rather on the conduct of a particular defendant which led to the introduction of this product into the market (Whittaker 2005: 5). It was realized, however, that this approach did not fit the reality of product liability cases. Such cases normally involve enterprises, where it is difficult to point to a conduct of a particular person, and generally require a more in-depth analysis of the condition of products which caused damage. Relatively modest developments took place in legal systems where the concept of 'fault' was firmly set as a requisite of liability – there the focus remained on the defendant's conduct, but the burden of proving 'due care' (this requirement may have been expressed in different terms in different countries) was shifted onto the defendant. In some legal systems this was merely the question of applying general provisions of civil liability (normally civil codes) which established the presumption of fault (Czechoslovakia). In Poland, where no presumption of fault was prescribed by the Civil Code, as well as in the United Kingdom where no such presumption existed in common law, courts used the *res ipsa loquitur* principle (its Polish derivative was the concept of *anonymous fault*). Many product liability systems, however, went further than merely facilitating the proof of fault. They abandoned the requirement of fault and focused on the concept of 'defect' instead (Hungary, France).

Whether in systems retaining the requirement of fault or in those which abandoned it, the notion of 'defect' presents very significant challenges in the practice of product liability. The analysis of 'defect' may indeed lead the courts to some extent back to the analysis of the defendant's behaviour.

Evolution of liability standards in product liability – from conduct ('fault') to defect ('strict liability') and ... back again to conduct?

Ironically, in spite of the very clear evolution of civil liability standards away from the requirement of 'fault', in product liability cases this evolution may indeed have been more circular: starting from focus on conduct (fault), to emphasizing defect, and then through a consumer expectations test or a risk/utility test back to conduct again.

While traditionally grounded in general civil liability rules and thus following the similar tendencies to those explored above, the specificity of product liability demands a carefully considered and tailored approach. Product liability is now classified by Koch and Koziol as strict liability limited by its focus on the cause of harm (2002: 402). The specificity of product liability cases, especially those involving complex products, often leads the analysis back to the evaluation of the defendant's behaviour – from the point of view of what is, or should be, expected of him. This has not been a uniform or a straightforward development throughout Europe and beyond (the reasons for the occurring divergences are explored below). Going back to Koch and Koziol's arguments, one may note that because dangerousness of products is normally less of a general phenomenon but rather an irregularity, strict liability here may be motivated by the need to share risks (2002: 413). Thus, following this train of thought one may argue that the urge to objectivize liability is not as strong here as it is in other areas of law. Further, the ultimate legislative and judicial output may be limited by the specified defences and other considerations – such as the scope of recoverable damage (2002: 413).[66]

In truly 'strict' product liability systems the conduct of the defendant ought not to weigh upon his position in the case. The focus ought to shift onto the product and away from the defendant. However, both in Western and in Central European product liability law even if the language of 'fault' disappears from legal practice, its spirit often remains. Some considerations typical of the 'fault discourse' continue to play a significant part in product liability litigation. The concepts of reasonability, predictability, foreseeability, avoidability,[67] as well as the socio-economic context seen through risks and benefits of products, remain relevant in contemporary strict liability systems (Cane 2006: 103). Strict product liability, or as the book develops this concept later, a more objective liability standard,[68] does not do away with all the 'fault-typical' considerations. The picture is further complicated by the fact that product defects may have different origins and forms, and thus there may be a need for a tailored, diversified approach even within a single 'product liability system'. This approach, involving 'boxing' of types of defects into manufacturing, design and failure to warn defects, has been formalized in the United States – most recently in *Restatement (Third) of Torts: Products Liability* 1998 (Owen 2005, Stapleton 2005: 302, Goldberg 2003: 38, Bagińska 2000), where 'strict' liability is contemplated only for 'manufacturing defects', and the other two types of defects

66 See Koch and Koziol for a detailed elaboration on the justifications for strict liability (2002: 407–13).

67 See the English case *A v National Blood Authority* where the court exercised some effort in dismissing the relevance of avoidability in cases based on the Product Liability Directive. Predictability and avoidability undeniably play some role in the development risk defence established by the Directive – see below.

68 Following Stapleton's classification mentioned above, full strict liability ought to cover all risks, and the forms of 'strict liability' existing in the context of product liability today do not comply with this requirement.

entail the reasonability criteria typical of fault liability.[69] Even beyond the United States, however, it has been almost universally accepted that design and failure to warn defects require consideration of the reasonable course of conduct the defendant ought to have engaged in (Lenze 2005: 104, Miller and Goldberg 2004: 354). Two competing approaches to establishing product liability were advanced: the one focused on consumer/social/public expectations,[70] and the one entailing elements of the risk/benefits analysis.

The US jurisprudence exhibits a clear tendency to move away from the 'expectations' test – as it is considered that the 'expectations' are difficult to establish outside the realm of a contractual relationship or in complex design cases where no specific expectations may exist (Miller and Goldberg 2004: 357, 360). The US courts rather moved towards the approach based on balancing the product's costs and benefits (risk/utility) (Miller and Goldberg 2004: 361). Obviously this risk/utility test may present its own problems: the risk and utility may not be fully known in complex products, and may be difficult to quantify even if known. It is clear from the US experience that a one-size-fits-all approach may well be impossible to establish in the product liability context, and the 'boxing' exercise may be the necessary prerequisite for creating liability standards which the courts are able to consistently interpret in cases before them.

To see the evidence in support of this statement one only needs to look at the Product Liability Directive and its impact in Europe. Although the Directive clearly moves away from 'boxing' of defects in its substantive provisions (Article 6), it is unable to offer a sustainable alternative approach which would allow the intended complete shift of focus onto 'expectations' (epitomized in Howells' 'abstract approach' [2005a: 141]) and away from the sources or nature of the defect in question. Although academics such as Howells go out of their way in creating a consistent theoretical basis for the 'expectations' standard proposed by the Directive,[71] the practice of European product liability continues to present a confusing picture. The efforts of national courts to interpret the standard of safety which "a person is entitled to expect" (Article 6 of the Directive) in complex cases involving defects in design or even in manufacture do not generate a uniform or consistent approach. Here one needs to refer back to a number of general issues which this book emphasizes. In the face of the intricate nature of product

69 According to Miller and Goldberg, the *Restatement (Third) of Torts: Products Liability* 1998 "has abandoned the doctrinal labels of strict liability and negligence and established separate functional definitions of liability for three types of defect" (2004: 351) – see §2(a) for manufacturing defects, §2(b) for design defects, and §2(c) for warning defects.

70 The tests have been expressed in various terms, although their main features remain relatively uniform.

71 He suggests that strict liability ought not to have regard to physical defect in a product, but should rather be inferred from a breach of "general perceptions of safety reasonably held" (Howells 2005a: 141).

liability law and product liability cases, as well as the often ambiguous framework of the provisions of the Product Liability Directive (analysed below), national approaches to product liability continue to be material in shaping the reality of product liability at present. The notion of 'defect' which, as it was elaborated above, took over the place traditionally occupied by the limitations of 'fault', continues to be influenced by these approaches. Thus, countries which more naturally stirred towards 'strict liability' – such as France or Hungary – have no problems in applying the approach which Howells would refer to as 'abstract' – focusing on legitimate consumer expectations. In other countries with similar legal and judicial culture and methodology (like Poland or the Czech Republic) it may also be easier to apply this standard. Other countries, such as the United Kingdom, may continue enquiries into the exact nature of the physical defects in products.[72]

Obviously, the main points of focus here are the challenges faced by Central European laws and judicial practice. A short introduction is due at this point before the more detailed exegesis in Part II. A relative simplicity of legal issues which Central European courts have had to deal with so far, already hinted upon in Chapter 2, does not allow one to determine with certainty which approach will be taken by them in future. On the one hand, their approach moved quite clearly towards focusing on defect and away from subjective considerations of fault, especially in Hungary. On the other hand, they have not so far dealt with a complex design defect or a latent defect case and it is impossible to predict the position they will take. Before the implementation of the Product Liability Directive, the tendency followed by the courts of Central Europe was to gradually abandon the requirement of fault (objectivization of liability, this mainly in Hungary), or to base this concept on a set of objective criteria (objectivization of 'fault', mainly in Poland). The 'fault'–'defect' evolution was most advanced in Hungary, with Poland in the process of developing a presumption of fault, *res ipsa loquitur* rule (or often its counterpart – the concept of 'anonymous fault'),[73] and *prima facie* evidence of 'defect'. Żuławska suggested that the adoption and development of the 'anonymous fault' notion demonstrated the "new approach to *delictual* capability", the approach resembling strict liability theories (1983b: 142, 3). According to her the "new" kind of producer's liability, appearing throughout the legal systems of the "highly developed" countries, finds its foundation in the *cuius commodum, eius periculum* principle, as well as in the deterrence function of liability. Increasing the stringency of liability encourages improvements in the quality of products, and renders this increase economically viable (1983b: 142,

72 See judgements of English courts: *Foster v Biosil* (2000), or *Worsley v Tambrands Limited* (2000).

73 A. Szpunar wrote about the process of creation of this concept (1985a: 154 et seq.). It relieved the plaintiff of the duty of proving 'fault' of some ascertainable person within the company whose activity caused the defect, only requiring the proof of weaknesses or defects in the normal operation of this entity or even such type of entity.

3). The Czech regime also utilized the presumption of fault, but it was relatively underdeveloped in this respect. Czech and Hungarian regimes had the advantage of presumption of fault prescribed by their Civil Codes, which was widely used in product liability litigation (Weir 1983: ch. 5, p. 9, s. 34). The evolution of product liability systems in Central Europe reached the point where 'fault' was either redundant as a feature of product liability (Hungary) or at least was easier to show (Poland and Czechoslovakia). In Hungary the liability standard so created was much stricter that the liability established by the Product Liability Directive. Apart from Hungary (where the concept of 'social expectations' was developed), the classification into manufacturing, design and warning flaws always featured in Central European jurisprudence, first of all applied to the various forms of 'fault' and, as the systems evolved towards more objective liability standards, also to defects.

Other factors affecting liability standards – defences in product liability law

The standards of liability applied in product liability cases around the world are far from uniform and unambiguous, and one could indeed wonder, using "doctrine, history, economics, procedure, sociology, or simple cynicism", what exactly is strict about the 'strict' product liability (Bernstein 1992: 207). The Product Liability Directive only increased this confusion. Apart from limiting its scope of application by the specific delimitation of the notion of 'defect', and the specific understanding of recoverable damage, it introduced a whole list of factors which allow the defendants to escape liability. While according to Stapleton's classification the regime introduced by the Product Liability Directive was contemplated as one of 'hindsight strict liability' limited by the requirement of 'defect' (1994a: 233), the introduction of the development risk defence (Article 7(e)) confused the initial intention and it is not certain where exactly on her map of standards one should place the regime of the Directive. The defence utilizes an enquiry into what a reasonable course of conduct for the defendant should have been – he can avoid liability if he proves that "the state of scientific and technical knowledge at the time when he put the product into circulation was not such as to enable the existence of the defect to be discovered". Other available types of defences – proof that the defendant did not introduce the product into circulation (Article 7(a)) or that the product was not manufactured for sale or any other economic purpose or not manufactured in the course of a business (Article 7(c)) – are the result of the specific nature of product liability law and its links with markets. However, other defences only increase the impression of uncertainty with regard to the liability standard, as they clearly steer towards an analysis of the defendant's conduct. Such is the case with the defence for manufacturers of component parts: "that the defect is attributable to the design of the product in which the component has been fitted or to the instructions given by the manufacturer of the product" (Article 7(f)), or indeed with the defence that "having regard to the circumstances, it is probable that the defect which caused the damage did not exist at the time when the product was put into circulation … or that this defect came into being afterwards" (Article 7(b)). The defences create the impression that the Directive is aimed at compensating victims of defective products only as long as the defendant's conduct has not corresponded with the requirements of reasonability. The only element of true strict liability can be seen in the liability of suppliers, who under certain conditions are liable even though they have not contributed to the defect in the product. Some of the defences which the Directive introduced are quite typical of a fault liability system: thus they would also have been applicable under the Central European tortious liability rules, although it is clear that the Hungarian product liability system did not allow most of those defences.[74]

Concluding remarks

The notions of 'breach of contract' and 'tort' gained very complex characteristics in product liability systems. As examined above, the discourse focused on 'defective products', but it also involved the conduct of those who introduced these products into circulation. Product liability no doubt challenged the traditional approach to standards of civil liability, and the present position across Europe remains unclear. Taschner concluded that "product liability cases can, to a large extent, be solved by applying fault liability principles" (1986a: 9). He pointed out that the "heart of product liability remains the problem of causing damage by creating unavoidable risks" (ibid.). Taschner's views are consistent with the opinions of other prominent academic writers on the topic – William Posner, Jane Stapleton or Peter Cane, all of whom consider that the introduction of strict product liability will make a difference in a very small percentage of cases. In the light of the observations above it could be argued that nothing short of an insurance system could provide a truly 'strict' liability standard in product liability cases. The nature of product liability, its links with markets and the necessary balancing exercise which it involves always entail an enquiry into the defendant's conduct. While there may be a problem with creating a true 'strict' product liability, the purpose of the Product Liability Directive is undoubtedly establishing a harmonized approach to these issues. The position at present is far from harmonized, and the manner in which the 'fault'–'defect' evolution proceeded on the national level remains material in the interpretation of the liability standard indicated by the Directive. This book goes to some length in emphasizing the importance of national laws and judicial practice for European product liability law at present. Thus, the comprehensive analysis of internal developments in Central European contractual and tortious standards of liability in product liability cases (Chapter 4 and Chapter 5 of Part II) remains relevant also in cases governed by the provisions of the implemented Directive.

---

74 See Part II for an analysis of the implementation of the Directive by the Central European states and its implications.

Damage

'Damage' has been defined as "every wrong inflicted upon an interest protected by law, be it property, dignity, freedom, limb or life" (Wagner 1974: 147).[75]

It transpires from the analysis above that not all loss suffered by individuals is 'recoverable damage', and an even lesser part can actually be recovered (as 'damages') in a particular case. The 'damage'/'damages' (recoverable damage/compensation) distinction is followed here in order to emphasize the difference between 'damage' which the law allows to be recovered in specified types of liability (the "actionable heads of compensation" – Magnus 1990: 675) on the one hand, and 'damages' which are actually recovered by a particular claimant from a particular defendant on the other. 'Damages' were described as money paid "in satisfaction of an obligation to pay", resulting from a court's judgement, from negotiation or agreement, from a mediated resolution of a dispute, or "from a concession by one person (or the insurer) of an obligation to pay" (Allen, Hartshorne and Martin 2000: 1). The focus of analysis below remains on 'damage' rather than 'damages' – in the understanding that assessment of 'damages' is linked to a much greater extent with the rules of procedure and not with substantive liability rules (Allen, Hartshorne and Martin 2000: 3).[76] It was suggested that a discussion of 'damages' should involve recognition of why they are awarded and "what external influences will dictate payment and quantum of those damages" (Allen, Hartshorne and Martin 2000: 3). 'Damages' are influenced by the "rules and guidelines of calculation, including identification of which losses are to be taken into account in the calculation, who has the power to determine the calculation, and at what point in time the damages are to be calculated" (Allen, Hartshorne and Martin 2000: 2). Further, there is no "value-neutral, scientifically correct determination of the appropriate damages for particular loss – the award is made in accordance with the norms and values of the society in which it is enforced and is therefore subject to socio-legal analysis" (ibid.). 'Damages' are therefore relevant to some extent in the context of the analysis conducted here. Although the procedure leading to their assessment goes beyond the scope of the book, a somewhat superficial analysis of the results of this procedure (for instance remarks on the general tendencies in the amounts of awarded damages) is instructive in understanding the changing nature of civil liability, especially in Central European societies.

In fact, the scope of recoverable 'damage' and the assessment of 'damages' are determined by a wide range of factors including substantive law, practice, policy arguments, as well as economic and social context of law. The standard of liability introduced above, and the causal considerations analysed below, also play a significant part in assigning a particular damage to the breach of contract or a

75 This definition was provided with reference to Polish law, but it is no doubt applicable more widely.

76 In fact, the English legal system, in contrast to most civil law systems, considers assessment of damages as a matter of procedure – Hibbert (2007: 12).

tort/*delict*. Consideration of these matters in detail reaches beyond the scope of this book. Instead, the analysis below describes the most crucial developments within the area of 'damage' in civil liability. More detailed discussions can be found in monographs on contractual or tortious liability or on the law of obligations in general – both in Western and in Central Europe.[77] While this area of law has not so far been formally harmonized on the European Union level, a number of developments indicating convergence of certain principles concerning assessment and awards of damages can be observed. Some of them impact on product liability law and practice, thus they need to be elaborated further. The analysis here contrasts the developments in the Western and in the Central European law and practice.

As illustrated above, product liability law made its own mark on the general rules of civil liability. Indeed, recoverable 'damage' is one of the most characteristic features distinguishing product liability from other civil liability systems. It determines the application of product liability law as opposed to some other liability regime. It is generally understood that loss or damage to the defective product itself is not covered. There are also other limitations, often policy-motivated, introduced in product liability laws such as the Product Liability Directive analysed below.[78] Such limitations are the result of policy choices which are taken at the time the law is established: by legislators or by courts. Those choices are motivated by a variety of factors, many of which can be traced back to the inevitable relationship between product liability and consumer protection laws and policies, presented in the following section of the book. In order to fully appreciate them, however, one must first take a broader look at general developments in the scope of 'damage' in civil liability.

Civil liability rules distinguish a number of types of 'damage': the most rudimentary classification sees 'damage' of a pecuniary (material) and non-pecuniary (non-material) nature.[79] Pecuniary damage can concern property or a person. According to Central European legal thought, similarly to most civil law systems of Western Europe, it may involve actual losses (*damnum emergens*) or lost profits (*lucrum cessans*) (these concepts are unknown to common law systems – van Dam 2006: 1201, Magnus 2001b: 193). Non-pecuniary damage is more problematic in recovery and assessment. It is, however, an area of civil liability which receives a significantly greater attention at present than it ever did before

77 At present they are also being reviewed on a comparative basis – for instance in the Tort and Insurance Law Yearbook *European Tort Law* or in an overview of European Tort Systems, *Unification of Tort Law: Damages* (Magnus 2001a).

78 On the other hand, 'damage' is another example of incompleteness of the regime introduced by the Directive. National laws remain applicable in some aspects, the most important being non-pecuniary damage. See below for further elaboration.

79 In some legal systems this difference is reflected in legal terms used to identify them: for instance in Poland – *szkoda/odszkodowanie*, to mean pecuniary damage/compensation of such damage, and *krzywda/zadośćuczynienie*, to mean non-pecuniary damage/compensation of such damage.

(Nesterowicz 2007, Wałachowska 2007, Hradek 2004: 96). What can be observed throughout Europe and beyond is greater focus on the protection of an individual; although the resulting emphasis on non-pecuniary damage is by no means uniform (Faure 2000b). Overall, recovery of non-pecuniary damage remains limited for a number of reasons: first of all, neither contract nor tort liability laws, one of the primary aims of which is compensation, are comfortable with recognizing damage which it is difficult to quantify. While compensation of non-pecuniary damage may well remain in line with the compensatory aim of liability rules, as well as with their deterrence aim and the need for risk and liability apportionment, economic analysis of civil liability indicates that a wide availability of personal insurance may be a better option to obtain compensation of this type of damage (Faure 2000b: 144, 147). Whether non-pecuniary damage is widely recognized and indeed compensated or not, what is needed is a more systematic, consistent approach to its recovery (some legal systems indeed attempt to introduce such a systematic approach – the Czech law which established a tariff system for specific types of non-pecuniary damage is a good example).[80] The latter remark applies both to the civil liability rules in general, and the product liability law in particular. The European product liability systems are still extremely diversified with regard to recovery of non-pecuniary damage (Pasa and Benacchio 2005: 116), and the Directive leaves this issue to national law.

Another area where changes are quite dynamic concerns 'pure economic loss'. The need to adjust civil liability rules to the changing market conditions is the basis for this development. 'Pure economic loss' is not yet recognized in principle by Central European civil laws, in common with the French system (Radé and Bloch 2004: 41) and indeed some other continental systems (Austria – Koziol 2001: 11, Germany – Magnus 2001c: 95). The concept of 'pure economic loss' has been widely acknowledged to be theoretically imprecise (Bussani and Palmer 2003: 8). Economic loss is considered 'pure' if, what is very difficult to establish, it is not consequential upon any physical damage or loss, and does not constitute a value of a physical loss as set by a court (Bussani and Palmer 2003: 5). Its recovery is normally more common in contract law, and in tort law it is much more limited if at all possible. Some liability systems clearly limit the possibility of recovery of 'pure economic loss' in tort (English law), and others (like Central European or French law), while generally not excluding such recovery, "limit the extent of liability with other instruments such as causation, proof of damage, the duty of the victim to mitigate damages, etc." (van Boom 2004: 34, Magnus 2001c: 95). This approach can generally be observed in product liability regimes, where

80 See Chapter 5 of Part II. The European Court of Justice has recently expressed its views concerning non-pecuniary damage, concluding that the EC Directive on Package Travel (90/314/EEC) extended the scope of protection for consumers onto non-pecuniary damage caused by the lost holiday (Case C-168/00 *Simone Leitner*). The Directive did not expressly mention non-pecuniary damage, so it is particularly instructive to observe the importance which the Court afforded to this type of damage.

'pure economic loss' epitomizes the loss to the defective product itself and thus is not recoverable as a matter of principle (Cane defined 'pure economic loss' in the product liability context as the "cost of remedying defect or loss consequential on a pure defect of quality [1986: 45]).[81]

Civil liability laws of many European states contain the principle of total compensation – *restitutio in integrum* ("total reparation" – Magnus 1990: 676). Traditionally, however, the laws of contract and tort are focused on recovery of specific types of damage reflecting the aims which these civil liability rules are meant to fulfil. The aims were introduced above. While in contract, where the desired result is to restore the innocent party to the state which he would have been in had the contract been performed, the focus is almost solely on compensation of sustained losses, in tort other considerations play a much greater role. Contract law's purpose is to protect legitimate expectations, and tort law's purpose: to protect the "integrity of one's own sphere" (Magnus 2001b: 194). This is perhaps one of the reasons why tort liability appears to have been a more suitable liability system for defective products. Tort law's focus is on compensation, as well as on allocation of responsibility which entails a greater emphasis on balancing costs and benefits. Tort law allocates risks and costs of activities to those who in the eyes of the law are most able to bear them. Deterrence is a crucial postulate which affects this allocation. The punitive role of tort liability, advocated especially in the United States and also increasingly in Europe,[82] affects the concept of 'damage' and the amounts of 'damages' in cases where such punitive damages are in fact awarded. Punitive damages are starting to appear in Europe, if only in doctrinal writings, as a realistic option in reaction to a tort or even to a breach of contract (Lee 2007). In Central Europe, however, punitive damages have not developed as a regular feature of civil liability.[83]

With the realization of complexity of aims of civil liability in the United States and Europe comes the widened scope of the concept of damage. Further, the amounts awarded to claimants, especially for personal injury and non-pecuniary damage, are growing (Koch 2003: 515). On the other hand, regimes such as product liability very clearly articulate the boundaries in respect of particular types of damage.

While at present the role and framework of damage rules as well as the principles and procedures governing the assessment of 'damages' in Central Europe are becoming similar to the Western European approach, certain peculiarities still remain. Socialism had a notable impact on damage rules, and indeed on the reality of compensating civil claims, and to some extent the past continues to influence

81 See van Boom (2004) and Magnus (2001c) for more detailed analyses of developments with regard to 'pure economic loss'.

82 <http://europeanlawnetwork.eu/2007/05/16/punitiveexemplary-damages-in-european-law-systems-uk-france-czech-republic/>, see also: <http://www.psp.cz/kps/pi/PRACE/pi-5-268.pdf>.

83 Ibid.

the present developments. Some of the economic and political phenomena affecting them are explored in the following section of this chapter, but here the emphasis is on the legal environment. The philosophical introduction to this analysis mentioned that the role of the law of obligations was significantly limited during socialism. It is indeed difficult to point to an element of obligations other than damages where this limited role could be seen clearer. Socialist damage rules were much narrower in scope, and the practice of assessment and awards of damages indicates their insignificance. The main aim of the socialist economy was the satisfaction of social needs set by national plan (Eörsi 1979a: 153). If damage occurred as a result of a tort or a breach of contract, socialist law focused rather on specific performance ("[A]ctual performance of the defaulting party's undertaking" [Treitel 1979: 3]) than on damages (Eörsi 1979a: 153). It was generally agreed that pecuniary incentives (liquidated and unliquidated) were incapable of compensating non-performance of contracts or torts. They reduced the income of undertakings – hence the investment fund and the participation fund of the employees, and central planning did not often allow for purchase of substitutes with the money deriving from damages (Eörsi 1979a: 153).[84] Although Eörsi put forward the above contentions, he also acknowledged that referring to specific performance as the "natural" remedy in centrally planned economies, and damages as the "natural" remedy in market economies, would be a "gross generalisation and simplification" (ibid.). When observing Central European laws governing tortious and contractual damages, one can see the emphasis upon specific performance only in the Czechoslovak Civil Code. The Polish and Hungarian codes, although containing provisions on specific performance, also contain very clear provisions on damages which seem to, at least in written law, be favoured. Nevertheless, the scope of recoverable damages has been distinctly narrower in Central Europe. Recovery of 'pure economic loss' was severely limited. There were particular problems with recovery of non-pecuniary damage. In Hungary it was impossible to recover it until the amendment of the Civil Code in 1977, and in fact it remains problematic until today.[85] In Czechoslovakia, recovery of lost profits was impossible until the amendment of the Civil Code in 1991.[86] Non-pecuniary damage was recoverable before then, and Section 444 of the Civil Code suggested that a government decree would specify in detail the levels of compensation for pain and aggravated social position (Hradek 2003: 89).[87] Non-pecuniary damage has traditionally been recoverable in Polish tort liability, and as early as in 1969

84 In any event, in the economy of shortages (examined below), the chances of obtaining such substitutes were rather slim.

85 The draft Civil Code proposes replacing compensation of non-pecuniary damages with special indemnity compensation (see Chapter 6 of Part II for further information).

86 Act No. 509/1991 Coll., amending the Civil Code.

87 Hradek analyses the latest amendment of the Decree amending the Decree on Compensation for Pain Suffered and for an Aggravated Position in Society (2003).

the Supreme Court declared that no permanent health changes would be required for such compensation to be awarded.[88]

The striking feature of damages in the socialist Central Europe, if at all awarded, were the amounts. These were very low indeed, at least in comparison with awards for similar types of injury or damage in Western Europe. While the main reason for the low amounts was the general approach to civil liability and its role mentioned above, one cannot forget the significantly lower living costs, the fully covered health expenses, pensions and generous social security schemes – all contributing to the fact that there was simply no need for high damages awards.

At present, the Central European position is changing towards greater focus on non-pecuniary damage and on the protection of an individual in general. Damages awards are growing in scope and in amounts, and there is a clear emphasis on fine-tuning the protection for individuals and their property, and therefore also the amounts awarded in compensation of pecuniary and non-pecuniary damage, with the transformations in post-socialist societies. The salaries and costs of living are rising, as are the costs of healthcare, not all elements of which are provided free of charge as they were in socialist systems.[89] The Polish Supreme Court stressed recently that the improved living standards in Polish society ought to be material in determining the amount of compensation for non-pecuniary damage awarded to a claimant who suffered physical and mental pain as a result of a wrong diagnosis and the resulting chemotherapy.[90] In spite of these significant improvements, the approach to recovery of non-pecuniary damage remains inconsistent, especially among lower instance courts. Damages awards in general are unpredictable, and inconsistencies can clearly be observed. Unquestionably, the stage of 'transition' from the socialist approach still lingers across Central Europe. These developments have impacted on product liability law and practice and they remain relevant even after the implementation of the Product Liability Directive. Although the Directive is quite specific about the types of damage it covers, it leaves non-pecuniary damage and, more importantly, the assessment of damages in particular cases, to national law and to national courts. The process of assessment of damages is subject to national rules on causation and standard of proof and to other procedural rules governing damage assessment, and it remains dependent on the living standards, salaries and costs of living.

---

88 Judgement of 24 February 1969.

89 On the other hand, wider presence of first and third party insurance changes the civil liability landscape (this issue is not examined in the book): see Perram (1992).

90 Judgement of 10 March 2006. Kidney removal was assessed at 35 per cent of health detriment, and the resulting depression and anxiety at 10 per cent. The Supreme Court assessed the compensation for the non-pecuniary damage to be 150,000 PLN (around $60,000), which doubled what the district court awarded the claimant in the first instance.

Causation

Causal considerations play a very significant role in establishing civil liability and in determining its scope. Causal link is often difficult to verify, in particular in product liability cases involving complex products such as medicines or medical devices.[91] Here also very significant changes are taking place throughout Europe, and their detailed assessment goes beyond the scope of this book. While a more comprehensive analysis of causality in contractual and tortious product liability of Central Europe can be found in Part II of the book, the key trends are presented below and contrasted with the developments in Western Europe.

Causation still receives much more attention in the writings on tort than on contract law, and the book reflects this approach.[92] On the other hand, some tendencies to uniformly understand the causation test in contract and tort can be noted, especially in the English legal system (Nash 1998).[93] These tendencies have always been strong in Central Europe where the causation discourse is only gradually reaching the level of sophistication observed in the West.

Causation is a requirement of civil liability which is rarely defined in substantive laws, including product liability laws. Most Western European civil codes do not contain a definition of causal link (Van Dam 2006: 266), and among the Central European codes only the Polish one contains such a definition. The European Community law does not offer its own concept of causation, and the guidance from the European Court of Justice has so far been limited.[94] The Product Liability Directive confines its focus to "damage being caused by a defect in the product" (Article 1), but leaves the determination of causal tests and their application to national law, and to national courts in cases before them.

The very nature of causation requires a particular methodological approach to assessing its development in Europe. Van Dam (2006: 266) and van Gerven (2000: 466) point out that because policy reasons lie at the forefront of causation, one needs to look beyond theoretical concepts into practical application. Van Gerven indicates that such approach allows one to observe "the large extent of commonality" between various legal systems (2000: 466). Such level of

91 See for instance the English case involving oral contraceptives: *XYZ & Others* v *Schering Health Care Limited* [2002] which failed on the preliminary issue of causation.

92 This tendency can be noticed equally in Western Europe – as noted by Hart and Honoré (1985) – and in Central Europe – Czachórski (2002). For more detailed analyses of causation see: Honoré (1971); and comparative analyses: Van Dam (2006: 266–300), Spier (ed.) (2000); van Gerven, Lever and Larouche (2000).

93 *Galoo v. Bright Grahame Murray* [1995] – the Court of Appeal followed an assumption that no difference existed in tests of causation in contractual and tortious liability (Nash 1998).

94 This was mainly in the area of Member State liability for damages caused by breaches of EC law (Francovich and Brasserie principles – see below for a further explanation) or liability of Community authorities – see also: C-352/98 *Laboratoires Pharmaceutique Bergaderm SA and Gouplin v Commission*, and 4/69 *Lütticke v Commission*.

commonality was indeed observed in the seminal book edited by Spier, where causation tests and their practical application were examined in a number of European states such as France, England, Germany, Italy, Austria, but also South Africa and the United States (Spier 2000). The contributors to the book did, however, also point out significant divergences in the manner in which causation was understood and applied in the respective legal systems. The more practice-focused approach allows one to assess the nature of causation in Central European laws, seeking common tendencies and divergences with the Western European approach.

Van Dam describes causation as "an elusive phenomenon", "an elastic feature which can be stretched and shrunk according to the magnitude of … other requirements of liability" (2006: 268). What follows is that it is difficult to pinpoint exactly, especially looking at jurisprudence of courts of various European states, which issues belong to causal considerations and which are part of other elements or requirements of liability. In some legal systems causation overlaps with considerations of fault or negligence (the latter – in common law systems) – namely probability and foreseeability – and other elements of fault or negligence, such as scope of duty or scope of rule, "absorb a number of causation issues" (Van Dam 2006: 267). According to Whittaker, in fault liability systems "issues of fault and causation tend to merge" (2005: 55).[95] This is certainly the case in Central Europe where both contractual and tortious liability have been based on 'fault'. Thus one would look in vain for a detailed elaboration of causal issues in Central European jurisprudence. The product liability jurisprudence followed this approach, with courts analysing the conduct of defendants – sellers, manufacturers, importers – in detail according to the required standards of behaviour, and subsequently often referring to causality as a matter of course. The position is now changing with the greater use of objective, even strict liability. Central European courts deal very frequently with relatively complex causal issues much more comprehensively than ever before.[96] Also they are increasingly forced to see causation as to a large extent detached from the defendants' conduct and rather linked with some other objectively ascertainable event (such as a defect in a product), thus extending the scope of issues to be considered as part of the 'causation' discourse.[97] This phenomenon has been particularly clear in Hungary, where the evolution of objective liability was very dynamic indeed (Szalma 2003). Further, causation is gaining more prominence in jurisprudence because it serves the purpose of limiting the scope of recoverable damage in a particular case. Thus, causal considerations are given a major role in delimiting the scope of the defendant's liability. This phenomenon is by no means only present in Central

95 This issue was mentioned in the section above devoted to liability standards (also exploring the notion of 'fault').

96 See below, also: Chapter 5 of Part II.

97 This statement follows the considerations above – if causal issues are not taken over by the analysis of 'fault' or negligence, they become more distinct and indeed prominent.

Europe – Cane notes its operation in common law systems (Cane 2006: 119). It may become even more prominent in Hungary, where the draft Civil Code suggests that contractual liability, although objective, should only allow recovery of damages which were foreseeable at the time of contracting.[98]

Throughout Europe and in the United States, causal considerations are divided into two more or less distinct stages: factual considerations (causation in fact), and what Van Dam refers to as 'limiting causation' – legal arguments involving issues such as proximity and adequacy of cause, remoteness, foreseeability of harm and policy (floodgates) arguments (Van Dam 2006: 269, Spier and Haazen [in Spier ed.] 2000: 131). While these are very clearly separated in Western European academic writings, courts do not always expressly make the distinction. In Central Europe the two-stage test has rarely been explicit even in scholarly writings. Policy considerations were and still are incorporated into the factual causation test, and the 'adequate' or 'normal' causal connections[99] are only sought among those which satisfy both the factual requirements and proximity, equity or justice requirements. Product liability practice has obviously been affected by this approach, of which below. The analysis here follows the two-stage distinction of causal issues for clarity purposes and in order to indicate the possible tendencies for convergence between the Central European and the Western European approach. It is likely that with a much greater emphasis on policy arguments in doctrinal writings and in judgements of Central European courts the second stage of causal considerations will indeed become more distinctly pronounced.

Factual causation engages the principle of *conditio sine qua non*, also referred to as the 'but for' test in common law systems.[100] It focuses on establishing whether the damage would have occurred if the negligent conduct or a strict cause had not occurred (Van Dam 2006: 269). In simple cases the answer 'yes' means no causation and therefore no liability, but more complex cases may involve situations where the claimant was 'deprived of chance' or where a number of possible causes or a number of defendants may have contributed to the damage. In these difficult cases courts apply various techniques to arrive at solutions which comply with their policy aims, and with their sense of equity and justice (Van Dam 2006: 269). Thus, for instance, English courts modify the 'but-for' test using the language of justice and fairness:[101] emphasizing the contribution to the risk of

98 Draft Code: Section 5: 129, quoted and analysed in detail in Chapter 4 of Part II.

99 These are two main causation tests applied in the Central European legal systems – see below.

100 See the English case of *Barnett v Chelsea and Kensington Hospital Management Committee* [1969].

101 See the House of Lords judgement in *Chester v Afshar* [2004].

injury,[102] or developing the concept of loss of chance.[103] Here is where the second stage of causal considerations is utilized. This stage entails narrowing the scope of events which remain in factual causal connection to those relevant in the eyes of the law. Thus even if an event is a factual cause of a particular damage it will not necessarily be seen as such a cause by law (Cane 2006: 125). In fact, it has been argued that this stage of analysis ought not to be referred to as causation but as "responsibility" or "scope of liability" (Cane 2006: 119, Stapleton 2003b: 388). The arguments go back to the key question posed in civil liability cases: "should the defendant be held responsible to pay compensation?" (Cane 2006: 120) or more precisely – should the defendant provide the required compensation to the specified claimant? They focus, therefore, "on allocating responsibility for life's misfortunes" (Cane 2006: 129). Again, various legal systems approach these issues in various ways, and often a specific area of civil liability would have its own limitations. Product liability obviously has such limitations as well. Overall, the 'scope of liability' is verified by the aims of liability rules: they determine whether the particular damage suffered by the claimant is recoverable and not too remote or too unforeseeable. Foreseeability and remoteness, the concept of 'scope of risk,' or a risk-benefit analysis (Cane 2006: 125), the scope of recoverable damages, the standard of conduct expected of the defendant, all play a part in establishing the 'limits of liability'. Policy arguments, accompanied by the economic and social context of civil liability laws and practice, provide an additional dimension to the discourse. Thus, some damages are not recoverable because they are unforeseeable or too remote (whatever notion is actually used in a particular legal system), in other cases the defendants are not responsible for damage which it would not be economically efficient for them to prevent (risk-benefit analysis), still in other circumstances 'damages' may be reduced because an intervening event or the victim's conduct[104] also contributed to the occurrence of damage, and finally in other cases damages are reduced or liability denied because of availability of other forms of compensation. Product liability introduces its own peculiar requirements to the discourse. Courts and academics attempted to reconcile these requirements with the universal causation tests when developing product liability rules. The social and policy aims to compensate victims and encourage care in manufacture and distribution of products, the realization that professionals ought to be placed under a more stringent set of obligations, the decisions concerning risk/benefit calculation in manufacture of products, and availability or unavailability of other mechanisms of compensation, were all instrumental in shaping causation tests in

102 *McGee v National Coal Board* [1972], *Fairchild v Glenhaven Funeral Services Ltd and others, Fox v Spousal (Midlands) Ltd, Matthews v Associated Portland Cement Manufacturers (1978) Ltd and others* [2002], *Barker v Corus (UK) plc (formerly Saint Gobain Pipelines plc), Murray v British Shipbuilders (Hydrodynamics) Ltd, Patterson v Smiths Dock Ltd and others* [2006].

103 *Gregg (FC) v Scott* [2005].

104 See below for a short elaboration of the doctrine of 'contributory negligence'.

product liability cases. In fact, Western European courts' experience in dealing with such cases is notable (Van Dam 2006: 270–97), and Central European courts only gradually are developing a consistent approach to them. As mentioned in Chapter 2, relative simplicity of case law transpires very clearly from the early jurisprudence of Central European courts, not least in the area of product liability.

In developing causation tests to be applied by courts, Central European academic writers[105] were inspired by the developments in Western Europe, where they saw two main theories: the 'equivalence of the cause' (*conditio sine qua non*) theory, and the 'adequate causal connection' theory (Wagner 1974: 155, Czachórski 2002: 210, Hradek 2004: 95). The former theory has been criticized as too broad because it assumes that all events are equivalent to the extent that exclusion of either of the events as a cause of damage excludes the possibility of the damage (Czachórski 2002: 210). Each event, therefore, constitutes a condition *sine qua non* of the damage (ibid.). The 'equivalence' theory relies heavily upon the further elements of liability, and 'fault' in particular, as determinants whether the specific person whose conduct according to this theory caused the damage would be responsible (Wagner 1974: 155). It is not very useful in legal systems which use strict liability. Its weaknesses were meant to be modified by the theory of 'adequate causal connection'. This theory evaluates all the events that lead to the damage and chooses only the ordinary consequences while excluding the unusual (Wagner 1974: 155, Hradek 2004: 95).[106] Although it was concluded that other requisites of liability played no role here (Czachórski 2002: 211), certain writers criticized this theory for its emphasis upon foreseeability, and hence some links to the concept of 'fault'. For a limited time, Central European civil liability laws affected by the particular political and economic conditions of socialism offered their own theory of causal link following the thoughts explored in Soviet Russia. The theory of 'necessary and accidental causal links' reflected the common contention of socialist legal writers that law ought to use the same concept of causal connection as other sciences, and especially social sciences. Accordingly, only 'necessary' causal links could give rise to civil liability. In Poland, Ohanowicz wrote that: "[t]he test on the ground of which we distinguish the necessary causal connection from the accidental one are the *laws of nature* established by science and experience. In this way an objective conclusion can be reached" (1958: 45,

105 For an introduction to the topic see: in Poland – Czachórski (2002: 209 – 217), and for a source in English see Wagner (1974: 154–73); in Hungary – Harmathy (1998: 118); in the Czech Republic – Svestka and Knappova (2002), Fiala and Kindl (2007), and in English: Vondracek (1988: 377) and Hradek (2004: 94–6): analysis of the judgement of the Highest Court: NS ČR 22 October 2003, 25 Cdo 1455/2003.

106 As to what exactly is 'the ordinary' and what constitutes 'the unusual' the theory offers several solutions: either evaluating the circumstances from the point of view of the person whose conduct is assessed, or from some objective point of view, evaluating the events irrespective of their foreseeability at the time of the events (Czachórski 2002: 211).

46).[107] This theory was, however, described as only ostensibly different from the theory of adequate causal connection (Czachórski 2002: 212). Further, it did not offer an unequivocal solution in cases where loss of expected profits was the relevant damage (Wagner 1974: 158), or where inaction was the cause of damage (Czachórski 2002: 212).

The disputes on the most appropriate theory of causal link are still continuing across Central Europe, now devoid of the burden of the socialist ideology. Some writers consider, however, that the theories can only give a general guidance in solving various problems in this area of law. The guidelines must be flexible and ought to be applied reasonably (Czachórski 2002: 212). Hence, according to Central European academics common sense ought not to be abandoned (Wagner 1974: 159). These suggestions may be seen as a reflection of a change in approach to causation: towards an approach where the two separate stages – factual and legal causation – are indeed distinguished more clearly. However, at present Central European courts deal with causal link in a unitary fashion, seeking the 'adequate' causes among those indicated by the facts of the case, and by legal and equity principles. A Czech court judgement of 2003, declaring a mental disease, pain and suffering of a woman whose husband was killed in a car accident by the defendant as not being in an adequate causal link with the defendant's conduct is a good example.[108] It appears that at least part of the rationale for the decision was the conviction that the woman's non-pecuniary damage should not be recoverable from the defendant.[109]

Similarly with the rest of Europe, also in Central Europe product liability challenged the established causation tests with its own unique policy requirements and factual complexities. Initially, Central European scholarly writings on product liability did not devote much attention to the issue of causation, as causal issues were largely taken over by 'fault' analysis. With the greater prominence of objective liability standards came greater recognition of the specificity of product liability cases, and there was a very clearly discernible feeling of the need to protect and compensate victims of defective products, to require professionals to comply with a higher standard of conduct than the one imposed on consumers. Those policy arguments affected assessment of what was a foreseeable and adequate consequence of a defect, thus extending the scope of recoverable damage. They also affected decisions concerning the relevance of 'contributory negligence' of the victim for the amount of awarded damages (see below). At present Central European legal thought and jurisprudence are handling increasingly complex causal issues, and face similar challenges to those experienced by the rest of Europe. What are these challenges?

107 Translated by the author.

108 NS ČR 22 October 2003, analysed by Hradek (2004: 94–6).

109 This is quite a controversial outcome, and it does not reflect the general approach of Czech courts – Hradek (2004: 96).

With the developments in science, technology, and new methods of risk forecasting, assessment and prevention, causal issues are becoming more intricate – there is more science and technology in everyday life, and relationships between people reflect this. Product liability cases for instance often involve medicinal products or medical devices: complex products, produced and distributed by elaborate business ventures, meant to cure various underlying conditions. Establishing causation in such cases where medical evidence is not conclusive – many companies and people may potentially be responsible, and there is always a chance that the injury was caused by the underlying illness – is very problematic. Policy considerations often used to allocate risk and responsibility in such cases must reflect the contemporary market conditions and the needs of society. Further, recently another phenomenon put causality to an even greater test – the emergence of group litigation.[110] Here issues of causality are much more problematic in tort law than in contract law. The relatively recent phenomena of mass torts and toxic torts, which first came to the fore in the United States, involving large numbers of claimants and potentially large numbers of defendants, bring new legal and factual issues into the causality discourse (Goldberg 2003: 40). Such mass torts, often occurring in the context of product liability, entail two main causal problems: identifying the responsible defendant and establishing factual and legal causation *per se* (Hodges 2001). With regard to the former point – the product or substance in question may have been produced, introduced into the market or used by a large number of undertakings and persons. Demonstrating which one of those is responsible for the injury may be difficult if not impossible, and courts faced with this problem are adopting various methods of overcoming it. So far the most noteworthy examples come from the US courts,[111] but recently also English courts had to decide on the issue.[112] As far as the latter point of causation *per se* is concerned, problems may arise with regard to general causation (determination whether the particular product may on the balance of probabilities have caused injuries reported in the case) and with regard to attributing the tort to the particular injury of a particular person (Goldberg 2003: 41). Again, Central European scholarly writings and jurisprudence do not present interesting insights into these issues. There is no doubt that Central European doctrinal writers and courts are building their legal framework of causation in the context of these changes, but their experience with some of the problems mentioned above is not yet noteworthy (not least because group litigation is as yet relatively unknown to Central European civil procedures).

Another aspect of causal considerations merits a mention here: it has a significant impact on the 'damages' awarded to claimants. In most European legal systems, including Central Europe, 'damages' have been reduced in civil liability

110 This is a relatively recent phenomenon in Europe, as briefly described below. In the United States, group litigation has quite a long tradition.

111 Burden-shifting or market-share liability – see Goldberg (2003: 41).

112 The judgement in *Barker v. Corus (UK) plc* [2006].

cases where the victim has contributed to the damage. Sometimes liability itself is extinguished where the victim's conduct is seen as the true cause of the injuries or damages. It is often referred to as 'contributory negligence',[113] although there is no consensus or indeed uniformity across various types of liability whether it is negligent conduct that is required for the concept to operate. In Central Europe, especially as civil liability has been based on 'fault', the courts sought 'fault' in the conduct which would qualify the victim's conduct as contributory. With the development of product liability systems it emerged that courts were not eager to declare 'contributory negligence'. Victims of defective products were seen as being in a weaker position – both economically and as regards knowledge about the products. They were not required to know or enquire about the dangerous qualities of products if not advised about those by the manufacturers or sellers.

Further relevant issues

Civil liability cases entail a number of other crucial legal issues: those deserving a mention here are limitation periods and various elements of civil procedure. They are not analysed in detail, although some preliminary remarks are useful at this point.

Limitation periods are acknowledged throughout Europe as crucial instruments safeguarding continuity and finality of business transactions and ensuring reasonable insurance costs. The Product Liability Directive introduces very clear time limits, and these have been implemented by the Member States. The Directive follows a two-tier approach: a subjective period of three years conditional upon the victim's knowledge of the damage and the person liable, and an objectively determinable cut-off period of ten years which commences with the introduction of the product into circulation. The latter period may effectively expire before the subjective one even starts (for example because of latency of some injuries). Central European states also introduced such periods, which became applicable in cases covered by the Directive instead of their general civil liability limitation periods regulated by the civil codes (the two-tier approach is also adopted by the Czech Civil Code and the Polish Civil Code for general tortious liability cases). However, it appears that the Polish and the Czech judiciary may be uneasy about the cut-off period expiring before the subjective period starts. The Polish Constitutional Tribunal declared in 2006 that such an arrangement in tortious liability cases was unconstitutional where personal injuries were suffered.[114] This led to the amendment of the Civil Code.[115] Czech courts tend to refuse to accept that the cut-off period expires before

113 Although the book uses the notion 'fault' rather than negligence, here the concept 'contributory negligence' is referred to – this is indeed the universal term given to this legal phenomenon.

114 Decision SK 14/05 of 1 September 2006.

115 See Chapter 5 of Part II.

the victim has learnt of the damage.[116] These developments occurred in the context of general civil liability, not product liability, and it is yet to be seen what effect this approach will have in product liability cases. In the light of the 'maximum harmonization' nature of the Directive any detraction from the ten-year long stop prescribed by it is unacceptable, but on the other hand these attitudes of the prominent members of the judiciary may be disruptive to the desired application of this instrument. The signs of change in approach to limitation periods, especially as regards personal injuries, are also visible in other legal systems. Some English academics postulate rethinking of limitation periods which increase costs of litigation and constitute an obstacle to effective compensation of personal injuries (Patten 2006).

Another set of factors, which in fact contributes to some significant differences in approach to civil liability between various legal systems (with a clear dichotomy between civil law and common law countries), was articulated by Whittaker (2005) – these are various aspects of civil procedure. The procedural dimension of civil liability is not covered by the book, but it is important to note a number of examples at this point to demonstrate the complexity of civil liability and its practice. First of all, elaborate scientific and technological investigations into causal links are often very difficult in civil law systems because of lack of the requirement of discovery. Further, the manner in which expert witnesses are appointed also bears significance – in civil law systems courts nominate experts from official lists. A similar situation takes place in Central Europe. Of course these procedural issues are relevant with regard to all the elements of liability already discussed above, and the rules of burden of proof are the key to unravelling the position of the parties and their obligation to determine the existence of these elements. Clearly, there is a need for further research into this dimension of civil liability throughout Central Europe.

Harmonization of law of obligations in Europe – the position of product liability law

The analysis above demonstrated how important the general laws of obligations remain for product liability law, also the product liability system established by the Product Liability Directive. Consequently, the contemporary processes of legal harmonization and convergence of laws of obligations across Europe, mentioned throughout the analysis, have significant impact on the process of harmonization of product liability in Europe (analysed below). But the influences are mutual: product liability challenges the established legal principles and in many respects it impacts those pan-European-level developments in the laws of obligations. The latter are briefly assessed below.

116 Judgements 33 Odo 477/2001 and R 2/1992 – Hradek (2003: 132). Hungarian civil liability rules do not distinguish subjective from objective limitation periods, thus this problem does not occur there.

Convergence of European laws, so widely commented upon by comparative lawyers (Wagner 2006, Zweigert and Kotz, 1998, Legrand 1996), has now been reinforced by the European Union efforts to harmonize the laws of its Member States. The process of harmonizing European contract and tort laws inspired by the European Union is well under way. Harmonization of contract law is more advanced and it is said to constitute the "pacemaker for tort law" (Wagner 2006: 1005). The Common Frame of Reference[117] and the related review of Consumer *Acquis* commenced building the platform for future work on codifying European contract law based on "a multi-layered approach, combining elements of soft harmonization with the final goal of a European Civil Code" (Wagner 2006: 1004).[118] The work on harmonization of European tort law is gradually progressing through the review of the existing rules and seeking commonalities.[119] For instance, a large number of volumes were produced by the European Group on Tort Law, devoted to specific concepts within tortious liability such as fault, strict liability, causal link, damages, etc.[120] Some research undertakings emphasize the interdisciplinary links between various strands of civil liability and the importance of recognition of these links for the effective harmonization of European civil liability laws (von Bar and Drobnig 2002). The efforts to harmonize European laws have recently become more complex with the enlargement of the European Union. Central and Eastern European legal systems are now taking part in the process. As illustrated by this book, their peculiar, transition-style features introduce an entirely new dimension to the harmonization debate.

One can observe two inter-linked processes of convergence, approximation and harmonization across Europe: a formalized, legalized harmonization conducted by the European Union, and a more informal, academically-inspired discourse among comparative law scholars concerning convergence of European legal systems. The debate between the 'mainstream' comparative scholars such as Markesinis, Zweigert, Kotz, Van Gerven, Watson or de Cruz who observe the process of convergence as a natural and a relatively straightforward process of legal borrowing, approximation and transplantation, and those comparatists such as Legrand or Teubner who argue

117 See Report from the Commission, *Second Progress Report on the Common Frame of Reference* (2007). See also Draft Common Frame of Reference (2008).

118 Communication from the Commission to the European Parliament and the Council, A More Coherent European Contract Law: An Action Plan (2003); Communication from the Commission, European Contract Law and the Revision of the Acquis: the Way Forward (2004), Commission Green Paper on the Review of the Consumer Acquis of (2007). See also: Vogenauer and Weatherill (2005).

119 See for instance – the draft of the 'Principles of European Tort Law' developed by the European Group on Tort Law, published in Koziol and Steininger (2003: 562–71). See also Wagner (2005) and (2006). The recent developments within European substantive law concerning consumers – including contract and tort law – are explored by Hodges (2007a).

120 See European Group on Tort Law, *Principles of European Tort Law* (2005), Spier (2003, 2000, 1998, 1996), Magnus and Casals (2004), Rogers (2004), Widmer (2005), Koch and Koziol (2002), Magnus (2001), Koziol (1998).

that this process is far from straightforward if at all possible, obviously reaches far beyond the interests of this book. Nevertheless, it is crucial to enquire about the real prospects for harmonization of law of obligations in the new, enlarged Europe. It is clear from the point of view of both these processes that legal harmonization in Europe may well be more difficult than imagined initially. The law of product liability illustrates this complexity with great transparency. Although the Product Liability Directive is considered a "flagship of European tort law harmonization until now", it has been said that such sectoral harmonization efforts may not be successful (von Bar and Drobnig 2002: 42). There are views that separation of product liability from the general law of obligations is not justified. A conclusion from observing the debate of contemporary comparative lawyers, and indeed the practice of laws which were harmonized on the European Community level (such as consumer protection directives reviewed in the *Acquis* Review, or the Product Liability Directive), is that the problems with achieving true approximation of laws go beyond the palpable issue of sectoral fragmentation. There is no doubt that the wider processes of convergence and harmonization of laws of obligations, now joined by the post-socialist states, are going to be crucial for harmonization of European product liability law.

PRODUCT LIABILITY AND CONSUMER PROTECTION – DEVELOPMENTS IN THE WEST AND IN CENTRAL EUROPE; THE IMPACT OF THE PRODUCT LIABILITY DIRECTIVE

INTRODUCTION

The development of product liability laws in Western Europe, and later also in Central Europe and the rest of the socialist region, was closely linked to the emancipation and strengthening of the role of consumers,[121] and to the recognition of their specific position within markets.[122]

> In the mind of the consumer, services, and even more so goods, constitute the principal if not the only area which fits into the modern concept of 'consumerism'.
> Calais-Auloy (1981: 12)

This statement summarizes the idea that consumerism[123] is inherently related to using goods or services, acquired either under a contract or otherwise. The core

121 See below for an elaboration of the concept of 'consumers'.

122 These developments occurred in the context of another new phenomenon in the modern society – the development of the 'welfare state'. This phenomenon is not analysed here (see Teubner [1986a] for a comprehensive review of the evolution of the 'welfare state').

123 This notion is used in the book to denote a movement, a policy or an approach promoting consumer interests and not in a pejorative sense of "greed, stupidity, and

parts of consumer protection laws are those aimed at safety and quality of products and services. The analysis below seeks the roots of product liability law, and continues to build its theoretical basis, through the developments in consumer law and policy in the 'West' and in the 'East'.

Consumer law is an integral, "sectoral" part of economic laws – the laws of the market (Hodges 2007b: 1243). Developments in modern market laws, and particularly the birth of consumerism, challenged the traditional legal structures within which product liability cases were contained. They ultimately led to the birth of autonomous, distinct product liability systems.[124] These challenges appeared in the United States and later in Western Europe, and they also took place in the socialist Central Europe and other socialist states. The 'West'–'East' differences in the manner in which they were recognized and responded to are explored below.

Initially, product liability was not recognized as a separate legal regime. It was based on contractual relationships between sellers and buyers. Following the principle of *caveat emptor* buyers were protected by law only in very specific circumstances: such as a breach of an express promise by the seller, or a fraud (Borrie and Diamond 1981: 17–21). The 'consumer-focused' product liability laws were gradually introduced in the second half of the twentieth century, and in Central Europe since the late 1970s and 1980s. Both in the 'West' and in the 'East' they reflected fundamental socio-economic and technological changes. On the one hand, growing incomes and standards of living enabled people to enjoy an increasing variety of goods and services. On the other hand, they gave rise to far-reaching inequalities in peoples' economic and social status. The products and services available to consumers were offered by enterprises growing in power and size, able to produce very complex products much faster and in higher quantities than was ever imaginable. Such products were capable of causing damage reaching beyond the buyer, his family and friends, to reach mere bystanders. The traditional concept of 'consumer buyers' rooted in contract law was no longer useful in the context of product liability. It was indeed taken over by much wider concepts of 'consumers' based upon a lack of professional knowledge about products (this element was emphasized in Europe, both Eastern and Western – Łętowska 1999, Maczonkai 1996, Mortelmans and Watson 1996, Bourgoignie et al. 1987), or poorly represented within society (this element was emphasized in the United States – Friedman 1978), irrespective of their relationship with the professionals who manufactured or introduced the product into the market. On the other hand, commercial chains leading to the ultimate victims of defective products were

insensitivity to want" (Douglas and Isherwood 1996: vii).

124 This in spite of some opposition from the academia and legal practitioners: Gilmore (1970: 116) stated that to isolate product liability in order to conduct its separate analysis would distort the debate on liability; while Simitis referred to the speech of a 'well-known' German barrister during the 1968 meeting of the German Lawyers' Association, in which the latter criticized the efforts to establish a specific regime for product-related injuries as "an unjustified import of a typically American 'good'" (1986: 100).

extended to involve various types of suppliers, wholesalers and retailers. The consumers had no opportunity, no sufficient means and knowledge to ensure the required quality of the products and services, and redress for damage caused by those products or services was not easy to obtain. These were the circumstances in which courts started establishing product liability regimes. Contract law which so far governed market relations often gave way to tort law – as much less limited in scope and generally more suited to the modern market conditions. Product liability laws as we know them today, although based upon traditional forms of civil liability, have their distinct features attributable to the general trends in the consumer protection movement. Further, the transformations within consumer policies and laws taking place at present[125] – a more integrated, comprehensive approach to regulating markets in the spirit of better regulation and competitiveness on the one hand and greater consumer protection and their access to justice on the other – result in transformations of the role and nature of product liability law and practice. These transformations are starting to gain ground in Central Europe.

The remainder of this chapter commences with setting out the broad conceptual framework of consumer policy and law, and the role of product liability law within these arrangements, and continues by presenting and to some extent contrasting the approaches of the European Union and the Central European states.

PRODUCT LIABILITY, CONSUMER LAW AND CONSUMER INTERESTS

Contemporary product liability laws, in common with other consumer laws, constitute a form of state intervention in markets. Such consumer laws are aimed at redressing what economists refer to as 'market failures' – imbalances in the respective market power of market participants. Consumer laws achieve this aim by shaping behaviour of market participants, or by providing redress, also financial redress of damage sustained as a result of those 'market failures'. Most to some extent combine the behaviour modification and the redress/compensatory functions. Although the compensatory function is paramount for product liability, both the prospect of product liability litigation and the decisions given by courts as a result of litigation which does take place, are also to establish a deterrence effect.[126] The analysis below depicts the process of shaping consumer laws – both in Western and in Central Europe – providing the context for the development of product liability law.

Two separate issues arise here: one, the links between product liability and consumer protection, and two, the prevalence, or lack thereof, of consumer interests within product liability law and practice. Both have shaped product liability law,

125 See below for an elaboration of these transformations on the European Union level.

126 See above for a detailed examination of the aims and roles of the law of obligations, in particular tort law.

and are explored below. The former has been quite widely agreed upon by academic writers – the links contributed to the development of product liability into what it is today. They appear strong enough for most scholarly writers to contain product liability law within a wider field of consumer protection law (for instance Howells and Weatherill 2005).[127] The latter is a much more controversial issue.

POLITICAL AND DOCTRINAL RESPONSES TO THE NEED TO PROTECT CONSUMERS AND THEIR IMPACT ON PRODUCT LIABILITY

Markets and their failures: balance of market power

As mentioned above, the raison d'être of consumer protection laws is the need to offset the "gross disparities of effective economic power" between businesses and consumers (Bourgoignie et al. 1987: 10). The idea of market power focuses on the ability to influence outcomes within the market environment. This ability can be achieved by various means – using rewards, coercion, or beliefs in superiority of a group due to its legitimacy or expert knowledge (Rezabakhsh, Bornemann, Hansen and Schrader 2006, Howells and Weatherill 2005: 16, Friedman 1999, Grønmo and Ölander 1991, French and Raven 1959). The balance of power within markets determines for instance how much pressure there is on businesses to produce safe, good quality products. The pressure may be the effect of competition with other businesses, and of consumer 'voice'. Weatherill and Howells use the well-known economic idea of 'perfect markets' to portray the situation where quality, price and safety of products are optimal: determined by market forces and the voice of consumers. In a perfect market "it is competition which acts as the key regulator ensuring that individual greed does not lead to exploitation" (Roper and Snowdon 1987: 11), and the consumer is an autonomous unit capable of making economic decisions on the basis of his or her own choice. Obviously, markets in reality are not 'perfect', and economists developed a concept of 'market failures', the features of which are, for instance, monopolies which deny consumers a free, informed choice, or dominant businesses abusing their position. Thus, the need for state intervention arises (Lipsey and Chrystal 1995: 11).

The strive for redressing market balance inspired consumer protection laws across Western Europe, but in a strictly socialist, centrally planned and state-owned economy it would be difficult to envisage ideas about stronger or weaker positions of businesses or citizens where both these groups were subservient to the wider interests of the state and thus to a large extent, at least formally, equally handicapped. The concept of 'market failure' was not known to socialist political or economic thought – the "socialist economy was per definition not a market

127 Yet, neither of the definitions of product liability given above refers to consumers. Also the substantive provisions of the most crucial legal instrument regulating this area of law in Europe – the Product Liability Directive – do not mention consumers. Articles 4 and 8 of the Directive refer to an 'injured person'.

economy and could not be admitted to have failed in any way" (Bakardjieva Engelbrekt 2006: 9). However, with changes to the traditional socialist economic thinking which commenced in the late 1970s and 1980s (described below) came an increased recognition of the need to monitor and redress the position of market participants – businesses and consumers. The doctrinal and political approach in Central Europe changed with the gradual materialization of elements of market economy. The weaker bargaining position of consumers in dealings with professionals permeates the writings of Nesterowicz on product liability (1970s in Poland), the seminal work of Łętowska on consumer protection law (1980s in Poland), Maczonkai's excellent observations on product liability law in Hungary (1990s), and Svestka's writings on consumer protection law in Czechoslovakia and the Czech Republic (1980s and 1990s).

Courts took account of these developments in product liability cases. Providing market balance lies at the heart of product liability law, which apportions risks inherent in products and thus ultimately decides whether these risks ought to be internalized (borne by those who manufactured or sold them) or externalized (borne by consumers). Why and to what extent should risks carried by products be internalized? Stapleton points out that product liability is the responsibility for commercially supplied products (1994a: 7). Such a description reflects the recognition of stricter obligations placed on commercial (professional) market participants.[128] Various theories as to why professional business people ought to bear the risk of loss caused by defective products manufactured, sold, or in any other way handled by them appeared in the 'West' and some were echoed in Central Europe after the market economy ideas appeared there. Economic theories, which gained most popularity in the United States in the writings of Prosser or Posner, used the argument of the cheapest cost avoider.[129] Non-economic theories of liability, much more prominent in Europe, used Aristotle's idea of 'corrective justice' (Stapleton 1994a: 174), and established a theory of moral enterprise liability (taking risks "in pursuit of financial profit" as a basis of liability – Stapleton 1994a: 186, Łętowska in Poland 1999: 90, 91, Svestka in Czechoslovakia 1989).

State intervention in markets – rationale and techniques

Regulating markets, and especially regulating the position of consumers, is a political process that goes beyond economic considerations of perfectibility of markets (Howells and Weatherill 2005: 7–8). According to Howells and Weatherill, consumer law involves questions of "how our society views the citizen" (ibid.). The contrast between Western and the Central Europe in this regard has been remarkable, although the two are becoming more similar. Harvey

128 The Product Liability Directive contains an exemption from liability if the defendant proves he did not manufacture or distribute the product in the course of his business (Article 7c).

129 See Fluhr (2007) for a review of the economic theory of product liability.

and Parry noted that "any informed view of the law …" ought to involve the knowledge of certain "assumptions" as to the economic, philosophical and political "nature of consumerism", and that the state, when creating consumer protection law, "proceeds on some of these assumptions" (1996: 6). Essentially, regulating markets and protecting consumers is determined by a particular style of governance: it concerns lawmaking techniques, regulatory techniques and enforcement mechanisms. The foundations of market regulation and consumer protection translate into specific mechanisms which serve these purposes. It is of course far beyond the scope of this book to assess these matters in detail. However, drawing on the rationale for the choice of mechanisms for protecting consumers allows a greater understanding of the role and framework of product liability which is a specific mixture of legislation and jurisprudence.

Trubek defined consumer protection policy as a policy of government intervention in "market place transactions", including intervention by law (Bourgoignie et al. 1987: 1); and consumer protection law as "the sum total of the ways in which a state constitutes, defines, and intervenes in markets for the purpose of protecting the ultimate consumer of goods and services" (Bourgoignie et al. 1987: 6). Consumer protection law thus becomes, according to Trubek, "a series of relationships, direct or indirect, between state institutions … on the one hand and private economic actors on the other" (Bourgoignie et al. 1987: 6). The evolution of consumer protection policies and laws of the Western European Member States of the European Union commenced with the recognition that the traditional, liberal legal approaches to the governance of market relations were unsatisfactory (Bourgoignie et al. 1987: 90). The 'modern political economy of consumer protection' established by Trubek is a vision of consumer protection law as it stands at present throughout Europe and beyond. In contrast to the traditional or 'classical' vision, the modern approach does not take perfectibility of markets for granted. It favours state action as "supplementing if not supplanting market determination" (Bourgoignie et al. 1987: 7).

The fundamental premise justifying the need for consumer protection within the law of the European Community and its Member States has been lack of sufficient knowledge and awareness on the part of consumers (Łętowska 1999: 13). The European Community approaches consumers as market participants who suffer from deficiencies of information about the goods and services they acquire (Wilhelmsson 1996). Łętowska pointed out that at the time consumer policy was starting to shape up within the European Community, the American ideology of *public interest law* (consumer protection as a response to insufficient representation of this group – Handler 1979, Friedman 1978) was rejected as too speculative and needing further elucidation (1999: 13).[130] The European Community rather wished to see consumer law and policy established by public authorities, not by the

130 Public interest law attempts to fill the gaps in the legal framework of the society by providing adequate representation of groups which are perceived as underrepresented (Łętowska 1999: 9).

individual demands of consumers. This approach ties in with the general regulatory technique which is dominant on the pan-European and the national level across Europe. Although some level of convergence can be observed (Kelemen and Sibbitt 2004), the discrepancy in approach continues until today: between the 'regulation through litigation' in the United States (ibid.), and an emphasis upon regulation of consumer affairs by public authorities in Europe. Evidence of convergence can be seen on the one hand in the United States' attempts to deal with some of the most negative implications of class actions (Class Action Fairness Act of 2005) and tort litigation in general, and an increased level of regulative intervention in markets (for instance: The Sarbanes-Oxley Act of 2002). On the other hand, the EU is looking at wider and more pervasive methods of private enforcement of law, for instance competition law (Commission Green Paper Damages actions for breach of the EC antitrust Rules)[131] and recently also consumer law (EU Consumer Policy Strategy 2007–2013), and class action mechanisms and other representative and collective enforcement methods are being introduced on the Member State level.[132] What are the implications of such divergent approaches for product liability law, the essence of which is indeed private enforcement?[133] They may well be one of the reasons for the greater 'litigiousness' of the American consumers in comparison with the European consumers (as pointed out by Markesinis 1990).[134] Although more research would be required to ascertain these contentions, it seems that in a regime focused upon public regulation of markets product liability law and practice may have a different role, importance and scope than in a regime focused upon private enforcement. The role of product liability in the American 'regulation through litigation' system may well be to a much wider extent behaviour modification and not merely compensation of losses. In European systems, behaviour modification is more often done with the use of public regulatory mechanisms, and product liability mainly realizes compensatory functions. This statement should obviously be taken with reservations which were indicated in the Introduction to this book: the existence of other methods of compensating victims of accidents, civil procedure rules, other mechanisms of accessing justice and the costs of litigation

131 See also: Howells and Wilhelmsson (1997). See the literature on the US approach: Kagan (2003).

132 For an overview of the development of collective enforcement mechanisms in Europe see: Hodges (2007a).

133 Product liability could be described as a 'litigation-heavy' system.

134 See Markesinis (1990) for an elaboration of some reasons which contribute to 'litigiousness' of societies (he analyses litigation rates, a more general propensity to litigate as a result of factors such as awareness of rights or costs of access to justice, as well as the numbers of cases fought to the end). Although one of the key thoughts of the article is that the differences with regard to litigation trends in England, Germany and the United States are not as significant as one might think, Markesinis stresses that the area where litigation rates in the United States have been high – higher in fact than in England – is product liability (1990: 268).

are also important here.[135] Further, the European approach is far from uniform: in particular, the United Kingdom exhibits much greater similarities to the US system than other European states.

Central Europe has undergone an unprecedented transformation as regards the theoretical basis and the mechanisms of state intervention in markets. In the initial stages of socialism such state intervention was solely based on the Marxist theories of central planning.[136] Control of markets was aimed at realizing socialist political aims. Thus, the interests of businesses (largely state-owned) and consumers were secured only to the extent that they complied with the interests of the socialist state. Market laws were present in primary legislation, for instance civil codes, but much more frequently they were contained in measures placed outside such legislation. This phenomenon was introduced in Chapter 2, which elaborated upon the separation of relations between state-owned enterprises ('socialist organizations') from ordinary civil law and the jurisdiction of civil courts, and on the concept of 'normative acts'. Initially, consumer interests suffered from lack of recognition, in particular as a result of the socialist 'holist' philosophy which opted for interests of the state in favour of individual interests (Łętowska 1999). With the gradual transformation in socialist legal and economic thought came an increased recognition of consumer rights. Socialist states enacted laws protecting consumers – both within and outside the civil codes. The particular feature of the socialist consumer policies and laws (and more generally – market policies and laws) was, however, that these were very often ineffective. The lack of efficient public enforcement of consumer laws was not compensated by a greater emphasis on private actions of consumers through litigation or other private enforcement mechanisms. The courts, which began building product liability regimes on the basis of general civil liability provisions, were ultimately unable to remedy the situation. Although in the absence of effective competition and efficient state regulation of market practices during socialism litigation was very often the only means consumers could use to ensure their interests were satisfied, it was largely inaccessible because of peculiar problems with access to justice and legal culture, analysed below. The position of product liability law was therefore quite peculiar: it was a crucial behaviour modification and compensation mechanism which could not be used effectively because of the peculiar workings of socialist political, economic and legal systems. After the transformation in the early 1990s Central European states commenced establishing fully-fledged consumer protection policies and laws. These have been influenced by the European Community policies and laws, and thus absorbed the regulatory approach to consumer law. They still,

135 Economic theories of liability, not analysed in detail in the book, provide another way of assessing the reasons why people opt for litigation or not – see Fluhr (2007).

136 The issue of economic planning of Central European markets, although undoubtedly vital in depicting the true state of these markets, is not examined in detail. For such a detailed analysis of Eastern European economies and their weaknesses see: Lewis (1994: 219–23) and Lavigne (1974).

however, retain some peculiar elements of systems in transition, emphasized in the final part of this chapter. Their impact on product liability is as yet not entirely certain.

The analysis below explores the developments in consumer policies and laws in the 'West' and in Central Europe. The Western European developments are portrayed by looking at the European Union and its consumer laws, their interaction with national consumer laws of the Member States, as well as the role, characteristics and effect of the Product Liability Directive.

CONSUMER PROTECTION POLICY AND CONSUMER PROTECTION LAW IN THE EUROPEAN COMMUNITY: THE ROOTS, THE ROLE AND THE EFFECTS OF THE PRODUCT LIABILITY DIRECTIVE

Introduction

This part of the book explores the European Community involvement in consumer protection, and the role of product liability in this process. Building European consumer law involves positive regulatory activities which the Community undertakes in order to harmonize laws of its Member States.

European consumer law witnessed an unprecedented expansion. The process of harmonization of Member States' laws with a view to building an internal market is by no means complete at present, but the Community is gradually taking over regulation of the legal position of European consumers (Micklitz 2007: 35). Efforts to build a truly harmonized consumer protection regime continue, having recently gained an entirely new dimension of a greater integration into market laws and policies. These developments are depicted below with a view to exploring the roots and nature of European product liability law.

The European Community and its legal system

The European Community, known until 1992 as the European Economic Community,[137] constitutes a vital part of the First Pillar of the European Union.[138] The laws of this structure have been declared by the European Court of Justice as being

137 Treaty establishing the European Economic Community of 1957 was amended by the Treaty on European Union of 1992 (Maastricht Treaty) and became the Treaty establishing the European Community (EC Treaty). The latter was consolidated by the Treaty of Amsterdam of 1997. The Treaty of Amsterdam changed the numbering of articles of the Treaty establishing the European Community, and the book uses the new numbers. For an elaboration on the history of the European Communities see Craig and de Búrca (1998: 3–48), also the web page of the European Communities: <www.europa.eu.int>.

138 The Treaty of Maastricht established the 'three-pillar' structure for what was henceforth to be called the European Union (Craig and de Burca 1998: 25).

supreme over the laws of the Member States[139] and, under certain circumstances, to have direct effect.[140] The sources of law of the European Community have been divided into two categories: primary sources (the EC Treaty belongs to this category) and secondary sources (by virtue of Article 249 of the EC Treaty these are Regulations, Directives, Decisions, Recommendations and Opinions – where the first three types are legally binding) (Weatherill and Beaumont 1999: 150–53, Craig and de Búrca 1998: 105–10). Consumer law has been introduced into the legal system of the Community primarily by means of Directives. A Directive is "binding, as to the result to be achieved, upon each Member State to which it is addressed, but (leaves) to the national authorities the choice of form and methods" of implementation. (Article 249 EC Treaty).[141] Although Member States have discretion in the choice of "form and methods" of implementing Directives, the obligation to implement them by the set deadline is by no means compromised. It is crucial to note at this point that if a Member State fails to implement the Directive on time or fails to implement it correctly, the principles of direct and indirect effect start operating for the benefit of all those individuals upon whom the Directive conferred rights (Weatherill 2003a: 141–66). Since the judgement in the case of Francovich and Others v Italian State[142] a Member State may also be held financially liable for any losses suffered by an individual which remain in

139 Case 6/64 *Flaminio Costa v ENEL*; confirmed by the ECJ in the case 11/70 *Internationale Handelsgesellscheft GmbH* and the case C-213/89 *R. v Secretary of State for Transport, ex parte Factortame*. For further elaboration on the problems of supremacy see for example: Craig and de Burca (1998: 255–95) and the literature referred to there.

140 Case 26/62 *NV Algemene Transporten Expeditie Onderneming van Gend en Loos v Nederlandse Administratie der Belastingen* – direct effect of Treaty Articles, cases 41/74 *Van Duyn v Home Office*; and 148/78 *Pubblico Ministero v Tullio Ratti* – direct effect of Directives. For a further explanation of the notion of direct effect, its weaknesses with respect to Directives, and the concepts of indirect effect and state liability, see for instance Craig and de Burca (1998: 163–212), Prechal (1995), Pescatore (1983) and the literature referred to there.

141 On the enforceability of the European Community Directives with regard to product liability law see: Kelly and Attree (1997: 30–34).

142 Cases C-6/90 and C-9/90. See Weatherill (2003a: 167–86).

causal link with the state's sufficiently serious failure to implement a Directive or to implement it correctly (state liability).[143]

In spite of this unique legal order established by the European Community,[144] the latter does not possess the traditional attributes of statehood.[145] Although it enjoys wide lawmaking powers, their source must come from the EC Treaty. Article 5(1) of the Treaty stipulates that the Community "shall act within the limits of the powers conferred upon it by this Treaty and of the objectives assigned to it therein". The limited lawmaking power of the Community is referred to as "the principle of attributed competence", and is said to demonstrate the fact that the European Community is not sovereign (Weatherill 2003a: 59). Thus any piece of Community legislation must have a legal basis in the EC Treaty (Article 253) and may be annulled in case of lack of such an adequate legal basis. ECJ judgements in the cases *Germany v European Parliament and Council*,[146] *R v Secretary of State for Health, ex parte British American Tobacco*[147] and, in the context of consumer law, *Germany v European Parliament and Council*[148] elucidate this rule. The Community shares most of its legislative powers with the Member States, and the distribution of powers is subject to the principles of subsidiarity (Article 5.2 of the EC Treaty) and proportionality (Article 5.3). Even in areas which, like

143 The conditions for this liability as used today were established in the joint cases *Brasserrie du Pecheur SA v Germany and R v Secretary of State for Transport, ex parte Factortame and others* (Cases C-46/93 and C-48/93). The crucial condition amounts to an assessment whether the Member State's failure to implement the directive or implement it correctly has been a 'sufficiently serious breach' of EC law. The latter is considered to be a 'manifest and grave disregard' of the Member State's discretion (*Brasserie*).

144 For the latest developments see the Presidency Conclusions of the Brussels European Council (21–2 June 2007), and the Treaty of Lisbon amending the Treaty on European Union and the Treaty establishing the European Community of 13 December 2007. At the time of completing the book the Treaty has not been ratified by all Member States, and thus its provisions are not analysed here. It is, however, unlikely that the new Treaty would have any material impact on the legal effect of the Product Liability Directive.

145 See for instance: Caporaso (1996).

146 Case C-376/98 *Federal Republic of Germany v European Parliament and Council of the European Union* (annulment of the Directive 98/43 EC on the approximation of the laws, regulations and administrative provisions of the Member States relating to the advertising and sponsorship of tobacco products, adopted on the basis of Articles 57(2) of the Treaty (now Article 47(2) EC), 66 of the Treaty (now Article 55 EC) and 100A of the Treaty [now Article 95]).

147 Case C-491/01, *R v Secretary of State for Health, ex parte British American Tobacco (Investments) Ltd and Imperial Tobacco Ltd* (refusal to annul the Directive 2001/37/EC on the approximation of the laws, regulations and administrative provisions of the Member States concerning the manufacture, presentation and sale of tobacco products, adopted on the basis of Article 100A [now 95] of the EC Treaty).

148 Case C-233/94 *Germany v European Parliament and Council of the European Union*.

product liability, have been regulated by a Community directive, a certain level of discretion remains with the national authorities (both within the legislative sphere – the content of the law, and within the judicial sphere – its interpretation and practical application). The precise scope of Member State discretion obviously depends upon the directive in question. The options and omissions (analysed below) of the Product Liability Directive are quite considerable, and thus national law remains applicable in some respects. Further, in the spirit of the principle of procedural autonomy of Member States the Directive does not indicate the mechanisms for its enforcement in practice. The reliance on national courts to apply and interpret European Community law was mentioned above. National courts are a key element of the enforcement mechanism within the European Union – the European Court of Justice stressed their obligation to follow EC law.[149] In *Centrosteel* the Court concluded: "when applying national law, whether adopted before or after the directive, the national court that has to interpret that law must do so, as far as possible, in the light of the wording and the purpose of the directive."[150] The national courts are guided in these efforts by the opportunity to refer preliminary questions to the European Court of Justice (Article 234 of the EC Treaty), and thus the legal system of the European Community operates in the context of dialogue between national courts and the European Court (Komárek 2006). However, this situation has the potential to lead, and indeed leads to the appearance of discrepancies in the application and interpretation of law by national courts, as demonstrated by consumer protection law including product liability law (explored below).

Development of the Community consumer policy

Introduction – the birth of consumer policy

The Treaty of Rome of 1957 did not contain an express provision aimed at protection of the interests of consumers[151] (Weatherill and Beaumont 1999: 1030, Kelly and Attree 1997: 6, Bourgoignie et al. 1987: 96). When the Treaty was being drafted (1956–57) "consumer protection as a matter of government concern was still in its infant stages within the Member States" (Mortelmans and Watson 1996: 38). Instead of opting for a positive legislative intervention for the protection

149 Case C-106/89 *Marleasing SA v La Comercial Internacional de Alimentacion SA* (doctrine of indirect effect), Case 6/64 *Costa v ENEL*, Case 11/70 *Internationale Handelsgesellschaft*, Case C-231/89 *R v Secretary of State for Transport, ex parte Factortame (Factortame II)*; Case C-48/93 *R v Secretary of State for Transport, ex parte Factortame (Factortame III)* (supremacy of EC law). For a further analysis of the issue see for instance: Weatherill (2003a: 159–66), Maher (1994).

150 Case C-456/98 *Centrosteel Srl v Adipol GmbH*, para. 16.

151 There were a number of remarks concerning consumers in other contexts: former Articles 39, 40, 85, 86, 92 EEC Treaty (now 33, 34, 81, 82, 87 EC Treaty).

of consumers, the implicit assumption of the Treaty seemed to be that the well-functioning common market would serve the interests of all the citizens of the European Community (Artis and Nixson 2001, Mortelmans and Watson 1996: 38, Bourgoignie et al. 1987: 98).[152] The 'productivist' stance of the Community entailed the major focus being upon economic integration and hence upon providing optimal conditions for active participants of the common market (Łętowska 1999: 14). The principal aim of the Community was "raising of the standard of living and quality of life" of the European citizens through the establishment of the "common market" (Article 2 of the EC Treaty).[153] At present the aim is to create an "internal market" (Articles 2, 3 and 14 of the EC Treaty) which comprises "an area without internal frontiers".[154] Its four key elements are the freedom of movement of goods, of persons, of services and of capital (Article 14 of the EC Treaty, El-Agraa 2001: 1–2). The Community uses various mechanisms to build the internal market: the key instrument being legal harmonization, or approximation, of laws of the Member States in order to eliminate trade barriers.[155] The process of creating the internal market continued even after the initial deadline of 1992 which was set by the Single European Act 1986 (Weatherill 2003a: 289, Cecchini 1988). While the benefits of the internal market have been widely documented, barriers to its effective functioning still persist.[156] It has been recognized that in order to create an effectively functioning internal market, harmonization of European law (including consumer law) must be revisited.

One could no doubt say that consumer law has seen extraordinary progress within the European Community. Since the 'Paris Summit' in October 1972

152 For an interesting insight into the initial approach of the Community towards consumers see Bourgoignie et al. (1987: 99–102).

153 Article 2 of the EEC Treaty read that the task of the Community was, "by establishing common market and progressively approximating the economic policies of Member States, to promote throughout the Community a harmonious development of economic activities, a continuous and balanced expansion, an increase in stability, an accelerated raising of the standard of living and closer relations between the States belonging to it".

154 See Weatherill (2003a) for an elaboration of the progress in building the internal market, and the distinction between the internal market and the common market (initial aim of the European Economic Community).

155 The book focuses on positive harmonization – introduction of EC legislation bringing closer together the relevant national laws (Weatherill and Beaumont 1999: 150–53, Craig and de Búrca 1998: 105–10). Negative harmonization, consisting in eliminating rules of Member States which disrupt the operation of the internal market (Weatherill 2000: 221–342, 569) is not analysed here. On the assessment of some other mechanisms for creating the internal market (the use of the country of origin principle and the mutual recognition doctrine) see for instance Majone (2005).

156 See Review of the Consumer Acquis, also the Summary – The Impact and Effectiveness of the Single Market (1996), The Macroeconomic Effects of the Single Market Programme after Ten Years (2002), Internal Market Strategy – Priorities 2003–2006.

it was clear that the Community was determined to broaden the scope of its activities to areas not directly involving economic matters, in other words to establish "a community with a human face" (Bourgoignie et al. 1987: 98).[157] As mentioned above, in contrast with the United States, where consumer protection policy has been motivated by the perceived need to combat lack of consumer representation in society (*public interest law* – Łętowska 1999: 9, Friedman 1978: 5), the European Community policy has since its beginnings been understood as involving action, especially legislative action, by central authorities. Consumer protection was developed as a policy through a series of Consumer Action Programmes and Plans.[158] The Council adopted the first Consumer Protection and Information Programme in 1975, subsequently followed by an action plan.[159] The plan distinguished five fundamental consumer rights: to protection of health and safety, to protection of economic interests, to redress, to information and education, and to representation (Kelly and Attree 1997: 10). The statements made in this plan and in the future plans introduced a positive approach to protecting consumers. The "modern economy of consumer protection" was thus initiated on the Community level (Bourgoignie et al. 1987: 97, 98). The plans and programmes which followed the first plan set the main goals to be translated into hard law measures. Bourgoignie pointed out that the plans and action programmes, adopted by a unanimous vote in the Council of Ministers, "grant(ed) the Community institutions full legal authority to initiate consumer measures" (Bourgoignie et al. 1987: 99). According to Kelly and Attree, the first plan "sowed the seeds" of the Product Liability Directive (1997: 10, Łętowska 1999: 75).[160]

Building European consumer law – the need to harmonize and policy caveats

Following the soft law measures, the Community commenced incorporation of consumer protection policy into the EC Treaty. The Single European Act of 1986

157 Bourgoignie referred to calls from "a number of actors on the European scene" for the establishment of an EC consumer policy in the early 1970s, but he also cautioned that the motives for these calls were "varied and to a degree conflicting" (Bourgoignie et al. 1987: 96–7).

158 For a detailed analysis of the beginnings of consumer policy of the European Community see Howells and Weatherill (2005: 120–29) and Kendall (1994).

159 Preliminary Programme of the European Economic Community for a Consumer Protection and Information Policy, 1975.

160 See also the Preamble to the Directive, and the Commission in its three Reports on the Application of the Directive European Commission: *First Report on the Application of Council Directive on the Approximation of Laws, Regulations and Administrative Provisions of the Member States concerning Liability for Defective Products*, the *Report on the Application of Directive 85/374 on Liability for Defective Products* of 2001, and the Third Commission Report of 2006.

introduced Article 100a (now 95),[161] and consumer protection acquired the status of a Community policy owing to the revision of the EC Treaty by the Treaty of Maastricht of 1992 (Article 129a[1] (now 153)[162]).

The similar need for finding the appropriate balance between the interests of industry and the interests of consumers which could be noticed on the national level of the Member States also motivated the European Community actions in the area. However, this search for balance gained an additional, cross-border dimension. The interests of trade and industry in the internal market assume a great need for 'open borders' (Bourgoignie et al. 1987: 2). It is clear that the initial premise of the drafters of the Treaty of Rome was a correct one – open borders do benefit consumers (by increasing competition which triggers lower prices); however, they may also inhibit their position. This occurs because of, in the words of Trubek, "*de iure* and *de facto* regulatory gaps" – where political and other types of pressures impede the passage of consumer protection laws or their enforcement (Bourgoignie et al. 1987: 3). On the other hand, the existence of divergent consumer protection laws on the Member State level can inhibit open borders (Howells and Weatherill 2005: 108–18).[163] Trubek therefore identified two motives for the European-level consumer protection laws: "the need for positive action at the European level where national diversity threatens open borders" and "the need for central European action where the creation of a common market weakens Member States' efforts" to protect consumers (Bourgoignie et al. 1987: 24). These policy arguments have been reflected throughout a considerable number of European consumer protection measures (including the Product Liability Directive) gradually building the 'European consumer law' system, although the balance between business and consumer interests has not always been clearly established. The complexity of these considerations is growing due to changes occurring within the European Community consumer laws and, more generally, market laws. The transformations which we see today reflect an increased emphasis on the redefinition of the business/consumer balance. They also entail a different outlook on the harmonization of product liability law in Europe (Sengayen 2007). European consumer law is being reviewed and reconsidered: entailing the reassessment of its internal structure and balance, its substance, clarity and consistency, as well as its effect and application throughout the European Union.

161 Article 95 gives the Council the power to adopt measures with the aim to establish the internal market.

162 This provision reads: "1. In order to promote the interests of consumers and to ensure a high level of consumer protection, the Community shall contribute to protecting the health, safety, and economic interests of consumers …."

163 On several occasions the European Court of Justice declared a national measure aimed, or deemed to have been aimed, at consumer protection, in breach of Article 28 of the Treaty of Rome. Not a great number of judgements actually endorsed the consumer protection exception to Article 28 established by the case *Rewe-Zentrale AG v Bundesmonopolverwaltung fur Branntwein* (120/78) *(Cassis de Dijon).*

What does it mean to protect European consumers, how should harmonization of European consumer law proceed, and indeed how far should it reach into the national legal systems?[164] Product liability law and the Product Liability Directive are key elements in this comprehensive reassessment.

Changes in the structure and the internal balance of European consumer law

The internal structure and balance of European consumer law are transforming, and the position of product liability laws has been redefined accordingly. In order to understand these transformations it is instructive to adopt the methodology of tracing a typical market activity of a typical consumer (assuming that there is indeed such a phenomenon in a Community of 27 Member States). Morris described three distinct stages in this process of acquiring goods or services: 'shopping', 'buying' and 'consuming' (1980: ix). It seems essential that consumers should be protected during all three stages, but different kinds of protection are required during each one.

Morris suggests that in the 'shopping' stage, when the consumer searches for the right product, it is the adequate information, protection against misleading practices, and safety of goods and services which must be ensured. During the 'buying' stage the transaction is being concluded. The law must safeguard fairness and binding effect of the contracts. By the 'consuming stage' Morris understood "using, eating, displaying, or consuming in other ways" (1980: x). Products and services should not be harmful to consumers or their property and ought to satisfy their needs in accordance with their reasonable expectations. Product liability laws feature rules aimed at protection during the last, 'consuming' stage. Two distinct tendencies can be observed with regard to the structure and balance of consumer laws and policies in the European Union. One trend concerns the developments within substantive consumer law, and the other relates to enforcement and procedural aspects of the existing consumer law.

Let us first of all observe substantive law developments. On the one hand, the focus of consumer protection measures is now very much on the stage of 'shopping'. Laws aimed at providing consumers with adequate information on products and services are being gradually introduced in Europe: the Timeshare Directive,[165] the Package Travel Directive,[166] the Doorstep Selling Directive,[167]

164 The links of consumer law with the 'laws of obligations' analysed in the previous chapter are clear. Thus, one ought to see this process together with the above-mentioned attempts to harmonize and/or codify European contract and tort laws (some coordinated by the European Union and others, independent academic endeavours).

165 Directive 94/47/EC.

166 Directive 90/314/EEC.

167 Directive 85/577/EEC.

the Distance Selling Directive[168] and the Price Indication Directive[169] introduce information requirements for commercial parties in consumer contracts. The new Directive on Unfair Commercial Practices[170] prohibits aggressive or misleading commercial practices.[171] Further, extensive legislative effort can be noticed in the 'buying' stage, particularly with laws safeguarding fairness of consumer contracts and their terms. The law shifted from merely ensuring enforcement of contracts to granting the consumer the time to think, change his mind (Doorstep Selling Directive and Distance Selling Directive), as well as making the binding effect dependent on the fairness of the contract (the Unfair Contract Terms Directive 1993).[172] Within the 'consuming', post-marketing stage, which is traditionally the domain of product liability laws, product safety became a flagship issue (Hodges 2006). Geddes wrote that the Product Liability Directive was a part of a "comprehensive code governing the obligations of producers and suppliers in respect of the safety of the goods … which they sell, and their liability in the event of those goods … causing death or injury, or damage to private property" (1992: 1).[173] Another crucial element of this code has been the General Product Safety Directive.[174] Adopted on the basis of Article 95 of the EC Treaty, the Directive represented the so-called 'New Approach' to harmonization of safety standards by the European Community – horizontal harmonization. It was to add to the already existing safety measures of the European Community, so far consisting of vertical instruments (Hodges 2006, Micklitz 1997: 50).[175] It introduced the 'General Safety Requirement' and dealt with the post-marketing control of products through various institutions (on the national and Community level) and emergency actions including recalls. The Directive has now been replaced by the General Product Safety Directive of 2001 which improves the effectiveness of post-marketing control measures.

In the light of these legislative developments, the role of product liability law appears to be more than ever one of a 'last resort' measure. On the other hand,

168 Directive 97/7/EC.

169 Directive 98/6/EC.

170 Directive 2005/29/EC.

171 Note that the scope of the Directive is very wide, and it applies to all three stages mentioned above.

172 Directive 93/13/EEC.

173 Geddes also mentions safety of services and liability for services – this in the light of the existence, at the time of writing his monograph, of the proposed Directive on the Liability of Suppliers of Services (OJ 1991 C12/8), which has since been abandoned. See, however, the Report from the Commission on the safety of services for consumers COM (2003) 313 final.

174 Directive 92/59/EEC has now been replaced by Directive 2001/95/EC.

175 The 'Pink Book' of those (updated annually) has been drafted by the European Commission Directorate General on Enterprise and Industry – accessible from <http://ec.europa.eu/consumers/cons_safe/prod_safe/other_EU/cons_prod_en.htm>.

the European Commission continues to stress its importance.[176] The relatively recent examples of food crises – those involving "mad cow disease" or dioxins – illustrate the undeniable fact that, as the Commission put it, "there is no such thing as zero risk".[177] The Commission convincingly argued that society must "adopt a system which is best suited to developments with a view to ensuring the best possible compensation of victims suffering damage from products".[178] However, product liability law, based on the traditional concepts of obtaining justice through private or sometimes collective litigation is often unlikely to provide such 'best possible compensation'. There are a number of reasons, some mentioned in the course of further analysis below, for this peculiar incapacity of product liability. They are related to the nature of product liability law, its links with markets, and its coexistence with other compensation mechanisms (not examined in the book), as well as to the nature of the Product Liability Directive and its impact across Europe, and to procedural aspects of the law (again, the latter are not examined here). The nature and effect of the Directive are explored in a further part of this chapter, and the initiatives within the area of civil procedures and access to justice appearing within the European Community policies and laws are considered directly below.

The effective enforcement of law by consumers has received growing attention on the European Community level.[179] Access to justice is a notion which plays an increasingly important role in European policies and laws[180] – with the work of the Directorate General for Justice, Freedom and Security, the establishment of 'EJ-Net' which hosts comprehensive information about the judicial systems of the Member States,[181] the Community framework of activities to facilitate the implementation of judicial cooperation in civil matters,[182] and several pieces of

---

176 Green Paper on liability for defective products of 1999. See also Second Commission Report on Product Liability Directive of 2001.

177 European Commission, The Commission Adopts a Green Paper on Producer Liability (1999) at p. 2.

178 Commission Adopts a Green Paper on Producer Liability, at p. 2.

179 See Commission of the European Communities Consumer Redress 1984; Supplementary Communication from the Commission on Consumer Redress 1987; Council Resolution on consumer redress 1987; Green Paper: Access of consumers to Justice and the settlement of consumer disputes in the single market 1993; Commission Communication Action plan on consumer access to justice and the settlement of consumer disputes in the internal market 1996; and recently the Consumer Policy Strategy and Consumer Action Programme for 2007–13.

180 See Action Plan of the Council and the Commission *on how best to implement the provisions of the Treaty of Amsterdam on an area of freedom, security and justice* 1998; and Tampere European Council 1999 – Presidency Conclusions.

181 See the Council Decision 2001/470/EC of 28 May 2001 establishing a European Judicial Network in civil and commercial matters.

182 Council Regulation 743/2002 of 25 April 2002 establishing a Community framework of activities to facilitate the implementation of judicial cooperation in civil

hard law which have so far been enacted.[183] Various consumer protection Directives suggest enforcement mechanisms involving actions by consumer organizations as representatives of the collective or individual interests of consumers.[184] The Community involvement in regulation of civil procedure extends also to funding of litigation, with the Legal Aid Directive harmonizing legal aid in cross-border disputes.[185] Access to justice for consumers, considered essential for proper functioning of the internal market (Hodges 2007a: 97), was set up as a policy and legislative priority according to four factors: simplification of rules, out-of-court solutions, protection of collective interests, and enhancement of legal aid (Hodges 2007a: 97).[186] Access to justice is therefore seen as a mixture of in-court and out-of-court measures. While efforts to simplify and make cheaper civil litigation in consumer disputes are clear, there is no doubt that pre-litigation advice and information, and alternative dispute resolution (Zemans and Thomas 1999: 65–88, Smith 1997: 5, Cappelletti and Garth 1978) are growing in importance. On the one hand, an approach which focuses on individual or group/representative action in obtaining redress can be noted as increasingly potent on the Community agenda (Hodges 2007a). Already detected by some academics, the climate in Europe is changing towards greater emphasis on private and collective litigation (Kelemen and Sibbitt 2004, Hodges 2007a). As indicated in the Lovells Report, procedural matters, access to justice and 'litigation culture' may well constitute a barrier to trade of a much greater strength than any differences in substantial laws of liability. The Community may well be prompted to extend its activities in the area of civil procedure and access to justice by the prominence these issues receive on the national level. Member States recognize the importance of enforcement of law, civil procedure and access to justice and they are reforming their civil procedure rules, enacting class actions or other types of group or representative proceedings (Hodges 2007a). On the other hand, in recognition of the limited role of litigation in providing effective redress, the European Community has been developing other ways of satisfying consumer claims, without the use of litigation. Both the Member States and the European Commission recognized the specificity of a consumer dispute, mostly relating to disparities between "the economic value at

matters.

183 See for instance: European Parliament and Council Regulation 805/2004 *creating a European Enforcement Order for uncontested claims*, Regulation 861/2007 establishing a European Small Claims Procedure. See also: Amended Proposal for a Regulation of the European Parliament and the Council creating a European order for payment procedure COM (2006) 57 final.

184 See in particular Directive 98/27/EC on injunctions for the protection of consumers' interests.

185 Directive 2002/8/EC to improve access to justice in cross-border disputes by establishing minimum common rules relating to legal aid for such disputes.

186 See also: Green Paper: Access to justice and the settlement of consumer disputes in the Single Market (COM(93) 576).

stake and the cost and duration of its judicial settlement".[187] A number of Member States adopted out-of-court dispute settlement mechanisms, and the European Community followed this tendency – initially by means of Communications and subsequently by establishing a network of bodies responsible for settlement of consumer disputes.[188] Alongside the alternatives to litigation, other avenues of compensating victims of defective products are being considered, for instance along the lines of the Nordic no-fault compensation schemes.[189] These initiatives accompany introduction of such compensation schemes in other Member States of the European Union (France and the United Kingdom), aside from the Nordic countries. While harmonization of civil procedures across the European Union has no doubt commenced,[190] it will certainly involve comprehensive reviews of national procedural laws and legal cultures. It is bound to be cumbersome, and its future is uncertain. At present the Community powers to legislate in this area are very limited. These issues have paramount importance for such 'litigation heavy'[191] areas of law as product liability.

---

187 "Most consumer disputes are characterised by the disparity between the economic value at stake and the cost and duration of its judicial settlement. To remedy the specific problems of consumer disputes, several Member States have opted for out-of-court mechanisms whose flexibility may be more attuned to the needs of both consumers and professionals: the low cost, rapidity and informal nature of these procedures are their main attraction", European Commission DG Health and Consumer Protection <www.europa.eu.int/comm/dg24/policy/developments/acce_just/acce_just04_en.html>.

188 See: Communication from the Commission *on the out-of-court settlement of consumer disputes* COM(1998) 198 final; Commission Recommendation *on the principles applicable to the bodies responsible for out-of-court settlement of consumer disputes* COM(1998) 198 final; Communication from the Commission of 4 April 2001 *on widening consumer access to alternative dispute resolution* COM(2001) 161; Commission Recommendation *on the principles for out-of-court bodies involved in the consensual resolution of consumer disputes not covered by Recommendation* 98/257/EC (COM(2001) 1016). A network of out-of-court bodies – European Extra-Judicial Network (EEJ-Net) – was established as a pilot project. For a list of EEJ-Net clearing houses by country see: <http://ec.europa.eu/consumers/redress/out_of_court/eej_net/acce_just14_en.htm>.

189 The Report of the Rosselli Foundation on the Development Risk Defence of 2004 recommended an introduction of a no-fault compensation scheme.

190 For academic reviews of the process of harmonization of European civil procedures see: van Rhee (2000), Kerameus (1995).

191 As mentioned above, this notion is used here to distinguish product liability (the heart of which is civil litigation) from other areas of consumer law – those focused largely on public regulation and enforcement – such as product safety or unfair commercial practices.

Changes in the role of consumer law – European consumer law as market law – the growing convergence of market laws and policies

Both on the political and academic arena, European Community consumer law is progressively being much more closely coordinated with other 'market laws'. First of all, Article 153(2) of the EC Treaty stipulates that "(c)onsumer protection requirements shall be taken into account in defining and implementing other Community policies and activities". Consumer policy is at present considered "the essential corollary of the progressive establishment of the internal market"[192] (Hodges 2006, 2007a, Howells and Weatherill 2005). This approach is visible in the proposed Community action programme for 2007–2013, which combines health and consumer protection,[193] and in the EU Consumer Policy Strategy 2007–2013, which develops the action programme.[194] While the aims outlined in the previous programmes – a common high level of consumer protection, proper enforcement of consumer protection legislation and a stronger voice for consumers (Consumer Policy Strategy 2002–2006) – remain relevant, the programme stresses that modern consumer protection policy and law must meet the challenges of complex, sophisticated markets, increasingly involving cross-border transactions (as confirmed in the recent Eurobarometer study of September 2006).[195] Thus, in order to satisfy the two key objectives: ensuring a common high level of protection of consumer health and safety and of protection of economic interests, the Commission proposed four main streams of action: better understanding of consumers and markets (through research), better consumer protection regulation (by identifying priorities, involving consumers in regulation making, developing the Review of the Consumer *Acquis*), better enforcement, monitoring and redress, and improvement in information and education of consumers. While the interaction between businesses and consumers has always been at the forefront of the European Community activities in the sphere of consumer protection, the emphasis on greater integration and coordination between the interests of these two key participants of the internal market has never been greater.

---

192 Consumer Policy Strategy 2002–2006 COM(2002) 208 final, p. 1.

193 Communication from the Commission *Healthier, safer, more confident citizens: a Health and Consumer Protection Strategy* Proposal for a Decision of the European Parliament and of the Council establishing a Programme of Community Action in the field of Health and Consumer Protection 2007–13. The programme recognizes similar objectives of health and consumer protection policies (protection of health and safety, information and education of consumers) and types of action required to achieve them (information, consultations). On the other hand, specificities of these two areas are stressed, and particular objectives of consumer protection policy are set out separately.

194 Communication from the Commission EU Consumer Policy Strategy 2007–13. *Empowering consumers, enhancing their welfare, effectively protecting them*, COM(2007) 99 final.

195 DG Sanco, Eurobarometer 252 *Consumer Protection in the Internal Market* of September 2006.

EC consumer law continues to be aimed at redressing the balance between consumers and businesses. In view of the contemporary approach to market integration demonstrated by the Lisbon Agenda[196] and in particular the Better Regulation goal of the European Union,[197] it appears that this course of action may no longer be a blunt expression of preference of one set of interests over another (Sengayen 2007). The approach to market regulation has shifted towards a more inclusive view of interactions between consumers and businesses. It is increasingly emphasized that laws aiming to protect consumers fundamentally concern business practices. By establishing consumer rights, they introduce obligations for businesses. The goals of enabling businesses to "get on with their business" and making sure consumers "get the full benefit of the internal market" are placed side by side in strategic documents of the European Community.[198] Consumer protection policy is seen as an integral part of market integration policy, and the existing European consumer protection law is being reviewed for its impact on the internal market.[199] Academic writers also increasingly present this somewhat more 'holistic' approach to product liability law and consumer law more generally – starting with the seminal work of Jane Stapleton (1994a), and including Kelly and Attree (1997), and Weatherill and Howells (2005).

---

196 Ten-year strategy adopted by the Lisbon European Council, the aim of which was initially to "make the European Union the most competitive and dynamic economy in the World" (Lisbon European Council Presidency Conclusions). See also: <http://www.ec.europa.eu/public_opinion/archives/ebs/ebs_215_en.pdf>, and *Extracts from Presidency Conclusions on The Lisbon Strategy by Theme. European Councils: Lisbon (March 2000) to Brussels (June 2004)*. On the revised strategy see Communication from the Commission to the Council and the European Parliament *Common Actions for Growth and Employment: the Community Lisbon Programme* SEC[2005] 981.

197 Communication from the Commission to the Council and the European Parliament, *Common Actions for Growth and Employment: the Community Lisbon Programme* SEC[2005] 981.

198 See the explanation of the main thrust of the 'Better Regulation' strategy: <http://ec.europa.eu/growthandjobs/areas/fiche03_en.htm>, and Howells and Weatherill (2005) for an academic view of consumer law as part of the law of the market.

199 The idea of the review of Consumer *Acquis* (reviewing the implementation of the eight key consumer directives, not including Product Liability Directive) was introduced in the Consumer Policy Strategy for 2002–2006. See the outline of the Review in Commission Communication on European Contract Law and the revision of the *acquis*: the way forward COM(2004); see also the conclusion of the first, diagnostic phase of the Review – Green Paper *on the Review of the Consumer Acquis* COM(2006) 744 final.

Changes in the effect of European consumer law – greater, closer, 'maximum harmonization'?[200]

In the spirit of the new approach to consumer law and market law, the Community embarked on the review of the existing laws governing markets, including the Review of the Consumer Acquis.[201] The main aim of the Review of the Consumer Acquis has been to assess the substance and impact of the key consumer law directives.[202] The inquiry into the substance of the Directives seeks ways in which their provisions can on the one hand be updated to reflect the challenges of the modern markets and on the other hand be better synchronized – heading towards a more horizontal and less sectoral regulation of consumer affairs. As far as the practical application of the directives is concerned, the focus is on tackling differences which were observed among various Member States.[203] The reviewed directives are 'minimum harmonization' measures – thus Member States may choose to detract from them and introduce more stringent obligations for businesses and more extensive rights for consumers. In such a 'minimum harmonization' system, a "'pure' model of an integrated market is sacrificed to the possibility of local preference", subject to observance of free movement of goods principles (especially Article 28 of the EC Treaty) (Howells and Weatherill 2005: 135). It was indicated that this approach may result in barriers to trade and thus, apart from proposals for an introduction of a 'horizontal instrument', suggestions of possible 'maximum harmonization' appeared in the Green Paper on the Review of the Consumer Acquis.[204] Thus, not even concerns over the need to protect consumers to the greatest possible level would be able to justify introduction or preservation of rules which depart from the provisions of the Directives.

The 'maximum harmonization' model has been the subject of criticism by academics who postulate the risk of depressing of standards of consumer

---

200 Following the approach taken when referring to various types of 'liability standard' (above) – using a single quotation mark to emphasize the distinctive meanings given to notions of 'fault' or 'strict liability' – 'maximum harmonization' is always mentioned here with the use of a single quotation mark. The manner in which this notion is understood by the European Community authorities – the European Commission and the European Court of Justice – is quite specifically tailored to the reality of European Community law.

201 Part of a wider exercise of the Review of the Single Market (see Consumer Markets Scoreboard: Communication from the Commission of 29 January 2008).

202 There are eight Directives being reviewed: 99/44 EC on Sale of Consumer Goods and Guarantees, 98/6 EC on Price Indication, 98/27 on Injunctions, 97/7 on Distance Selling, 94/47 on Timeshare, 93/13 on Unfair Contract Terms, 90/314 on Package Travel and 85/577 on Doorstep Selling.

203 See the EU Consumer Law Acquis Database <http://www.eu-consumer-law.org/index.html>.

204 The suggestion is to revise the legislation, "based on full harmonization complemented on issues not fully harmonised with a mutual recognition clause" – Green Paper on the Review of the Consumer *Acquis*, at page 15.

protection existing at the national level (Howells and Weatherill 2005: 110, 133–7, Weatherill 2002). Does the model indeed entail the inevitability of such a result? The Green Paper on the Review of the Consumer *Acquis* clearly expresses the determination to make the internal market work for all its participants. Although the introduction of 'maximum harmonization' Directives may well lead to lowering certain standards of protection in some Member States, one ought to see this potential legislative development in the context in which it occurs. The emphasis on greater coordination and synchronization of the existing consumer law, coupled with attempts to improve access of consumers to justice which can be observed at present (introduced above) offer a perhaps less ominous vision of the future of consumer law than those academic writings would indicate. It is of course beyond the scope of this book to assess the impact of the planned reforms. It is unclear whether the Commission's suggestions will lead to concrete legislative output heading in the direction of 'maximum harmonization', especially in the light of the aforementioned principle of 'attributed competence'. So far, among the main sources of EC consumer law it is only the Product Liability Directive which constitutes a true 'maximum harmonization measure'.[205] The example of the Directive indicates that national laws, procedures and legal cultures still impact the practical application of a legal instrument which the European Court of Justice refers to as a 'complete harmonization' mechanism.

Product Liability Directive as a case study in 'maximum harmonization'

While at first the position of the Product Liability Directive was not entirely clear (Stapleton 1994a), the European Court of Justice now very strongly emphasizes the 'maximum harmonization' point.[206] The main argument for advancing this approach is ensuring that the producers–insurers–consumers balance is preserved.[207] The Product Liability Directive is therefore a case study of how 'maximum harmonization' operates in practice.

In fact, a number of questions appear when one considers the aims and the results of 'maximum harmonization': is such an exercise necessary, how to

205 The Unfair Commercial Practices Directive, while heralding maximum harmonization, allows temporary detractions from it.

206 See the following ECJ judgements: Case C–52/00 *Commission of the European Communities v. French Republic*; Case 177/04 *Commission of the European Communities v. French Republic*, 14 March 2006; Case C–154/00 *Commission of the European Communities v. Hellenic Republic*; Case C–183/00 *Gonzalez Sanchez v. Medicina Asturiana*; Case C–203/99 *Veedfald*; Case C–402/03 *Skov AEg v. Bilka LavprisvarehuscA/S and Bilka Lavprisvarehus A/S v. Jette Mikkelsen, Michael Due Nielsen*; Case C–127/04 *Declan O'Byrne v. Sanofi Pasteur MSD Ltd, Sanofi Pasteur SA*.

207 The Preamble talks about a "fair apportionment of risk between the injured person and the producer" (Recitals 2 and 7). The Third Commission Report on Product Liability Directive refers more precisely to the balance between claimants, manufacturers and their insurers (at page 8).

strike a balance between the interests involved in the substance of the law, can 'maximum harmonization' achieve this balance, and can it achieve any other aims it is supposed to achieve? The analysis of the Directive conducted below follows these questions. According to the recent activities focused on the Directive – the Third Commission Report, the Lovells and Rosselli Reports,[208] meetings of expert groups, and the jurisprudence of national courts[209] – the prevailing view is that the desired producers–insurers–consumers balance has been satisfactorily achieved. On the other hand, opinions that the Directive is unable to accomplish the aims it has set out to realize can increasingly be heard (Fairgrieve and Howells 2007, Sengayen 2007). Remarkable differences can be observed in the implementation, application and interpretation of the provisions of the Directive by national legislative authorities and national courts. The legal basis and the very need for an EU-level regulation of product liability have always been questioned, and these controversies are now resurfacing in academic writings.[210] As the harmonization of European law becomes a much more multi-level, multi-discipline, coordinated enterprise, it is becoming clear that the notion of 'maximum harmonization' needs to be revisited. The approach of the European Court of Justice, which often uses the notions 'complete', 'full' and 'maximum' interchangeably when referring to harmonization, is misleading. The Product Liability Directive has not achieved 'complete harmonization' of product liability laws in the European Union; it is unlikely to achieve such harmonization in the near future, and it is uncertain whether achieving it would in fact be beneficial. The European Commission advocates the need for 'maximum harmonization', but it exhibits a much more realistic approach to it. In its Reviews of the application of the Directive it emphasizes the differences in application among the Member States, but surprisingly they are not perceived to have an appreciable effect on the market (Fairgrieve and Howells 2007: 966). The Commission concludes that "total harmonization in the broadest sense is not only unrealistic, but also not necessary in view of the limited impact (if any) that its absence would have on the Internal Market."[211]

208 Lovells Product Liability in the European Union, A Report for the European Commission 2003; Fondazione Rosselli Analysis of the Economic Impact of the Development Risk Clause as provided by Directive 85/374/EEC on Liability for Defective Products Study for the European Commission of 2004.

209 The jurisprudence in the area of product liability on the national level is assessed by a number of professional and academic research journals and projects: the European Product Liability Review (Lovells), the Product Liability Database (British Institute for International and Comparative Law), and the European Tort Law Series (here the focus is on tort law in general) – *Tort and Insurance Law Yearbook* (edited by the European Centre of Tort and Insurance Law – Koziol/Steininger [eds]).

210 Atiyah argued that there was no single system of product liability in the United States; therefore it seemed to him that the European Community did not need to unify its Member States' rules concerning this issue (1995: 232). For renewed concerns see Fairgrieve and Howells (2007).

211 Third Report on Product Liability Directive, p. 8.

The Product Liability Directive has been subjected to a very comprehensive doctrinal exegesis[212] and providing one more study, apart from being a somewhat futile exercise in the light of lack of changes in its substantive provisions, is by no means the purpose of this book. The analysis below imposes its own focus on the issues. The key question is the legal effect of the Directive, its impact and enforcement. A more detailed analysis of the provisions of the Directive is also provided in Chapter 6 of Part II of the book, where their implementation by the Czech Republic, Hungary and Poland is portrayed.

Back to the roots – the rationale and the legal basis of the Directive

Obviously, the roots of the Directive are in the European consumer protection policies analysed above. However, it is useful to reinstate them here because they throw some light on the aims of this legal instrument.

The legal basis for the adoption of the Product Liability Directive has been comprehensively examined by many writers on the topic (Howells 2005b, Whittaker 2005, Weatherill 2003a, Faure 2000a, Stapleton 1994a, Howells 1993).[213] The "engine" of the reform envisaged by the Directive was "social and political" (Stapleton 2002: 1230). Although the social pressures triggered by the Thalidomide tragedy were mounting, accompanied by the consumer-friendly attitude of the European Commission and the Member States, concerns against a very strict liability burden imposed on the industry were also voiced (Stapleton 2002: 1231).[214]

The need for regulation of product liability issues at the European Community level was set out in the Explanatory Memorandum to the Product Liability Directive of September 1976.[215] The Memorandum accompanied the draft Directive at the time it was first published.[216] It was noted that the remedies provided to consumers who suffered damages caused by defective products differed among the Member States, and that these divergences distorted free movement of goods and fair competition within the common market. According to the Memorandum, in strict

212 See for instance: Whittaker (2005), Gnela (2000), Jagielska (1999), Kelly and Attree (1997), Stapleton (1994a), and further literature referred to in the bibliography.

213 Whittaker (2005: 439) continued Stapleton's discourse on the weak legal and theoretical basis of the Directive (1994a).

214 See for instance the Economic and Social Committee Report on Proposal for a Council Directive on Liability for Defective Products, COM(76)372 final at 41–5; also the report of the Legal Affairs Committee of the European Parliament EUR. PARL.DOC. (COM 246)26 – (1978).

215 EEC Directive on Liability for Defective Products, Explanatory Memorandum of September 1976.

216 Commission Proposal for a Council Directive Relating to the Approximation of the Laws, Regulations, and Administrative Provisions of the Member States Concerning Liability for Defective Products, 1976.

liability regimes (France, Luxembourg or Belgium)[217] the risk was passed on to the producer at the same time affecting the prices of goods and insurance, while in the systems with the requirement of proof of negligence (United Kingdom or Germany) the producer could often escape liability. The producers may have been discouraged from selling their products in the Member States with more stringent liability rules.[218] These developments did not, in turn, have a beneficial effect for consumers (Geddes 1992: 1); and the consumer protection ideas, even though not explicitly mentioned in the EC Treaty, were gaining recognition among the Community decision-makers. Systems of liability for defective products based on the requirement of fault were criticized in the Memorandum as often leaving the victim without protection. A strict liability regime was considered capable of putting the victim in a better position to recover compensation. Such a strict liability regime should, it was believed, be introduced throughout the European Community. For the reasons given above the harmonization of the Member States' laws concerning product liability was considered essential.

Article 100 (now 94) of the Treaty of Rome, which was used as a legal basis for the Directive, concerns harmonization of laws which directly affect the establishment of the common market. Here is where the controversy lies – it appears to some that the differences in national product liability laws may not have been significant enough to actually have an appreciable effect on the common market. Stapleton challenged the argument that differences in costs caused by discrepancies in product liability regimes would be more significant than, for instance, differences in fuel or insurance costs (1994a: 55–8).[219] She argued that the Directive could not and would not be capable of achieving the purpose it was established to aim towards (1994a: 53–60), and hence suggested that no legal basis existed within the European Community law for its adoption (1994a: 56). She claimed that, far from introducing harmonization, the Directive was likely to lead to further divergences between the product liability regimes of the Member States – divergences of implementation and translation, or divergences by omission in areas left for the national regulation (1994a: 54, 55). While the idea of 'maximum

217 These were the states which ratified the Council of Europe Convention on Products Liability of 27 January 1977 – the international law instrument which predated the Product Liability Directive and in some respects introduced a stricter product liability than the Directive. It was ratified by only four states (Whittaker 2005: 433) and never exerted any significant impact on European product liability law.

218 Explanatory Memorandum 1976.

219 Stapleton uses the judgement of the European Court of Justice in the case *Alsthom Atlantique v Sulzer* (Case C-339/89) to show that the European Community approach to the issue of different liability regimes as affecting the operation of the common market is not entirely unequivocal. In the judgement the ECJ held that the method of interpreting Article 1643 of the *Code Civil* by the Cour de Cassation – establishing a presumption that a professional supplier of goods was aware of any defects in the goods – did not constitute impediment to trade between Member States as long as the rule applied without distinction to foreign and domestic trade and did not favour domestic trade.

harmonization' may help vindicate the existence of the Directive, it is clear that Stapleton's vision was correct. Declaring 'maximum harmonization' is incapable of providing the uniformity of product liability laws in Europe. Furthermore, it appears that such uniformity is not required, as according to the Commission the existing differences do not significantly disrupt the internal market.

Scope of the Directive – inducing harmonization or diversity?

The Directive introduced liability which the Commission and many commentators, also Central European scholars, refer to as 'strict', 'objective' or 'liability without fault' (Whittaker 2005: 481–2, Howells and Weatherill 2005: 222–4, and in Central Europe: Łętowska 2001, or Maczonkai 1996). For some Member States this was not a new approach to product liability cases. They applied strict liability standards before the adoption of the Directive: either a general product liability system established by courts (France, Luxembourg and Hungary) or a system established by the legislator for specific products (the German pharmaceutical liability scheme). Does this mean that the Directive achieved the levelling-up of liability standards among the Member States? The 'producers'[220] and in some cases also the suppliers of a defective product are rendered liable for death, personal injury and some types of property damage[221] caused by the product which they introduced into the market. The liability is, at least in principle, independent of the level of care exercised by them. Article 1 stipulates that the "producer shall be liable for damage caused by a defect in his product". All the injured person is required to prove is "the damage, the defect and the causal relationship between the defect and damage".[222] The multitude of defences available to producers, however, shifted the standard of liability away from strict liability and, according to some commentators, towards 'super negligence' (Stapleton 1994a: 228). In this respect one may be justified in concluding that the Directive led to relaxing the liability standards, at least in some Member States. This position finds its roots in the widely proclaimed need for providing balance between the interests of businesses and of consumers. The need for legal certainty, consistency and predictability of outcomes – true legal harmonization – lies at the basis of this balance. Is this the outcome which the Directive achieves?

220 Article 3.

221 Article 9.

222 Article 4. Professor Taschner – the 'father' of the Directive, in his speech *Basic Problems of Product Liability Law from a Comparative Perspective* at the British Institute of International and Comparative Law in London on 22 October 2003 stressed that the Directive was "defect limited, not fault limited". Only the defect and the damage are regulated in the Directive. As mentioned above, the notion of causal link, although an important requisite of liability, was left to national law.

On the one hand, the net of liability was set quite widely – to include producers, importers, own-branders and suppliers.[223] On the other hand, the Directive left crucial elements of the 'liability jigsaw' – deciding whether contributory actions by victims ought to impact producers' liability, rules on suspension or interruption of the three-year' limitation period,[224] the rights of recourse of producers against persons responsible for the damage,[225] deciding whether the regime of the Directive would cover non-pecuniary damage,[226] and all procedural aspects of product liability cases – to the discretion of national authorities (Fairgrieve and Vaqué 2005: 3, Whittaker 2005: 436–7). Some other concepts, although stipulated by the Directive, did not receive any further explanation: for instance the causal link between defect and damage,[227] the assessment of damages, or the required burden and standard of proof.[228] The divergences in Member State-level implementation are deepened by the options and "add-ons" established by it – the development risk defence[229] and the ceiling for personal injury damages[230] (Fairgrieve and Vaqué 2005: 3). Other concepts used by the Directive have been defined in very general terms and may lead to discrepancies in application. Indeed, some fundamental notions which the Directive introduced — 'defect' is the best example — leave large scope for varying interpretations by national courts in specific cases before them. The jurisprudence of national courts of various Member States offers varying explanations of the meaning of 'defect' (Fairgrieve and Howells 2007: 967–70).[231] Some further elaboration of the implications of these elements of the Directive for Central Europe can be found in Chapter 6 of Part II.

While it is certainly true that the main aim of the Product Liability Directive is to render the producers of defective products liable for death, personal injury or damage to personal property caused to consumers (Kelly and Attree 1997: 11), it must be stressed that the Directive is "the product of a painstaking

223 Article 3 of the Directive.

224 The limitation period is regulated in Article 10.2.

225 Articles 5 and 8.1.

226 Article 9.

227 Specified in very general terms in Article 4.

228 Burden of proof is mentioned in general terms in Articles 4 and 7 of the Directive.

229 Articles 7(e) and 15.1(b).

230 Article 16.1.

231 See for instance: the English judgment in *Foster v Biosil* (2000) (breast implant not defective although it ruptured in the claimant's breast – indication that the claimant ought to have shown the 'source' of the defect), and the Austrian judgement OGH-Urteil: 406 94/04h – bystander injured by a premature explosion of fireworks, Supreme Court held that in the regime established by the Directive it was unnecessary to point out a particular product flaw, and thus the fireworks were defective because a premature explosion was not something a person is "entitled to expect". See also Whittaker (2005: 481–94) for an explanation of systemic, substantive and procedural reasons for differences in the understanding and practical application of 'defect' in England and in France.

compromise reached over many years between the interests of producers and those of consumers" (Geddes 1992: 9). Stapleton argued that as a result of this compromise the Directive was "one of the high water marks of Euro-fudge and textual vagueness" (2002: 1231). The Directive was adopted during the time when the approach of the Community to consumer issues was still largely 'productivist' – harmonization of consumer protection laws was to serve the interests of the market. Thus, while the intention of the Commission might have been the increase in the level of protection for European consumers, the Directive in fact establishes a liability standard which is less stringent than in some Member States' national laws, including Hungary. An American commentator of the Product Liability Directive contended that by favouring strict liability the Act favoured litigation as a means of settling disputes, and it appeared to aim at redistributing the wealth away from corporations (Bernstein 1992: 210). Other commentators confirmed this role of the Directive as a gesture for consumers (Whitehead 1989: 63). It is still, however, difficult to establish this role of the Directive because of its compromise nature. Indeed, the Directive presents a confusing picture of a liability system with a great many theoretical and substantive gaps and inconsistencies.

The essence of 'maximum harmonization' under the Directive and the remaining unanswered questions

The idea of 'maximum harmonization' entails the existence of uniform, unyielding rules across the European Union. It is the foundation of legal certainty for businesses and consumers. It is the response to the remaining differences in Member States' laws governing business activity and the resulting obstacles to intra-Community trade.

How does the 'maximum harmonization' work in the context of the Directive? The jurisprudence of the European Court of Justice explored this question in some detail.[232] The key point remains the interpretation of Article 13 which stipulates that the Directive "shall not affect any rights which an injured person may have according to the rules of the law of contractual or non-contractual liability or a special liability system existing at the moment when this Directive is notified".[233] A number of crucial questions arise here: is it indeed possible for Member States to retain their existing contractual and non-contractual liability regimes

232 Case C–52/00 *Commission of the European Communities v. French Republic*; Case 177/04 *Commission of the European Communities v. French Republic*; Case C–154/00 *Commission of the European Communities v. Hellenic Republic*; Case C–183/00 *Gonzalez Sanchez v. Medicina Asturiana*; Case C–402/03 *Skov AEg v. Bilka LavprisvarehuscA/S and Bilka Lavprisvarehus A/S v. Jette Mikkelsen, Michael Due Nielsen*; Case C–127/04 *Declan O'Byrne v. Sanofi Pasteur MSD Ltd, Sanofi Pasteur SA*. For the analysis of the status of the European Court of Justice see Poiares Maduro (1998).

233 The Preamble refers directly to a special liability system in the pharmaceutical products' sector – Recital 13.

which provided a higher level of protection for consumers; can they implement the Directive in a way as to provide such a higher level of protection; or could the implementation of the Directive mean an effective reduction in the level of consumer protection in the existing national laws?[234] The approach to these issues is relevant also in the assessment of the Central European product liability regimes, as both their legislation implementing the Directive and the pre-existing regimes have at times been more advantageous for consumers.

The jurisprudence of the European Court of Justice is clear: the Directive introduced a "complete harmonization" of the product liability laws of the Member States. It was a result of "a complex balancing of different interests" including "guaranteeing that competition will not be distorted, facilitating trade within the common market, consumer protection and ensuring the sound administration of justice".[235] In the Spanish *González Sánchez*[236] case the Court indicated that implementation of the Directive may mean that the level of protection of victims of defective products effectively becomes lower than it was under national law.[237]

The Court held that it was not within the Member States' discretion to establish provisions more advantageous for consumers in the laws implementing the Directive, and thus to disturb the set balance between the interests of businesses and consumers.[238] This concerned, for instance, the 500 Euros threshold which was not introduced by France[239] and by Greece.[240] Both these countries were in breach of the Directive. However, while maintaining such a strict stance on the introduction of the threshold in the first place, neither the Court nor the Commission appear troubled by the fact that most Member States actually see this threshold as a deductible (Fairgrieve and Howells 2007: 974). This is but one of the examples of inconsistent implementation of this legal instrument on the national level.

Another controversial issue considered by the European Court of Justice in a number of judgements was supplier liability, which under the Directive is merely subsidiary.[241] The questions concerned provisions implementing the Directive as well as the pre-existing liability regimes. The Court extended the effects of 'maximum harmonization' upon both. France and Denmark have had significant problems with regulation of supplier liability, not least because the law existing before the implementation of the Directive provided for it to be the same as the producer's

234 For an analysis of the evolution of approach to the issues see: Stapleton (1994b) and Sengayen (2007).

235 Case C-52/00, para. 29.

236 Case C-183/00.

237 Case C-183/00, para. 34.

238 Case C-52/00, paras 14–16; Case 154/00, paras 12–14.

239 Article 3 of Law No. 98-389 of 19 May 1998 on liability for defective products.

240 Law No. 2251/94 on consumer protection.

241 Article 3.3 of the Directive. Supplier's liability is contingent upon two conditions: that the producer cannot be identified and that the supplier does not inform the injured person of the identity of the producer, the importer or his own supplier within reasonable time.

liability. While in France this was explicitly strict liability, in Denmark it was based on 'fault' but in practice interpreted virtually as 'strict liability' (Fairgrieve and Howells 2007: 976). French law implementing the Directive provided for liability of suppliers as being the same as liability of the producers,[242] and following an ECJ judgement it was amended by *Loi No* 2004-1343 *de simplification du droit*[243] to state that the supplier would be liable even if he advised the victim within reasonable time of the identity of his own supplier, as long as the producer was unknown (Article 1386-7 of the Civil Code). Following another judgement which considered the last amendment insufficient, France amended Article 1386-7 of its Civil Code again in 2006, this time complying with the Directive.[244] Denmark[245] provided in Law No. 371 of 7 June 1989[246] that the supplier ('intermediary') was liable directly to "injured persons and subsequent intermediaries in the distribution chain".[247] The Law followed that after satisfying the claim of the injured person the intermediary would take over the latter's rights against any operators higher in the distribution chain.[248] The response of the European Court of Justice was unequivocal: Member States cannot extend strict producers' liability onto suppliers in this manner. The Court also held that the Directive did not preclude "application of other systems of contractual or non-contractual liability based on other grounds, such as fault or a warranty in respect of latent defects".[249] The problem is that while the Danish Ministry of Justice is now considering amendments to the Law by which producer's fault liability is extended onto the supplier, this amendment may also be contrary to the Directive because in court practice producers' 'fault' liability was "very strict" (Fairgrieve and Howells 2007: 976). The judgement in *Bilka* indicates that Article 13 covers liability regimes other than 'strict' liability for defective products. A question which presents itself is: would it also cover a liability system based on 'fault' but interpreted by courts to create a system where

242 Case C-52/00.

243 Two inconsistencies: inclusion of damages below the threshold of 500 EURO prescribed by Article 9b of the Directive (Article 1386-2 of the Civil Code) and the requirement that producers wishing to benefit from the development risk defence or regulatory compliance defence (Article 7 d and e of the Directive – Article 1386-12 of the Civil Code) ought to prove they have taken "appropriate steps to avert the consequences of a defective product" were rectified by *Loi No.* 2004-1343 *de simplification du droit* – Law of 9 December 2004. Law of 9 December 2004.

244 Case 177/04.

245 *Bilka*, Case C-402/03.

246 Amended by Law No. 1041 of 28 November 2000.

247 Case C-402/03, para. 12.

248 To be precise, suppliers would take over the liability of economic operators placed further up the production and distribution chain (Case 402/03 para. 9). Further, it was indicated in the ECJ judgement that the developments in the case law meant that sometimes the producer was liable even if not at fault (para. 9). See below for a short assessment of the uncertain implications of these developments.

249 Case C-154/00 para. 18; Case 52/00 para. 22; Case 183/00, para. 31.

'fault' did not need to be proven? Such systems were present in some Member States, for instance Hungary (Sengayen 2005), and indeed Denmark. Obviously if one considers the spirit of 'complete harmonization' and its aims, such court-made strict liability could not prevail. The judgement of the Court in *Bilka* recognized these developments within the case law of Danish courts.[250] It may be assumed that the Court does refer to both – the written provisions of Danish law (the Law implementing the Directive) and the established case law – when it concludes that "a national rule under which the supplier is answerable, beyond the cases listed exhaustively in Article 3(3) of the Directive, for the no-fault liability which the Directive establishes and imposes on the producer" is precluded by the Directive (Sengayen 2007).[251] This conclusion is in line with the approach of the Court to the idea of 'maximum harmonization' as well as to the understanding of the role of national courts in the enforcement of EC law.[252]

What became clear was that 'strict' product liability is now solely regulated by the Directive, and no other pre-existing national laws (written or court-made) or the laws implementing it may detract from it for the benefit of consumers. The European Court of Justice interpreted Article 13 to mean that Member States' discretion to regulate strict product liability "is entirely determined by the Directive itself and must be inferred from its wording, purpose and structure".[253] Harmonization of laws, regulations and administrative provisions in the matters regulated by the Directive is complete and no provision of national law based on the same ground as the Directive may provide for greater advantages for injured persons. On the other hand, as mentioned above, the Directive does not provide a completely harmonized system of liability. Apart from omissions, options, add-ons and the resulting inconsistencies in implementation which were indicated above, the practice of product liability on the national level exhibits striking divergences.

The role of national courts – judicial methodology, legal culture and the complexity of European product liability law

Indeed, for the full picture of European product liability law one must refer to judgements of national courts. National courts play a crucial role of enforcing the

---

250 "Developments in the case-law had the result (...) that in certain cases the producer was held liable even in the absence of fault. The supplier was answerable for the liability of the economic operators further up the production and distribution chain" (Case C-402/03, para. 9, also para. 41).

251 Case 402/03 para. 45.

252 The role of national courts in contributing to the operation of the European Union's legal system was explored above. See also the following section of this chapter for a further elaboration of the implications of this phenomenon for product liability practice in Europe.

253 *Bilka*, Case C-402/03, para. 22.

wording and purpose of the Directive. There, however, comes the problem which is inherent in the EC law enforcement system. Its necessary reliance on cooperation between national courts and the European Court of Justice creates potential for incoherence and mistakes in the interpretation of law (Maher 1994: 234–42). In the light of the inconsistencies in interpretation of the Directive which are already being noted, one may question whether this reliance on national courts can indeed lead to satisfactory results. There is still scope and need for a clarification (by the European Court of Justice and by the European Commission) of the desired approach to various elements of the Directive (Fairgrieve and Howells 2007).

The way Member States' courts approach the Directive can be traced back to a number of phenomena: their general approach to European Community law,[254] and the strength and role of national product liability laws before the implementation of the Directive.[255] Some national courts (Spanish, Italian or French – Whittaker 2005: 450–65) often attempt incorporating the approach of the Directive into the rules of product liability existing before its implementation, taking into account the general principles of the law of obligations. Courts of other Member States (for instance English courts) represent a position of a much greater focus on the Directive, with some comparative remarks of how its provisions are seen in other legal systems.[256] Here the enquiry ought to go back to the shape of national legal and judicial systems and the role of courts and jurisprudence in them (analysed in Chapter 2). In civil (and also post-socialist) systems, the role of the courts is predominantly to apply written law, and here writers such as Fairgrieve and Howells see the explanation why those courts use a much wider discretion in interpreting the Directive. They simply are not required to provide extensive justification for their approach (2007: 967). This position remains in contrast with the common law courts which have traditionally been required to give comprehensive justifications for their decisions (Fairgrieve and Howells 2007: 967).

Throughout Central Europe, wide-ranging transformations of the regulatory and judicial systems are affecting the position of courts and the judicial methodology, especially as regards the new obligation to follow the European Community law. The phase of transition which the judicial systems of Central Europe are still undergoing, described in Chapter 2 (Galligan and Matczak 2006, Kühn 2004, Tichy 2002b: 76), is material in shaping the approach to European law on the one hand,

254 This issue is not analysed in detail in the book – see Jarvis (1996).

255 Whittaker provides an excellent analysis of the reasons for the discrepancy in the approach to the Directive between France and England – with the French product liability regime based on strict liability principles and the French courts' efforts to extend contractual liability boundaries beyond contractual parties in order to assist victims of defective products, and the English negligence-based system (2005: 28, 444).

256 The judgement of Burton J in *A v. National Blood Authority* is an excellent example of this technique. See Stapleton (2007) for an elaboration of benefits and dangers of the comparative approach in tort litigation. For an introduction to the methodology of the use of comparative law by the judiciary see Cavinet, Andenas and Fairgrieve (2004).

and to complex liability systems such as product liability on the other. The views which Central European judiciary hold of the European Community law are being shaped with mixed success and consistency. While higher courts tend to be more receptive to European rules, lower courts present varied attitudes: from following these rules with flair and openness to a blunt refusal to follow them.[257] As mentioned above, so far one can observe no significant judgements concerning the provisions of the implemented Directive in Central Europe, so it is yet to be seen what the approach of Central European courts to this legal instrument will be.

Another factor contributing to the divergences in interpretation of the provisions of the Directive is the complex nature of product liability law and its links with the political and economic context (the key elements of which were explored above) in which it operates. Again, here Central European courts operating within the period of economic transition are challenged by the new context of product liability rules.

The rules of civil procedure which the Directive left untouched also undoubtedly create scope for divergent outcomes in product liability cases before courts of different Member States (Whittaker 2005: 75). An example of the consequences of this position is the English case of *O'Byrne* in which the European Court of Justice dealt with the issue of defendant substitution in the context of the ten-year long stop provided by Article 11 of the Directive.[258] The Court did not provide a clear rule here, but rather referred to national procedural laws which were to be applied in the spirit of the Directive and in accordance with its 'personal scope'.[259] The leading model of the European legal order remains the dependency of European substantive law on national procedure (Delicostopoulos 2003: 599, Maher 1994: 232). While this approach may well help greater assimilation of European law within national legal orders,[260] one cannot help noticing that it leads to significant discrepancies in application of such crucial provisions of the Directive as the ten-year long stop. It is by no means certain that the *O'Byrne* case would have a similar effect in France or Germany. Again, the discussion comes back to the role

257 The latter is a rare occurrence indeed, but it has been noted in a number of cases in Poland. Courts refused to apply European regulations or to follow judgements of the European Court of Justice because these had not been translated into Polish. Their argument was the need for legal clarity and certainty, but Andrzej Wróbel – the Polish Supreme Court Judge – suggested that lack of translation was no defence to refusal to follow EC law (interview in *Gazeta Prawna* No. 246, 19 December 2006 – see above – Chapter 2 footnote 46). Potentially such refusals to follow EC law, or cases where this law was followed incorrectly, may lead to compensation claims against the state under the *Francovich* (Cases C-6/90 and C-9/90) principles (see the recent case of *Traghetti del Mediterraneo* C-173/03 on national courts), and/or the need for the court in question to reopen the case (*Kapferer* case C-234/04).

258 Case C–127/04.

259 Case C–127/04, para. 38.

260 Maher (1994: 232) indicates that "despite the problems that the application of national rules can cause, national judges are more likely to entertain a Community law point as a matter of course, if no extraordinary procedures are required".

of national courts in enforcing and interpretation of the Directive. It is clear that the Directive does not always induce a truly harmonized product liability regime. Whether the harmonization which it formally established is a 'maximum' one or not, national courts are grappling with their own laws, in their own political and economic reality. Because of its contextual focus, this book may throw some light on the challenges faced by Central European courts.

Official reviews of the Directive and possible future reforms

In the First Report on the Application of the Directive (1995) the Commission saw a very limited impact of the Directive within the Member States.[261] On the other hand, it confirmed that the Directive had "contributed towards an increased awareness of and emphasis on product safety".[262] In 1999 the European Commission adopted the Green Paper on Liability for Defective Products with the intention to ascertain a growing impact of the Directive and to seek support for its possible reform.[263] The Green Paper received around a hundred responses from industry, insurers and consumer representatives.[264] The general state of affairs was concluded not to be different from the situation in 1995 – the experience with the application of the Directive remained limited. The major reasons for this were summarized as late implementation and the continuing relevance of the national tortious and contractual liability rules.[265] Further, the information concerning the practical application of the Directive and true differences between the Member States' product liability regimes was recognized as being 'scarce'.[266] The Commission concluded nevertheless that the Directive "constitute(d) a significant element of the legal environment in which intra- and extra-Community trade (wa)s conducted".[267] Although the Commission confirmed that the Directive created a "well-balanced and stable legal framework" respecting the needs of consumers and producers, it also noticed its coexistence with the national systems.[268] The latter remained popular, seen as more protective or simply better known.[269] It was observed that the Directive contributed to the increased level of safety of products, through its deterrent effect (assisted by the product safety legislation) and availability of

261 COM(95) 617 final.

262 COM (95) 617 final, at p. 2.

263 The two main questions asked by the Commission in the Green Paper were: how has the Product Liability Directive worked in practice, and to what extent should it be modified (COM(1999) 396 final).

264 The responses to the Green Paper of 1999 can be found at the following internet address: <www.europa.eu.int/comm/internal_market/en/goods/liability/replies.htm>.

265 The Second Report on Product Liability Directive, at pp. 28, 30.

266 Ibid., at p. 28.

267 Ibid., at p. 8.

268 Ibid.

269 Ibid.

compensation in cases of unavoidable injuries.[270] When analysing responses of the interested parties to the Green Paper regarding specific issues such as "maintaining the balance", burden of proof, development risks, financial limits, prescription and liability periods, suppliers' liability, and damages, the Commission stressed that it was impossible to create a position satisfactory for all involved.[271] However, no conclusive evidence was provided that the contemporary shape of the regime should be changed.[272] With the aim to collect more comprehensive data regarding these issues, and to assess the possibility of reform of the Directive, a study (conducted by Lovells) was completed in 2003 (Meltzer, Freeman and Thomson 2003). The study was aimed first of all at providing a comparative analysis of the practical effect of the product liability regimes in all the Member States, of the differences between them, and also at assessing the possible future of product liability legislation. It confirmed the findings presented in the Second Commission Report. Although the national product liability systems of all Member States were said to "rest on a common basic framework" including the Directive[273] and contract and tort law rules, differences were pointed out "in terms of claims being brought and their outcome".[274] Most respondents attributed the differences to the existence of the optional provisions in the Directive relying on the national liability rules which have not been harmonized, differences in implementation and interpretation of the Directive, differences in assessing damages, different procedures and levels of access to justice, and, last but not least, differences in consumer attitudes.[275]

The Third Report on the Product Liability Directive of 2006 did not recommend any amendments to its substantive provisions, but indicated several areas within the product liability system which may need to be monitored, not least in the light of the potential "opening the way towards greater harmonization": these are the burden of proof, the concept of defect, the development risks defence, the regulatory compliance defence, the minimum threshold, and the issues related to novel products, design defects and failure to warn.[276]

---

270 It was concluded that many cases were settled out of court, in particular when the facts were clear. While the out-of-court settlements were considered more advantageous than court proceedings by many representatives of industry, consumer organizations criticized the settlement proceedings for their confidentiality and a stronger position of producers and insurers (Second Report at p. 10).

271 "Victims want the highest level of protection at the lowest cost, while producers ask in particular for ceilings and for the shortest possible liability period" (Second Report at p. 12).

272 Ibid., at p. 28.

273 The Lovells Report concludes that "(I)n most respects, the Directive has been faithfully implemented in each Member State" (Executive Summary, at p. 5).

274 Executive Summary at p. 6.

275 Ibid., at p. 6. In fact, many respondents claimed that in their view the differences in procedure and access to justice were more significant than divergences in substantive law (Executive Report at p. 6).

276 Third Report on Product Liability Directive, pp. 9–11.

The future of the Directive, the future of 'maximum harmonization'

Harmonization of European product liability laws is by no means complete. Although the Directive aims at harmonization of the national rules relating to product liability (positive integration), Joerges argues that harmonization does not necessarily mean uniformity, and an application of a common Community principle may differ from one Member State to another (1993: 322). One ought to consider the fact that, as Freeman pointed out, "the practical impact of any product liability law will be a function of the procedural, social and cultural factors that influence the prevalence of civil liability in any given country" (2003: 3).

While there is a lot to be said for stable, consistent maximum consumer protection rules on the European level, speaking of completeness of harmonization is unrealistic. Establishing 'maximum harmonization' laws in the European Union does not entail declaring immediate victory, but rather setting out a long-term programme of legal approximation, coordination and convergence. The European Union should see 'maximum harmonization' as a process moving towards deeper and wider harmonization of law and procedure (Sengayen 2007). Product liability law and consumer law in general are systems of rules, practices and legal cultures, and need to be seen as such. The complex nature of product liability entails the impact on its practical operation of the general law of obligations, consumer law, other legal mechanisms providing compensation to victims of defective products, public regulation of product safety, as well as political and socio-economic factors accompanying the functioning of markets.

Harmonizing product liability laws entails a much more comprehensive undertaking than a mere adoption of a Directive, especially when the latter is an ambiguous instrument leaving significant areas of the regime to be decided by national laws. Now more than ever the Directive constitutes a component in the system of rules governing markets and protecting consumers, opening "the way towards greater harmonization".[277] Present day harmonization of European substantive and procedural laws involves greater coordination and search for consistency between various civil liability regimes and their practical application. A more inclusive approach to market regulation can be seen in the spirit of improving competitiveness and 'better regulation'. The enlargement of the European Union to include post-socialist countries is a new challenge to the process of harmonization of European law. Central European states for instance bring their own legal, political and socio-economic heritage into the equation. The internal market-building process has become an even more complex exercise. The Community is said to be faced with "new regulatory and enforcement structures and, more generally, with new attitudes towards consumer protection".[278] These are bound to take time to transform along the lines of the patterns evolving in the European Community.

277 This role was indeed stressed in the Preamble – Recital 18.

278 Consumer Policy Strategy 2002–2006, p. 5.

A number of conclusions may be drawn from looking at the European product liability system. The key one from the point of view of this book is that changes which will affect this liability system in the foreseeable future are rather placed outside the realm of the Product Liability Directive (Stapleton 2005). Central European states, now fully part of the process of harmonizing European law, also need to take on this comprehensive transformation challenge. Below is a closer look at what it may involve for them with regards to markets and consumer protection.

MARKETS AND MARKET LAWS IN CENTRAL EUROPE, AND THE DEVELOPMENT OF PRODUCT LIABILITY SYSTEMS

The analysis above presented the links between product liability on the one hand and the policies and laws of markets on the other, and their implications within Western Europe. Below the development of Central European markets and market laws is portrayed within the same conceptual framework. The emerging market economies, and consumer protection policies and laws, established a foundation and context for the birth of product liability systems.

Socialism features strongly in this analysis. It was a political and economic system with a remarkable impact on markets and their main *dramatis personae*. With the demise of socialism the position of Central European consumers and businesses was radically transformed. First of all, the shift from centrally planned economy to market economy changed the shape and organization of markets. The laws regulating business practices adopted an entirely new basis, a new form, and gained a new force. Further, the importance of law in society grew, and so did the exposure of society to law (Galligan and Kurchiyan 2003). Market policies and laws, including consumer laws, started following the Western European models much closer than ever before. With this explosion in legislative and regulatory output, there is also a renewed emphasis on enforcement of law. New institutional frameworks and procedural mechanisms are being introduced. Nevertheless, regulation of markets in Central Europe has yet to arrive at the complex, thorough, multi-level, more inclusive approach occurring in the European Union.[279] The position of product liability laws within these transforming market systems is changing, and its future is as yet not entirely certain. The analysis below ventures into predicting this future to some extent, based on the position at present and drawing upon the experience of Western European states and the United States. Following on from this venture, some predictions concerning the future of the project of harmonizing European product liability law in general are made in the final conclusions to the book.

279 Here the analysis refers to the concepts of better regulation and responsive regulation, the judicialization of society, the more inclusive and multi-disciplinary approach to market regulation in the European Union explored above.

Because the main determinant of the transformations taking place in Central Europe was socialism and its demise, the enquiry below separates two historical periods – before and after the year 1989.

Before 1989: socialist markets and laws and their gradual collapse – the birth of consumer protection and of product liability

Introduction and setting the scene

As with the developments in the 'West' explored above, the materialization of product liability laws in Central European jurisprudence can be directly linked to the greater focus on consumer interests within laws and markets. How did this phenomenon occur in the socialist Central Europe?

Initially, consumers were very rarely the addressees of rules or procedures. The interests of the state were at the heart of market laws. In the late 1970s, however, references to consumers and their position in socialist markets appeared in academic writings and court judgements.[280] Consumers were increasingly seen as the weaker parties in market relations or, in the context of product liability, victims of products with less knowledge and resources than businesses, although the market and the law were still largely focused on the interests of the state. Safety and quality of goods were commonly understood as the greatest challenges faced by consumers, and at first the law was mainly concerned with those challenges (Sengayen 2002, Łętowska 1999: 5). Although there were no written product liability provisions, courts started building the foundations of distinct product liability systems. The case law analysed in Part II of the book indicates attempts to facilitate the victims' position in product liability litigation. Numerous advantages of tortious liability prompted the shift in the courts' attention from contract to tort as a basis for product liability cases.[281] Further, in the last ten to twenty years of socialism the courts seem to have realized how inadequate the then solutions regarding dangerous products were (for many reasons – explored below), and the systems evolved from 'fault-based' to 'strict' liability (Hungary), or at least reached the stage where 'fault' could be established relatively easily (Poland, Czechoslovakia).

In spite of the developments towards a market-economy-style regulatory approach, the situation was unsatisfactory. It was assessed above what type of political and economic thought and action are conducive to creation of an efficient market law and an efficient consumer law. It was also mentioned that socialist Central European consumer laws were limited in scope and, even if in existence, ineffective. The lack of clarity in determination of the balance of interests between businesses and consumers, central control of markets by the state, lack

280 Formal, legal definitions of consumers appeared after the demise of socialism – with the appearance of the plethora of consumer protection laws deriving from the European Union.

281 This apart from Czechoslovakia – see below.

of effective competition, and the resulting lack of the desired impact of market laws and policies were the core features of socialist systems. These are explored below, with the enquiry structured to reflect the key phenomena – the ideology and political thought, the market as it functioned during socialism, and the types of state intervention in it. Ultimately, conclusions can be drawn concerning the laws of the market and their practical application during socialism, and the role of product liability (a 'litigation-heavy', private-enforcement-based system) within the overall scheme.

Socialist ideology – the key obstacle to effective market regulation and consumer protection

The omnipresence of the socialist ideology resulted in a very peculiar approach to market regulation. It meant lack of a political will to enact substantive consumer protection laws and procedures on the one hand, and the lack of adequate institutional and enforcement framework on the other. It affected legal culture: neither the legal profession nor the market participants (businesses and consumers) approached market laws with confidence.[282] Lack of adequate regulatory and institutional framework, lack of belief in the utility of the existing framework, social distrust of law and public authorities, legal and judicial formalism, were the stifling attributes of socialist legal cultures (explored in Chapter 2 which looked at the distinguishing features of socialist legal thought and legal method).

In other words, the political doctrines and ideology of socialism by no means facilitated the position of market participants. Even during the later years of socialism (late 1970s and 1980s) the populist 'holist' vision of the social/general interest being more significant than an individual's interest was dominant (Łętowska 1999: 2). Such an attitude was present, although not always expressly articulated, in the political and legal writings as well as the legal practice of the *époque*. It contributed to the widespread view that it would be against the ideals of socialism to protect the 'selfish' interests of an individual consumer, especially given that this protection was very often directed against a state-owned undertaking (Łętowska 1999: 2). In fact, both the consumer interests and business interests were totally subservient to the interests of the state. Thus, lack of a consumer protection focus was not accompanied by a strong support for businesses.[283] Market regulation was largely random, arbitrary and dependent on the state agenda. The laws intended to protect consumers were virtually non-existent.

282 See for instance: Friedman (1997, 1986) for an explanation of the notion of 'legal culture'.

283 On the other hand, however, it ought to be noted that in disputes between consumers and businesses the economic interests of the latter had a relatively greater recognition because they were seen (at least to some extent) as the personification of the 'system', the state, within market relations.

Further obstacles to effective market regulation and consumer protection were the very specific economic conditions of centrally planned markets. Even if some market laws did in fact exist, they were "in the state of hibernation", as they could not have been applied in these market conditions (Bakardjieva Engelbrekt 2006: 7). To some extent, socialist countries experienced systems of "competition law without competition" and "consumer law without consumerism" (Bakardjieva Engelbrekt 2006: 7–8). These issues are investigated below.

Socialist markets, their evolution and impact on the position of consumers

In classic centrally planned markets neither businesses nor consumers had any significant market power, if indeed they had any. In the 'economy of shortages' – both shortages of means of production and of consumer durables (Kozminski 1992: 354) – businesses were forced to use political pressure, corruption and illegal exchange in order to operate. They could not make independent decisions regarding quantity or characteristics of their products. Managers were unable to control their employees' wages or indeed their number – the policy of over-employment was aimed to compensate for absenteeism and short supply of means of production (Kozminski 1992: 354). Finances of businesses were centrally controlled and planned. Political ideologies significantly affected economic life. Kozminski stressed that this situation led to the printing of "empty money". As a result, consumers who did not have access to special stores for the privileged elite[284] had to queue for hours to obtain the most basic consumables or food, or buy them on the black market for prices much higher than those determined by the state (Kozminski 1992: 354).[285]

After the shift of market policies away from the stricter socialist rule during the 1970s, the market conditions started changing. The changes were described by Kozminski who drew a distinction between "privileged countries" such as Czechoslovakia (the ninth industrial nation in 1938 and the only European country which emerged with a reinforced economy after the Second World War) and "reformist" countries such as Hungary and Poland (1992: 356–7). Let us now observe these transformations.

In Hungary, after a short period of strict socialist rule, the policy of compromise led to what is sometimes described as "Kadarism" or even "goulash Communism" (Kosztolanyi 1999: 1). According to Kosztolanyi, a very simple rule was the following: Hungarians were able to enjoy many privileges, such as a variety of available food or consumer durables, so long as they did not oppose the general

284 In Poland – PEWEX, where one had to pay in dollars.

285 The author of this book queued for over four hours for a small bag of coffee in June 1985, and even longer for a chocolate bar in July 1986. Her entire family queued for a number of days for a vacuum cleaner in the late 1970s. With regard to the latter queue – this was a very well organized enterprise, with a nominated head of the queue, with a sign-in list, and a rota for the members of the queue.

socialist policy (ibid.). Consumer durables such as television sets or other electric appliances were very expensive (only domestic brands were offered), but Hungarian banks were quite eager to offer credit to consumers willing to buy them (Kosztolanyi 1999: 1). Further, although waiting time for cars (again, virtually always domestic or other socialist countries' production) and telephones was sometimes longer than the consumer's life,[286] the availability of a greater variety of products and credits made it easier to acquire them than elsewhere in the socialist world. The Hungarian market was relatively well equipped with consumer goods. Availability of a greater selection of products in the market was stimulated by more intensive competition, and competition has the capability to provide higher quality and safety (Gnela 2000: 177). Also the attitudes of the legal profession to consumer problems were much more in line with the Western European tendencies.[287] Although consumer policy was not something the government would openly admit to, consumer awareness and confidence in Hungary were probably higher than in many other Central and Eastern European countries, including Poland and Czechoslovakia. The importance of a free market and activities aimed at gaining profit was acknowledged in policy and academic writings (Harmathy 1998: 98). Ultimately it was recognized that the interests of consumers were not always uniform with the interests of undertakings, and the Civil Code was amended in 1977 to give effect to these changes in approach to consumers (ibid.).[288] These changes are described below.

The Czechs, although trying to avoid direct confrontation with the Soviets, did not manage to escape their intervention in 1968. After the intervention the policy of 'normalization' was adopted and Czechoslovakia achieved some economic progress. Private economic activity, although not as dynamic as in Hungary, was growing in scope and size. The supply of products and competition in the market was not satisfactory, but probably better than in Poland which is analysed below. The consumer confidence and legal awareness were poor. The legal formalism and positivism described in Chapter 2 led to the situation where the development of market law and civil law in general was not steady and lacked the solid basis of doctrinal writings and comprehensive case law. The relatively steady progress of the Czechoslovak market ultimately did lead, however, to wider changes in approach to market regulation and consumer protection, of which below.

Poland suffered from lack of political stability and frequent changes of political leaders for most of the socialist period in its history. After Stalin's death the liberal approach of the new leader of the Polish United Workers' Party (PZPR) Władysław

286 This led to the Parliamentary debate as to whether applications for phone lines ought to be inheritable (Kosztolanyi 1999: 1).

287 This is a revised part of the article published by the author (Sengayen 2002: 426).

288 The amendment of the Civil Code led to the control of contracts by courts. Administrative control, so popular in other socialist jurisdictions, was not considered capable of reaching the same objective; hence it was not trusted (Harmathy 1998: 98).

Gomułka was very soon reversed back to strict socialism. His successor Edward Gierek, intending to improve the quality of life in Poland, used foreign credits. For a brief period of time the shops were full of produce. After this short-lived and very peculiar time of 'economic progress', Poland found itself in an even deeper crisis than before, now burdened with debts. Following the dramatic price increases, strikes broke out in 1980. The establishment of Solidarity, martial law and a deep economic crisis followed.[289] In spite of some level of transformation towards market economy, within policy circles, academic writings, and ultimately in regulatory and judicial activities, the position of consumers and indeed other market participants in such political and economic conditions was very fragile. The lack of incentives for undertakings to produce safe, good quality products was striking.

Evolution towards a market economy model

As mentioned above, socialist states attempted, though initially largely unsuccessfully, to conduct effective regulatory control of the market. The aim was undoubtedly to ensure safety and quality of products and services. These attempts were constrained by the socialist political and economic systems explained above. Central planning was unable to ensure care on the part of businesses to provide such safety and quality. Lack of healthy competition deprived the efforts of the authorities of any significant power to encourage the desired market behaviour ("competition law without competition" – Bakardjieva Engelbrekt 2006: 7). Lack of an adequate regulatory and institutional framework which would be able to induce such behaviour was striking, and the weaknesses of this framework were not properly supported by any other enforcement mechanism (for instance product liability systems). Even if the systems such as product liability had operated successfully (which they did not, for reasons explored below), the entire regulatory market system was imbalanced and could not operate efficiently.

The situation started changing with the gradual movement towards greater appreciation of market philosophy as opposed to a strict socialist philosophy. Throughout Central Europe the regulatory policies were gradually changing towards greater recognition of the fact that the interests of undertakings ('socialist organizations') were not necessarily uniform with the interests of the society as a whole, and consumers in particular. Especially in the 1980s the contention that the consumers' interests ought to be protected to a greater extent gained strength among the legal profession. Svestka elaborated upon the "reconstruction of the direction of the national economy taking place in the socialist countries" (1989: 92, 93). This reconstruction was concerned with the spirit of initiative and enterprise, free competition and commencement of liquidation of monopolies (ibid.). Administrative means of regulating national economy started giving way to economic means (ibid.), but on the other hand there was recognition of the need to

289 For a more detailed analysis of the history of Central Europe see Lewis (1994).

establish a firm legislative and procedural framework enabling individuals to enforce their rights in market relationships. These changes placed new requirements upon the regulators and the legal profession. The lawmakers were challenged to amend the unsatisfactory legal provisions, and the judges had to interpret the existing legal provisions in a manner consistent with the new tendencies. The specific time when these ideas became popular depended upon the level of economic and social development of a particular state, this development remaining under the influence of political conditions. Hungary was the first country to change its political philosophy into a much more free-market-focused one. The first true recognition of the needs of the markets, and the needs of consumers, took place directly after the economic reforms in Hungary during the 1970s. The Civil Code was amended in 1977 towards a greater control of contracts by courts (Harmathy 1998: 98), and administrative planning was no longer treated as an effective means to ensure the progression of the market in the desired direction.[290] In 1984 Hungary adopted the Act on Prohibition of Unfair Economic Activity which regulated unfair trade practices, cartels and abuse of a dominant position.[291] As regards the product liability regime, this was also the time when the courts started realizing that the existing solutions were unsatisfactory, and searched among the rules available to them to provide more effective remedies (ultimately establishing a 'strict liability' system). Czechoslovakia followed shortly, although its changes to the socialist ideology and their effect upon consumers were narrower in scale and scope. There is, however, no doubt that the need for consumer protection was recognized there, at least during the 1980s. Czechoslovak scholarly writers elaborated upon the situation of consumers[292] ("the so-called non-professional contractual party", a party "lacking experience and professional product knowledge") as being in the "weakest economic position" (Svestka 1989: 91). During the 1980s the problems of consumers were widely recognized in Czechoslovak law, both in the Civil Code and in other regulations, especially in the field of administrative law (regulating product quality, technical standards, or prices) (Svestka 1989: 92). The contention that "protection of the interests of citizens as buyers, e.g. consumers in general, is not resolved by the very act of take-over of the means of production and planning" (ibid.) became very popular. Among the legislative, regulatory, and judicial reforms, Svestka mentioned control of 'common trade conditions', instalment and credit sales, obligatory statutory guarantees, and also remedies provided to those who sustained damages caused by defective products (ibid.).

290 Harmathy, when referring to the Hungarian market after the 1970s reforms, spoke clearly of the "economy in transition to a special kind of mixed market and planned economy" (1998: 98).

291 Act IV of 31 October 1984. See Cseres (2004) and Várady (1999) for a more detailed analysis of Hungarian competition law and policy.

292 Svestka refers to them rather as 'citizens as buyers' and 'third parties', or simply 'citizens' (1989: 90, 92). He also, sporadically, uses the notion 'consumers' (1989: 92). Knappova and Wilhelmsson concentrate on "the citizen as consumer" (1989: 131).

Market regulation and control of competition was however not satisfactory, subject to the Commercial Code which was not amended. The issue of liability for defective products indeed received some attention in the Czechoslovak doctrine of law. The doctrine postulated preventive measures aimed at securing quality, but also distribution of risks through compensation of losses caused by defective products (Svestka 1989: 94). Compensation was to cover the losses and, even more important, be easily obtainable (ibid.). Polish consumer protection policy suffered for a long time from lack of attention caused by serious political and economic crises, and hence in Poland the change took place latest. Łętowska wrote in the early 1980s of the necessity to accept the need for a greater protection of consumers and thus to abandon the socialist ideals in this sphere (1983: 401).[293] The scholarly writings concerning consumer protection were numerous even before this point, but they seemed to have focused solely upon the matters of liability for defective products.[294] This position was baffling in a country with probably the least developed 'consumer awareness'. Polish courts were relatively active in interpreting the general liability rules towards greater protection for the victims of the defective products which constantly flooded the Polish market. In terms of other issues concerning consumers, the Polish legal and economic system was truly unsatisfactory. Although, in common with Czechoslovakia, commercial guarantees were obligatory,[295] significant obstacles on the way to obtaining remedies under these guarantees existed in the market where 'the money was chasing the products'[296] (Sengayen 2002: 425). Enacted regulations aimed at securing the desired quality of products were never fully applied in practice. In Poland the attitude towards consumers and markets in general finally changed in the late 1980s. The Act *on Countering Monopolistic Practices in the National Economy* was adopted in 1987,[297] although it did not regulate unfair commercial practices like the Hungarian Act. Very shortly after these modest transformations took place the peaceful revolution broke down socialism and transformed it into a totally different reality. The markets of the entire post-socialist Europe were faced with new challenges, not very often perceived as such by regulators or the legal profession (Łętowska 1999: 3, 4).

The features of Central European product liability laws were introduced above and will be analysed comprehensively in Part II. There is no doubt that

293 See also Wasiak (1985) or Żuławska (1985: 41–9).

294 Sołtysiński (1970) wrote a study postulating introduction of contractual liability of the producers of defective products; liability based upon the legal construct of a 'guarantee promise' (see Chapter 4 of Part II); see also Nesterowicz (1979: 4–19).

295 Their content was regulated by the Civil Code. They were obligatory until the amendment of the Polish Civil Code on 28 July 1990. For more detailed analysis of the Polish legal and commercial guarantees system, see Sengayen (2002: 403–37).

296 As opposed to the markets where 'the products chase the money' – capitalist markets saturated with consumer durables (Łętowska 1999: 5).

297 Act of 28 January 1987, later repealed.

the seeds of these relatively comprehensive, progressive, and indeed often 'strict' or at least 'objective' liability systems were sown at the time when socialism, although transforming in the ways described above, still prevailed. What could one say about the role of product liability at that time? It was clearly an important legal mechanism which was increasingly used by consumers (and, interestingly, businesses)[298] injured and suffering significant damages as a result of contact with defective products – the plague of socialist markets. On the other hand, its relative 'success' and popularity did not entail the results which a Western European commentator would expect. In the absence of effective regulatory regimes, product liability law was unable to provide both the behaviour modification and the compensatory role which it normally is designed to play. Although used in a number of high-profile cases, it did not and could not fulfil the needs of the socialist markets. Product liability law without the context in which it functions in the 'West' – market economy, competition and other mechanisms of market regulation, control, enforcement and compensation – could not function effectively. Further, civil procedure, judicial systems and the unsatisfactory access to redress (high costs of litigation, very poor availability of legal aid, unavailability of good quality legal advice, lack of means of alternative dispute resolution) meant that many cases of damages caused by defective products did not result in compensation.

Consumer protection law and market law in general, were largely ineffective, inconsistent, and did not play their intended part during socialism. Below is an examination of the way in which they transformed after 1989.

After 1989

Introduction

Throughout Central and Eastern Europe the socialist leaders began round table discussions with the opposition groups in 1989. The 'peaceful revolution' which swept the region began in Poland and Hungary in 1989 and reached Czechoslovakia later the same year (Lewis 1994: 226–59, Kozminski 1992: 259). The 'revolution' recommenced the development of democracy and initiated the gradual re-

298 In fact, the development of product liability systems in relations between businesses (normally – 'socialist organizations' – the most common form of economic presence in socialist markets: state-owned enterprises and cooperatives) shows very interesting attempts of courts to use product liability as a replacement for an ineffective quality and safety regulatory regime. This took place in Poland and Czechoslovakia where relations between 'socialist organizations' were regulated and settled separately from other types of relations. These very specific systems of economic and legal relations developed their own product liability regimes, more stringent than the ordinary systems of liability for defective products (Dobiasova 2003, Gnela 2000: 175–9, Svestka 1989: 90). In Hungary there was no such separation, but on the other hand the product liability system developed by courts was very stringent indeed.

establishment of healthy market relations. The process of reform in Hungary, referred to as "the most persistent economic reformer of Eastern Europe",[299] was undoubtedly less chaotic than in many other former socialist states. In contrast to Poland, Hungary adopted a "gradual transition" strategy of development, which entailed a "managed", slower, and less radical introduction of market relations (Kozminski 1992: 365). Foreign investors had access to the Hungarian market already before the 'revolution',[300] and the market could be characterized as bearing some signs of freely operating competition between enterprises even in the times of socialist domination. In this country the transformation towards the desired liberal democracy was, to a much greater degree than in other post-socialist states, achieved solely through constitutional change (Lewis 1994: 285).[301] The "gradual transition" model meant that the dissolution of the administrative infrastructure of the government was not as wide-ranging as in Poland, and thus the continuity of the regulatory process was secured (Kozminski 1992: 366). Czechoslovakia – before the Second World War a country with very strong democratic traditions and a high standard of living – was also considered relatively well developed and well placed to "make the leap to a market economy".[302] The "leap" it made followed the Hungarian "gradual transition" example rather than the Polish model explained below (Kozminski 1992: 363). Poland, already weakened by strikes and the martial law of 1981, entered the new era burdened with significant debts, a disorganized economy and unsettled political life. It seemed a more effective reconstruction strategy to adopt a "shock treatment", "accelerated transition" model, also entailing a rapid disintegration of the administrative and institutional framework existing before (Kozminski 1992: 366). While new administrative structures were being built, the process of creating new rules and regulations governing market relations and protecting consumers was slower than in the two other Central European states.

Economic transformations, new market ideologies and the unsatisfactory position of market participants

Economic transformations followed this 'peaceful revolution'. The flow of poor quality foreign goods (Kozminski 1992: 365) into Central Europe soon ended

299 *The European Community and its Eastern Neighbours* Study 1990 at p. 23.

300 *The European Community and its Eastern Neighbours* Study 1990 points to a number of examples of foreign investors, such as General Electric or General Motors, actively involved in the Hungarian market (at p. 23). Harmathy states that, even during the period of planned economy Hungary was "a member of the international business community without interruption" (1998: 15).

301 For a more detailed analysis of the constitutional change in Hungary in 1990 see Harmathy (1998: 9, 10).

302 *The European Community and its Eastern Neighbours* Study 1990 at pp. 24 and 25.

as a result of competition from domestic producers and more stringent safety laws. Very shortly the number of private companies in Central Europe would be significant, and competition in consumer markets would ensure supply of better quality products. Irrespective of these significant changes, however, the position of consumers was still unsatisfactory (Łętowska 1999: 2, 3).[303] More generally, the economic and regulatory situation on the post-socialist markets was unsatisfactory for all market participants.

The regulatory and institutional framework was still relatively poor. Laws intended to ensure fair competition and consumer protection were being introduced with a significant dose of hesitation. Contrary to what one might have expected, the attitudes of regulators and the legal profession did not significantly shift in the direction of modern 'market-economy style' thinking. Even though the socialist ideology no longer stood in the way, there was no overwhelming enthusiasm for market laws, and consumer laws in particular. According to Łętowska, Poland commenced building capitalism as it was when the country left it at the start of the Second World War (1999: 3) (this could no doubt be noticed also in other countries of Central Europe, although it was not so overwhelming in Hungary).[304] It was believed that the free market was capable of protecting interests of all its participants, including consumers (Łętowska 1999: 3).[305] In the period of socialist domination the state took over regulation of all the economic presence in the market, and it was falsely proclaimed as best equipped to effectively protect citizens' interests. Because such belief was in fact detrimental to consumer and business interests, the disillusionment with state intervention in the market after the end of socialism was significant (Łętowska 1999: 3, 4). Free market ideas were welcomed as an infusion of healthy, fair competition, and it was hoped that the free market on its own would be capable of curing the ills of the post-socialist markets and provide consumers with an adequate level of protection (Sengayen 2002). For instance, shortly after the end of the socialist period the Hungarian Constitutional Court took the view that freedom of contract was one of the most fundamental rights in the new reality (Harmathy 1998: 104), and only some time later did the Court realize the need for protection of weaker contractual parties and thus for limitations of freedom of contract. The Czech regulators and legal profession have also undoubtedly suffered from the described illusion.

303 Łętowska's contentions concern Poland only, but their relevance can be extended to the entire Central Europe. The conditions which contributed to the situation described by Łętowska were present, although with various strength and at slightly different historical moments, throughout the region.

304 The Hungarian scholars and the legal profession were much greater enthusiasts of the regulatory involvement of the state in markets – see Kornai (2001).

305 Kozminski refers to "simple-minded 'zealots' within the professional circles of economists and within the post-communist governments" (1992: 367) carrying similar views.

This position still to some extent lingers across Central Europe, creating a picture of political, economic and legal systems in transition. The postulates of the need to balance the market coordination – by the state, by the market itself, and by self governance and civil society – are gaining ground (Kornai 2001). Changes towards such a market economy regulatory model are taking place gradually, mostly as a result of influences of the European Union policies and laws.[306]

Relations with the European Union and their effect on the position of consumers

Below is a short analysis of the development of relations between the European Union and Central Europe culminating in the 2004 enlargement. Depicting this process enables a better understanding of the rationale behind the changes in market regulation and consumer protection in Central European countries.

As mentioned above, in a short time after the demise of socialism post-socialist states undertook significant reforms of their political, economic and social systems (Lewis 1994). In recognition of these transformations, the European Communities became interested in strengthening the relations with the newly freed countries. The European Commission was asked to draw up proposals for association agreements in order to establish a "special type of relationship reflecting geographic proximity, shared values and increased independence" (Gower 1999: 5). The Association Agreements ('Europe Agreements')[307] were not very explicit about the future chances for membership of the European Union, only referring to the membership as the "final objective" (Gower 1999: 5). Nevertheless, it was clear that the process of "merging the CEECs back into the Western part of Europe, and re-establishing a sense of belonging that they have always claimed" had begun (Curzon Price, Landau and Whitman 1999: 13).[308] Article 68 of the Polish and the Czechoslovak Agreements and Article 69 of the Hungarian Agreement stipulated the obligation to approximate national law to the *acquis communautaire*,[309] the

306 See Bakarjieva Engelbrekt (2006), Cseres (2004) and (Várady) 1999 for more detailed analyses of the market transformations in post-socialist states.

307 Association Agreements between the European Union and the Central European States – Hungary, Poland and Czechoslovakia – were signed in December 1991. See: Commission of the European Communities Background Brief (1992). In January 1993 the Czech Republic and Slovakia became independent states and the Agreements needed to be signed again with these states separately (Henderson 1999: xvi). The Europe Agreements "provide the framework for bilateral relations between the European Communities and their Member States on the one hand and the partner countries on the other. The … Agreements cover trade-related issues, political dialogue, legal approximation and other areas of cooperation …" <www.europa.eu.int/comm/enlargement/pas/europe_agr.htm>.

308 Gower referred to the "major shift in EU policy" (1999: 7).

309 The *acquis communautaire* are "all the rights and obligations, actual and potential, arising from the Treaties, EC law and the jurisdiction of the Court of Justice plus declarations, resolutions and international agreements adopted within the Community framework" (Gower 1999: 18).

following provisions of the Agreements containing the most crucial areas of law to be dealt with, and among those the law of consumer protection. In the Commission Report 'The Challenge of Enlargement' presented to the Lisbon European Council in June 1992, enlargement was envisaged as an "historic opportunity" and placed at the forefront of the Community agenda.[310] In 1993 the Copenhagen European Council set out the main criteria which the countries aiming to access the Union had to meet (Gower 1999: 7, 8).[311] The associated states were to be capable to "take on the obligations of membership", and the preparation was to involve establishment of political stability, democracy and protection of human rights, the rule of law, and a well-functioning market.[312] The relations between the Union and the post-socialist countries evolved further as a result of the Essen European Council, where the Commission was asked to prepare "concrete proposals to draw together all the various EU policy instruments into a coherent strategy to prepare the countries of CEE for accession" (Gower 1999: 9).[313] During the meeting of the Council, the Commission was invited to draft a White Paper to be presented at the Cannes European Council the following year.[314] While the White Paper was welcomed by the post-socialist states as an implicitly drafted "action plan" for them, it also stressed the areas which the Commission considered of particular significance, including the "legal approximation" concerning economic laws of the associated states (Gower 1999: 9). The "legal approximation" was to involve, apart from adopting a significant volume of legal instruments,[315] ensuring their practical operation through establishing relevant enforcement and administrative procedures (ibid.). The impact of this however obvious requirement on consumer law or on market law in general is notable. Although the book does not attempt to comprehensively examine issues such as the widely understood access to justice – mechanisms for private and collective or representative enforcement of the law, civil procedure rules, methods of funding civil litigation, or access to alternative dispute mechanisms – these issues are no doubt of paramount significance and beg further investigation.[316]

As mentioned above, the Europe Agreements contained provisions which expressly mentioned consumer protection. These provisions prompted the process

310 Commission of the European Communities, *Europe and the challenge of enlargement* 1992: 9.

311 Council of the European Union (1993).

312 Ibid.

313 See Commission of the European Communities, The Europe Agreements and beyond: a strategy to prepare the countries of Central and Eastern Europe for accession 1994, and Follow up to Commission Communication 1994.

314 Commission of the European Communities White paper: preparation of the associated countries of Central and Eastern Europe for integration into the internal market of the Union 1995.

315 "80,000 pages of EU law" (<www.europa.eu.int/pol/enlarg/overview_en.htm>).

316 See Hodges (2007a) for an introduction to the developments in this area at the European Community level.

of implementation of various consumer protection directives, including the Product Liability Directive. Article 69 of the Czech Association Agreement provided:

> (T)he Contracting parties recognize that the major precondition for the Czech Republic's economic integration into the Community is the approximation of the Czech Republic's existing and future legislation to that of the Community. The Czech Republic shall endeavour to ensure that its legislation will be gradually made compatible with that of the Community.

Article 70 stipulated that the approximation of laws would extend in particular to: (among other areas) protection of health and life of humans, animals and plants, and consumer protection. The Europe Agreement concluded between Hungary and the European Union contained Article 67 which required Hungary to approximate their laws to the laws of the European Union. In Article 68 specific fields of interest were listed, and among them consumer protection including product liability. The Hungarian Act on Product Liability of 1993 contains a short Preamble which elaborates upon the motives for the adoption of the Act:

> (t)he participation of Hungary in the international economic integration process, the safety of international trade, the protection of the interests of consumers, and the requirement of focusing on offering more advanced and higher quality products require that manufacturers, while maintaining prevalent conditions of production, should be held liable for damages caused by defective products to a greater extent than generally expected.[317]

Later the Preamble refers to the "achievements of the approximation of laws on product liability within Europe".[318] Such a Preamble is unique among the Central European product liability acts. What is also unique is the reference of the Preamble to the existing achievements of the case law, and the need for their consolidation in a written piece of legislation (Kalman, Lelkes and Domokos 2003: 4). The Association Agreement of the European Union with the Republic of Poland contained Article 68 obliging Poland to approximate its laws to the laws of the European Union. Article 69 enumerated the most crucial areas and included consumer protection laws (Szostak 1995: 53). The Legislative Council of the Republic of Poland very soon after the Agreement came into effect established that product liability law ought to be one of the areas of priority for reform.[319]

317 English translation of the Act provided by the Hungarian Ministry of Justice (Judit Bartfai).

318 Ibid.

319 Statement of the Legislative Council of 3 March 1994 *w sprawie dostosowania prawa polskiego do systemu prawa Unii Europejskiej* (on the adoption of the Polish Law to the system of law of the European Union), *Biuletyn Rady Legislacyjnej* 1994, no. 1, p. 90.

Poland and Hungary formally applied for membership of the European Union in 1994, and the Czech Republic did the same in 1996 (Gower 1999: 10, 18). The 1996 Intergovernmental Conference leading to the signing of the Treaty of Amsterdam, although primarily concerned with the internal reforms within the Community structures, did so with regard to the future enlargement.[320] The 1997 summit in Luxembourg prepared the scene for negotiations which were to be held with six countries including the Central Europe as defined in this book. The accession negotiations began in 1998.[321] In 1999 the Treaty of Nice was signed, where the Member States undertook to "streamline their decision-making" by reforming the main institutions of the European Union.[322] In 2001 in Gothenburg, the European Council concluded that enlargement negotiations would be completed by 2002 and the enlargement would take place in 2004.[323] In 2002 the European Commission confirmed that the ten applicant countries would join the Union in 2004, and the Copenhagen European Council formally welcome the new Member States (subject to ratification in their national referenda).[324] The Treaty of Accession[325] was signed on 16 April 2003. The referenda in the three Central European states ratified the accession process. With the moment of joining the Union (1 May 2004), the obligation to follow all the *acquis communautaire* (including the Product Liability Directive which had already been implemented by that time by all Central European states) became legally enforceable. The process of implementation of the Directive in Central Europe is explained in more detail in Chapter 6 of Part II.

New approach to market regulation and new consumer protection policies

Market regulation became the major point of focus for Central European authorities after the initial free market enthusiasm mentioned above. The relationship between the state and market participants has changed dramatically, and this was closely linked to market regulation techniques. The importance of economic power and wealth of Central European industry was increasingly recognized, and there was realization that regulatory involvement of the state ought to assist in building those. On the other hand, the ideology of market economy entailed the need to rectify the newly recognized market failures and to introduce the language of equality of bargaining power in business-to-business and business-to-consumer relations.

320 For the analysis of the reforms undertaken by the Communities in order to prepare for accession of the new Member States see for instance: Deubner (1999: 119–28), Phinnemore (1999: 71–85).

321 <www.europa.eu.int/pol/enlarg/overview_en.htm>.

322 Ibid.

323 Ibid.

324 Ibid.

325 <http://www.europa.eu.int/comm/enlargement/negotiations/treaty_of_accession_2003/table_of_content_en.htm>.

The need for providing a balance between business and consumer interests was voiced in political and academic writings of the early 1990s. It was very influential in the debates leading to the implementation of the Product Liability Directive, illustrated bellow. On the one hand, industry was still relatively fragile and often incapable of withstanding the modern regulatory challenges of high safety and quality standards, the threat of hefty public fines, or civil litigation. On the other hand, consumers who were now faced with a new market economy with all its challenges and opportunities required assistance. There was a renewed focus on clear, comprehensive primary legislation (as opposed to 'normative acts' so widely used by socialist authorities). This legislation became increasingly inspired by the European Union and its market regulation philosophy.

Consumer agenda was being widely advanced in political circles. The end of socialism marked the beginning of belief in an inevitable improvement of the position of consumers. As noted above, this improvement did not appear immediately and until today the position can be categorized as far from satisfactory. The continuing changes in economic policies, introduction of new market laws, and the changing attitudes of the legal profession determined slow but steady progress in increasing consumer awareness and confidence. The consumer movement, which in Poland began formally in 1980 and in Hungary in 1988, gained more strength, and the role of consumer associations was developing (Kozminski 1992: 366). The quality and safety incentives for manufacturers and other professionals dealing with products – the result of increased competition, stronger regulatory structures of the state, and consumer movement – were also growing. As mentioned above, a significant part of improvements in consumer policies can be attributed to the pressures deriving from the European Union and the hopes for membership in this structure. Below is a brief account of the developments in the field of consumer policy.[326]

In 1997, Hungary adopted the Act on the Protection of Health and Consumers. It provided basic consumer rights reflecting parts of the European Community *acquis*.[327] The Act contains provisions aiming at protection of life, health, safety, and property of consumers, provisions ensuring consumer information and education, provisions establishing mechanisms for enforcement of consumer law, and the operation of central and local governmental bodies and consumer associations protecting consumer interests. Subsequently, further pieces of European Community consumer legislation were implemented, and the process advanced so significantly indeed that this chapter of negotiations was provisionally

---

326 See <http://ec.europa.eu/consumers/strategy/scene_en.htm> for a country-by-country review of consumer policies, laws, institutional enforcement structures, consumer organizations and consumer redress in all the EU Member States, including the Central European countries.

327 Act CLV of 1997. <www.europa.eu.int/scadplus/leg/en/lvb/e16103.htm>. The Act is available in Hungarian at: <http://net.jogtar.hu/jr/gen/hjegy_doc.cgi?docid=99700155.TV>.

closed in 2002.[328] In spite of significant delays in implementing the Consumer *Acquis*, Poland ultimately sped up the development and also provisionally closed the chapter in 2002.[329] No consumer protection act was adopted in Poland, which rather focused upon separate regulation of specific issues. The progress of the Czech Republic was also noted as unsatisfactory by the Commission, although the chapter was closed in 2002.[330] In 1992 the Czech Consumer Protection Act was adopted,[331] establishing a wide range of rights for consumers. Further substantive law measures, those inspired by the European Community and those adopted on a purely national basis, are being adopted throughout Central Europe until today. In fact, the development of consumer law is still very dynamic.[332]

Apart from establishing a system of substantive legal provisions, Central European states also focused on building an institutional-regulatory framework for protection of consumers. Various state bodies were set up, both within the consumer protection acts and outside their scope, in order to adequately secure enforcement of consumer rights (Bakardjieva Engelbrekt 2006).[333] In fact, the importance of the process of implementation of the European Community *acquis* rests with, apart from the weight of the newly adopted black-letter legislation, the emphasis upon mechanisms of enforcement virtually unknown before. As mentioned above, the European Union considers the enforcement of laws, establishment of the pertinent administrative and judicial structures, and coordination of institutions involved in the enforcement procedures, of paramount importance. It requires the same approach from the new Member States. The approach is a novelty in the post-socialist states where law enforcement, especially with regard to consumer protection law, did not receive adequate attention.

Below is a more detailed analysis of these developments within the Central European states which shape the contemporary policy of consumerism.

---

328 Ibid. See Commission Reports on the progress of Hungary: COM(97) 2001 final, COM(98) 700 final, COM(1999) 505 final, COM(2000) 705 final, SEC(2001) 1748 final, COM(2002) 700.

329 <www.europa.eu.int/scadplus/leg/en/lvb/e16106.htm>. See the Commission Reports: COM(97) 2002 final, COM(98) 701 final, COM(1999) 509 final, COM(2000) 709 final, SEC(2001) 1752, COM(2002) 700 final.

330 <www.europa.eu.int/scadplus/leg/en/lvb/e16107.htm>. See the Commission Reports: COM(97) 2009 final, COM(98) 708 final, COM(1999) 503 final, COM(2000) 703 final, SEC(2001) 1746, COM(2002) 700 final.

331 Available in Czech at: <www.mpo.cz>.

332 It is reviewed on the following website: <http://ec.europa.eu/consumers/strategy/scene_en.htm>.

333 Again, these developments are assessed on the following website: <http://ec.europa.eu/consumers/strategy/scene_en.htm>.

Building the regulatory, institutional and 'individualistic' model of consumerism

The consumerism which is being built in Central Europe follows examples of Western European states, and is clearly inspired by the European Union approach. Above it was explained how neither the public regulation nor private litigation were adequate mechanisms for market control or consumer protection during socialism. As a result, both these types of regulatory and redress mechanisms are being developed in parallel at the present time. Thus the title of this section: the model of consumerism which is being built is a regulatory, institutional one, but also a more 'individualistic' one: while public regulation and public authorities are considered to be major forces in protecting consumers, the latter are also encouraged – through strengthening of the role of consumer associations, reforms of various procedural mechanisms for seeking redress, including courts and Alternative Dispute Resolution bodies – to take law enforcement into their own hands.[334]

The European Union is the key inspiration for establishing new market laws and regulations, new institutional structures, and the emphasis on the power of public authorities to enforce the rules effectively. On the other hand, signals from the European Union and various Member States (analysed briefly above) are of an increased emphasis on individual and collective consumer redress. How are these developments taking ground in Central Europe?

Central European states implemented the existing EC consumer directives, including those evaluated in the Review of the Consumer *Acquis*.[335] They deal with substantive consumer rights, and with their enforcement by consumer associations or public authorities (Injunctions Directive 98/27, Consumer Protection Cooperation Regulation 2006/2004).[336] Central European states have established a comprehensive institutional regulatory and enforcement framework for consumer law, which is based on the primary role of public enforcement bodies which exercise their functions with the support of consumer associations funded by the state. In the Czech Republic, the Trade Inspection and the Regional and Local Trades Licensing Offices have the key role in enforcing consumer law, with the power to issue injunctions and to impose fines. The key non-governmental organizations which support their role are: the Consumers Defence Association of the Czech Republic[337] and the Czech Consumers Association.[338] The main regulatory and enforcement bodies in Hungary are the General Inspectorate and the Regional Inspectorates for Consumer Protection,[339] again with injunctive and

334 For a review of these developments in each Central European state: see <http://ec.europa.eu/consumers/strategy/scene_en.htm>.

335 See the Consumer Law Compendium and EU Consumer Law Acquis Database: <http://ec.europa.eu/consumers/rights/cons_acquis_en.htm#comp>.

336 See <http://ec.europa.eu/consumers/strategy/scene_en.htm>.

337 Websites: <www.spotrebitiele.info>, <www.consumers.cz>.

338 Website: <http://www.regio.cz/spotrebitel/>.

339 Website: <http://www.fvf.gov.hu/>.

punitive (fines) powers. They cooperate with a range of consumer associations, above all the National Association for Consumer Protection.[340] The Polish Office for the Protection of Competition and Consumers (the President of the Office, the central office and the local offices) is the main competition and consumer law regulatory and enforcement body. According to the Act on the Protection of Competition and Consumers of 16 February 2007,[341] the President of the Office has injunctive and punitive powers in cases where consumers' interests have been breached. He is supported by regional and municipal consumer ombudsmen (financed from the local budget)[342] and non-governmental organizations (again, financed from the public purse) – the Consumer Federation[343] and the Polish Consumer Association.[344]

On the other hand, litigation, civil procedure and access to justice are undergoing a significant overhaul. Here the impact of the European Union is not so overwhelming,[345] but the need to reform the handicapped court structures, litigation systems and out-of-court dispute resolution mechanisms is clear.[346] Central European states are amending their Civil Procedure Codes with the aim to make litigation more efficient, speedier and generally more suitable to the new reality.[347] The transformations also extend to the judicial attitudes and judicial methodology, analysed in Chapter 2 above. Both the role of the judiciary in society, and their own approach to their role, are undergoing crucial changes. Legal training for judges and other members of the legal profession (training concerning new legislation – especially the law of the European Union, new political and economic conditions, as well as computer literacy) is taking place on a much wider scale.[348] While these reforms are progressing with impressive speed and dynamism, it is obviously a much

340 Website: <www.ofe.hu>.

341 Available in the Polish language at the website of the Office: <http://www.uokik.gov.pl/pl/regulacje_prawne/polskie_i_wspolnotowe_akty_prawn/podstawowe_regulacje/polskie_akty prawne/>. Parts of the Act (analysed in English by the author) will soon appear on the EU Consumer Law Acquis Database: < http://www.eu-consumer-law.org/>.

342 The description of the role and the list of all consumer ombudsmen can be found on the following website: <http://www.uokik.gov.pl/pl/ochrona_konsumentow/rzecznicy/>.

343 Federacja Konsumentów – <www.federacja-konsumentow.org.pl>.

344 Stowarzyszenie Konsumentów Polskich – <www.skp.pk>.

345 The European Union has recently stepped up its efforts to harmonize aspects of Member States' civil procedures – see above. Particular emphasis is presently seen in the area of collective consumer redress: see <http://ec.europa.eu/consumers/redress/collect/index_en.htm>.

346 See: Bukovská (2002), *Access to Justice Country Report: Czech Republic*, Kádár, Pardavi and Zádori (2002) Hungarian Helsinki Committee, *Access to Justice Country Report: Hungary*; Bojarski (2002), *Access to Justice Country Report: Poland.*

347 At the time this book was being completed, the Polish Civil Law Codification Commission was finalizing a draft act on group litigation (a generic, opt-in mechanism).

348 See for instance: 'Efficient Court' – guidelines prepared by the Polish Judge Association IUSTITIA (<www.iustitia.pl>).

more complex effort to alter the elements of legal culture mentioned in Chapter 2 of Part I. These are bound to remain and to some extent determine the distinctive nature of post-socialist states within the civil law family.

The newly created bodies responsible for consumer protection are increasingly active in regulating market behaviour, business practices, fair competition, and in pinpointing and remedying conduct infringing consumer interests. Consumer organizations, various civic initiatives and the media are also progressively more dynamic in bringing consumer issues to the public arena, although problems with financing and human resources remain. The increased competition and enhanced public control, as well as activities of consumer organizations and other consumer initiatives, inspire businesses to strive for better safety and quality of their products and services. Self-regulation and establishment of codes of conduct are still rather rare, but they are no longer completely foreign in Central European business vocabulary.[349]

The role of product liability in the newly established markets and their regulatory framework

What is the place of product liability law among those new regulatory structures and the new concept of consumerism? There is no doubt that it continues being a crucial area of consumer law, perhaps even more crucial than in some other European states because new forms of compensation mechanisms (mostly private and social insurance) and new deterrence mechanisms (public enforcement mentioned above) which exist there are only now being built in Central Europe. The growing importance of product liability law – both for consumer protection and for balancing the interests of market participants – could be observed very soon after the end of socialism, when the dissatisfaction with the existing consumer protection systems was voiced by politicians and academics alike (see below).

It is not absolutely clear which direction Central European systems will take: whether the number of product liability cases will indeed increase. With the greater emphasis on private enforcement, individual and collective redress as well as the reforms in civil procedures, organization of legal profession and funding of civil litigation, product liability – an example of a 'litigation-heavy' branch of consumer law – may well flourish. On the other hand, while other methods of settling disputes and obtaining redress are being established, product liability may be used rather rarely. The number of court judgements in this area of law remains very low at present, although as mentioned above this is not necessarily the sign of insignificance of the system but rather the characteristic feature of product liability as remedy.

349 Some initiatives in this area, especially those taken in Poland, were mentioned on the following website: <http://ec.europa.eu/consumers/strategy/scene_en.htm>.

Assessment of the existing product liability systems – dissatisfaction and reform proposals

In spite of significant progress achieved in the field of remedies for product-related injuries in Hungary and Poland, a great number of politicians, legal practitioners and academic writers called for a reform very soon after the end of socialism. The need for reforming the Czechoslovak product liability regime was also acknowledged by politicians and academics. Below is the analysis of these postulates. After the Association Agreements with the European Union were signed, another impetus for reform of Central European product liability regimes appeared with the inevitable implementation of the Product Liability Directive. It is useful to depict the political and academic climate before the implementation of the Directive, as it to some extent determines the destiny of this new legal mechanism in Central Europe.

After the initial euphoria and fascination with free market ideas, the reforms of product liability law epitomized by the Directive were widely welcomed throughout Central Europe. They were welcomed irrespective of the fact that national product liability rules often already resembled the Directive. They were seen as part of a much wider system of consumer protection rules, reflecting the ideas of market economy, fair balance of market interests and healthy market relations. They were to some extent understood as having their origins in the legal systems (French, German, Austrian law) which constituted models for Central European civil laws.

The Hungarian contractual and tortious liability regimes analysed in Part II seem to have provided an excellent opportunity for redress for victims of defective products. The reform movement commenced earlier than in other Central European states, and already in early 1980s Hungary achieved considerable progress in establishing a 'strict' product liability regime. Nevertheless, one of the members of the Hungarian Parliament who initiated reforms of consumer protection laws, and among those also the product liability law reform in the early 1990s, postulated 'defencelessness' of the Hungarian consumers against manufacturers of defective products (Kecskés 1994: 68–101). The regime which already in fact surpassed the level of protection offered by the Product Liability Directive was considered unsatisfactory from the point of view of consumers.[350] The MP stressed the importance of factors lying outside the scope of the substantive liability regime. An academic commentator of Hungarian product liability law – Maczonkai – concluded that it was indeed impossible to ascertain the true position of Hungarian consumers by analysing court judgements. How often did cases such as those analysed in Part II of this book find their way to courts? More importantly, how consistent were the courts in following the breakthrough judgements (Maczonkai 1996: 115)? Unfortunately, data on these

350 It is by no means submitted that the politician considered the regime of the Directive unsatisfactory. Rather he concluded that the sum total of protection provided to Hungarian consumers was inadequate.

issues is unavailable (Maczonkai 1996: 115, Kecskés 1994). Maczonkai conducted quite a comprehensive analysis of the existing case law on product liability in Hungary, but he also concluded that the very nature of product liability litigation involving rare cases with considerable damages and significant costs does not allow one to ascertain the true situation by looking at decided cases. The number of cases reported in the literature was small, and it would be an overstatement to claim that Hungarian product liability regime was satisfactory based upon this insignificant number of judgements. On the other hand, the circumstances surrounding the operation of product liability laws – political attitudes, economic conditions, attitudes of the legal profession and consumer awareness – are all of relevance for ensuring adequate remedies for consumers. The implementation of the Product Liability Directive, which in the case of Hungary entailed no more than, in most aspects, condensing or simply summarizing in a written document the already existing principles, is therefore not likely to combat the said 'defencelessness'. It is the transformation of the 'context' of the law that should achieve this aim. It appears that Hungarian political and academic thought was largely prepared for the challenges of the new, market-focused consumer policies and laws.

Among the Czechoslovak legal scholars there were those who, satisfied with the fault-based regime of liability for defective products, claimed no reform was desired in general. According to them, strict liability ought to be introduced, if at all, only for certain specific products such as medicines and chemicals (see the analysis of the viewpoints of the doctrine by Svestka 1989: 103). The motive set forth by this group was securing the interests of all those involved in the market for products – hence not only the consumers, but also the industry. The argument was that the presence of strict liability rules in the area of manufacturing of products would discourage the innovation and technological progress, as well as prevent the improvement of labour organization methods (Svestka 1989: 103). Another group of Czechoslovak scholars emphasized social justice in distributing the risk of losses onto those who were in a position to avoid the damage caused by defective products (Svestka 1989: 104). This group concluded that consumers, as economically weaker, inexperienced and lacking professional knowledge about products, were the least able to avert the risk. Hence, the liability for defective products ought to be strict, and not based upon fault which may or may not have existed and does in any event require a considerable effort to show. Among the proponents of this view there were those who contended that sellers should be made strictly liable to consumers, and others who claimed that manufacturers should be liable. Svestka argued that the former option was an easier one from the point of view of the buyers, as the seller is known and is usually placed geographically closer to them (1989: 105). Further, sellers' liability is 'only provisional', as, after having settled the consumer's claim, the former can recover the damages from manufacturers. Still, the advantages which the ability to sue the seller provides to buyers do not necessarily remain in the case of victims other than buyers.[351] Svestka seems to have forgotten about this, indeed crucial, group, probably following the general tendency in Czechoslovakia in the times when his paper was written. Another part of the group of strict liability proponents argued the need for strict liability of manufacturers of defective products, or their importers (Svestka 1989: 106). Such liability regime seemed to them to better satisfy the postulate of fairness and social justice than placing the liability on the sellers. The fundamental requirements of their liability would be the defectiveness of the product, the damage caused to the consumer, and the causal relation between those. This group also took into consideration victims other than buyers, concluding that rendering the manufacturer liable avoids the hurdles of privity of contract. Even this group was, however, still cautious in attempting to strike a fine balance between the interests of industry and the interests of consumers. Svestka points out their will to place the provisions on strict product liability, once they arrive, outside the Civil Code (1989: 107).

The Polish doctrine of law used examples of the United States or the existing Member States of the European Union as a rationale for reform of the existing regime, which was considered unsatisfactory by many (Nesterowicz 1979, Łętowska 1983). The regime based on fault, although as a result of some groundbreaking judgements facilitated with the concepts of 'anonymous fault', *res ipsa loquitur* or evidence *prima facie*, was seen as inadequate and far from the achievements of American and Western European regimes (Gnela 2000, Łętowska 1999, 1983, Nesterowicz 1979). The increased risks for consumers carried by the progress in the fields of science and technology were noted and legal writers postulated the change in allocation of risks following such dangerous activities (Nesterowicz 1979). Most representatives of the Polish doctrine of law adopted the *eius periculum, cuius commodum* theory in order to justify the stricter liability of producers, sellers and even importers (Nesterowicz 1979, Łętowska 2001: 125). On the other hand, the implementation of the Directive in Poland took place relatively late (in 2000), and this was partly the result of the recognition that the fragile position of Polish industry may not warrant the burden of a new strict liability regime. This issue is explored further in Chapter 6 of Part II.

In the light of the internal movement prompting the reform within the substantive product liability law, Central Europeans were quite receptive to the new approach to product liability and consumer protection brought in by the Directive. It was, of course, also acknowledged that the essence of the required reforms lie elsewhere than in substantive product liability laws, and the major elements of the reform process were explored above.

351 Also, in cases where the seller is for some reason judgement-proof, the situation for a victim of a product sold by that seller is far from satisfactory if there is no possibility of taking action against another participant in the chain of supply.

Conclusions to Part I

On the one hand, Part I of the book has built the foundations of the further substantive analysis of the Central European product liability regimes. On the other hand, it constitutes a largely self-contained multi-disciplinary survey of a number of phenomena surrounding product liability laws and their practice in Europe, seeking answers to the following questions: why is Central European product liability law 'in transition', and what are the key features of this transition? It even ventures into searching for the possible impact of the transition on the wider process of harmonization of product liability law within the European Union.

Part I showed the complex nature of product liability and demonstrated the intricacy of the process of its harmonization in Europe. The insights into the complexity of product liability were provided by observing its legal, economic and social context, and the manner in which these phenomena developed in Western and Central Europe. It is clear that product liability law has very specific features and aims. Part I showed what these are, and demonstrated how they evolved in Western and Central Europe. While the nature of product liability requires certain common political, economic and legal features necessary for its very existence, it also entails very close links with the political and regulatory framework, market and consumer law, economic and social models of a particular country. Central European systems retain their own specific mark on the approach to the role, features and context of product liability law and practice.

PART II
Product Liability Systems in Central Europe – Domestic Contract and Tort Law, Implementation of the Product Liability Directive

Introduction

Part I demonstrated the peculiarity of Central European product liability regimes by exploring the history, the role, the context and the main features of product liability law in the 'West' and the 'East'. Part II is devoted to substantive law of product liability and its practice in Central Europe. It portrays the development of national contract and tort law rules, as well as the provisions implementing the Product Liability Directive. Many similarities with the evolution of the law and practice in Western Europe are noted. Tortious liability gradually replaced contractual liability. The requirement of fault upon which tortious liability was traditionally based was transformed into a much more objective liability standard.

In accordance with the historical development of product liability regimes across Central Europe, Part II starts with an examination of contract liability (Chapter 4), follows with tortious liability for 'fault' and the national 'strict liability' rules (Chapter 5), and concludes with the implementation of the Product Liability Directive (Chapter 6).

Chapter 4
Contract Liability

INTRODUCTION

Contract law of the Czech Republic, Hungary and Poland was shaped similarly with the contract laws of other civil law systems, although for some time it gained a range of characteristics brought in by socialism.

Although contractual liability was the primary form of product liability, the evolution of product liability systems in Central Europe tended to steer away from contract law (as with the developments in the United States and Western Europe). Contract law was seen as unable to fulfil the requirements of the new liability system – a system which was to play a very specific role in modern market economies.[1] The focus on bilateral transactions and the consequent restriction to those 'privy to contract' did not fit the reality of modern markets in which those injured by defective products on the one hand and those who were in the best position to bear liability on the other were often excluded from the scope of liability. Its focus on pecuniary damages also did not reflect the growing emphasis on the protection of an individual and the resulting focus on compensation of non-pecuniary damage. The analysis below explores how Central Europe did use contract law in product liability cases and presents attempts to overcome some of the weaknesses of contractual liability. Ultimately, however, it is clear that contract law was not considered adequately equipped to handle product liability cases. The exception to this rule remains to some extent the Czech Republic, where contractual liability is still chosen whenever there is a contract between the injured person and the defendant (seller, supplier or manufacturer).[2]

As a rule, contractual liability arises out of a failure to fulfil a contractual obligation or a failure to fulfil it correctly (Gnela 2000: 122, Jagielska 1999: 23). When goods are transferred under a contract,[3] liability may arise when their quality

1 See Part I for the analysis of the role played by product liability. See Pasa and Benacchio (2005: 101): they point out that "the rules which sustain product liability answer to different needs and criteria" than rules governing consumer contracts.

2 It is unclear how the implementation of the Product Liability Directive will affect this approach by Czech courts.

3 Although very often goods are transferred under contracts of sale, and these contracts are the key focus of this chapter, it must be remembered that many other types of contracts have a similar result, such as loan, rental, licence, (Gnela 2000: 123) barter, exchange, gift, bailment, hire-purchase (Atiyah 2001: 7–22).

or safety do not correspond with the contract (Gnela 2000: 122).[4] Damage which arises in such situations may be limited solely to the defective product (normally occurring when the product is not of an expected quality), or it may extend onto other property or a person (Jagielska 1999: 25). It can have a pecuniary or non-pecuniary nature. Generally, damage limited to the defective product does not trigger product liability. Cases related to the inadequate or unsatisfactory quality of products are singled out by many legal systems and regulated by distinct regimes of liability, again relatively independent from ordinary contractual liability.[5] They are not analysed here (Sengayen 2002).

THE HISTORICAL BACKGROUND AND FEATURES OF CONTRACTUAL PRODUCT LIABILITY IN CENTRAL EUROPE

In common with the rest of Europe, Central European contractual liability for defective products is the creation of courts. Historically, the defective nature of goods was considered to be a form of non-compliance with the contract of sale. The seller–producer was the most appropriate person to be held responsible for making (usually hand-making) and delivering safe goods (Jagielska 1999: 21). In the beginning of the twentieth century, however, the market conditions changed. On the one hand, the distribution chains leading to the ultimate consumers have grown (hence, reducing the possibility of quality and safety control by the

4 In academic writings of Central Europe this situation was described as delivery of a product not of the contractually stipulated quality or safety, or alternatively, delivery of a product with defects not known to the buyer (Jagielska 1999: 23).

5 The regime of legal and commercial guarantees is autonomous because its purposes are not necessarily similar to the purposes of contractual liability in general. While in case of an 'ordinary breach' of contract the principal remedy is compensation, in cases of inadequate quality of a product it is perceived that the remedy should rather focus on ensuring performance (exchange of the defective product for one without defects, repair or decrease in the price) or the possibility of a quick termination of the unsatisfactory contractual relationship (Łętowska 1999: 294). Legal and commercial guarantees are primarily aimed at satisfying the needs of consumers who, as the ultimate users of products, are particularly interested in obtaining a satisfactory product, hence the need to abandon the strict application of the principle *pacta sunt servanda* in these liability regimes (ibid.). In the Polish Civil Code legal and commercial guarantees are regulated by Articles 556–82, in the Czechoslovak Civil Code, Sections 247–56, in the amended Czech Civil Code, Sections 596–600 regarding contracts of sale and barter in general, and Sections 616–27 regarding 'Sale of goods in shops' (additional requirements upon those selling goods in the course of a business), and in the Hungarian Civil Code, Articles 305–11. Central European states implemented the Directive 1999/44/EC *on certain aspects of the sale of consumer goods and associated guarantees* (Consumer Sales Directive) – see EU Consumer Law Acquis Database: <http://www.eu-consumer-law.org/directives_en.cfm>. See Sengayen (2002) for the analysis of Central European guarantee laws.

sellers). On the other hand, products have become complex and often dangerous, capable of injuring not only the buyers but also their family, friends or even mere bystanders. The legal changes gradually started following the economic and social transformations, albeit not as accurately as one might expect. Courts operating within the realms of contract law, although gradually vitiating the privity limits, could not handle the new reality effectively. When American and later Western European courts started introducing changes into their liability regimes in the 1930s, recognizing tort law as the panacea for inadequacies of contract law, Central Europeans recently freed from the domination of the Empires[6] were not yet concerned with these issues. After the Second World War the Civil Codes were enacted throughout Central Europe. While on the one hand they were marked with socialist ideas, the general principles of contract liability were still very much cognate with the liability rules of Western European civil law systems. After the initial stagnation caused by strict adherence to the philosophy of socialism, and following the political and economic changes described in Part I, Central European courts started using these general principles and attempted to apply them in product liability cases. They encountered similar problems to those tackled earlier in the 'West', and took relatively dynamic steps to overcome them (analysed in this chapter).

A short note introducing the main principles of the Central European contract law and their implications for product liability is due at this point. As mentioned in Part I, Central European civil law has been constructed around the concept of 'legal acts'.[7] A contract is defined by the Central European doctrine of law as "a mutual legal act, that is one involving two parties" (Czachórski 2002: 127)[8] or as a "lawful act done with the aim of achieving a legal effect" ('juristic act' – Harmathy 1998: 95).[9] A contract is said to consist in a "wilful intention of the parties, aimed at creation, amendment or termination of legal effects" (Czachórski 2002: 127).[10] Central European contractual liability, in common with other continental liability regimes, is based upon the requirement of 'fault'.[11] The 'fault' is presumed, and in product liability litigation this presumption means that the victim of a defective product must show other requisites of liability: breach of contract, damage, and the causal link between them. The defendant, on the other hand, needs to prove he was not 'at fault'. In the evolution of the Central European product liability regimes the latter task was rendered increasingly difficult. In Hungary the view of the courts

6 See Chapter 2 of Part I for an account of the history of Central European legal systems.

7 Terms 'juristic' and 'lawful' are also used by academic writers.

8 Translated by the author.

9 The concept of 'legal acts' (or 'juristic acts' as it is sometimes referred to) was introduced in Chapter 2 of Part I.

10 Translated by the author of the book.

11 The contractual 'fault' is often interpreted in a different manner than in tortious liability. See the analysis below.

evolved towards disregard of the existence or non-existence of 'fault', hence effectively leading to 'strict liability'. In Czechoslovakia and the Czech Republic the defendants needed to show they exercised due care in fulfilling contractual obligations. Although there were cases when the defendants could avoid liability, such cases were not very frequent (Svestka 1989). The Polish contractual product liability regime required the party in breach (usually the seller) to show maximum care.[12] The liability of professionals was stricter than that of non-professional contractual parties. Although there was a very strong conviction throughout Central Europe that contractual 'fault' was different than tortious 'fault', the two-stage structure of the concept (objective and subjective element)[13] was common in contract law as well. Further, similarly with the evolution of tortious liability explored below, here the courts increasingly focused on the objective elements. In the context of product liability this meant an increased focus on the defects in products and less focus on the defendant's conduct.

FREEDOM OF CONTRACT, ITS LIMITS AND ITS INFLUENCE ON CENTRAL EUROPEAN PRODUCT LIABILITY SYSTEMS

Part I explored some more generic issues related to freedom of contract and the development of its limitations concerned with the need to protect consumers in Western Europe. Freedom of contract is a crucial legal principle, but it is explored here only with regard to its particular implications for contractual product liability. What are these implications? Freedom of contract gives rise to one of the most characteristic features of contracts – the possibility of broadening or limiting the scope of liability. Product liability regimes appeared as a result of mass markets and mass production. The key feature of these is a standard form contract (an adhesion contract). Such contracts are particularly challenging for consumers, as they may contain exemption clauses by which professionals purport to limit their liability for a breach of contract. Modern legal systems have therefore reduced the scope of freedom of contract to prevent this situation from occurring to the detriment of consumers. At present freedom of contract is limited by similar constraints in Central Europe as there exist in Western Europe, mostly for reasons associated with the need for protection of consumers (Howells and Weatherill 2005: 14–18).

Since the nineteenth century the principle of freedom of contract has been the leading feature of most traditional contract law regimes (Wagner 1974: 43).[14]

12 See the analysis of Article 472 of the Civil Code, below.

13 Described in Part I, and in more detail below and in Chapter 5 of Part II.

14 Łętowska pointed out that even in the nineteenth century, when freedom of contract was the principal concept governing market relations, purely formal equality was not considered 'fair' or 'just' (1999: 4). However, giving formally equal rights to contractual parties together with the manner in which the then markets were operating was believed to have been sufficient to ensure equality of opportunities for market participants

While formally contract laws of socialist Central Europe have also been functioning based upon respect for the principle of freedom of contract, this principle was virtually abandoned or, according to other writers, severely restricted (Wagner 1974: 45).[15] The rationale for this phenomenon was to some extent explored in Part I, which depicted the key characteristics of the socialist ideology and its impact on markets and laws in Central Europe. Wagner wrote that freedom of contract was widely believed to have been a crucial feature distinguishing "a traditional legal system from a socialist one" (1974: 44). He also, however, contended that this was only true to some extent – as an absolute freedom of contract did not exist in the Western European jurisdictions, and even the socialist legal systems knew this freedom (ibid.). According to Marxist philosophy, freedom of contract could not operate effectively in capitalist markets where differences in wealth determined the stronger position of the "industrial colossus" capable of imposing its terms upon weaker parties (Lasok 1973: 12). However, socialism did not offer a system able to fight these disadvantages of capitalism successfully. Lasok pointed out that "in a system of state monopoly and the scarcity of consumer goods still persisting in the socialist world the citizen has practically no choice and little satisfaction from complaints. … with the predominant proportion of the '*contrat-type*' in the socialist system the comparative discussion about the freedom of contract has been denuded of any real significance" (1973: 12, 13). Contracts between two 'socialist organizations'[16] were very often the consequence of an administrative decision (in these cases one could refer unambiguously to an obligation to conclude a contract). Decisions on concluding these contracts as well as their contents, directly linked to central planning of the national economy, were strictly regulated (Czachórski 2002: 138). The main aim of such contracts was the realization of centrally planned economic tasks. Civil Codes of many socialist countries contained specific provisions on planned contracts. In relations not involving two 'socialist organizations' freedom of contract had much more importance during the socialist period. It was obviously limited by factors influenced by socialism,[17] but also other factors, increasingly resembling the Western European rationales for restrictions in freedom of contract.[18]

(1999: 4). Wagner added that the rule of freedom of contract, "triumphantly asserted in the XIX century, during the period of economic liberalism", was even then restricted by "considerations of public order and morality" (1974: 44).

15 For a more detailed examination of the principle of freedom of contract, its effects and limitations in the socialist states see Wagner 1974: 43–64.

16 See Part I for an explanation of the meaning of this term, and how these relations were to some extent more distinctly regulated than relations between other market participants.

17 Mostly economic and political factors, examined in Part I.

18 Again, see Part I for an elaboration of the changes within the Central European civil laws accommodating the restrictions on freedom of contract in order to protect consumers (especially the amendments to the Hungarian and the Czech Civil Codes).

At present, after the repeal of the provisions on planned contracts and other rules affected by the socialist ideology, the picture of freedom of contract in Central Europe resembles the one in Western Europe.[19] Poland, Hungary and the Czech Republic implemented the Unfair Contract Terms Directive which comprehensively harmonizes the rules concerning control of contractual clauses in business-to-consumer contracts.[20]

CONTRACTUAL LIABILITY IN THE CIVIL CODES

The following analysis of provisions of Central European Civil Codes is conducted in chronological order – the Hungarian Code was adopted first, with the Czech and Polish Codes analysed respectively.

The Hungarian Civil Code (Act IV of 1959 *on the Civil Code of the Hungarian Republic*)[21] to some extent combines regulation of contractual liability with tortious liability.[22] Article 339[23] is to be applied in conjunction with Article 318[24] (Harmathy 1998: 113). Section 318 paragraph 1 of the Code provides:

> The provisions on tort liability shall be applied to liability for breach of contract and to the extent of indemnification, with the difference that such indemnification may not be reduced, unless otherwise prescribed by law.[25]

---

19 For reasons of space, clarity and consistency the issue of control of contracts, and in particular the control of unfair contract terms and the situation in Central Europe with regard to this problem, have been omitted from the scope of the book. Suffice it to say that at the moment all the Central European states implemented the Unfair Contract Terms Directive. In Hungary the control of unfair terms in contracts took place, although on a less grand scale, also during the time of socialism – see Wagner (1974: 11, 47), Zoll (1997), Harmathy (1998: 104), Gnela (2000: 148).

20 Council Directive 93/13/EEC of 5 April 1993 *on unfair terms in consumer contracts*. See EU Consumer Law Acquis Database for further information concerning the implementation of the Directive: <http://www.eu-consumer-law.org/directives_en.cfm>.

21 *évi IV. törvény a Polgári Törvénykönyvről*. Available online (in English) at: <http://www.angelfire.com/mn2/reformclub/hunc1.html>. The analysis below rather refrains from using this online version, however, and instead refers to translations provided by the Ministry of Justice and if these are not clear, by legal practitioners.

22 It is inspired by the Austrian ABGB, which stipulates in Paragraph 1295 subs. 1: "Everyone is entitled to demand compensation of the person who did him harm by fault; the harm may be caused by breach of contract or may have no relation to a contract" (Koziol 2005: 11).

23 In Part Four Obligations, Title II Tort Liability and Liability for Unjust Enrichment, Chapter XXIX General Rules of Damages.

24 In Part Four Obligations, Title I Contracts, Chapter XXV Breach of Contract. Common Provisions Pertaining to Breach of Contract.

25 This is the translation provided by the Hungarian Ministry of Justice – analysed by Dr Gáros Péter (Department for the Codification of Civil Law) at the Institute for European

Another, perhaps clearer translation of the same provision provides:

> In respect of the liability for breach of contract and of the level of the compensation for damages, the rules on the liability for damages caused outside contractual relations shall be applied, with the difference that the compensation for damages shall not be lowered, except provided otherwise by law.[26]

There is no significant difference between these two translations, apart from the fact that one of them refers to tort liability and the other to liability for damages caused outside contractual relations. It was already explained in Part I that these terms are often used interchangeably.

Section 339 paragraph 1 of the Code, which is also analysed below in Chapter 5 concerning tort liability, specifies:

> (1) Someone who causes damage to another in violation of the law, shall be liable for such damage. He shall be exempted from that liability if he proves that he has acted in a manner that is generally expected in the given situation.
>
> (2) The court shall, under special and equitable circumstances, be entitled to grant partial exemption from liability to a person for damages.[27]

The defendant can thus be exonerated from liability if she can prove that she has taken all steps expected in the circumstances (fault liability – Harmathy 1998: 113). In contrast to tort, liability cannot be reduced on equitable grounds (as prescribed by Article 318 paragraph 1, referring to Article 339 paragraph 2). For the purposes of assessing the operation of the contractual product liability regime in Hungary these provisions are examined in detail below.

An additional basis for claiming compensation in contractual relations is established by Article 310 of the Code. In addition to claiming redress for breach of warranty rights (in implementation of the Injunctions Directive 99/44/EC), Article 310 allows the claimant to be compensated for damages "resulting from deficient performance", unless the defendant proves that "he has acted in the manner that can generally be expected in the given situation".[28]

The Draft Hungarian Civil Code significantly changes the manner in which contractual liability is regulated. First and foremost, it is aimed to separate the

---

and Comparative Law, Oxford University, in February 2006.

26 Translation by Éless and Németh (*Hungary* Response to the Commission's Green Paper *Damages Actions for breach of the EC antitrust rules*), at p. 2. The issue of limiting compensation is further analysed in Chapter 5 concerning tort liability – it refers to Section 339, paragraph 2 of the Civil Code which provides that compensation of damages may be reduced "under special and equitable circumstances" ('the Conception' to the Draft Code).

27 Translation provided by the Hungarian Ministry of Justice.

28 Ibid.

regulation of contractual and tortious liability. As mentioned in Part I, the Draft introduces a new outlook on the law of obligations. It contains a new general part on obligations as a whole, supplemented with largely separate regulation of contracts and torts. The new provisions concerning contractual liability are now contained in Part Two *Common Rules of Contracts*, Title V *Breach of Contract*, Chapter I *Common Provisions pertaining to Breach of Contract. Liability for Damages caused by Breach of Contract*, Sections 5:128 and 5:129.

Section 5:128:

> Someone who causes damage to another by way of a breach of contract, shall be obliged to repair the damage. He shall be relieved from liability if he proves that the breach was due to circumstances which are out of his sphere of interest and beyond his control, and not foreseeable at the time of the conclusion of the contract.

Section 5:129:

> (1) The injured party may be entitled to damages covering his actual loss.
>
> (2) Consequential losses and unrealised profit shall only be repaired to the extent to which the injured party proves that the possible consequences of the breach of the contract were foreseeable at the time of the conclusion of the contract.
>
> (3) In case of damage caused intentionally or with gross negligence, the injured party may claim damages also for losses, which were not foreseeable until the breach of the contract.[29]

As explained further in 'the Conception' (Regulatory Syllabus of the Draft Civil Code), contractual liability will no longer be based on fault. The change is said to be in line with the "international commercial standards" such as those introduced by the 1980 Vienna Convention on international sale of goods (Article 79)[30] and to some extent also the Principles of European Contract Law 1998.[31] 'The Conception' explains that contractual liability rules are mostly concerned with commercial dealings, where liability ought to be divorced from considerations of any efforts undertaken by contractual parties.[32] 'The Conception' stresses the

29 Draft provided by the Hungarian Ministry of Justice – analysed by Dr Gáros Péter at the Institute for European and Comparative Law, Oxford University, in February 2006.

30 United Nations Convention on Contracts for the International Sale of Goods, 1980 (CISG) (incorporated into Hungarian law by Decree No. 20 of 1987).

31 'The Conception', p. 143.

32 This approach reflects the new focus of civil law – the newly created market economy. 'The Conception' explains that so far civil law, and particularly contract law, was focused upon private dealings (contract law following the requirements of private

role of contractual liability in the business context as being risk distribution as opposed to penalizing "faulty conduct".[33] The sanctions for contractual breaches ought therefore to satisfy "bankrupted legitimate expectations" irrespective of the existence or non-existence of fault.[34] 'The Conception' points out that the approach of the Draft is not a novelty in the Hungarian legal system. It merely incorporates into written law the current practice of Hungarian courts which for some time have seen contractual liability as based on objective standards (enabling the defendant to exculpate himself only if circumstances beyond his control were shown).[35] While an objective liability standard is the general rule, the requirements of specific contracts, those not concluded in the business context, are also to be recognized by the new Civil Code (for example contracts for medical treatment) – here liability is to be regulated separately and is to retain the fault requirement.[36] Consumer contracts are not mentioned at this point. These contracts are to some extent regulated separately within the Draft, where the provisions of implemented EC consumer directives are incorporated. The Draft is based on the concept of unity of civil law, and thus the implemented consumer directives, which so far were contained in various legislative and administrative mechanisms – the Civil Code, the Consumer Protection Act of 1997, government decrees, and other legislative and administrative acts – are largely incorporated into the Civil Code.[37] A number of sanctions for traders breaching their obligations are included there. In the context of product liability, however, general provisions regulating contractual liability will apply. It will be interesting to see the effect of the shift to strict liability on product liability cases, although in the light of the developments in case law illustrated below this effect may seem quite insignificant.

The Czech civil law is also largely based on Austrian ABGB, and, as mentioned above, the latter does not distinguish between contractual and non-contractual liability (Tichy 2002a: 107). Each subsequent repeal or amendment of the Civil Code took over this construction. Neither the doctrine of law (Sedláček)[38] nor the

---

transactions with some adjustments and special provisions for business transactions – this created inconsistencies and lack of clarity which did not serve business interests even during socialist times – at p. 105). 'The Conception' specifies that needs of business transactions must be recognized in the rules of contractual liability because these transactions are very important for national economy.

33 At p. 142.

34 Ibid.

35 Judgements: Gf. II 30 137/1980: BH 1981/330; Gf. V. 30 605/1981: BH 1982/524 – quoted in 'the Conception', at p. 143.

36 'The Conception', p. 143.

37 'The Conception', p. 108.

38 J. Sedláček (1932: 669 *et seq*). See, however, J. Krčmář (1932: 301), who acknowledged that there was a certain degree of difference between contractual and non-contractual liability and they ought to be treated as existing alongside each other. However, he did not explain further what this would have meant in practice.

judicial practice[39] questioned this approach, which remains in the Czech law until today. The relevant provisions of the Civil Code will, therefore, be analysed twice throughout the book.

Before the significant amendment of the Czechoslovak Civil Code in 1991,[40] the Code contained Sections 420 and 421. Although they to referred both contractual and tortious liability, the sections separately regulated liability of legal and physical persons (the latter referred to in the Code as 'citizens', the former as 'organizations'). Contractual liability was seen within the framework of a breach of duty. The legal duties mentioned by the relevant Sections of the Czech Code can derive from legal provisions (in which case the breach is treated as a tort)[41] or from a contract or another type of agreement (breach of contract, breach of the agreement) (Vondracek 1988: 377).

Section 420 read:

> 1. A citizen is liable for damage which he has caused by infringement of a legal duty.
>
> 2. A citizen is exonerated from liability if he proves he was not at fault in causing the damage.[42]

Section 421 read:

> 1. An organization is liable to a citizen for damage which it has caused by infringement of a legal duty.
>
> 3. An organization is exonerated from liability if it can prove that it could not have prevented the damage even by the exertion of every effort which can be required from it. An organization, however, cannot be exonerated from its liability by pleading that it was following the orders of superior organs.[43]

The Code was amended in 1991 and now Section 420 (which can be found in Part Six *Liability For Damage and For Unjustified Enrichment*, Chapter 2 *Liability for Damage*) refers to liability of all persons. It reads:

> 1. Everyone shall be liable for damage caused by violating a legal duty.

39 The decisions of the Czechoslovak Supreme Court No. 6207 and No. 2398.
40 Act no. 509/1991 Coll., came into effect on 1 January 1992.
41 See the development of these ideas in the following chapter concerning torts.
42 From the commentary of the Code by Vondracek (1988: 375).
43 Ibid., p. 378.

> 3. A person who proves not to have caused the damage shall relieve himself of the liability for it.[44]

The rationale behind such a change of approach towards uniform treatment of all persons was given in the explanatory report of the amended Section 420, which stipulated that the amendment was "the result of a newly conceived, real equality of rights between subjects of civil law relationships" (Dobiasova 2003: 2). Another change was the apparent omission of the express reference to 'fault' in the new Section 420. This issue is analysed further in Chapter 5 on tort liability, but it does not appear to be the case that general civil liability became strict as a result of this amendment (especially in the light of the fact that a distinct strict liability provision was introduced in Section 420a, again analysed in Chapter 5). On the other hand, the amendment certainly indicates a certain level of 'objectivization' of liability (Tichy 2005: 53), which may have been the reinforcement of earlier jurisprudential attempts aiming to objectivize civil liability (those are analysed below in the context of product liability litigation).

It is crucial to indicate at this point that the regulation of contractual liability in the Czech Republic is likely to change further with the imminent introduction of the new Civil Code, a number of drafts of which appeared recently (Hradek 2006, Tichy 2002a: 118–20). The author obtained an unofficial translation of the draft Civil Code as it stood in August 2006, with some changes incorporated in 2008, from Tichy and Hradek (the authors of the translation). At first sight, the draft Code appears to introduce some confusion with regard to the tendency to regulate contractual and tortious liability by the same provisions, introduced by the previous Codes. According to Tichy, "the draft makes a significant differentiation between law of tort liability and contractual liability" (2002a: 119). Division 2 *Duty to compensate damage*, Subdivision 1 *General provisions*, Section 2412 of the draft (as translated by Tichy and Hradek) stipulates:

> Everybody is obliged to compensate damage he has caused by a culpable breach of legal obligations towards others.

This provision can be found in Chapter Three of the draft Code, which is entitled 'Tort Liability', not in the 'General Liability' chapter as before. It appears to stress the requirement of fault in civil liability, which is not expressly stated in the current Civil Code. Although Section 2412 does not expressly differentiate between different types of legal obligations, and thus seems to apply both to contractual and tortious duties, Section 2416 provides:

> (1) A person that has caused damage by breaching a *contractual obligation* may release himself from liability to compensate damage if it is proved that he was

44 From the translation of the Code provided by Monika Dobiasova of the Czech Ministry of Trade and Industry.

> prevented from performance of the obligation temporarily or permanently by force majeure representing an extraordinary, unpredictable and non-avertable obstacle preventing the contracting party from performance of a contractual obligation, which force majeure occurred independently of the person's will.
>
> (2) A contracting party may not invoke an obstacle resulting out of its personal relations, an obstacle occurring only after the time when the party was already in delay with the performance, nor an obstacle, which, under the contract, the party was obliged to overcome by securing a respective permit or otherwise.[45]

These two provisions, if interpreted together, create a puzzling picture of contractual liability. Although Section 2412 indicates liability for fault, Section 2416 shows that contractual liability is stricter than liability in tort (where fault is presumed, of which below). The fact that Section 2416 expressly mentions and indeed so exhaustively defines only the *force majeure*, implies that this indeed may be the sole defence in cases of contractual liability. The draft appears to be a step towards separation of contractual from tortious liability, and towards stricter contractual liability.

The Polish Civil Code of 1964 regulates contractual liability in Book 3 'Obligations', Title 7 'Performance of obligations and the effects of non-performance', Division 2 'The effects of non-performance of obligations'. Article 471 stipulates:

> The debtor is required to repair the loss resulting from non-performance or incorrect performance of an obligation, unless the non-performance or the incorrect performance are the results of factors for which the debtor is not responsible.[46]

The provision seems to be referring to obligations in general, not only contractual obligations. This is only ostensibly misleading, as Article 487 of the Civil Code concerning 'obligations arising from contracts'[47] refers to Article 471 as the one applicable, and tortious liability is regulated in a separate provision – Article 415, analysed in Chapter 5.

Two main elements of Article 471 need to be examined in detail as particularly relevant in the product liability context. First of all, the conceptual frame of the notions of non-performance and incorrect performance by the debtor, and,

45 Emphasis added.

46 The provision remained unchanged since it was first inserted into the Code in 1964. Translated by the author.

47 In fact, the Code uses the term 'mutual contracts' – this is the result of the fact that contracts do not require consideration, reciprocity (necessary in common law systems), to be legally valid in Poland.

secondly, the cases in which the debtor would not be responsible. The analysis is conducted in a further part of this chapter.

Below is an examination of how the provisions mentioned above were interpreted by the Central European courts and doctrine of law for the needs of the product liability systems. The analysis follows the structure of the main elements of civil obligations elaborated on in Part I: it observes developments in the concept of breach of contract, and the role of 'fault' and 'defect' in it, the notion of contractual damage, and causal considerations. It then portrays other significant issues such as burden of proof and time limits for claims. It concludes with an evaluation of the benefits and weaknesses of contractual liability in the product liability context.

BREACH OF CONTRACT: 'CONTRACTUAL FAULT' AND 'DEFECT'

INTRODUCTION

The rationale behind the methodological approach to analysing together these seemingly separate elements of civil liability ('fault' and 'defect') was explored in Part I. In the development of product liability systems, with the transformation of the liability standard into a more objective one, the language of 'fault' gave way to the much greater emphasis on 'defect'. This gradual progression towards a 'defect-focused' liability did not, however, entail a complete abandonment of all the elements of the 'fault' discourse – such as reasonability, predictability and other considerations pertaining to the conduct of defendants. The analysis below portrays this evolution.

In the context of contractual liability for products, a breach of contract does not have to consist in supplying a dangerous product (which is normally a requirement for tortious liability), but simply a product of an inferior quality. According to the Polish doctrine and case law, lack of the required safety or quality in a product is generally understood to be an example of an incorrect performance of a contract (Pajor 1982: 114, Skąpski 1976: 118, 145, Jagielska 1999: 24). A similar position can be seen in the Czechoslovak and Czech case law and scholarly writings[48] (providing a defective product to the buyer gives rise to the seller's liability: Svestka 1989: 96–100),[49] and in Hungary (Maczonkai 1996: 110–11). However, it is universally accepted that only those defects which lead to consequential damage (damage outside the defective product itself) can give rise to product liability.

In fact, this focus on the condition of supplied products grew throughout the evolution of product liability systems, turning away from the common feature of Central European contractual product liability systems – the requirement of

48 Czechoslovak and Czech case law were very clear in distinguishing the liability for "defects of a sold product and liability for damage or loss caused by a sold defective product" (Svestka 1989: 96). See below.

49 'Sellers' were referred to by Svestka as 'trading corporations'.

'fault'. In general, contractual liability puts much less emphasis on 'fault' than tortious liability – this tendency can clearly be observed in Central Europe. The prevalent view is that the contractual 'fault' is a different concept than tortious 'fault'. Although Central European scholars see 'fault' in its broadest sense as including an objective and a subjective element, the objective element in contractual liability is "contractual unlawfulness" (Gnela 2000: 124). This 'unlawfulness' is interpreted differently from the 'unlawfulness' in tortious liability. It is a breach of contract – an incorrect fulfilment of a contractual promise. The subjective element, in turn, is "not exercising due care" when fulfilling an obligation (Żuławska 1987: 196, 197).[50] The reality of modern market relationships required reconsideration of the requirement of 'fault' in contract law, especially as regards the level of care required of a professional contractual party.[51] Following doctrinal postulates and court decisions, contractual liability in Central Europe has become much more objective in standard, often bordering on strict liability. In many cases, including those involving product liability, defendants' conduct and the level of care exercised by them played very little if any part in the decisions of courts to establish their liability. The courts in Central Europe recognized the specificity of business-to-consumer contractual relations, which generally entailed much more stringent liability standards than the Civil Codes would indicate. More fundamental changes of contractual liability standards are under way in Central Europe at present. Contractual liability is affected by developments on the European Community level, in particular by various consumer protection directives, and other international law instruments – such as the Vienna Convention on International Sale of Goods (CISG)[52] – which also require changes in the contractual liability standard. These developments may well be formalized in the forthcoming Civil Codes of Hungary and the Czech Republic. Both the Hungarian and the Czech drafts and commentaries to them indicated such a possibility. The Polish Codification Commission has not so far noted any suggestions of this kind ('Green Book').

EMERGING PRODUCT LIABILITY SYSTEMS – BREACH OF CONTRACT – FROM CONDUCT TO DEFECT

The Hungarian Civil Code gives no definition of a breach of contract (Harmathy 1998: 111). 'Fault', however, is clearly one of the key elements of contractual liability.[53] Thus, the defendant must prove she has taken all the necessary steps which would be expected in the circumstances (Harmathy 1998: 113). In product liability cases before Hungarian courts it has not been an easy task for defendants

50 Translated from Polish by the author.

51 See Part I (p.97) for a general introduction to these issues.

52 United Nations Convention on Contracts for the International Sale of Goods, 1980, CISG <http://www.uncitral.org/pdf/english/texts/sales/cisg/CISG.pdf>.

53 There are specific provisions envisaging strict contractual liability (Harmathy 1998: 113, 114), but their analysis falls outside the scope of the book.

(Harmathy 1998: 114). Harmathy even suggested that not much importance has actually been attached to the seller's conduct, and a much more crucial factor in determining liability was "the fact of the defect of the good" (ibid.). In fact, from the case law of Hungarian courts it may be inferred that contractual product liability does not require the existence of 'fault'. Although, in common with Poland, Hungary did not recognize the difference between *obligation de moyens* and *obligation de résultat*, standards of care varied depending upon the circumstances (Article 339, paragraph 1 specifies that all measures expected in the given circumstances must be taken) (Harmathy 1998: 114).

One of the first cases concerned with liability for defective products in Hungary was the 1960 'paint case' (Benedek-Világhy 1965: 301–6). The defective paint was supplied to the entrepreneur (house painter) by a retailer.[54] The paint in the can had different qualities to what the painter expected based upon the information on the can. The painter suffered damage, as the paint was unsuitable for its intended use (Maczonkai 1996: 110). The court rendered the seller liable for the damage, and the basis for his liability was the incorrect information concerning the qualities of the product (thus, the product had an 'information/warning defect'). It was made clear that a very high level of care was required of a party who breached the contract by providing a product with false or incomplete instructions and warnings. In fact, the retailer did not have the opportunity to check the contents of the can of paint, but he could not avoid liability merely by showing that the cause of defect was beyond his control (Maczonkai 1996: 110). Thus the Hungarian court adopted a mechanism very similar to the French '*obligation de garantie*', where a party who is in breach of contract cannot defend herself by claiming that the breach was beyond her control (ibid.). This approach to the issue of contractual 'fault' was repeated in the 'chickens' case (Maczonkai 1996: 110).[55] The retailer was held liable for the death of chickens supplied by him to a farmer. The defect in this case was caused by the chicken breeder who had not handled the animals properly during the process of incubation (example of a 'manufacturing defect') (Maczonkai 1996: 110). The 'turnip cabbage seed case' (Maczonkai 1996: 110), where it was held that the damage caused by inadequate quality of the seeds rendered the seller and the producer liable,[56] ultimately established the approach of the courts to contractual product liability. Although some enquiry into the defendants' conduct was undertaken, ultimately the standard of liability was objective. 'Fault', on which contractual liability was based according to the provisions of the Civil Code, in the practice of product liability no longer constituted a relevant factor.

54 Central European product liability cases, especially the early ones, did not distinguish between consumers and small entrepreneurs – protection was provided for both (although see the remarks concerning the separate regulation of relationships between 'socialist organizations').

55 Also cited by Tamás Tercsák (1993: 224).

56 See below for an elaboration of the concept of 'assistant in performance' which enabled producers to be liable in contract.

Contractual product liability became liability for damages caused by defects in products, irrespective of the level of care exercised by the person liable.

The Czech law requires the presence of 'fault' in contractual liability, and a defendant is able to avoid liability if he proves that he was unable to prevent the damage "with his utmost effort (care) which could have been required of him in the particular situation" (Svestka 1989: 98). The jurisprudence applying this provision in product liability cases did not go as far as in Hungary, and the defendants' conduct remained material in establishing their liability. It has therefore been relatively easier for a 'trade corporation' (seller) to adduce satisfactory evidence of proper conduct than it has been for the manufacturer (normally liable in tort)[57] (Svestka 1989: 101). It was considered more likely that sellers had no influence over the condition of products they sold. Svestka offered a number of examples where a 'trade corporation' was in fact held liable: a breach of an obligation concerning assessment of quality of products, or a failure to make use of adequate practices concerning marketing, storage and maintenance of products (such as: unsuitable storage conditions, neglect in inspections and tests of products, failure to monitor products introduced into circulation and to remove defective products from circulation, or selling expired products) (ibid.). The Supreme Court of the Slovak Socialist Republic in the judgement 29/75 of 1975[58] awarded damages in a case between a buyer of poor-quality cement who suffered consequential damage and a seller. While the courts understood supplying a product which caused damage or loss as a breach of contract (Svestka referred to a "defective-dangerous" product [1989: 103]), it was clear that the conduct of sellers played a very significant part in their liability. This may be gradually changing at the present time. The Czechoslovak civil liability regime has undergone a significant transformation recently, although the precise implications for product liability cannot yet be assessed because of a negligible number of judgements. It appears that the transformations in jurisprudence leading to a more objective liability have been reinforced by the 1991 amendment of the Civil Code:[59] Section 420 abandoned the express reference to 'fault' (these changes are described further in Chapter 5). Tichý argues that "fault, as a characteristic of 'subjective liability' has become a less important prerequisite for liability for damage" (2005: 53).

Although Polish courts were clearly determined formally to retain the requirement of 'fault'[60] in contractual product liability, the standard of care required of defendants was becoming more stringent. During socialism this process started in the activity of arbitration bodies resolving disputes between

57 See Chapter 5.

58 Judgement of the Supreme Court of the Slovak Socialist Republic Cz 29/75. From the contribution of Dobiasova to the Product Liability Database (BIICL).

59 Law No. 40/1964 Coll. (Civil Code) amended by Law No. 509/1991 Coll.

60 This 'fault' was referred to as a 'contractual fault' by Gnela (2000: 124), although Dąbrowa (1968: 142) claimed that in civil obligations one ought to understand fault as a homogeneous concept (common for contract and tort).

'socialist organizations'.[61] In such disputes the existence of fault of the seller was of no importance, as the mere fact of damage caused by the defect in a product was held to determine liability (Cincio-Podbiera 1988). Further, ordinary civil courts avoided emphasizing 'fault' as a material factor in contractual product liability (Gnela 2000: 137).[62] This approach allowed liability to be easily established based solely on the existence of damage caused by a defect in a product. The result of presumption of fault was that the victim of a breach of contract was only obliged to show that she had suffered damage as a result of the breach, and it was the party in breach who had to show that she had exercised all due care.[63] By virtue of Article 355.1 of the Civil Code "the debtor is obliged to exercise care generally required in the particular type of relations (due care)".[64] The requirement of 'due care' applies unless a law provision or a legal act (for instance the contract itself) specify otherwise (Article 472 of the Code). In cases involving professional sellers, the requirements of 'due care' have been very high indeed (Gnela 2000: 140). On the other hand, some doubt was cast upon the exact meaning of 'due care' (Żuławska 1987: 197, Stelmachowski 1984: 87, 88). In relations between 'socialist organizations' it was rather understood as being 'the highest level of care' (Gnela 2000: 126). Such 'highest' level of care was also required from other (non-state) professional parties in other contracts, but lack of uniform interpretation created a level of uncertainty as to the precise meaning of 'due care'. The amendment of the Civil Code in 1990[65] changed this situation for the benefit of non-professional parties in contracts. Since this amendment Article 355.2 reads: "due care of the debtor acting in the course of a business shall be assessed with reference to the professional character of the activity."[66] The liability of the professional contractual parties is therefore more stringent than the liability of non-professionals. The amendment prompted Gnela to express the opinion that at present 'fault' is a rather objective concept in professional contractual liability, and hence in product liability cases 'due care' is insufficient to exonerate the defendant (2000: 127). Thus, according to her, unforeseeable risks ought to be borne by the professionals rather than the consumers (ibid.). Indeed, the tendency in Polish civil law and product liability jurisprudence has been to create a system

61 The tendency was motivated by political reasons: the need for improving the quality of products for the benefit of the national economy (Gnela 2000: 128). The Arbitration bodies went even as far as holding that only a *force majeure* could exonerate the organization in breach of contract (a decision of an administrative body rendering the performance of the contract impossible was treated as such *force majeure*) (Gnela 2000: 128).

62 The statement is based on the jurisprudence of the District Court of Kraków – Pajor (1989).

63 'Due care' – *należyta staranność* – translated by the author (Article 472 of the Civil Code).

64 Translated by the author.

65 Act of 28 July 1990 on the amendment of the Civil Code.

66 Translated by the author.

of liability for damage caused by defective products where 'fault' was not a material factor. What is increasingly emphasized is the notion of 'defect'. Since the first product liability cases this has been the key concept in contractual product liability. In the cases of the Fiat 'Multipla'[67] and the 'P-70' car[68] the Supreme Court held that supplying a car with defects capable of causing an accident was a breach of contract of sale.[69] On the other hand, a certain amount of doubt was cast upon the exact meaning of the notion 'defect', and whether this notion ought to mean the same in cases of contractual and tortious liability.[70] Ultimately both the civil courts and the arbitration bodies understood a 'defect' according to the wording of Article 556.1 of the Civil Code: the provision directly regulating legal guarantees for poor quality products (although product liability still only covered those defects which caused consequential damage).[71] Among various types of defects the Polish product liability jurisprudence noted manufacturing defects, design defects (these two were not always clearly distinguished) and information/warning defects (Gnela 2000: 140).[72]

DAMAGE

Part I provided an outline of changes taking place within the concept of 'damage' in Central European civil law. These changes concern contractual and tortious liability: they cover the role and scope of recoverable damage, the substantive law and its practice (assessment of damages). Below is a more detailed analysis of these changes in contractual liability. The remarks concerning the limited role of damages and indeed the limited role of the law of obligations in socialist states are not repeated here. The analysis focuses on the present-day approach to contractual damage and its implications for product liability.

67 Judgement of the Supreme Court of 6 February 1963.

68 Judgement of the Supreme Court of 28 April 1964.

69 In spite of holding that breach of contract had occurred, the Supreme Court preferred to base the liability of the defendants in both of these judgements upon tort. See the further analysis of the judgements in Chapter 5 of Part II.

70 Gnela pointed to some unpublished judgements of the Polish Supreme Court, where at times the Court held that a 'defect' ought to be interpreted uniformly throughout the civil law regime, and in other judgements it clearly distinguished a 'dangerous characteristic' from a 'defect' in the understanding of the rules on guarantees (2000: 138).

71 Article 556.1 establishes when a product is defective: it is when the defect decreases its value or utility, taking into account the purpose stipulated in the contract or implied from the circumstances or the normal use of the product; if the product does not possess qualities of the existence of which the seller assured the buyer, or if the product was sold in an incomplete state (legal guarantee) (Polish *rękojmia za wady fizyczne*). (Translated by the author.)

72 Unpublished judgements of the Supreme Court: II CR 187/87, II CR 100/87, IV CR 31/88 (Gnela 2000: 140).

Across Central Europe, general principles of the law of obligations governing damage and its assessment are used in Central European product liability cases. In the Czech Republic and Hungary, the same provisions of the Civil Codes apply to cover contractual and tortious damage (indeed, these provisions[73] are analysed in more detail in Chapter 5). In Poland, in spite of some commonality, there are specific provisions concerning recovery of damages in tort.[74] Whatever the case may be, contractual liability, with its specific social and economic role, requires a specific approach to damage, and so does contractual *product* liability. What are these specificities?

First of all, while contractual liability normally covers pecuniary damage with no specified limits as to scope, contractual *product* liability only applies to damage occurring outside the defective product which caused it. Guarantee laws are applicable to the damage confined to the product (Sengayen 2002).

Further, contractual damage has an unquestioned pecuniary character – the debtor is required to ensure that economic interests of the creditor are protected (Gnela 2000: 142). Non-pecuniary damage is normally not recoverable in contract. The Central European approach to this issue has not, however, been conclusive. On the one hand, the recovery of non-pecuniary damage has been limited and often completely excluded by judicial practice throughout Central Europe (courts tended to use causation to limit the scope of recoverable damage solely to pecuniary damage), also in product liability cases. The Polish Supreme Court allowed recovery of non-pecuniary damage in contractual liability in the judgement of 6 July 1966,[75] but it has not always followed this approach (Nesterowicz 2007, Gnela 2000: 143). In other judgements, the Court rather attempted to declare that non-pecuniary damage caused to the buyer of a defective product ought to be recovered according to the rules of tort law (Gnela 2000: 143).[76] At present there are signs of potential change of approach to non-pecuniary damage in Poland (see below). Also the Czech Republic and Hungary are attempting to introduce more clarity and consistency into the principles governing recovery of non-pecuniary damage. These efforts have a more universal character (concerning both contract and tort): Czech and Hungarian courts never explicitly stated that non-pecuniary damage was not recoverable because the case was based on contractual liability – they rather used the rules of causation and thus limited the scope of recoverable damage to achieve the same result. The attempts to facilitate the recovery of non-pecuniary damage also, therefore, do not make the explicit contract/tort distinction. These attempts are introduced in more detail in Chapter 5 on tort liability. They include

73 The Czech Civil Code: Sections 13–16, 442–50, the Hungarian Code: Articles 355–60.

74 General provisions on the scope of recoverable damage in civil obligations: Articles 361–3 of the Civil Code. Specific provisions concerning damage in tort: Articles 444–8 of the Code.

75 OSPiKA 1967/7-8.

76 Unpublished judgement of 22 September 1986, IV CR 279/86.

the Hungarian Draft Civil Code which proposes replacing compensation of non-pecuniary damage with a special indemnity compensation, where the requirement to document the exact scope of harm is abandoned; and the Czech Decree of 2003 on the tariff system for compensation for pain and "aggravated position in society" (Hradek 2003: 89). Overall, one may expect a greater emphasis on recovery of non-pecuniary damage in Central European contractual liability in future. Indeed, the Polish Codification Commission working on the draft Civil Code indicated that non-pecuniary damage may be made recoverable in contract law, and this suggestion is supported by some scholarly writers (Nesterowicz 2007).

Contractual damage is normally understood to include physical losses (*damnum emergens*) and lost profits (*lucrum cessans*)[77] (Gnela 2000: 142). Both personal and property damage can be recovered. As mentioned above, provisions of the Civil Code concerning damage and its assessment are applicable to both contractual and tortious liability. However, in practice the courts limited recoverable damage to comply with the requirements of the contractual liability system (greater focus on pecuniary damage, compensation rather than deterrence or punishment): predominantly by causal considerations. This tendency will no doubt continue in future, although one can also observe signs of legislative input in order to systematize and clarify damage rules and assessment in contractual liability. For instance, the Draft Hungarian Civil Code implements this approach and by doing so it introduces some differentiation between contractual and tortious damage rules. The Draft limits "lost profits and other losses" in contractual liability by the principle of reasonable foreseeability.[78] Thus, although the main principle remains full compensation, 'the Conception' to the Draft explains that "liability shall not exceed the measure of loss that the non-performing party foresaw or could reasonably have foreseen at the time of the conclusion of the contract as a likely result of its non-performance based on the facts and circumstances attending the conclusion of the contract."[79] 'The Conception' links the notion of foreseeability with predictability, but stipulates that the standards of behaviour expected from the parties are "objective" (at pp. 143–4). 'The Conception' follows that the requirement of foreseeability can be the best measurement of damages for lost profits and other consequential loss, better in fact than the direct reference to 'breaking the chain of causation' which has been used by courts so far (at p. 144). An important thing to note is that, as 'the Conception' suggests, reasonably foreseeable damage would become one of the requisites of liability ("prerequisite element of liability, and not an element of excuse" at p. 144) to be shown by the claimant ("the burden of proof lies with the aggrieved party") (ibid.).[80]

77 Serious difficulties were noted in recovery of lost profits in Central Europe, especially in the Czech Republic – see below (Harmathy 1998: 115).

78 'The Conception', p. 142.

79 At p. 143.

80 This suggestion, if adopted, rather diminishes the importance of changes in contractual liability standard from 'fault-based' liability to 'strict liability' (the Draft

THE BURDEN OF PROOF AND CAUSAL LINK IN PROCEEDINGS INVOLVING CONTRACTUAL LIABILITY

Central European rules on burden of proof resemble the classic civil law tradition rules on the issue: the obligation to prove lies with the claimant (the victim of a defective product in product liability litigation).[81] Accordingly, in cases involving contractual product liability, the victim of a defective product must prove the breach of contract, and the damage resulting from the breach. Certain developments in Polish case law, however, determined the use of presumptions as to the damage and its exact measure (Gnela 2000: 141). Further, because of the existence of presumption of fault in contractual liability in Central Europe, it is for the defendant to show that she exercised due care.

The principles governing causal link are understood uniformly in contractual and tortious liability. They are analysed in Chapter 5 concerning tortious liability. Here it is important to stress once again the important function of causation – it has been used by Central European courts to determine the scope of recoverable damage. Thus, the theory of 'adequate' or 'normal' causal links applied throughout civil liability was interpreted here to fit the needs of contractual liability.

LIMITATION PERIODS FOR CONTRACTUAL CLAIMS

As a result of the implementation of various European Community Directives in the area of consumer contracts, specific limitation periods apply to specific contracts or contracts concluded in specified circumstances (such as distance contracts or those concluded outside the business premises of the trader). With regard to warranty claims for products, limitation periods were established by the implementation of the Consumer Sales Directive.[82] In the Hungarian Civil Code the warranty claims arising from a breach of a consumer sales contract are limited by the six months and two years' periods running from the time of performance, subject to some exceptions (Article 308, Rein and Kohegyi 2006: 164). The Czech Civil Code (Section 620.1) specifies similar limitation periods, although it establishes exceptions for groceries, foodstuffs and animals.[83] The Polish *Consumer Sales Act* of 27 July 2002 specifies the same limitation periods

---

analysed at p.168 above).

81 For instance, Article 6 of the Polish Civil Code stipulates: "The burden of proving a fact lies with the person who draws legal consequences from this fact" (translated by the author).

82 Directive 99/44/EC. On the specific provisions of Polish, Hungarian and Czech law implementing the Consumer Sales Directive see: EU Law Consumer Acquis Database and the Consumer Law Compendium.

83 See the Consumer Law Compendium, at p. 641.

in Article 10, again with some exceptions. Further analysis of these issues goes beyond the scope of this book.

General contractual liability has different limitation periods and these are applied in product liability cases. In Poland Article 118 of the Civil Code, which establishes general limitation periods for civil claims, applies to most contractual claims. It specifies the term for bringing claims is ten years unless a legal provision specifies otherwise. Obviously contracts may also specify different limitation periods. The Civil Code also contains specific limitation periods for claims arising from contracts of sale involving business persons: Article 554 establishes a two-year limitation period. Neither the Hungarian nor the Czech Civil Codes differentiate between contract and tort law claims. The Hungarian Code established a period of five years from the time when the damage occurred for bringing all claims (Article 324.1).[84] The latter period starts running from the "due date of the claim" (Rein and Kohegyi 2006: 164). The Czech Code establishes a general limitation period of three years from the date when the "right could be exercised for the first time" (Section 101).[85] However, claims for damages have a limitation period of two years from the day "when the damaged person learnt of the damage and of the liable person", and in any case they become "statute-barred ... three years and, as for damages caused intentionally, ten years from the day when it came to the event from that the damage arose; this rule shall not apply to damages to health" (Section 106).[86]

UTILITY OF CONTRACT LAW RULES IN THE PRODUCT LIABILITY CONTEXT – THE LIMITS OF PRIVITY AND ATTEMPTS TO VITIATE THEM

Contractual liability provides for recovery of quite a comprehensive range of damage – including the value of the defective product and damage in other property or persons, although the scope of damages recoverable under the rules of contractual product liability is narrower. The developments analysed above demonstrate that it was not easy for sellers to escape liability if the products sold by them caused damage to the buyer's person or property. These advantages of contractual product liability were, however, overshadowed by the unavoidable existence of the principle of privity of contract. The privity rule, explained in Part

84 BIICL Product Liability Database, <http://www.biicl.org/plf/index.asp?contentid=889>.

85 <http://ec.europa.eu/civiljustice/time_limits/time_limits_cze_en.htm>.

86 <http://ec.europa.eu/civiljustice/time_limits/time_limits_cze_en.htm>. See Chapter 5 for an elaboration of the manner in which this provision was applied by Czech courts. This dichotomy – distinguishing subjective and objective limitation periods (Hradek 2003: 132) – can also be seen in the Polish Civil Code, in regulation of limitation periods for tortious liability (described in detail in Chapter 5).

I, has been one of the general principles of contract law across Central Europe. The rule, in its horizontal and vertical dimension, severely limits the scope of application of contractual product liability law. It is thus impossible for victims of defective products other than buyers to take action in order to gain redress, and on the other hand those most likely to have had influence on the quality and safety of products – manufacturers – can often escape liability as not being parties to the contract of sale under which the victim has obtained the product. The three analysed Central European states had found very specific ways to deal with the problem of privity of contract. These are analysed below.

The progressive attitude of Hungarian courts, clearly seen in their approach to the issue of contractual fault, has been continued in the area of privity of contract. In the analysed 'paint case' the claimant brought the action against both the seller and the producer, but the court refused to impose liability upon the latter for the reason of the lack of a contractual link between the claimant and the producer (Maczonkai 1996: 110). A similar attitude could be seen in the 'chickens case'. A breakthrough came in the judgement of the 'turnip cabbage seed case'.[87] Here the seeds did not produce an expected harvest, and the buyer sued the seller as well as the producer. The court held that both of them were liable in contract, as the seller was the 'assistant in performance' of the producer (Maczonkai 1996: 111). The 'turnip cabbage seed case' opened the possibility of suing every producer, including the producers of component parts, together with the sellers. Maczonkai considered the development of the concept of 'assistant in performance' as a particular advantage of the Hungarian contractual liability system over the Product Liability Directive and the Hungarian Product Liability Act.[88] The Directive sets the producers (Article 3) as the primary defendants in product liability litigation, only to offer the subsidiary liability of suppliers (Article 3.3). The rationale behind this solution seems very clear: the Directive carries with it an assumption, not expressly articulated, that the consumers are faced with "a big producer and a small retailer" (Maczonkai 1996: 111).[89] Howells, however, very rightly pointed out that the situation could very easily be reversed in the contemporary markets, full of large retailers (1993: 30). Thus, the Hungarian solution to the problem of privity indeed seems to have been more advantageous for consumers. The victim of a defective product could sue the retailer together with the producer, instead of taking action against only one of those (Maczonkai 1996: 111). One significant drawback of the 'assistant in performance' concept was, however, that it did not allow victims other than buyers to take action. Instead of remedying this weakness remaining within the contract law remedies, the courts rather focused on the law of tort, considered more suitable for product liability litigation.

87 Cited by Maczonkai (1996: 111) and Tercsák (1993: 224).

88 The Act implementing the Directive into the Hungarian legal system – Act X of 1993.

89 See also the Preamble to the Directive.

The Czechoslovak and Czech product liability litigation seems not to have suffered from the restrictions of privity of contract. The courts were very flexible in holding the sellers liable in contract and the manufacturers liable in tort, with the possibility of their joint and several liability irrespective of the different legal bases of action (Svestka 1989: 96–100).

The Polish doctrine and case law regarding product liability has very rarely been focused upon combating the challenges of privity of contract (Gnela 2000: 154). There were, however, a number of proposals of scholarly writers designed to render contractual liability more accessible for victims of defective products. Sołtysiński considered privity of contract as a very significant obstacle to victims seeking redress, and set up a doctrine of a 'guarantee promise' (1970: 173). The doctrine was based on the existence of trademarks, quality marks and other types of marks and information encouraging consumers to buy a particular product. These statements assuring the consumer of the particular quality of the product established, according to Sołtysiński, an obligation on the part of their author (mostly the manufacturer) (1970: 173). Such a unilateral obligation created, he continued, an obligation relationship between the manufacturer and every person who bought the product, hence even the ultimate buyer – the consumer (ibid.). It was therefore possible to envisage an action brought by a consumer against the manufacturer, based on liability *ex contractu*, for breaching the 'guarantee promise'. This revolutionary approach to advertisements and any other information about products made available to consumers was not, however, accepted by the Polish doctrine and practice of law at the time. It was considered that such practice would discourage the producers and other professionals from informing consumers about products, for instance through advertising. It seems that at present the issue of liability of producers for the content of advertisements has been comprehensively regulated by the European Community, albeit not always in the sphere of civil obligations.[90] Sołtysiński's theory was aimed at establishing contractual liability as the most proper avenue of redress for victims of defective products, although its main weakness was the fact that it did not provide a solution to the problem of the horizontal aspect of privity. Victims other than the buyer would be unable to establish the existence of an obligation relationship with the manufacturer based on his 'guarantee promise'. Further, the theory has not taken into account situations where the person introducing a product into the market has uttered no explicit 'guarantee promise'. The conception introduced by Żuławska (1983a) meets some of these criticisms. She contended that liability for defective products ought to be based upon a specific legal act (*quasi-contractus*) of the producer (1983a: 279). She declined the possibility of placing product liability in the sphere of contract law or tort law, and argued that it should be an independent type of liability. Again, her theory was not taken up by the courts. It seems that, in common with Hungary, Polish legal profession declined the possibility of curing

90 The Consumer Sales Directive 99/44, the Misleading and Comparative Advertising Directive 97/55, and recently the Unfair Commercial Practices Directive 2005/29.

the shortcomings of contract law and headed towards tort liability as a more suitable regime for product liability cases.

CONCLUSIONS

In spite of the existence of some features characteristic of socialist legal systems, Central European contractual product liability regimes resembled the regimes established by Western European courts. Similar tendencies in the development can be noticed, including the dismissive attitudes towards contract law – as unable to satisfy the claims of all those involved. This finding has great importance for the entire process of adopting the European Community *acquis* in the field of product liability, and the overall transformation within Central Europe. It is significant for the manner in which this transformation should be understood.

Chapter 5
Tort Liability

INTRODUCTION

While the development of product liability in Central Europe commenced within the field of contractual liability, very soon emphasis shifted to tort. The limitations of contractual liability rules were a strong motivation for Central European courts to seek other avenues of redress for victims of defective products.

Chapter 5 shows in a comparative manner the evolution of tortious product liability in Central Europe, including the legislative, judicial and doctrinal aspects of this evolution. The narrative commences with substantive rules of liability based upon fault. Here it must be remembered that Central European notions of fault are conceptually much closer to the French *la faute délictuelle* (Whittaker 2005: 42) than to the English negligence, and the book uses the language and methodology of fault, not negligence. The chapter observes the case law of Central European courts accompanied by doctrinal writings, which interpreted the general tortious liability provisions to create more objective liability standards reaching and crossing the boundaries of strict liability. It draws parallels with law operating in Western Europe and with the Product Liability Directive. It shows that, at least in certain aspects, Central European tortious product liability regimes were quite advanced in protecting victims of dangerous products. Specific provisions of civil codes establishing 'strict liability' which were used in product liability cases, albeit very rarely, are also analysed. This chapter is followed by the investigation of the measures which implemented the Product Liability Directive and their impact on product liability regimes of Central Europe.

GENERAL TENDENCIES IN THE DEVELOPMENT OF CENTRAL EUROPEAN TORTIOUS PRODUCT LIABILITY REGIMES

SETTING THE SCENE

Until the implementation of the Product Liability Directive by the Czech Republic, Hungary and Poland, there was no specific tort regime of product liability in the written laws of these countries. In common with the Western European systems, tortious liability for defective products assumed growing importance as a result of judicial activity. Its legal bases were, with certain minor exceptions,[1] general tortious liability rules in the civil codes. Tortious regimes of product liability developed gradually, albeit with different features and impact in each country. The civil law roots of the Central European legal systems contributed to the courts' fidelity to the text of the codes. However, differences in approaches of Central European courts to product liability issues reached even beyond the dissimilarities suggested by the pertinent black letter laws. They were conditioned by developments explored in Part I. The Civil Code of Hungary (1959), of Poland (1964) and of Czechoslovakia (1964) were adopted in an era of belief that socialist markets could effectively secure the interests of all citizens, also the citizens in their 'consumer role' (Svestka 1989: 92, 93). No provisions for the protection of consumers were originally embedded in the Codes, apart from certain contractual remedies in cases of sale of defective goods. Part I depicted how the socialist ideology and policy of the state – the main if not the only owner of manufacturing and trade enterprises – affected this absence of will and the conceived lack of the need for consumer protection laws. It was also shown how the realization that the socialist market ideals were as such not capable of securing protection for consumers arrived later on, conditioned by the political changes and transformation within markets, throughout Central Europe. Following these changes, the courts started to interpret progressively the available provisions of the civil codes in cases involving defective products.

RATIONALE FOR THE SHIFT IN EMPHASIS FROM CONTRACT TO TORT

As explored in the previous chapter, privity of contract was a very serious obstacle in providing remedies to all victims of defective products. In common with the Western European legal thought in the area of product liability, the Central European scholars proposed various solutions to the barriers created by privity. Some efforts to extend the scope of contractual liability were also noticeable in jurisprudence. They were not, however, as successful here as in Germany or Austria where the concept of tort is narrower than in the rest of Europe; or in France where the *non-cumul* rule prevented many victims of dangerous products from relying on tort laws (Łętowska 1999: 81).

The Hungarian legal system seemed to be a relatively good ground for such legal developments. Even Hungarian courts soon realized, however, that tort law constituted a more adequate environment for product liability claims. Maczonkai, who assessed the evolution of contractual product liability, pointed out that even the very impressive developments in the Hungarian jurisprudence concerning the concept of 'assistant is performance' were incapable of confronting the 'horizontal

---

1 See the following section on the 'specific tortious liability provisions' in Central European Civil Codes and their application in product liability cases.

limits'[2] of privity of contract (1996: 111). The Czech regime of product liability saw flexible application of contract liability if a contract between the victim and the seller existed, and tort liability where there was no contract (liability of manufacturers and also importers).[3] With both these types of liability functioning on the basis of the same provisions of the Civil Code, such a dichotomy did not have very serious implications for victims of defective products. Polish courts never fully utilized the projects presented by academic writers, outlined in Chapter 4, and headed directly towards tortious liability as a response to the limitation of contract law.[4] Very soon after the first product liability cases reached the courts, it was stressed that even those in a contractual relationship with the victim may be liable in tort. According to Nesterowicz, the reason for abandoning contract law in product liability cases by Polish courts was the "weakness" of contract law rules, especially of the laws on legal and commercial guarantees (1979: 10, also Sengayen 2002).

Throughout Central Europe, tort gave victims of defective products the possibility of suing those most likely to have had influence upon the safety and quality of products. On the other hand, it offered a practically unlimited range of claimants, from the buyer and his family and friends, to his employees, and even mere bystanders, the chance to sue. Hence, the very popular contention that tort is capable of overcoming the shortcomings of privity of contract was also put forward in Central Europe (Gnela 2000: 173, Maczonkai 1996: 111, Nesterowicz 1979: 10). Łętowska points out a broad scope of application of the concept of tort, allowing inclusion of most cases which the doctrine and practice of law wish to see within the scope of product liability (1999: 86). With the *non-cumul* rule not applicable throughout Central Europe, victims of defective products could bring a tortious liability claim even if the defect constituted a breach of a contract.[5]

The benefits of tortious liability, from the perspective of victims of defective products, were universally recognized in the jurisprudence and doctrine of law of Central Europe. However, because of a much greater level of separation of contractual and tortious liability in the Polish Civil Code, those benefits are much clearer there. The possibility of joint and several liability of a number of possible defendants was a particular advantage (Łętowska 1999: 87). The Polish Civil Code contains a general provision on joint and several liability in Article 441. Article 344 of the Hungarian Civil Code describes this type of liability (Harmathy 1998: 118), but as a result of the use of the concept of 'assistant in performance', such liability

2 Victims other than buyers being prevented from obtaining remedies.

3 Information about importers' liability – from an interview with Monika Dobiasova.

4 Because of a much more significant level of separation of contractual from tortious liability in the Polish Civil Code, these 'limitations' were greater than in the two other Central European legal systems – see below.

5 As mentioned above, Czech courts did not use this opportunity. For a further elaboration of the approach to *non-cumul* principle across Central Europe see below.

was also possible in contract law.[6] The Czech Civil Code envisages the possibility of joint and several liability in Section 438 (Vondracek 1988: 392–3), and it seems to be of no importance in product liability cases that the basis for the seller's liability is contract and for the manufacturer's liability, tort (Svestka 1989: 100). Other 'advantages' of tortious liability – those relating to the scope of recoverable damage or limitation periods – were also observed in Poland. Łętowska discusses the very advantageous provisions of the Polish Civil Code concerning personal injuries and their recovery in tort (Articles 446–9), analysed below (1999: 87). So far, contractual liability has not covered non-pecuniary damage (Jagielska 1999: 181), although changes in this regard are now heralded by some academic writers (Nesterowicz 2007, Wałachowska 2007) and the Codification Commission (Nesterowicz 2007). Some contract claims have shorter limitation periods than those prescribed for tortious claims (Pyrzyńska 1996: 276). According to Article 118 of the Polish Civil Code, the period for bringing all claims is ten years; but under Article 554 claims which arise out of sale contracts concluded in the course of a business of the seller must be brought within two years. Claims in tort, on the other hand, are subject to the limitation period of three years from the time the victim learnt of the damage and the person liable to repair it. In any event, however, tortious claims expire ten years after the tortious event (Article 442, para. 1 of the Civil Code).[7]

From what were undoubtedly general rules on tort liability, the courts of Central Europe established a very specific set of rules. These rules, however impressive they may seem, were not always comprehensive, clear and uniformly understood; and the regimes functioned poorly in the overall political and socio-economic conditions of Central Europe. Below is the analysis of the provisions of the Civil Codes which served as a basis for the development of product liability regimes, followed by the account of the evolution of the courts' approach in the area and the opinions of the doctrine of law. Particular emphasis is placed upon assessing the efforts to create a more objective standard of liability.

6 See Chapter 2.

7 See below for an interpretation of this concept, and the analysis of the 2006 judgements of the Polish Supreme Court and the Polish Constitutional Court, the latter of which declared the unconstitutionality of the rule that the limitation period of ten years starts running from the time when the tortious act took place. The Civil Code was amended following the judgement of the Constitutional Tribunal (see below). In the Czech and Hungarian Civil Codes no significant differences can be seen in the limitation periods between contractual and tortious claims (Article 324.1 of the Hungarian Code, Section 106 of the Czech Code, analysed in Chapter 4).

I. PRODUCT LIABILITY SYSTEMS BASED ON GENERAL TORTIOUS LIABILITY PROVISIONS – 'FAULT-BASED' LIABILITY

GENERAL TORTIOUS LIABILITY PROVISIONS IN THE CIVIL CODES

Following the French *Code Civil* (*general civil delictum*) and contrary to the German regulation of specified protected interests (Van Dam 2006, Wagner 2006) Central European Codes contain a general prohibition of torts. This position has been retained in the draft codes as well. Although such a general approach was referred to by Eörsi as a "positive achievement of socialism",[8] it became rather more particularized in the judicial practice (similarly with other legal systems using the approach – Wagner 2006). In the product liability context, courts needed to apply the general liability provisions to cases where defective products caused damage. Below is the analysis of these general provisions. Again, it is provided in chronological order – the Hungarian Civil Code was adopted first, with the Czechoslovak and Polish Codes passed later.

The Hungarian Civil Code of 1959 contains Article 339 which defines tort liability.[9] It stipulates:

> (1) Whoever unlawfully causes damage to another shall be bound to compensate the same. He shall be relieved of such responsibility if he can prove that he has been acting in such a way as might, as a rule, reasonably be expected in the given situation.
>
> (2) The Court, having regard to the circumstances of the case deserving special appreciation, may partly relieve the person, responsible for the damage, of his responsibility.[10]

The concept of tort contains an opportunity for the defendant to exculpate herself on the condition that she proves she acted in a generally accepted manner in the given circumstances (Maczonkai 1996: 112). Further, courts may reduce liability on equity basis (Article 339.2). Following the words of Harmathy it may be said that the wording of Article 339 suggests "liability based on fault with a reversed burden of proof" (1998: 115). This rule was not uniformly understood by doctrinal writers. Some considered that it was not based on fault at all (Harmathy 1998: 115). It is apparent where such views may have come from, considering the wording of the provision. The concept of unlawful conduct used there implies

8 Quoted by 'the Conception' at p. 170.

9 It is the first article in Title II 'Responsibility for Damages Caused out of Contract and for Unjust Enrichment', Chapter XXIX 'General Rules Referring to Compensation of Damages'.

10 Civil Code of the Hungarian People's Republic, 1960.

an objective approach to torts. According to established theories in Hungary and other Central European states ‘unlawfulness’ constitutes an objective element of the broader concept of ‘fault’, the concept which should involve an objective as well as a subjective (‘fault proper’) element.[11] Ultimately, the majority view is that the provision is “the formulation of the rule of liability based on fault and … a parallel one to the rule on strict liability (Art. 345)[12] and to other special rules on liability” (Harmathy 1998: 115).

The draft Civil Code contains Section 5 regulating tortious liability, which does not significantly differ from Article 339.[13] It stipulates:

> A person who causes damage to another person in violation of the law shall be liable for such damage. He shall be relieved of liability if he is able to prove reasonable conduct under the circumstances.[14]

What is interesting, however, is the text of ‘the Conception’ which accompanies the Draft Code. While on the one hand it clearly opts for retaining the general liability standard based on ‘fault’, it emphasizes the need for an objective rather than a subjective standard of conduct. ‘The Conception’ stresses the need for this general provision to be flexible enough to enable courts to interpret it in the “changing social environment” and there is a strong indication that in many cases (especially those involving businesses and “organised multinational corporations”) the standard of conduct would be very stringent.[15]

As mentioned above, Section 420 of the Czechoslovak Civil Code regulates both contractual and tortious liability. It used to read:

> (1) A citizen is liable for damage which he has caused by infringement of a legal duty.
>
> (2) A citizen is exonerated from liability if he proves that he was not at fault in causing the damage.[16]

11 See the analysis below for a detailed analysis of the two elements, as well as certain arguments indicating that there are indeed great similarities between the objective element of fault and the objective (strict) liability.

12 Article 345 is examined further below, in the part concerning ‘specific tortious liability provisions’ in Central European Civil Codes.

13 The main difference is in fact the omission of the second paragraph – the one concerning the possibility of discretional reduction of liability in special circumstances.

14 Quoted by ‘the Conception’, at p. 171.

15 ‘The Conception’, p. 171.

16 Vondracek (1988: 375).

Liability of legal persons (organizations) was set out in a similar fashion, although the possibilities of exoneration were different. By virtue of the former Article 421:

> (1) An organization[17] is liable to a citizen for damage which it has caused by infringement of a legal duty.
>
> (3) An organization is exonerated from liability if it can prove that it could not have prevented the damage even by the exertion of every effort which can be required from it. An organization, however, cannot be exonerated from its liability by pleading that it was following the orders of superior organs.[18]

Both provisions endorsed a breach of a legal duty as a precondition for liability. Vondracek pointed out that such legal duties could be divided into two categories. He mentioned duties imposed by written law (including the general duty of care – Section 415, which reads: "Everyone must act so as to avoid damages to health, property, nature and environment"[19]), and duties arising from contracts and agreements (1988: 377). The latter category was already the subject of analysis in Chapter 4. Tortious liability concerns breaches of those duties which have been imposed by law. What duties exactly have been imposed by the Czechoslovak and Czech law upon those dealing with products professionally shall be seen in a later part of this chapter. The existing division between liability of physical and legal persons entailed a specific approach to product liability cases. It seems clear why Article 421 has been the legal basis for early Czechoslovak product liability litigation. Most sellers and manufacturers of products are legal, not physical, persons. Doctrinal writers established the theoretical framework for liability of such legal persons. Vondracek wrote that in cases where the liability of legal persons was involved, the act or omission in question would be committed by an organ or an employee of the legal person (1988: 378). The liability would be "removed" from these persons and "assigned" to the legal person (Vondracek 1988: 378). According to Svestka, the necessary conditions for Czechoslovak tort liability have been both of a subjective and of an objective character (1989: 97). The wording of Section 421 suggested that the subjective element of fault on the part of the defendant would be presumed. However, as in the Hungarian code, this subjective element was not explicit, at least not in relation to legal persons. The presumption of fault would be rebutted by the tortfeasor upon showing that the damage caused could not have been prevented in the particular case even if the 'objectively assessable due care' was exercised (Svestka 1989: 98, Vondracek 1988: 375). The objective requisites of liability – the unlawful conduct, damage

17 For the concept of 'socialist organizations' see former Sections 18–21 of the Czechoslovak Civil Code (Vondracek 1988).

18 Vondracek (1988: 378).

19 From the translation of the Czech Civil Code provided by Dobiasova.

and causal link – had to, in turn, be established by the aggrieved party (Rubeš 1970: 450, Vondracek 1988: 375).

The Code was amended in 1991[20] and at the moment Section 420 concerns 'any person'. It holds:

> (1) Any person is liable for damage which he caused by breaching a legal obligation (duty).
>
> (3) A person (an entity or an individual) shall be relieved of his liability if he proves that he did not cause the damage.[21]

This amendment also seems to have removed the subjective requirement of fault from the list of requisites of liability. The commentary to the Civil Code by Trade Links suggests that the features of liability are now: a breach of a legal obligation, damage caused, and a causal link between the damage and the breach (1996: 123). Trade Links also point out that the liability for damage has become liability of an 'objective' character (ibid.). It may be contended that this point is going too far, and that the wording of Section 420 is simply imprecise.[22] To support the latter argument the comparison ought to be drawn between the new Section 420 and the old Section 421, this one undoubtedly based upon fault (as confirmed by courts and doctrine). Tichy also points out that, "in addition to the general principle of liability for fault (Section 420), the Civil Code was in 1991 supplemented by a principle of strict liability as a second pillar" (Section 420a)[23] (2002a: 118).[24] It is indeed extremely difficult to establish an authoritative opinion of Czech courts, as the number of judgements since the amendment of the Civil Code has been truly insignificant (Tichy 2002a: 120–23).[25] The situation may well be clarified by the Draft Civil Code, the unofficial translation of which was provided by Hradek and Tichy. The draft retains a similar dichotomy of tortious liability – there is a separate provision concerning strict liability, analysed below, and a provision establishing liability clearly based upon fault. Division 2 *Duty to compensate damage*, Subdivision 1 *General provisions*, Section 2412 of the Draft Code stipulates:

20 Act No. 509/1991 Coll., effective from 1 January 1992.

21 Translation of the Czech Civil Code provided by Dobiasova.

22 In an on-line interview with the author of this book (September 2003) Dobiasova pointed out that according to her the regime was still based upon "presumed culpability".

23 Section 420a is analysed in the following section of the book on 'specific provisions of tortious liability'.

24 Remarks in brackets added by the author of the book.

25 This remark refers to judgements of higher instance courts. As mentioned in Chapter 2 of Part I, lower courts' decisions are not often published in Central Europe.

> Everybody is obliged to compensate damage he has caused by a culpable breach of legal obligations towards others.

The Draft reiterates presumption of fault existing in the Code currently in force. It also introduces a definition of negligence,[26] which is a new development. Section 2415 provides:

> (1) It shall be understood that a person who caused damage has caused such damage due to his negligence.
>
> (2) A person acts negligently if not acting sufficiently carefully and with such knowledge and skills as may be usually expected within private relations from an average person. If however, such person claims to possess specialist knowledge or skills, or is engaged in activity necessitating specialist knowledge, skills or care, such person's activity shall be deemed negligent if it fails to display the same.

The Polish Civil Code was preceded by the Code of Obligations of 1933, Articles 134 and 135 of which were similar to the present regulation of tortious liability in the Civil Code.[27] By virtue of Article 415 of the Civil Code of 1964:

> Whoever by his fault caused a damage to another person shall be obliged to redress it.[28]

From the text of Article 415 it could be inferred that the person who suffered damage needed to prove that it had been caused by the 'fault' of another. In relationships between consumers and businesses this may be a difficult or even an impossible task. The difference between the Polish regulation of tort liability, placing the burden of proof of 'fault' on the victim, and the Czech and Hungarian regulations offering the benefit of reversing the burden of proof (through providing for presumptions of fault), appears to be crucial from the point of view of victims of dangerous products. Did the Polish regime, however, indeed offer

26 The translation of the Draft provided by Tichy and Hradek refers to 'negligence'. The book, however, follows the terminological choice made at the outset, and continues referring to 'fault'.

27 The Polish codification of tortious liability resembles the French and the Swiss codifications (Articles 1382 and 1383 of the French *Code Civil*, Article 41 of Swiss Code of Obligations). Article 1382 of the *Code Civil* '*Tout fait quelconque de l'homme, qui cause á autrui un dommage, oblige celui par la faute duquel il est arrivé, á le réparer*' only refers to intentional torts, as confirmed in Article 1383. The latter provision contains an identical rule for negligent acts (Wagner 2006: 1006).

28 This is the first article in Title VI 'Czyny niedozwolone' (Torts), Book III 'Zobowiazania' (Obligations) of the Code. Translated by Wojtasiewicz (2000).

them less than the other two jurisdictions? The jurisprudence of Polish courts has attempted to facilitate the position of the claimants – in some cases they were not required to prove fault at all. The doctrine of law played a crucial part in this inner transformation of tort for the purposes of product liability.

Below is an assessment of the ways in which Central European courts and legal doctrine interpreted these general provisions for the purposes of the product liability regimes.

THE JURISPRUDENCE OF CENTRAL EUROPEAN COURTS AND THE DOCTRINAL RE-INTERPRETATION OF LAW – EVOLUTION OF TORTIOUS PRODUCT LIABILITY REGIMES

INTRODUCTION

General rules of civil law liability based on fault were the core of product liability litigation in Central Europe. The judgements and doctrinal views analysed below show how these general rules were applied in the product liability context.

Hungarian courts established a product liability system practically crossing the boundaries of strict liability. Czechoslovak and Czech courts were relatively far behind their Hungarian counterparts in terms of development of strict product liability rules. The Polish product liability regime also did not reach as far as the Hungarian one in rendering the manufacturers, or sellers, strictly liable. Overall, however, attempts to objectivize liability standards in product liability cases have been clearly visible across Central Europe. The efforts of the Central European judiciary were assisted by legal scholars who developed various ideas and concepts to facilitate the operation of the product liability systems.

Below is a detailed analysis of the characteristics and requisites of the tortious product liability regime as established by the Central European case law and doctrine. The structure of the analysis reflects the need to deconstruct the product liability system by assessing each of its component parts. First of all, the analysis turns to those liable and those benefiting from product liability laws.

THE TORTFEASORS AND THE VICTIMS – EVOLUTION TOWARDS ‘CONSUMERISM’

Introductory remarks

Civil Code provisions which served as legal bases for tortious product liability systems did not limit the persons liable or those able to recover compensation for losses. The development of Central European product liability entailed introducing such limitations, reflecting the links of this specific liability system with markets, mass production and consumption. On the tortfeasor side the focus was on business, professional liability, and there was a growing preference for manufacturers or importers as opposed to direct sellers. The philosophical context of these developments was presented in Part I. On the victim side, courts and academic writers gradually introduced the arguments of a weaker market position, a lesser access to information, and the language of 'consumerism' was increasingly used.

Below is a more detailed assessment of the Central European approach to the main *dramatis personae* of product liability regimes.

Persons responsible for damages caused by products

For the reasons specified in Part I, tortious liability for defective products was generally placed on 'professionals', those who in the course of business introduced defective products into the market. A stronger market position and greater knowledge about products was seen as the justification for their liability (Mohmand 2002: 168).[29] These arguments became much more prominent in court judgements and academic writings when liability was becoming more objective, even strict. Further, in Hungary and in Poland, the *eius periculum cuius commodum* rule[30] was advanced as another root cause for more stringent liability of businesses. The obvious advantage of tortious liability – the absence of privity of contract constraints – enabled a much wider class of potential tortfeasors to be considered. Hungarian and Polish law allowed the use of tort law even if the damage constituted a breach of an existing contract. While this meant that even direct sellers could be liable in tort, the courts and the representatives of doctrine of law wished to see the manufacturer being held liable (Nesterowicz 1979: 5). It must be said that the latter approach initially might have resulted from the 'fault-based' liability standard (manufacturers were most likely to have actually been 'at fault' with regard to defective products), but later the arguments of a stronger market position and profits (mentioned above) gained support. The Czechoslovak regime suggested the liability of the manufacturer in tort, unless the manufacturer had a contract with the victim, in which case contract liability was suitable (Svestka 1989: 100, 102). Apart from manufacturers, however, other actors in the distribution chain could also bear liability. The fact that the introduction of dangerous products into the market and not their production has been endorsed as a tort leading to product liability, made it possible for all those taking part in the process of supplying the products to be included within the group of possible defendants. Although Czechoslovak and Czech law was quite ambiguous in this respect, Dobiasova pointed out that Section 420 of the Civil Code "is based on thesis of liability of everybody for the damage caused by violation of law",[31]

29 Taschner emphasized that private activity, irrespective of who performs it, falls outside the scope of product liability law (1986b: 257).

30 Which, in simple terms, can be translated as "whoever gains from an activity, ought also to bear the risks which the activity entails".

31 From a telephone interview with Dobiasova, June 2003.

indicating that manufacturers would not be the only possible defendants in product liability cases.

Below is a closer examination of the development of case law and doctrine in this area.

The Hungarian case introducing the idea of product liability in tort – the 'motorcycle accident' case of 1973[32] – focused upon the seller's liability. There was no privity of contract between the victim (the person riding the motorcycle) and the seller; hence the difficulty to award damages using contract liability rules. The court held that selling defective products gave rise to the retailer's liability in tort. The justification for this statement – the close factual relationship between the breach of contract by the seller and the injuries suffered by the driver – was thought quite weak by Maczonkai (1996: 112). Nevertheless, even the weakness of the theoretical basis of the judgement could not diminish its value in setting the new direction in the development of product liability law. A few years later the 'chemical spray' case of 1977 commenced the practice of placing the liability on the manufacturers, for the purposes of this case those who did not adequately instruct the consumers of their products.[33] The later case of defective slippers[34] reflected a debate taking place at the time among Hungarian legal scholars and practitioners: those in favour of tortious liability of manufacturers and those arguing that in the case of an existing contract the seller ought to be sued. The Supreme Court held that causing damage gave rise to a "direct relationship between the person causing the damage and the damaged person" (Kalman, Lelkes and Domonkos 2003: 3). The manufacturer was held liable for producing slippers with a very slippery sole. The landmark case of 'colour television sets' of 1984[35] ultimately confirmed a number of key principles in the Hungarian product liability system, some of which (like abandoning the 'fault' requirement) are analysed below. The clear preference was for manufacturer liability as opposed to seller liability. Although the topic was not explored in depth by the Hungarian courts until recently, theoretically there is no obstacle to tortious liability of other actors taking part in the distribution chain.[36]

Liability of sellers (trading corporations[37]) in the Czechoslovak contract law regime was examined above. The manufacturers (manufacturing corporations[38]) could be liable together with the sellers, or alone. It was of no importance for

32 Quoted by Maczonkai (1996: 111).

33 Quoted by Maczonkai (1996: 112). The manufacturer was held not to have fulfilled his duty of care towards those using the product.

34 Supreme Court Decision No. 1986/12/501, analysed by Kalman, Lelkes and Domonkos (2003: 3).

35 Quoted by Maczonkai (1996: 113).

36 Liability of importers was considered in a case based on provisions implementing the Product Liability Directive – see below.

37 Expression used by Svestka (1989).

38 Ibid.

their joint liability that they were liable according to different liability systems. The manufacturers would be liable for a 'common delict' (Svestka 1989: 101). If, as happens in most cases, the manufacturer was a legal person, liability would be 'assigned' to the manufacturer and 'removed' from the employee who actually committed an act or omission in question (Vondracek 1988: 378). Interestingly, it is shown below that the scale of duties placed upon the manufacturers was larger than the scale of sellers' duties. Further, Section 420 and, before the amendment of the Civil Code, Section 421 have referred to anyone who caused the damage to another, hence other participants in the distribution chain could also be held liable.[39]

In Poland the very similar cases of defective cars – Fiat 'Multipla' (1962) and 'P-70' (1963) – based on the Code of Obligations of 1932, introduced the idea of the sellers being liable in tort to the injured buyers. Similarly to the Hungarian courts, the Polish Supreme Court attempted to provide some underlying principle of the tortious liability of a contractual party. The fact that the products had caused personal injuries was the starting point in this search for the rationale.[40] The Court found that selling a motor vehicle, which by its very nature could easily cause injury to a person's health, with technical defects capable of causing an accident, was not only a breach of contract but also a breach of the general duty not to put human life and health in danger.[41] In the 'P-70' case the Court explored this issue from a different point of view, holding that supplying a defective product by a seller was not only a breach of contract, but could also be a tort provided it constituted a breach of a provision of law or the 'principles of community life'.[42] It must be acknowledged that this type of reasoning is relatively more appealing than the approach of the Hungarian court in the 'motorcycle case'. The case of Fiat 'Multipla' also made it clear that the seller could be held liable jointly with the manufacturer, or, more precisely in this case, the importer of the product.[43] In the 'chemical spray' case of 1972 both the seller and the producer of the spray were held liable to the plaintiff for insufficient warnings of the dangerous nature of the product and not supplying protective gas masks. In the 1980s the courts gradually abandoned the idea of tortious liability of the seller and concentrated upon the manufacturer or importer. The case involving the sale of a cake containing a

39 Dobiasova – Product Liability Database Report (BIICL).

40 'Fiat Multipla case', II CR 96/62, at pp. 40, 41.

41 II CR 96/62, at p. 44.

42 See Part I (pp.28, 29, and 61) for the explanation of the meaning and role of this general clause.

43 The car in question was produced by Fiat in Italy, and imported into Poland by Motoimport – a state-owned company with a monopoly for importing foreign motor vehicles. Motoimport attempted to, unsuccessfully, strike down the claim of the victim by pointing out the lack of any contractual link with the latter. The Supreme Court confirmed the view of the District Court of Lódź that a company with a monopoly for importing foreign cars into Poland had a duty not to import dangerously defective vehicles, and could be held liable in tort to all those who suffered the ill consequences of a breach of this duty.

pin (1981) which was swallowed by the buyer is an interesting example of the manufacturer's liability. Although the manufacturer and the seller of the cake were the same legal person (Hortex)[44] the court did not pay attention to the latter and concentrated upon the former role of Hortex. The doctrine of law widely approved the tendency of concentrating on the manufacturer, as according to them he was the person who had the greatest influence upon the safety and quality of products (Nesterowicz 1981, Szpunar 1985a). In the light of the prevailing requirement of 'fault' on the part of the defendant this was clearly an approach ensuring legal and factual consistency.

While in the light of the statement above the manufacturers' liability was welcomed by Polish courts and representatives of the doctrine of law almost unanimously, the liability of importers to the same extent as that of manufacturers was much more difficult to accept, as it was recognized that it might to a certain extent involve elements of a more objective liability standard. In earlier cases the courts rather did not envisage such a possibility. The case of Fiat 'Multipla' (1962) shows that the absence of a contractual relationship was not sufficient justification for the importers to strike down the claims of victims of products imported by them. However, the importers were not liable for hidden defects, those not detectable with the exercise of a due level of care. It could be implied from the early judgements that, as importers merely acquired products from producers, they were assumed not to have as much control over the quality and safety of products as the latter. The level of care required of them was therefore lower. This issue is elaborated upon in a further part of this chapter, the part devoted to the issue of fault. Here it is necessary to point out that with the case of the defective 'Wartburg', of 1984, the importers' duties became as stringent as those of the manufacturers. Hence, the legal basis of importers' liability being Article 415 of the Civil Code, "a legal person importing cars made abroad for the purpose of their introduction into the national market, accepts liability towards those injured (by the cars) to the same extent as the foreign manufacturer would."[45] According to the Supreme Court this was "the only proper approach, complying with the principles of social co-operation and the social and economic aim of introducing imported cars into the Polish market".[46] Surprisingly, the reasoning of the Court in this case very much resembles the reasoning behind the Product Liability Directive, although both these legal instruments were certainly adopted on a different political and economic arena. The Supreme Court held:

> This attitude complies with the general system of co-operation of member states of the Socialist Camp. Making the liability of importers of goods more stringent in the light of the present difficulties in obtaining remedies directly from the

44 The cake was made by Hortex and sold in a Hortex shop.

45 II CR 57/84, p. 75. Translated by the author of the book. Words in brackets added by the author.

46 Ibid, at p. 79.

> manufacturer becomes necessary in relation to dangers brought about by the developments in production and market relations. Adopting a different view might as a consequence lead to lack of possibilities of obtaining compensation for losses caused by a defective product ....[47]

The Supreme Court wished to secure the rights of victims of defective products in the circumstances of growing international commercial exchange. The Court followed the opinions of doctrinal writers calling for equal treatment of manufacturers and importers as regards their liability to victims of defective products. Those calling for a change in attitude were for instance Sołtysiński (1970: 169) and Nesterowicz (1979: 9). Unfortunately the Supreme Court, having focused upon the aforementioned economic and social factors, failed to provide precise legal foundations for such heavy duties of importers. Doctrinal writers, including those who wrote the commentary to the judgement in the 'Wartburg' case (Szpunar and Łętowska 1984) tried to fill in this gap and provided their own understanding of how legally the liability of the importers ought to be shaped. The conceptual question was: should the importers be liable for their own conduct (in other words, can their own actions be treated as a tort), or for the conduct of the manufacturers? According to Szpunar and Łętowska, the importers are very specific professional traders, and as such ought to be liable for their own conduct of introducing unsafe goods into the market (1984). Without the importers, the particular product would not appear on the market of a particular country. Their conduct has therefore the same impact upon the market from the point of view of the victim as the conduct of the manufacturers.

Hungarian and Polish doctrine and case law have developed tortious product liability from the liability of sellers to the manufacturers' or importers' liability. Their Czechoslovak counterparts, on the other hand, conducted a very clear division of the possible defendants and bases of their liability, being contract for the sellers, and tort for the manufacturers.[48] Notwithstanding these differences in approach, all the Central European jurisdictions envisaged the possibility of joint and several liability of a number of actors present in the distribution chain leading to the ultimate consumer. This issue is further examined below.

Victims of dangerous products – heading towards 'consumerism'

Who could benefit from Central European product liability laws? In Part I it was submitted that the birth of contemporary product liability laws was linked to the recognition of the specificity of the position of consumers within markets. In Central Europe, until the Product Liability Directive started exerting its influence, the notion 'consumers' was not mentioned very often with relation to product

47 Ibid, at p. 79. Translated by the author.

48 This unless the manufacturer actually had a contractual relationship with the victim of his product (Svestka 1989: 100, 102).

liability issues (Gnela 2000: 182). Initially, socialist systems did not recognize the importance of consumers' position, and instead required that the relations between state-owned undertakings ('socialist organizations') be distinguished as particularly important for national economies. Separate *arbitrazh* regime available for dealings between state undertakings in Poland and in Czechoslovakia contained product liability rules for its own use (these were strict liability systems).[49] With the political and economic changes taking place in the late 1970s and early 1980s, product liability systems were established by courts and scholars, increasingly following the 'consumer rhetoric'. Thus, although the notion 'consumer' might not have always been used, and protection was afforded to small entrepreneurs as well as private individuals, the language of weaker market position and poorer access to information about products and services was notable very early on.

Another *raison d'être* of tortious product liability regimes has been to assist persons otherwise barred by privity of contract from bringing claims. Hence, compensation is to be independent of the victim's status or relationship with the tortfeasor. Central European jurisprudence in the area of product liability headed in this direction as well.

Below is a short analysis of the developments in court judgements and doctrinal views concerning the potential claimants in product liability cases.

Hungarian civil liability rules refer to 'anybody' (Article 339 of the Civil Code) when determining possible claimants in a tort action. The first case establishing tortious product liability of the seller – the 'motorcycle case' mentioned above, made it clear that this liability would be available to any victims of defective products who did not have a contractual relationship to fall back on.[50] Product liability cases involved mainly consumer victims, although the courts did not refuse protection to entrepreneurs or businesses whose property or health was damaged by defective products. In fact, already examined contract liability cases[51] did involve entrepreneurs, and the same tendency could be observed in tortious liability.[52] The key rationale for using product liability rules has been to protect those whose position as opposed to the tortfeasor's was somehow economically weaker, and there was an informational imbalance to the detriment of the victim.

A similar approach could be seen in Czechoslovakia, especially with regard to the focus on lack of sufficient knowledge about products and services, and generally a weaker market position of claimants in product liability cases. According to the

49 These special liability systems no longer exist. At present, liability in business relations is regulated by the Civil Codes in Hungary and Poland (subject to normal civil liability rules) and by the Commercial Code in the Czech Republic (Act No. 513/1998 Coll.) (here liability is strict). Product liability in business relations is not analysed in this book.

50 Further, because the *non-cumul* principle did not apply in Hungary, tortious liability was also available to those in an actual contractual relationship with the seller.

51 The 'paint case' and the 'chickens case'.

52 The 'chemical spray case' and the 'bee case' – Maczonkai 1996: 110.

former Section 421 of the Czechoslovak Civil Code, "an organization is liable to *a citizen* for damage which it has caused by infringement of a legal duty."[53] The amended version of Section 420 reads: "any person is liable for damage which he caused by breaching a legal obligation (duty)." The concept of a 'citizen' as a victim of a tort, which has now disappeared from the regulation of civil liability, was also present in doctrinal writings of Czechoslovakia (Svestka 1989). It was a wide concept, including those in a contractual relationship and those outside a contractual relationship with the tortfeasor (Svestka 1989: 100). Such a wide approach to victims of torts has remained after the concept of 'citizens' disappeared from the Civil Code.[54]

The Polish Civil Code offers protection of tort law to 'another' person (Article 415) – hence anyone injured by the tortfeasor. Adopting this provision as a legal basis of the product liability system meant that the courts allowed anybody who suffered damage, irrespective of lack of a contractual relationship with the tortfeasor, to bring a claim. Such an approach was confirmed by the Supreme Court in the case of the 'P-70' car.[55] The Supreme Court pointed out, when considering an appeal from the judgement of a district court, that once it was decided that liability of the seller should be based on the law of tort, it was of no importance whether one of the claimants in the case (the buyer's wife) was not a party to the contract of sale. Similarly with the two other Central European systems, Polish courts allowed claims of entrepreneurs as well as private persons: for instance an owner of a poultry farm,[56] an owner of a sugar beetroot plantation,[57] or a person renting a farm for business purposes.[58] In the latter case the defendants unsuccessfully tried to strike down the claim pointing to the victim's professional experience with chemicals.[59] This approach was not, however, always followed, and in the case of another chemical used on a sugar beetroot farm[60] the Supreme Court refused protection to the owner of the farm, arguing that, as a professional, he ought to pay attention to the smell of the chemical and realize he received the wrong one. As a matter of fact the protection was, nonetheless, generally provided to a wider category of persons than merely non-professionals, as long at the informational imbalance between the claimant and the defendant could be established.

53 Emphasis added.

54 Note, however, the tendency highlighted above: Czech courts used tort as a basis of liability when there was no contract between the victim and the defendant in the case.

55 II CR 540/63, OSN 1965/32.

56 Judgement of the Supreme Court of 3 VI 1986, II CR 131/86 – unpublished, Gnela (2000: 182).

57 Judgement of the Supreme Court of 21 VI 1985, I CR 127/85 – unpublished, Gnela (2000: 182).

58 Judgement of the Supreme Court of 28 VI 1972, II CR 218/72.

59 The victim used to work for the seller, dealing with the type of products which caused his death.

60 Judgement of the Supreme Court of 26 V 1986, II CR 127/86 – unpublished, Gnela (2000: 182).

'PRODUCTS' WITHIN THE SPHERE OF APPLICATION OF CENTRAL EUROPEAN PRODUCT LIABILITY LAWS

Introductory remarks

The concept of products arrived in Central Europe together with the wider appearance of various elements of market economies (entailing greater presence of consumer durables on the market), and the greater influence of 'Western' market economy and philosophy. With the transformations in socialist markets and laws came the appearance of litigation which was referred to as 'product liability' litigation following the Western European and US examples. Such developments appeared in scholarly writings and in the jurisprudence of courts. The source of transformations towards mature tortious product liability regimes was the very realization of the complex and often dangerous nature of 'products'.

This new arrival on the Central European legal scene caused some terminological confusion in the systems which until then operated on the basis of the traditional civil law concept of 'things'. Central European civil codes define, or at least refer to, the concept of 'things'.[61] The Hungarian Civil Code avoids defining things, rather referring to them as 'subjects of property'.[62] According to Article 45 of the Polish Civil Code, "[T]hings, in the understanding of this Code, are only material goods."[63] The Czech Civil Code defines 'things' in Section 119 which reads: "[T]hings shall be divided into movable things and real estate."[64]

As product liability systems developed across Central Europe, it gradually became clear that the two notions are not to be understood uniformly: thus not all *things* can be within the scope of operation of *product* liability laws.[65] There are some things which, mainly because of their peculiar characteristics, or the manner in which they were manufactured, prepared or acquired, do not justify the stricter than ordinary tort liability – product liability. On the other hand, courts and scholars realized that a wide understanding of 'products' was an advantage for those injured by dangerously defective 'things'. If a thing is not at the same time a

61 The concept of 'things' was utilized by, for instance, laws on legal and commercial guarantees – in Articles 556–82 of the Polish Civil Code. The Czechoslovak and Czech Civil Code is largely inconsistent in its use of terminology relating to 'things': Sections referring to contracts of sale (Sections 590–611) use the notion 'object of sale', Sections referring to special provisions on 'Sale of Goods in Shops' (Sections 612–18), 'goods' or 'things', Sections referring to liability for defects (Sections 619–27), 'things'.

62 Article 92.1 of the Code stipulates: "[G]oods directly serving or promoting the satisfaction of the citizens' personal requirements (family homes, furnishings and articles for personal use, etc.) are subjects of personal property."

63 A great many representatives of Polish doctrine of law wrote about the concept of 'things' – see for instance Wasilkowski (1963: 8).

64 Translation provided by Dobiasova.

65 As a consequence, it is assumed here that a 'thing' is understood as a concept wider in scope than a 'product'.

'product', liability for damages caused by it is still possible, but not according to product liability rules.[66]

Both in Europe and in the United States, commodities which have not been produced or which have not been in mass circulation, have not always been seen as 'products'. Blood and human body parts, electrical energy, subjects of intellectual property rights, or computer software (Łętowska 1999: 93) have generally been subjects of controversies as to their possible treatment as subjects of product liability laws. How have the Central European countries coped with the concept of 'products'? The assumption that the source of tortious product liability is the introduction of a dangerously defective product into the market, and not its production, would normally allow the inclusion of not only manufactured goods, but also goods which have not been manufactured or constructed, but merely acquired, within the list of the possible subjects of this liability.[67] Was this the approach which the Central European courts and scholars adopted?

Food and agricultural produce

These goods may or may not have been in some way processed. There is no doubt in the practice and doctrine of law, both in the 'East' and the 'West' of Europe, that processed agricultural produce may potentially give rise to product liability. Natural, unprocessed produce, on the other hand, has been a more controversial subject. The division introduced initially by the Product Liability Directive and causing some confusion among the scholars and lawyers dealing with product liability – the division into unprocessed and processed products – did not seem to exist in the civil law regimes of Central European countries. Hence, it has been possible to classify even non-processed goods as possible subjects of product liability cases, although after a brief glance at the case law in the field, one cannot help concluding that cases involving manufactured or processed goods were common indeed.

Wasilkowski, in his widely approved in Poland definition, considered 'things' as "material parts of nature in their primary or processed state, but separated (in a natural or artificial manner) to the extent that in socio-economic relations they can be treated as independent goods" (1963: 8). Although the contention must remain in the sphere of theoretical considerations, in Poland and other Central European countries there would be nothing preventing the courts from the use of the product liability laws to offer redress to a person injured by such produce. On the other

66 It must be added here that regimes other than general product liability law may at times provide for strict liability of those dealing with certain, specifically defined goods (such as liability for medicines in Germany). These regimes, which also operate in Central Europe (mentioned below) shall not be examined in any detail in this book.

67 The Czechoslovak regime did not explain what exactly it considered as the source of product liability – whether it was the production or the introduction into circulation of defective products. See below for a further explanation.

hand, the standard of liability ('fault-based' liability) normally applied in product liability cases, as well as causation requirements, may well effectively prevent liability for products where no specific conduct of the defendant is seen as having 'caused' the damage. Lack of significant experience of these jurisdictions with unprocessed products in product liability cases cannot offer any fabric for definite conclusions.

Blood and human body parts

The controversy around the possible classification of these goods as 'products' for the purposes of product liability laws could also be observed in Central Europe, even some time before the implementation of the Product Liability Directive. The debate was by no means solely concerned with the legal dimension of the issue. Philosophical, moral and ethical arguments for adequate treatment and classification of those 'goods' deriving from a human body were also put forward.[68] The debate presented below does not encroach upon these issues, and concentrates on the legal side of the problem. The discourse began with the question whether these 'goods' ought to be 'things' within the meaning of the civil codes. No consensus has been achieved so far. Concurrently, courts and scholarly writers made attempts to compensate those who have suffered as a result of transfusions of contaminated blood. They tried avoiding, with mixed success, using general tortious liability provisions of the civil codes based on the requirement of 'fault'. Applying established product liability laws which very often abandoned this requirement was one of the options for securing such compensation, although not the only option. Introducing stricter liability standards for such 'products' was said to enable risks related to them to be internalized by their suppliers (Łętowska 1999: 94). The suppliers ought to be in the best position to reduce to a minimum the risks carried by these 'products' – by warnings or instructions, testing the blood and organs, the proper control mechanisms, and post-market control mechanisms (Łętowska 1999: 94) – and to take out insurance policies to cover any liability exposure.[69]

The Central European Civil Codes, framed in a general manner, have not given any suggestion as to the distinct treatment of cases involving blood or human body parts. In Poland the doctrine of law presents a viewpoint that, while a human being or a human body are not 'things', the situation is different as regards body parts separated from the body, including blood (Grzybowski 1985: 411, 412). The latter, until they become attached to a human body again, are according to

68 In Poland the literature concerning these issues is impressive: Safjan (1992: 51–9), Góralczyk (1997: 86–100), and many other papers referred to in the above. In Poland, where the main part of the population is Catholic, religious concerns were also reflected in the academic writings.

69 These arguments are relevant also to products such as computer software, considered below.

this theory 'things', or, according to a more cautious view, 'things *sui generis*' (Katner 1985: 30).[70] Gnela, however, continues to claim that neither of these views is correct (2000: 84, 288, 289). Her contention extends even to the period after the implementation of the Product Liability Directive into the Polish Civil Code.[71] This approach could potentially deprive victims of, for instance, transfusions of contaminated blood of remedies from which those using product liability laws are able to benefit (Mohmand 2002: 231). It is with such victims in contemplation that, claims Mohmand, product liability regime was established at all (ibid.). While so far liability of hospitals for transfusion of contaminated blood or body parts has been based on the requirement of 'fault' (courts used the general tortious liability provisions), academic writers suggested the need for a special liability system, perhaps even one resembling a Nordic compensation scheme (Hodges 2006, Nesterowicz 2001). Similar division of academic opinion can be seen in the two other Central European states (Dobiasova, Weeks).[72] Thus far, Hungarian courts have awarded compensation to persons who suffered as a result of a transfusion of contaminated blood or human organs on the basis of special liability rules concerning healthcare. The courts which have been considering a large number of claims from persons contaminated with Hepatitis C virus (statistics show that 1.7 per cent of the Hungarian population has the virus) awarded compensation on the basis of the Act on Public Health 1997 (Kovács 2003). Blood is generally deemed to be a medicine in these cases (Kovács 2003, Menyhárd 2004: 244). Czech courts have attempted to avoid using the general liability provision of Section 420 of the Civil Code, and often use Section 421a (introduced in 1991) which provides for absolute liability (it is unequivocally stated that the person liable "cannot relieve himself of liability in any way") for damage caused "by circumstances originating in the nature of a tool or other thing used in performing an obligation".[73] Section 241a explicitly allows its application in cases of "medical, social, veterinary and other biological services".

The issues involving safety and quality of, and liability for blood and human body parts reach into the wider context of healthcare, health insurance, medical liability and transplantology, not explored in this book. Central European states are gradually harmonizing these issues with the approach of the Western European

70 Compare the view of the House of Lords in the recent case of *A and others v National Blood Authority and another* (2001). Burton J clearly classified blood as a product, and the contaminated blood in the case was referred to as a 'non-standard product'.

71 It is clear that the Directive does not suggest any precise solution to this problem. Hence, national legal orders must cope with it individually.

72 Interview with Monika Dobiasova (Czech Ministry of Trade and Industry) conducted on-line in June 2003; Interview with Troy Weeks (Clifford Chance, Budapest) by telephone in September 2003.

73 Translation provided by Dobiasova. Thanks to Professor Lubos Tichy for verifying the judicial practice on this issue.

countries, and the European Community has a particularly important role to play here.

Movables attached to other 'things'

It has generally been assumed across Central Europe, in common with other legal systems as well as the Product Liability Directive, that only movable things could be subjects of product liability laws (Łętowska 1999: 94). Łętowska argued that any product which took part in the mass circulation of goods could be the subject of product liability, and immovable goods therefore should be excluded from the category as not being in mass circulation (1999: 94).

The problem of movables attached to other 'things' involves components and the question whether they ought to be treated as independent 'products' or whether they lose their independent status. The connection of two or more goods into one can have various forms and create various types of 'products' as a result. Two main categories may be distinguished. The first group are 'simple' products where it is not possible without some chemical or technological process to separate them into their component parts again, and the total separation resembling the situation from the time before the connection is impossible (such as foods consisting of several ingredients, or medicines). The second group are 'complex' products which contain spare parts, each one of which has some independent purpose, at least until the connection, and can be separated from the rest (for example a car) (Grzybowski 1985: 417). From the point of view of a victim of a defective product (whether a 'simple' or a 'complex' one) it is crucial to be able to determine whether components are to be treated as distinct products. This is for a number of reasons. The first one concerns the persons liable in a particular case, and the more emphasis is placed on 'fault', the more important it is to identify who exactly caused the defect (the manufacturer of the component or the manufacturer of the whole product).[74] Another crucial point is the generally accepted key feature of all tortious product liability regimes – the possibility of recovery of only those damages which occurred outside the defective product itself. From the analysis of Article 2 of the Product Liability Directive it is clear that movables incorporated into other movables or into immovables are treated as independent products capable of causing damages or losses independently of 'the whole'. According to the Directive, the only damages recoverable, apart from death or personal injury, are damages to 'any item of property other than the defective product itself' (Article 9(b)). This approach entails that a defect in one of the components,

74 Even some 'strict' liability systems, such as the Product Liability Directive, emphasize the relevance of the person responsible for the defect in case of complex products – Article 7(f) of the Directive provides a defence to manufacturers of component parts – they will avoid liability is they can show that the defect was attributable to the design of the final product or the instructions given by the manufacturer of the final product.

although making the whole product defective, entitles the victim to recover the value of 'the whole' if the latter has been damaged by the defective component.

How have Central European product liability laws approached these issues?

The Polish Civil Code defines component parts of a 'thing' as "everything that cannot be separated from it without damaging or a crucial alteration of the whole, or without damaging or a crucial alteration of the separated thing" (Article 47.2).[75] Things connected with other things only for some temporary use are not to be treated as their components (Article 47.3). Further, equipment used for supplying water, vapour, gas, electricity and other similar equipment, if belonging to a public utility company, is not the component of the building or the land (Article 49). The legal effect of classifying a thing as a component of another is the loss of its independence as a separate thing, as well as a separate subject of property or other rights (Article 47.1). The Hungarian Civil Code, as already mentioned, avoids defining 'things', but it is possible to find regulation concerning components among the provisions referring to property. According to Article 95.1, "[T]he right of ownership comprises all that is permanently united with the thing in such a way that separation would produce the destruction of the thing, or a considerable decrease in the value or utility of the thing or of the separated part thereof (component part)." The Czechoslovak and Czech Civil Code defines components of a thing as "all that appertains to the thing according to its nature and cannot be separated from the thing without devaluation of the thing" (Section 120).[76] It also seems clear that components cannot be subjects of separate property rights: according to Section 135a "Accessions of the thing, even if they were separated from the main thing, shall belong to the owner of the thing."[77]

Central European Civil Codes have been quite clear about the component parts not being independent things. In theory, therefore, there seemed to have been no prospect of suing the manufacturer of the component which caused loss, or indeed recovering the value of the whole product if the component was defective. On the other hand, in 'fault' liability systems, naturally occurring questions would be: exactly which part of the product caused damage, and exactly who contributed to the existence of the defect. Thus, there was a potential for a conflict between the approach of the Civil Codes and the requirements of product liability litigation. In practice, no such conflict has been visible. The jurisprudence demonstrates attempts to scientifically determine the nature and source of the defect, with the use of expert witnesses nominated by courts. Once the defect has been ascertained, all those involved – manufacturers of final products and manufacturers of spare parts – could be held liable (separately, or jointly and severally).[78] With the development of more 'objective' liability standards, or even 'strict liability' in Hungary (see below for a detailed analysis), these enquiries focused on the defect itself and

75 Translated by the author.

76 Translation provided by Dobiasova.

77 Ibid.

78 Rights of recourse among defendants were, of course, not affected.

if it was the manufacturer of the final product who was sued by the victim, the manufacturer would have been held liable simply for the result – the defect in the final product. Neither of these developments could, however, change the position concerning recovery of the value of the whole if the spare part was defective – normally this was not possible in tort law.

In cases where a movable connected with an immovable caused damage or loss, remedy could not be sought according to the Central European product liability rules before the implementation of the Product Liability Directive. The avenue of redress was either through a general tortious liability provision, or particular liability provisions concerning liability for buildings and other immovables.[79] The situation undoubtedly required change with the implementation of the Directive.

Animals

The main tendency in the development of legal systems around the world in the area of liability for damages caused by animals has been the transfer of focus from the traditional 'thing-liability' to 'person-liability' (Weir 1983: ch. 5, p. 11, s. 40). According to the Polish Act on the Protection of Animals of 1997 "an animal, as a living being, capable of suffering, is not a thing". This means that Polish product liability law would not become involved in damages or losses caused by animals. Even before the Act on the Protection of Animals had been adopted, it seems that Polish law endorsed the classification of animals as specific sources of danger. The Civil Code contains Article 431, which reads: "He who keeps or uses an animal must repair damage caused by it, irrespective of whether it was

79 Dangers posed by components were in fact noted in cases involving buildings. The Polish Civil Code has provided for liability of a person 'in possession' of the building for losses or damages caused by collapse of the building or detachment of one of its parts. It is a strict liability rule. Obviously, such a provision did not provide a remedy to those victims who *were* the persons 'in possession'. Those persons, if injured by a part of a building, had to use Article 415 and its fault liability regime. This provision was used by the Polish Supreme Court in the judgement of 1 December 1986. The case involved the death of a young girl caused by poisonous substances present in the air of her parents' apartment. In fact, these highly toxic chemicals were used in the building process. The building company was held liable for the girl's death. The Court declared using the harmful substance in the building process to be a tort. It is likely that after the implementation of the Product Liability Directive a case of this nature could have a different outcome. The substance or material used by the builders could be held dangerously defective and its manufacturer could bear liability – irrespectively of his fault. Czechoslovak Civil Code does not contain any provision regulating liability for buildings (Weir 1983: ch. 5, p. 9, s. 35), hence, the general liability provisions need to be used. Article 354.1 of the Hungarian Civil Code provides that the owner of a building shall be liable for damages caused by the collapse of a part of it, or by structural defects (rule based on fault), but this provision is without prejudice to the victim's right to claim damages from the tortfeasor (Weir 1983: ch. 5, p. 9, s. 35).

under his supervision, got lost or run away, unless neither he nor a person he is responsible for are at fault."[80] The doctrine of law postulated various solutions to the problem of damages or injuries caused by animals. Czachórski distinguished two situations: Article 431 should, according to him, not apply if an animal was a mere tool in the hands of a person, but it should apply if the animal caused damage "of its own will"[81] (2002: 242). In the former situation the person shall be liable for his own actions according to Article 415 of the Civil Code. It is clear that neither of these situations would include wild animals, roaming free, where no such liability is possible. Both provisions are based on fault, but in the former case it is fault in supervision – culpa in custodiendo.[82] The Czechoslovak and Czech Civil Code does not contain any specific provision concerning liability for damages caused by animals, hence the general rules of liability must apply. In addition, the Hunting Act of 1992 or the Act on State Liability of 1998 have been used as legal bases for compensation of damages caused by wild animals (Hradek 2004: 91). The Hungarian Civil Code (Article 353.1) distinguishes between domestic and wild animals. The persons keeping wild animals are treated by the Code as performing an activity of high risk, and hence strictly liable. Those keeping domestic animals fall under the general principles of liability (Weir 1983: ch. 5, p. 12, s. 42). The strict liability of those "bearing the hunting rights" for damages caused by wild animals was additionally endorsed in the Act on the Protection of Wild Animals, the Wild Economy and Hunting of 1996 (Menyhárd 2004: 234).

Electricity

It is clear that the Product Liability Directive requires electricity to be treated as any other product. Can one observe a similar approach in the Central European civil laws before the Directive was implemented? The civil codes have generally not included electricity into the scope of 'things'. Here is where another significant change is likely to happen after the implementation of the Directive.

The subjects of intellectual property rights

Following the contemporary technological and industrial progress, more and more goods which traditionally would not be treated as 'products' at all, become potential dangers to those using them. Adopting the right approach to contents of a book or any other written piece of information, such as a leaflet or computer software, has become a challenge recently and the need for product liability laws to either accept liability for them or reject it has occurred. Central European countries before the implementation of the Product Liability Directive have not developed these issues. Surely they would not be classified as 'things' according to the traditional

80 Translated by the author.

81 Translated by the author. The Polish phrase is '*z własnego popędu*'.

82 The issue was analysed by Szpunar (1985c: 11).

definitions in the Civil Codes. The need for the implementation of the Product Liability Directive also did not solve this problem unequivocally, as the Directive has not regulated the issue in an unambiguous manner. Dobiasova clearly stated that the Czech product liability litigation has so far avoided this problem, as, even though there have been several cases involving defective computer software or components, these were settled out of court.[83] The Polish scholarly writers rather opted for not treating intellectual goods as products, although it was also argued that the position on computer software should perhaps be reconsidered in future (Czachórski 2002: 284).

THE ELEMENTS OF TORTIOUS PRODUCT LIABILITY IN CENTRAL EUROPE

Once the preliminary matters concerning the Central European tortious product liability systems have been explored, the core of the liability (its key elements) needs examination. Transformations which took place in Central European jurisprudence and doctrine of law concerning these issues have been remarkable. On the other hand, a striking feature of Central European product liability practice until now has been relative lack of complexity. Central European courts only recently started being faced with intricate design defects, cases involving latent side effects of medicines, or complicated causal issues involving a number of concurrent possible causes or multiple defendants. The consistent, well-grounded approach to these issues has not so far been established. The analysis below reflects this relative simplicity, and describes the challenges which are now presenting themselves.

One needs to tread carefully when structuring the analysis of the key elements of tortious product liability. The elements which are now taken for granted: defect, damage, and the causal link between the two, did not initially exist in this form in the 'fault liability' systems of Central Europe. This conceptual framework did, however, develop gradually in courts' jurisprudence and in doctrinal writings. Although one must be aware, therefore, that the dividing lines between these key elements were not always very clear-cut, the book offers an assessment which seems historically, doctrinally and conceptually manageable. The three main 'chunks' are the 'tort', the damage and the causal link. The 'tort' element is complex and its conceptual structure was radically transformed in Central European product liability systems. It is encapsulated in the legal construct of 'introduction into circulation of a defective product' and involves: the essence of the defect, 'fault' and its components, and of course the notion of 'introduction into circulation'. Because of the particular value of the 'fault' discourse in shaping Central European tortious product liability, this element is analysed in great detail,

83 The statement derives from the interview with Dobiasova (June 2003). She pointed out that large consumer organizations received inquiries concerning the manner in which to settle such disputes.

although it has not been considered useful to separate it from other considerations pertaining to 'tort'.

Generally, liability in tort finds its basis in a damage caused by one person to another, normally outside the bond of a contractual relationship (Czachórski 2002: 197).[84] In the words of Witold Czachórski – a very prominent representative of the Polish doctrine of law – the contents of a tortious obligation relationship are the innocent party's right to gain redress and the tortfeasor's obligation to redress the damage (ibid.) The requisites of tortious liability in Poland are usually held to include: some event with which law associates the obligation to compensate (normally, someone's conduct bearing the characteristics of 'fault' is required here), the damage, and the causal link between the event and the damage (Czachórski 2002: 198). In the Czechoslovak doctrine of law, the requisites of tortious liability – together forming the *corpus delicti*[85] (*skutková podstava*) – were: an act or omission by an individual having the characteristics of infringement or violation of a legal duty, the damage the extent of which can be proven, the causal link between the conduct and the damage, and finally the 'culpability' (intent or negligence) on the part of the particular individual (Fiala and Kindl 2007, Vondracek 1988: 375). In the Hungarian doctrine of law, the conditions for tortious liability were shaped similarly: unlawful conduct, causal connection, damage, as well as fault were mentioned (Harmathy 1998: 117). The clearly visible difference between the Polish approach on the one hand, and the Czech and Hungarian approaches on the other, is the treatment of the 'standard of liability' (as explained in Part I, 'standard of liability' involves the question how important the 'fault' of the defendant is in determining her liability). According to the Polish doctrine of law, 'fault' does not constitute another necessary requisite of liability, but merely the characteristic of the human behaviour to which law attaches an obligation to compensate (Czachórski 2002: 198). Czech and Hungarian writers rather see 'fault' as an independent requisite of liability. From the perspective of product liability regimes, this difference in approaches does not seem to matter, and indeed it has not affected the structure of this book. It is the particular value and conceptual content given to 'fault' which weighs upon the operation of product liability laws.

The 'tort' – its features and meaning in product liability cases

Introduction

The first step on the way to creating an effective product liability system based on the general provisions specified above was establishing whether an actual 'tort'

84 All Central European legal systems allow using tortious liability even if there was a contract between claimant and defendant. Czechoslovak and Czech courts did not use this opportunity (see Chapter 4 above, and also below).

85 German *Tatbestand* – Vondracek (1988: 375).

could be found in the activity of the producers, importers, distributors or sellers of products which caused damage. How did Central European courts and doctrine of law accommodate liability for defective *products* within liability for *torts*? The analysis below portrays how the general concept of 'tort' was developed into a legal construct which could be referred to as 'introduction into circulation of a defective product'.

The gist of a product liability case following the rules of general tortious liability has traditionally been in the considerations of 'fault'. It is a complex notion, not easy to grasp in the context of product liability. The existence of defect which caused damage was the ultimate requirement in product liability cases, but it was attributed to a breach of some type of a legal duty on the part of the defendant. The language of duties was engaged in assessing the existence of 'fault' (specifically – in assessing 'unlawfulness' of conduct – the objective element of 'fault').[86] Other elements of product liability discourse – predictability, avoidability, reasonable expectations and cost/benefit analysis – also featured very strongly in analyses of 'fault' in specific cases (in assessing the subjective element of 'fault' – 'fault proper'). Further, the structure of the civil process and the litigation culture in Central European states entails that issues which in other legal systems (especially the common law systems) would form part of causal considerations (like foreseeability) were also contained within the 'fault' concept.

The concept of 'fault' gradually became more objective, sometimes to the extent where it was no longer significant, replaced by the 'defect' discourse.[87] This transformation occurred in doctrinal writings and court judgements in the context of product liability, but it was also accompanied by more general changes of civil liability standards in Central Europe. These entailed a review of the key elements of 'fault'. Indeed, the tendency across Central Europe has been to objectivize some types of civil liability.

The development of Central European tortious product liability can be described as follows: while initially, according to the general principles of tort, the key point of focus was the analysis of the defendant's conduct with a view to establishing 'fault', with time attention shifted onto the condition of products and the damage they caused. The 'fault' discourse blended with other, more objective and targeted considerations of 'defect'. While in Czechoslovakia and Poland the 'fault' element remained valid to some extent, in Hungary it gave way entirely to these other considerations (focusing on the 'social expectations' test, although the courts also did not shy away from elements of risk/utility analysis). Hungarian courts created a liability system where the 'social expectations' with regard to products were the key factor determining liability.[88] On the other hand, it is still unclear whether the

86 See below for a detailed analysis of the elements of 'fault'.

87 A more detailed conceptual background to this transformation was presented at pp. 71-75, Chapter 3 of Part I.

88 This remark concerns liability for products which do not comply with public/consumer/social expectations – see Howells' 'abstract approach' explored at pp. 73-74,

consumer expectations test proposed by the Directive will sit comfortably with the Central European product liability practice. This is partly due to the complex character of product liability law, to the shape and effects of the Product Liability Directive, and partly because of the fact that the Central European practice will no doubt be influenced by the wider transformations in Central European civil laws. Obviously, the test is a novelty for the Polish and Czech courts. However, even the Hungarian courts may have problems with applying it consistently to cases before them. As mentioned above, Central European courts have so far been confronted with cases where defects were not very complex. While it is relatively straightforward to refer to 'social expectations' where a television set explodes in one's apartment, or if one slips on a rough surface wearing a slipper with a clearly unsafe slippery sole (examples of cases where Hungarian courts used the 'social expectations' test), there may be problems in applying the test in more complex design defect cases. Central European courts, in common with other courts in civil law systems (such as France or Austria) operate in a more principles-oriented environment, where no great need for detailed justification of judgements exists.[89] Thus, it would be easier for them to follow the route chosen by those other civil law systems where the focus is often on the consequences of the defect: on the damage, and where the defect itself is not closely examined (and neither of course is the conduct of the defendant). On the other hand, although product liability transformed in Central Europe from liability for 'fault' to liability for defective products and beyond, the analysis can never become completely divorced from the conduct of defendants – it is after all liability for defectively produced or designed products which found their way to the market. The future of the Central European 'defect' standard is not yet set in stone.

Let us now observe the evolution of the 'tort' in product liability systems: first through the doctrinal analysis of its main components, and following this through their interpretation by courts.

Gradual reallocation of interest – from a conduct-focused to a defect-focused approach

Until quite recently, Central European tortious product liability did not involve a very refined approach to the notion of defect. One of the reasons for this was the specific legal culture and the nature of legal practice which did not entail very complex legal issues (described in Part I). Nonetheless, there was an even more significant reason – one involving different elements of discourse. There is no doubt that 'defect' was a key factor in establishing liability, but in regimes based on the requirement of 'fault' an enquiry into the nature of 'defect' was translated

Chapter 3 of Part I (he suggests that there is no need to enquire about the exact physical source of defect in the product as long as it causes damage or injury in a way that contravenes such expectations).

89 See Chapter 2 of Part I for a further elaboration of the Central European legal and judicial systems and cultures.

into tackling the 'what went wrong' question – an assessment of the process which led to the introduction into the market of a product which caused damage. This approach entails classifying the conduct of the defendants to create design, manufacturing and instructions/warning flaws. Polish legal doctrine and practice also added flaws in 'observation', which derived from the professionals' failure to monitor products already introduced into circulation for possible defects and dangers not known before (Łętowska 1999: 93). This classification, or 'boxing', which more commonly is applied to classify defects in products, was pinpointed by academic writers and courts in Poland, and less comprehensively in Hungary[90] and Czechoslovakia. On the other hand, lack of comprehensive, learned scientific approach to these issues across Central Europe was sometimes striking. Especially the differences between the design and manufacturing flaws/defects were not always delimited precisely.

'Fault' was understood in Central Europe as consisting in a subjective ('fault proper') and an objective ('unlawfulness') element. Thus, the enquiry into the defendant's conduct had elements of a subjective look at the reasonability, predictability or avoidability considerations, and of any objective social or legal norms which the defendant might have breached.

When courts started shifting the liability standard towards a more objective (the Czech Republic and Poland), even strict liability (Hungary), their attention was increasingly on the product in question and not on the activities which led to its defective condition. The 'boxing' into various types of 'fault' was taken over by another classification – one to indicate types of defects involved, and the latter remains valid until today. The 'boxes' are emphasized with various levels of strength. Although it appears that in Hungary they were taken over by the more abstract 'social expectations' considerations, it is unclear what the position would be if a complex design defect case was being decided. What effect the implementation of the European Product Liability Directive will have on these developments is not entirely clear, although, as mentioned above, it may be assumed that the practice of product liability law will continue to be affected by the approach developed before.

It must be acknowledged here that these remarks, and indeed the structure of this section of the book, are the result of a complex research and assessment process, involving very often 'reading between the lines' of the very laconic judgements of Central European courts, and a number of in-depth interviews with Central European academics and practitioners. The structure of analysis adopted below does not therefore follow the structure and methodology that Central European courts or academic scholars expressly used. It is rather the approach which an 'external' observer, equipped with all the advantages of hindsight and

90 In Hungary the 'boxes' were not utilized in any great detail in spite of the fact that courts very quickly abandoned the focus on the defendants' conduct. They emphasized the result – damages and broken 'social expectations' – instead of a detailed analysis of the defect itself. See below for a further explanation of this process.

the knowledge of the Western European approach to these issues, would adopt. Further, the structure of the analysis below allows one to formulate conclusions concerning the main features of the product liability discourse in Central Europe at present, and correlating these with what is happening elsewhere in Europe. These conclusions are crucial in assessing the possible future of harmonizing the Central European systems with those of other European Union Member States. Part I elaborated on the importance of the internal product liability discourse (including the pre-existing rules, jurisprudence, academic writings and legal culture) in the process of harmonization; the process which, after all, consists in a day-to-day application of the provisions of the Product Liability Directive.

Because 'fault' was such an integral part of tortious liability, the analysis of the elements of 'tort' ought to start with it. Through the transformations within this concept one may see the emergence of other elements of tort and indeed the emergence of mature tortious product liability systems in Central Europe.

'Fault' – the roots of product liability

Introductory remarks

Although most defendants in product liability cases were legal persons, their liability was 'personalized' enough to be covered by the general liability provisions which describe responsibility for 'own actions'. The liability was related to the conduct of an employee or an organ whose responsibility was 'channelled' onto the legal person. In the words of Vondracek (a Czech scholar) "since juristic persons are considered mere intellectual or fictional constructions, they cannot commit a wrong but their corporate organs and employees can. Tortious acts committed by these individuals are imputed to the juristic person by a fiction of the law if they acted in the implementation of the juristic person's task" (1988: 378).[91] The crucial feature of such liability for own conduct is the 'fault' of the person concerned (Łętowska 1999: 96). Indeed, 'fault' has been the key part of the 'tort discourse' in Central Europe.

Conceptual framework of 'fault' in Central Europe

Central European doctrinal writers distinguish two 'component parts' of 'fault': the unlawful conduct ('unlawfulness'/'wrongfulness' – objective element) and the 'fault proper' (subjective element) (Czachórski [2002: 202] and Łętowska [1999: 96] in Poland, Szalma [2003] and Harmathy [1998: 118] in Hungary, Vondracek [1988] in Czechoslovakia).[92]

---

91 Vondracek uses the term 'juristic persons' instead of 'legal persons'.

92 Harmathy observed the practice of Hungarian courts, especially in cases of medical malpractice: they refrained from distinguishing the two factors and simply focused upon the fact of non-compliance with the professional rules of conduct, which is held to indicate the unlawful conduct as well as the existence of 'fault' (1998: 118). This practice

Such a division in Poland could have existed only within the doctrinal opinions and jurisprudence. The Civil Code mentions 'fault proper' but does not mention unlawfulness within the factors determining tortious liability. The Polish Civil Code has to a great extent followed the Code of Obligations of 1933, which in turn was based upon the French *Code Civil* of 1804. Following the latter, the conduct of the defendant was to have the 'characteristics of fault'. According to the majority of academic writers this meant that the conduct needed to be objectively and subjectively "negative" (Czachórski 2002: 202).[93]

In contrast to the Polish Civil Code, Czechoslovak and Hungarian codes do mention 'unlawfulness' as well as the 'fault proper', although they deal with the latter indirectly (through the exonerating circumstances).[94] They took the example of the Austrian civil law, and to some extent of the German civil law.[95] In the Hungarian Civil Code, "whoever *unlawfully* causes damage to another shall be bound to compensate the same" (Article 339). The 'unlawfulness' is visible at first sight, in contrast to the subjective element of fault. According to Harmathy, the "constituent elements of the rules on *delictual* liability are unlawful conduct, causal connection, and damage. In the case of the so-called general rule of Article 339 the *additional condition* is fault as it is interpreted in practice"[96] (1998: 117). Harmathy adds the last element, although earlier in his paper he acknowledges that according to a "rather influential opinion" in Hungary, the rule of Article 339 does not require the subjective 'fault proper' (1998: 115). The prevailing approach, however, adopted in practice by Hungarian courts, is to require the existence of 'fault proper'. The source of this requirement is Article 339 itself: it contains a basis for exoneration of the defendant if she proves she acted in a way expected of her in the particular situation. In the light of this statement, the developments in the product liability case law, leading gradually to the establishment of the regime closely resembling a 'strict liability' one, appear to have been in spite of, rather than according to, the Hungarian Civil Code. The developments in Czechoslovakia and the Czech Republic need to be analysed with regard to two time periods. Before the crucial amendment of the Civil Code in 1991, Sections 420 (concerning physical persons, referred to as 'citizens') and 421 (concerning

is a reflection of the movement towards the objectivization of the concept of fault, very dynamic in Hungary – see below.

93 Notion used by Czachórski.

94 See below – accordingly certain prominent representatives of the Hungarian doctrine of law have held an opinion that Article 339 of the Civil Code did not require 'fault proper' at all. Such contentions were also put forward in the Czechoslovak doctrine of law. Since the amendment of the Czech Code in 1991 the inexplicit subjective element of fault disappeared – this lead to even more suggestions of objective liability.

95 See the analysis of the main principles of Central European legal systems in Chapter 2 of Part I.

96 The italics added by the author of the book, in order to stress the particular importance of the manner in which the subjective 'fault' element is being treated by Harmathy.

legal persons, referred to as 'organizations') clearly contained both elements of fault: the objective "infringement of a legal duty" (420.1) and the subjective "fault" (420.2).[97] According to the amended version of the Czech Civil Code "any person is liable for damage which he caused by breaching a legal obligation".[98] The subjective element of fault seems to have been removed. Hence the statement by Trade Links that liability gained an objective character owing to the amendment of the Code (1996: 123). This statement was contested by Dobiasova, who claims that the Czech liability system is still based upon 'presumed culpability'.[99] It is also confirmed by some leading academic writers (Hradek 2006, Tichy 2005).

Changes within the framework of 'fault' in product liability cases

Two tendencies in the development of product liability theories and practice in Central Europe can be observed (Nesterowicz 1979: 13–19). The more cautious one has been the objectivization of 'fault', which following Nesterowicz can be described as abandoning the subjective element of 'fault proper' (1979: 16). It occurred in Poland and Czechoslovakia. The other, more progressive one is the objectivization of liability itself, rendering the liability for dangerous products independent of 'fault'. This one appeared in Hungary. Chapter 3 of Part I to some extent explored the difference between these two processes, arguing that objectivization of fault retained the focus on the defendant's conduct, albeit assessed according to objective standards; and objectivization of liability entailed a shift in focus from conduct onto 'events' causing damage (defects in products).

The analysis now turns to the systematic account of the evolution of both elements of 'fault', and indeed of the evolution of the concept of 'fault' itself, in Central European product liability law. It is difficult indeed to make the analysis manageable because although the general tendencies were similar across Central Europe, a great deal of discrepancies can also be observed. In order to ensure clarity and consistency, the discussion follows these general tendencies, and emphasizes the differences whenever applicable. This to some extent entails a distinct assessment of the developments in the three legal systems.

Subjective element of fault – 'fault proper' The 'fault proper' has been defined as a subjective, improper nature of a person's conduct, improperness of behaviour concerning the "moment of foreseeability and the moment of will" (Czachórski 2002: 203),[100] or a substantial claim of improper conduct (Łętowska 1999: 98). The particular defendant is held to be 'at fault' because in the particular circumstances she failed to behave in a way she should have, and could have, behaved. Two main theories have been put forward in Central Europe with regard to this concept:

97 The latter not expressly mentioned in Section 421 referring to legal persons, but indirectly present through the exonerating circumstances.

98 Civil Code of the Czech Republic, 2001, Trade Links.

99 Telephone interview with Dobiasova, September 2003.

100 Translated by the author.

the psychological theory and the normative theory (Czachórski 2002: 204, Dąbrowa 1968). According to the psychological theory the improperness of the defendant's behaviour ought to be judged according to her mental attitude towards the behaviour or towards the consequences of this behaviour. Normative theory focuses upon the manner in which this mental attitude can be judged by an outside observer (Czachórski 2002: 204). The Polish legal system seems to have favoured the normative theory, and the Czech and Hungarian systems rather favoured the psychological theory. These preferences are very closely related to the manner in which tortious liability in general, and the concept of 'fault' in particular, have been regulated by the Civil Codes. The Polish Civil Code requires the plaintiff to prove the 'fault' of the defendant, while the Czech and Hungarian Codes introduce presumption of 'fault'. Vondracek pointed out that the Czechoslovak legislator had introduced the presumption of 'fault' because the 'fault proper' had been considered as the "state of the mind", not "directly perceptible to others: a tortfeasor himself knows best the part which he has played in the alleged course of events" (1988: 375).

In addition to this general conceptual approach to 'fault proper', product liability adds its own characteristic features to the debate. Essentially, defect becomes the integral part of the considerations of 'fault' in product liability cases. Reasonability, predictability, avoidability, discoverability and risk/benefit analysis, all play a part in determination of the manner in which the defendant (manufacturer, importer or retailer of a defective product) should have behaved.

First of all, business nature of the defendants' activities determined a high standard of conduct – higher than would be demanded of an ordinary individual. This approach can be clearly seen throughout Central Europe. Further, the analysis of a defendant's conduct was linked to the type of defect which the product exhibited, thus 'fault' was not simply 'fault' – it was 'fault' in design, in manufacture, in instruction/warning, in 'observation'. While the 'boxing' of types of 'fault' was not very comprehensive and indeed very explicit, one may certainly observe scholars and courts referring to 'fault', and subsequently also to 'defect' of a particular type. With differing levels of focus on 'fault', there was indeed an interesting complexity in the case law – one may either see references to types of 'fault', and, as the product liability systems developed, increasingly to the types of 'defect'.[101]

Design and manufacturing defects ('fault') were not often distinguished from one another. Indeed, what may in Western Europe have been design defects, were rather approached as flaws in the manufacturing process. Building presumptions of 'fault' or even abandoning the 'fault' requirement altogether seemed relatively straightforward here. Courts took the view that it was easier for the defendant to demonstrate the details of the design and manufacturing process than it would be

101 The roots of this transition were in changes of the liability standard – relaxing the 'fault' requirement and a greater focus on the defects in products (analysed in more detail below).

for the victim, and ultimately that it was easier for the defendant to internalize the risks of defects.

Instruction/information defects ('fault'), wider known as 'failure to warn' defects, were very common, and interestingly enough these cases often exhibited the courts' willingness to presume 'fault' or even to exclude its relevance. A closer observation of the exact defects involved in cases across Central Europe so far (clear misinformation of consumers with regard to very dangerous products – it was easy to predict possible damages and thus it was a reasonable step to warn consumers) exhibits a relative ease with which such developments could have been construed. Yet, it is difficult to predict the approach the courts would have taken if they were faced with a difficult case requiring a balance of costs and benefits of the product and the warnings.

Predictability and reasonability arguments were also used by Polish courts to establish a 'fault in monitoring' (referred to in Poland as 'observation fault'). This concerned situations where there were clear signals of injuries or damages caused by a particular type of product reaching the manufacturer or seller, and no steps were taken to warn consumers, change the design or manufacturing process, or take the product off the market. Here, again, Polish courts rather presumed 'fault' – the assumption was that the alternative cause of action to the one actually taken by the manufacturer would be required.

The courts of Hungary and Poland, as well as the Czechoslovak courts (although not as extensively as their Hungarian and Polish counterparts), have attempted to, if not indirectly abandon 'fault proper' in product liability cases, simply facilitate the burden of proving it. Whether the subjective element of fault was abandoned entirely or not, the major point of focus in product liability litigation became its objective element – 'unlawfulness'.

'Unlawfulness' – transformation, and decreasing reliance on safety standards and other regulatory requirements The notion of 'unlawfulness', whether mentioned expressly in the Civil Codes or not, has always been the necessary component of the concept of 'fault' in each Central European jurisdiction. When Central European courts and doctrinal writers consider 'unlawfulness' in product liability cases, they employ the language of duties – those explicitly established by law, or those contained in general clauses such as the 'principles of community life'. The existence of defect in a product which caused damage is linked to a breach of "objective standards; not fulfilling certain safety requirements and standards of conduct" (Nesterowicz 1979: 16), or acting against a general prohibition of putting the others' lives, health and property in danger.

As the product liability regimes were being established, 'unlawfulness' became an increasingly prominent factor. The tendency to increase the duties of those dealing professionally with products was clear (Łętowska 1999: 96). The absolute safety of products has never been required, but the level of the required safety was gradually increased. The considerations leading to establishing 'unlawfulness' involved complex factual and legal issues concerning the product itself: its construction and design, attached instructions and warnings, protective equipment attached to it, as well as the conduct of the defendant. With time, 'unlawfulness' often became the only element of 'fault' which was in fact considered.

In the absence of an express written provision concerning product liability, what such 'unlawfulness' has meant in the product liability context has not always been constant and clear in the Central European legal systems. The use of general liability provisions, whether those referring to tort (Poland), or those concerning both tort and contract (the Czech Republic and Hungary) as legal bases of the product regimes, entailed the questions: when and how these provisions could be breached in the context of introduction into the market of dangerous products. The Czech Civil Code mentions the breach of a "legal obligation (duty)" (Section 420), and the Hungarian Civil Code, unlawfulness of the defendant's conduct (Article 339). In Czechoslovakia, a 'legal duty' was held to include duties imposed by statutes or other legal provisions, as well as the general duty of care imposed by Section 415 of the Civil Code (Vondracek 1988: 377).[102] The last is not known to tort liability systems (Poland) which do not adopt a general presumption of fault (Szpunar 1970: 51). The Polish Civil Code does not mention 'unlawfulness', but courts generally considered it, searching for a violation of duties imposed by safety regulations, or breach of certain other legal provisions (Gnela 2000: 183, 184).[103] According to the Polish Supreme Court, supplying a product with a defect was a 'tort' as long as it constituted a violation of a binding legal provision or the 'principles of community life'.[104] The unpublished judgement of the Supreme Court of 11 December 1987 (the case of defective poultry feeding stuff) indicated particular provisions of Polish law contravened by the producer of the feeding stuff which did not contain sufficient quantities of vitamins and other nutrients (such as calcium) necessary for the proper growth of poultry.[105] The provisions introduced the duty to test every component before its use for manufacture of the final product, and to test the safety and assess the quality of the final product. A further obligation was concerned with provision of information to consumers about the characteristics of the products (Article 20 of the Act on Quality). The provisions mentioned above have been used by the Polish courts on numerous occasions in product liability litigation. For instance, an earlier judgement of the

102 Section 415 of the Czech Civil Code stipulates: "Everyone must act so as to avoid damages to health, property, nature and environment" – translation provided by Dobiasova.

103 In the product liability context these were for instance: the Act *on Normalization* of 27 November 1961, or the Act *on the Quality of Goods, Services and Buildings* of 8 February 1979 ('The Act on Quality').

104 See for instance the judgement of the Polish Supreme Court of 28 April 1964 (the case of the defective 'P-70' car), at p. 43. See pp. 28-29 and 61, Part I for the short explanation of the role of the 'principles of community life'.

105 These were: Article 20.1.5 of the Act on Quality and paragraph 3 of the Act of the Council of Ministers of 1979 *on the organization of quality control for goods, services, works and buildings*.

Supreme Court in the case of exploding television sets (1981) engaged Article 30 of the Act on Quality as the legal basis for treating the conduct of the producer of the television sets as a tort.[106]

It is clear that a breach of the legal duties mentioned above led to product liability. Would complying with the specified safety standards mean no liability? In other words, would a 'regulatory compliance defence' be a valid defence in Central European product liability systems? Further, the administrative rules governing virtually all aspects of market operation were comprehensive during socialism. Did they entail a pre-emption rule for manufacturers of products?

The debate on the possible introduction of a form of a regulatory compliance defence is taking place at present in European policy papers and academic writings (Fairgrieve and Howells 2007: 972–4, Mildred 2007, Third Report on Product Liability Directive). The Product Liability Directive has not so far adopted the regulatory compliance defence, although the Third Report on the Directive did emphasize the need to monitor this issue and indicated possible changes in future. The position in post-socialist countries is very complex because of the past experiences with inefficient safety regulation and its impact in civil litigation. Primarily, the tendency which occurred in Central Europe simultaneously with the evolution of product liability systems has been to abandon the absolute reliance upon the administrative rules concerning product safety and quality. It was acknowledged in academic writings and jurisprudence on product liability that following these norms was by no means a valid defence. It did not suffice to ensure that the product complied with the existing technical safety requirements (Łętowska 1999: 97). In Poland, this approach was pioneered by the 'Collegium of the Economic *Arbitrazh*'. In 1963 the 'Collegium' held that compliance with technical norms was but one criterion determining quality of products.[107] The Polish Supreme Court in the judgement of 4 December 1981 confirmed this view in the consumer context and in terms of safety, not quality of products.[108] In this case of 'exploding television sets', the conformity with safety regulations was no defence for the producer.[109] In Hungary a similar approach may be observed, curiously

106 What can be seen here is the direct use of product safety legislation in product liability cases. A phenomenon such as this can hardly be noticed in the regimes of Western Europe, where product safety is crucial at the stage of design and production, as well as post-marketing control of products, and product liability at the stage where some unavoidable injuries were caused. A greater coordination between product liability and safety laws could provide more clarity. On the other hand, the fact that the provisions of the mentioned Acts had to be used at all at this late stage in the chain of events leading to the injury demonstrates the unsatisfactory condition of the Polish regulatory regime, unable to secure enforcement of safety and quality laws.

107 GKA – 4 November 1963.

108 The Judgement of the Supreme Court of 4 December 1981, with the commentary of Żuławska.

109 The Supreme Court confirmed that compliance with the regulations was no defence, but it also suggested that the regulations had actually been breached by the

also in a case concerning exploding television sets (1984). In this landmark case the manufacturer pointed out that the television set had been licensed by the Commercial Quality Control Institute (state body). This line of defence was held unsatisfactory. The Czechoslovak and Czech case law also followed this tendency, supported primarily by an express provision of Section 421.3 of the Civil Code which stipulated that a legal person "cannot be exonerated from its liability by pleading that it was following the orders of superior organs".[110] Therefore, liability has not been excluded or reduced in a case where a machine's safety device was inadequate and caused damage, even though the safety device was installed following the instructions issued by the Ministry of Health (Vondracek 1988: 379).

In the light of the very clear rejection of the regulatory compliance defence, there was also no possibility for using the doctrine of pre-emption (assuming the predetermination of lawfulness of conduct by permits given by administrative authorities) in product liability cases (Harmathy 1998: 118). No apparent change of position is visible in jurisprudence or doctrinal writings, although the number of safety regulations, and indeed the regulatory activity of the administrative authorities, grows with the implementation of various safety standards deriving mostly from the European Union.[111]

Evolution – from 'fault' to defect and beyond – through the lens of the jurisprudence

Below is an assessment of the developments in Central European 'tort' of product liability introduced above, as seen through case law. Because of crucial differences between the analysed legal systems, each is assessed separately.

A short introduction is due at this point. It concerns the notion of defect, the specific understanding of which has indeed triggered the engagement of tort liability in product liability cases in the first place. The development of tortious product liability was prompted by cases where (even though a contractual relationship existed between the victim and the defendant) the defects in the products caused significant injuries and damages and thus the courts declared that not merely a breach of contract but also a tort (*delict*) has been committed. They were defects which entailed lack of safety as opposed to mere shortcomings in quality of

producers of the television sets. Żuławska agreed – the regulations required using non-flammable isolating materials. The producers in fact used materials which after three years of using the television sets lost their non-flammable character.

110 Translation provided by Dobiasova.

111 See the Baker McKenzie *General Product Safety Directive (GPSD) – Comparative Directory* 2006 for a comparative review of implementation of the GPSD throughout the European Union, and the website: <http://ec.europa.eu/consumers/safety/prod_legis/index_en.htm> for comprehensive information about implementation of European sectoral product safety laws.

products.[112] This emphasis on safety was very clear from the start and was indeed the distinguishing feature of the product liability systems.

Hungary The 'motorcycle accident' case of 1973 constituted a breakthrough in the attitude of Hungarian courts towards product liability cases. The wheel of the virtually brand new motorcycle became uncontrollable, started to shake, and as a result of these quite violent movements the driver lost control and crashed into another vehicle. The accident was serious and the driver suffered considerable injuries. Although the seller offered a warranty to the buyer, and this was clearly enforceable with regard to the value of the motorcycle which was destroyed, the person who suffered the injuries was not the buyer. His injuries were recovered because the court established the seller's liability in tort. First of all, the court stressed the defect in the motorcycle rendering it dangerous to drive, and held that selling such defective products in the market was in fact a tort (Maczonkai 1996: 111). The liability was placed on the seller, and the court established the seller's fault in the case using the general requirement of acting 'as expected in the given circumstances'. The fault did not concern manufacture or design, as it would be very problematic to impute such fault on the seller. The court stressed the seller's duty to ensure the product was safe when leaving the shop. However, the emphasized basis of 'fault' was the lack of instructions explaining proper use of the motorcycle. The seller did not provide such instructions to the buyer.

The same essence of 'fault' can be seen also in the 'chemical spray' case of 1977. The court analysed the qualities of the spray and concluded that it was not dangerous in itself, but was capable of causing loss or damage if not used properly. The spray was supplied by the manufacturer without instructions, the farmer did not use it properly, and the expected harvest was lost. The manufacturer was held not to have fulfilled his duty of care towards those using his product. The court held that 'fault' of the manufacturer was shown by the mere lack of instructions which should have been supplied with the product. Indeed, one could look in vain for a detailed assessment of 'fault' in this judgement: the mere lack of instructions indicated 'fault'. It can surely be pointed out that the Supreme Court "made a step towards developing strict liability for defective products under tort law" (Maczonkai 1996: 112–13), although the complete lack of instructions was quite a straightforwardly blunt example of breach of duty by the manufacturer.

112 There is a separate legal regime of contractual liability – often referred to as the system of guarantees for poor quality products in Central Europe (Sengayen 2002). Regime of liability for pure quality defects (lack of a required level of quality, loss of utility or value – Tenreiro 1997: 57) was regulated on the Community level by the Directive 1999/44/ *on certain aspects of sale of consumer goods and associated guarantees*. For an elaboration of differences between the Product Liability Directive and the Consumer Sales Directive see Tenreiro 1997: 56–61. The regime of the Consumer Sales Directive remains outside the scope of the book.

These two judgements still exhibited some emphasis on the defendant's conduct, and the analysis concentrated on the 'breach of duty' element. Further cases saw a shift of focus.

The case referred to by Maczonkai as the "landmark case of product liability" involved 'exploding television sets' (1984) (Maczonkai 1996: 113). Here the claimant's apartment and furniture were damaged as a result of a fire caused by the explosion of his colour television set. It appeared from the proceedings before the court that a certain type of television set, of which the claimant's was an example, were in fact defective and it was not uncommon for them to explode. The television sets – Videoton Color Star TV – became the subject of country-wide attention when a number of them exploded upon being switched on. In this case of, one can suppose, design defect[113] the producer was held liable for damages suffered by the owner of the television set. In fact, a number of cases concerning exploding television sets reached different courts, and the reasoning behind their decisions was far from consistent or uniform. The Supreme Court ultimately established requirements for manufacturers' liability and it must be stressed that they do not appear very different from the conditions typical for strict liability. On the one hand, the Court held that the plaintiff needed to prove the unlawfulness of the defendant's conduct, the existence of the damage, and the existence of a causal link between the conduct and the damage (Maczonkai 1996: 113). On the other hand, the manufacturer's conduct seemed completely irrelevant in the final decision. The defendant manufacturer attempted defence by claiming, following Article 339, that he had indeed acted properly in the given circumstances. The television set was licensed by the Commercial Quality Control Institute (a state body). As mentioned above, this was held to be insufficient defence. Further, even though in the case at hand the explosion was likely to have been caused by the changed fuse of a capacity greater than the previous one, the manufacturer's liability was neither excluded nor limited. Perhaps overwhelmed by the country-wide reach of this problem, the Court drastically limited the possibility of using Article 339 of the Civil Code defence of 'acting as expected in the given circumstances'. It held that the decisive factor in determining the defendant's liability were 'social expectations' (Maczonkai 1996: 113). Thus, if the product placed on the market does not meet this criterion, the existence or non-existence of the proper conduct, the existence or non-existence of 'fault' on the part of the defendant, are of no significance. Surprisingly, the Hungarian regime seems to have introduced liability more stringent than the Product Liability Directive. Nothing short of a *force majeure* could provide sufficient defence for the manufacturer.

Cases involving exploding television sets were very common indeed throughout the whole of Central Europe and other socialist countries. They are mentioned again below, in the examination of the Polish system.

The tendency which is clearly observable in the judgements analysed above is that, as liability became more stringent, the focus of the courts shifted from the

113 The type of defect was not sufficiently explored in the judgement.

defendants' behaviour to the defect in the product and the damage caused by it. The science of product liability also became more elaborate and comprehensive.

Czechoslovakia and the Czech Republic Section 421 (concerning legal persons only) of the Czechoslovak Civil Code was the most common legal basis for cases involving dangerous products. After the amendment of the Code in 1991, Section 420 took over the regulation of liability of legal persons as well as physical ones, and accordingly it became the basis for product liability litigation. Apart from this crucial amendment, another change took place in the Czech Civil Code at the same time. The subjective element of fault seems to have disappeared. What have been the implications of this complex legal matrix for product liability cases? Because a significant part of the Czechoslovak jurisprudence in this area was not published, one is forced to refer to the doctrinal analyses here.

Under the former Section 421.3 a legal person could escape liability if it showed "that it could not have prevented the damage even by the exertion of every effort which (could) be required from it". In the Czechoslovak Civil Code the reversal of the *onus probandi* was aimed at, according to Vondracek, avoiding the "situation where the plaintiff finds himself in insurmountable 'evidentiary distress' (*důkazní nouze*)" (1988: 376). Following the words of Section 421.3 it seems that exoneration was relatively difficult (Vondracek 1988: 378). In product liability cases the courts interpreted the provision of Section 421 of the Civil Code by holding that the defendant could defend himself if it was proven that he exerted an "utmost effort (care) that could have been required from the defendant as a whole, in the given situation, to prevent production of defective articles and their introduction into circulation" (Svestka 1989: 102). The manufacturer was required to show that due care was exercised throughout the process of production, and this may have been a difficult task. With sometimes a great number of persons involved in an activity of a legal person, the conduct of only one of them having the characteristics of 'fault' was enough for liability of the legal person to be established. The employee must have "performed an act which is necessary or customary in performing the duties flowing from, or closely connected with, his employment" (Vondracek 1988: 179). As long as this requirement was satisfied, however, the legal person would be liable to the victim of his conduct. Here certain similarities to the Polish '*anonymous fault*' (explored below) concept can be seen, although the concept as such was not explicitly recognized by the Czech courts and scholars. Svestka acknowledges that there may have been situations where the manufacturer was effectively able to escape liability, having proven he has taken all due care to avoid damage (1989: 102). He also points out, however, that a much greater burden of proof was placed by the Czech courts on the manufacturer than on the seller (the latter – in contract liability, which was also based upon a concept of presumed 'fault') (ibid.). The majority view concerning the 1991 amendment is that its impact on the standard of liability has not led to any changes in the court practice (Tichy 2002a: 118).

A similar shift in focus – from conduct to defect – could be noticed in the jurisprudence, although it must be said that the judgements very often lacked the depth of analysis which characterize modern product liability jurisprudence. While defect became more prominent, the courts and doctrine continued considering product liability in the context of 'fault'. The latter element prevailed until the Product Liability Directive was implemented. Nevertheless, it must be argued that the Czech tortious product liability regime was much worse equipped to secure the interests of victims of defective products than the Hungarian regime. The likelihood of Czech courts having let the victims bear the loss seems much greater than the likelihood of Hungarian courts having done a similar thing.

Poland 'Fault' as established by Article 415 of the Civil Code ("whoever by his fault caused damage to another person shall be obliged to redress it") was interpreted for the needs of the product liability regime in a manner which significantly differed from its ordinary understanding. It must be acknowledged, however, that 'fault' has always played a significant role in Polish product liability cases.

The case of a Fiat 'Multipla' (1963) introduced the idea of tortious liability for defective products in Poland.[114] Here the Supreme Court considered a judgement of a district court regarding liability of the importer (Motoimport) and the seller (Motozbyt) of a Fiat. The car had a manufacturing defect – the machinery holding the wheels in place was not properly welded to the floor of the car. This defect could have been discovered by the importer or the seller only if either of them removed the paint from the relevant place. Neither of them did, and the wheels of the car suddenly changed their position while the vehicle was being driven. The buyer suffered serious injuries, and the process of his recovery lasted eight months. On the facts of the case collected by the district court, the Supreme Court found no sufficient proof of fault on the part of the seller and importer (hence the case was referred back to the district court for a further examination of the relevant technical data). However, the Court held that as a matter of principle the severity of personal injury suffered by the individual in question determined the defendant's liability in tort. Thus, "sale of a vehicle which has technical defects capable of causing an accident – if the defects are a result of fault – justifies the liability of the seller of the car under Article 134 of the Code of Obligations 1933."[115] A later case of a defective 'P-70' car (1964)[116] followed this tendency, and the Supreme Court held that introducing into the market a car with a defect which could cause an accident violated the "principles of public security and of protection of human

114 OSN 1964/95.

115 OSN 1964/95, at p. 41. Translated by the author. The Code of Obligations preceded the Civil Code of 1964.

116 OSN 1965/32.

life and health".[117] It was therefore a tort in the understanding of Article 134 of the Code of Obligations of 1933.

Although the Supreme Court was willing to introduce tortious liability in these cases, it seemed too early for taking the liability system further and to imply 'fault' of the defendants. In the cases of the Fiat 'Multipla' and the 'P-70' car the district courts attempted to use the *res ipsa loquitur* principle, but the Supreme Court excluded this possibility. What followed these two judgements was a process of building a product liability system which, although distinctly based upon the requirement of 'fault', sought various ways to facilitate the proof of its existence. Increased focus on the nature of defects and the damages they caused did not, however, disturb the inherent tendency to refer to 'fault' in manufacture, in design, in warnings, or in monitoring (observation) rather than to manufacturing, design, warning or observation defects. In contrast to the Hungarian and Czechoslovak Civil Codes, the victim bore the burden of proof of 'fault' of the defendant.[118] The courts recognized very early that most of the product liability cases had involved the liability of legal persons, whose subjective 'fault proper' was difficult or even impossible to establish. With an intention to facilitate the task of the victim, the concept of '*anonymous fault*', widely accepted by the representatives of doctrine of law and the courts, has been devised instead.[119] This legal construct meant that as long as the victim was able to point to the fact of the defendant legal person as a whole not having acted in an expected manner, there was no need to search for a particular person within the structure of the latter who had been the cause of the defect. Hence, what may be observed here is the abandonment of the subjective characteristics of 'fault' and a movement towards the objective factors as determinants of the fault of legal persons. What the expected manner of conduct should actually have been depended largely upon who exactly the defendant was. The duties of the manufacturers significantly differed from the duties of the ordinary distributors or sellers. The importers, as already elaborated on, were in fact liable to the same extent as the manufacturers. Hence, they were held liable even for manufacturing defects, those impossible to have been detected without the deconstruction of certain parts of the product.[120] Although it was not expressly argued by the representatives of the doctrine or practice of law, a significant contribution towards strict liability can be clearly seen in this development.

117 OSN 1965/32, at p. 43. Translated by the author.

118 This according to Article 6 of the Civil Code, which stipulates that "the burden of proof of a fact lies upon the person who draws legal consequences from this fact" (translated by the author).

119 The concept derived from the case law concerning financial liability of the state (Żuławska 1983b).

120 See the judgement of the Polish Supreme Court of 26 March 1984, OSN 1984/186 ('Wartburg case'), where it held: "the importer of goods ought to be treated as the manufacturer, and he is liable in tort to the buyer and the third parties for damages caused by the defects in the product" (at p. 78).

Examples of defective products which were the subjects of product liability cases in Poland were, for instance, television sets manufactured negligently so that they exploded after a few years' use (1981),[121] a fruit cake containing a pin (1981), a car (Wartburg) with the steering system blocking suddenly while being driven (1984), a bottle of soft drink with the cap falling off to injure the eye of the plaintiff (1996), or a can of a spray for use in the bathroom containing gas which caused an explosion upon switching on of the washing machine (2000). The defects mentioned above were either manufacturing or design defects (the latter were referred to in Poland as 'construction defects'). In cases where a construction (design) 'fault' has been shown, the main if not the only defendant has been the producer. The producer could exonerate himself by claiming that in the then state of technological knowledge the design adopted did guarantee the required level of safety (in other words, using a development risk defence) (Łętowska 1999: 99). However, it was not a sufficient defence to claim that, taking into account the price of the product, designing a product complying with the safety requirements was impossible (Łętowska 1999: 99).[122] Cases of manufacturing fault saw the greatest transformation as regards liability standards. A good example of the transformation is the judgement in the case of a pin in a cake (1981). The district court had assumed that the pin must have been inside the cake. Having excluded all other possibilities, such as the pin being for some reason left on the plate on which the cake was served, the court went on to hold that the person liable for the presence of the pin in the cake was the producer. The Supreme Court confirmed the views of the district court. An interesting phenomenon which could be observed in the judgement is that the claimant – the person who was unfortunate enough to have swallowed the pin which then injured his throat – did not have to prove the 'fault' of the producer. The mere presence of the pin in the cake was held to have demonstrated the weaknesses in the production and supervision processes (Łętowska 1999: 99).[123] The Supreme Court continued to develop the reasoning used in the latter judgement in the case of 'exploding television sets'.[124] An expert's opinion confirmed that the specific type of television sets had a tendency to explode, and this was so even though they were not connected to the mains supply. The Supreme Court applied the concept of '*anonymous fault*': the claimant was relieved of the obligation to point to a particular person within the organizational

121 In contrast to the Hungarian 'exploding television sets' case, the issue of design was actually mentioned in the judgement involving the television set. It was not developed in any significant detail.

122 An example of this approach is the judgement in the 'Wartburg case' of 1984.

123 The manufacturer did not succeed in defending himself against this *res ipsa loquitur* presumption, and this was so especially in the light of the statement of one of its employees, who pointed to sugar used in production not being properly tested.

124 Judgement of the Supreme Court of 4 December 1981, with the commentary of Żuławska.

structure of the defendant responsible for the defect.[125] Not only the use of the cheap 'replacement materials'[126] in the production process, held the Court, but also the knowledge of the danger and failure to warn the users of the television sets of the imminent danger to their property as well as life and health determined the existence of 'fault'.[127] While the first point leaves no room for doubt with regard to the manufacturer's 'fault', the question of warnings and their relevance here has been more controversial. It is further examined below. In the 'poultry feed case'[128] the Supreme Court used the notion of '*anonymous fault*' again. It held: "supplying a defective product is the result of fault if the unit (legal person) which supplied the product knew or should have known that it was defective, and as a result of this it endangered the interests of the user."[129] The dangerous nature of the poultry feed was proven to be the result of defects in the components used for its manufacture, and the manufacturer of the feed was held to have been at fault "if those defects could have been discovered before the use of the component in the manufacturing process, or the defects of the goods could have been discovered during a routine technical control".[130]

Generally, in cases where 'manufacturing fault' has been established, it was difficult for the manufacturer or another person to defend themselves. Merely showing that all due care was taken in organization and control of production did not suffice (Łętowska 1999: 100). The maximum care had to be shown to have been exercised by all those taking part in the distribution chain (ibid.). The argument of *force majeure* was acceptable, but the manner in which the concept itself was understood by the courts rendered the proof an uneasy task. In the case of the Pepsi Cola bottle cap[131] the manufacturer of the bottle attempted defence by claiming *force majeure*. His arguments were rejected by the court of appeal of Katowice. According to the court, *force majeure* was an "unusual, external, impossible to prevent event, which is not an ordinary accident (*casus*). These are phenomena

---

125 Although used before by the Court, the concept could be said to have been definitely confirmed in this judgement, and accepted by the commentator – Żuławska – as an indication of the courts abandoning the traditional, subjective idea of fault centred around intentions and will (1983b: 142).

126 The use of replacement materials was indeed popular in socialist nationalized industries, as it was falsely conceived that it was more efficient and generally better for the national economy to use cheap materials, thus reducing production costs. Many 'rationalization motions' (*wnioski racjonalizatorskie*) to this effect were put forward within the industry, supported by the economic policy of the state (Nesterowicz 1979: 11, 12).

127 The evidence in the proceedings showed that the manufacturer knew about the fact that the television sets often burst into flames, and continued producing the sets without altering the production process (OSPiKA 1983, z. 2, poz. 55, at p. 141).

128 Judgement of the Supreme Court of 11 December 1987 (unpublished).

129 Commentary to the judgement in the 'poultry feeding stuff case', Nowe Prawo 4/1989, at p. 109.

130 Nowe Prawo 4/1989, at p. 110. Translated by the author.

131 Wokanda 2/1998, 40–43.

such as natural catastrophes (*vis naturalis*), the acts of public authorities to which an individual cannot oppose (*vis imperii*), and military acts (*vis armata*)."[132] The court indicated that all products, if used according to their ordinary purposes, ought to be safe and no accidents should occur. Such an accident (in this case the cap of a bottle of Pepsi Cola detached and hit the plaintiff's eye), allowed the court using the *res ipsa loquitur* rule, demonstrated either a defective technological process or its defective operation by the manufacturer.[133]

Other defects triggering tortious liability were 'instruction' (warning) defects, sometimes leading to very serious, even tragic consequences. Polish case law regarding this matter indicated a firm stance of the courts that inadequate warnings or wrong instructions concerning the product should lead to liability of those responsible. This type of 'fault' can be committed not mainly, as in design and manufacturing fault, by the manufacturer or importer, but also by the seller and any other distributor. There is no doubt that in certain cases the defendant may escape liability if adequate warnings were provided, but it appears that the approach ought to be carefully tailored to the needs of the particular case. Żuławska criticized the implication by the Supreme Court in the 'exploding television sets' case that the lack of warnings was one of the factors determining the manufacturer's liability (1983c: 144). It could not be assumed, according to her, that the fault would not have been established had the producer warned those using the television sets of the danger of explosion (ibid.). While warnings have importance in the context of legal and commercial guarantees, they must not, following the words of Żuławska, be considered in tortious product liability unless the dangerous characteristic of the product is one of its ordinary features (such as poisonous nature of some chemicals), and the user is able to sufficiently protect himself from those dangerous features (1983c: 144).[134] Clearly an explosion of an unplugged electrical device is not something that a reasonable person would perceive as an ordinary feature.

The following case is an example of a situation where proper warnings could have allowed the defendants to escape liability. In the case of a 'chemical spray' (1972)[135] a farmer and his son died while using the spray on their farm. The bottle of the spray contained warnings that it was dangerous and could cause poisoning, so it was recommended that a mask protecting from benzene ought to be worn. Unfortunately, masks of this type were not available on the market at the time. The warnings were written in very small print, but it was shown during the court proceedings that the victim knew about their content, as he, together with the seller, read them before purchase. Nevertheless, joint liability of the seller and the manufacturer of the spray had been established by the Supreme Court. The fact

132 Wokanda 2/1998, at p. 43. Translated by the author.

133 Wokanda 2/1998, at p. 42.

134 Here Żuławska refers to the judgement in the case of the 'chemical spray' of 1972, analysed below.

135 OSN 1972/228, 67–74.

that the product was dangerous as such did not make it dangerously defective. The crucial issue here was the inadequacy of warnings on the bottle containing the spray: indicating the poisonous nature of the spray was, according to the Court, insufficient when it was clear that the spray could lead to death. It was also suggested that the manufacturer of the spray was obliged to produce relevant protective masks if they were not available on the market.[136] The seller breached his duty of care because he knew or should have known that the gas masks recommended by the producer were unavailable (Łętowska 1999: 100).

Another crucial case, considered very shortly before the Polish implementation of the Directive came into effect, involved an airbag which suddenly inflated in a parked car injuring a little girl sitting on the front seat.[137] The reason for the inflation of the airbag was never found. It was held that the defendants (Ford Distribution – the Polish importer – and the dealer) were liable for the girl's serious injuries. First and foremost, the court pointed out that the main function of the airbag was ensuring safety, and it was entirely unpredictable and unnatural for it to inflate while the car was parked. However, the defendants' liability was based on their failure to pass on the information which they held (failure to warn). Apparently, Ford Motor Co. advised its dealers and service stations of the possibility of an inflation of the airbags in certain conditions (for instance a strong magnetic field), but the consumers were not warned of this possibility. While the result of this case might be applauded, and the court did manage to achieve the outcome which would also be likely to arise under the 'strict' liability regime of the Product Liability Directive (Bagińska 2002: 389), the rationale of the judgement could be questioned. One cannot help but revert to the judgement in the 'exploding television sets' case, and the critique of the commentator who argued that equipping products which are unreasonably, unavoidably and unpredictably dangerous with even very comprehensive warnings ought not allow defendants to escape liability.

Other goods dangerous *per se* – especially cigarettes (Łętowska 1999: 92) – have also recently appeared as subjects of product liability litigation in Central Europe. Attempts to make the manufacturers of cigarettes liable for death or personal injury caused to smokers in Poland have so far failed. In August 1999, Sławomir Lubicz-Sienicki commenced litigation before the district court of Kraków for non-pecuniary losses caused by his mother's death.[138] His mother died at the age of 59 after having smoked 40 cigarettes a day for 42 years. Sienicki's claim was that no

136 The victim did in fact attempt using a gas mask, but it was not the required one and it failed to protect him from the poisonous chemical. In this far-reaching judgement the Supreme Court was very clear in its position that it was unacceptable to start the process of manufacturing and distributing a dangerous product without at the same time securing adequate means of protection for its users.

137 *Rzeczpospolita* 19 April 2001.

138 See descriptions of the facts and the decision in English: <http://www.tobacco.org/news/47162.html>, <http://transcripts.cnn.com/TRANSCRIPTS/0001/09/wr.02.html>.

warnings of the danger of smoking appeared on the packaging of cigarettes for the first 30 years of his mother's smoking. The court, dismissing the claim, held that no 'fault' of the manufacturer could be found, as the dangerous effects of smoking have been widely known for a long time. This view is also presented by the representatives of legal doctrine: Łętowska argues that those products would not and could not trigger product liability (1999: 92). Their dangerous nature cannot be denied, but they cause damage during their normal use, and not, what Łętowska considers as a necessary factor of the operation of product liability, as an unintended, "side effect" of their use (ibid.).

Another type of fault recognized by Polish courts concerned 'observation' (monitoring). This type of fault can involve the manufacturer, the importer, or any other distributor and seller of products, if they failed to take account of events of injuries or damages suffered by those using their product and adequately warn others of the danger or take other remedying actions. In the case of 'exploding television sets' of 1983 the Supreme Court established the fault of the manufacturer on the basis of the fact that, knowing of the frequent cases of explosions of their television sets, it failed to take any steps to warn the users of the sets, or stop producing the television sets using the same materials.

The judgements analysed above indicate the tendency to make liability for defective products more objective, although they did not reach as far as those of Hungarian courts. By stressing the defects involved in cases before them, Polish courts focused less on the defendants' conduct. Again, one observes an increasingly more scientific, comprehensive approach to analysing defects. The language of 'fault' was still present, but it was rather tailored to the circumstances of the case and reflected what the judges would see as the equitable approach: from cases such as the 'Pepsi Cola bottle cap case' where very little attention was devoted to the defendant's conduct and most to the cap itself and the possible reasons why it could have suddenly burst, to the latest cigarettes case where it was declared that no 'fault' of the defendants could be established.

Introduction into the market (into circulation)

Central European scholars and jurisprudence almost universally adopted the notion of 'introduction into the market/into circulation' as indicating the moment from which liability begins, and indeed indicating the act which is the basis of defendants' liability. The Polish doctrinal writers (Gnela 2000: 175, Letowska 1999: 84, 85, 89, Nesterowicz 1979: 9) and courts did not initially approve of this view, but the voices of the opponents soon disappeared.[139] In the case of a defective Fiat 125p engine,[140] the Polish Supreme Court held:

139 In Poland, the *Guidelines of the National Economic Arbitrazh* of 1977 referred to "manufacturing products with defects"; Rembieliński and Pryca (1983: 99) followed the same approach.

140 OSN 1981/205.

> Producing a car with defects decreasing its value does not constitute a tort in the understanding of Articles 415 et al. of the Civil Code; while *introduction into circulation* of a dangerous – as a result of defective construction – product, if the defect became the cause of personal injury or damage to property, does constitute a tort.[141]

In Hungary, the 'motorcycle accident' case[142] demonstrated the courts' approach to this issue. It was held that *selling* a defective product constituted a tort on the part of the seller. A similar approach was subsequently adopted in the case where for the first time the manufacturer was held liable in tort to the victim of his product. The 'chemical spray' case involved a spray *supplied* by the manufacturer without instructions.[143] The Czech position is also relatively clear: the courts linked product liability to introducing a product into the market (they mention 'production' and 'selling' as well as 'introducing into the market', although this choice was determined by who exactly the defendant was, and upon his role with regard to the defective product). Svestka presents the possible defence of the manufacturer in cases of damages caused by defective products as being an "utmost effort (care) that could have been required from the defendant as a whole, in the given situation, to prevent production of defective articles *and* their introduction into circulation" (Svestka 1989: 102).[144]

The concept of introduction into circulation has not been formally defined for the needs of the product liability regime until today. According to Mohmand, the existence of the notion with no further definition in the Polish Civil Code as well as in other sources of Polish law[145] suggests the certainty about its unequivocal meaning (2002: 289).[146]

While no legally binding definitions exist, doctrinal writers continue to further elaborate the notion when building the theoretical basis and conceptual framework of the product liability systems. Polish scholars have been particularly prolific in this respect. According to Łętowska, the moment from which one can consider the possibility of product liability is the moment when a commodity actually becomes a 'product' – the subject of a transaction in the market (1999: 85). The first 'legal act' having the product as its subject would be the time when the potential for

141 Ibid. at p. 4. Emphasis added. Translated by the author.

142 Bírósági Határozatok (Court Decisions) 1973/1 No. 19.

143 Bírósági Határozatok (Court Decisions) 1997/1 No 31. Italicized words added by the author to emphasize the notion used by the court in this case.

144 Italics added by the author.

145 For example the Act on Normalization of 3 April 1993, as later emended; and the Act on the Health Conditions of Food and Nutrition of 11 May 2001.

146 Mohmand also suggests that the existing definition of 'introduction into circulation' in the Act on the Assessment of Compliance, Accreditation, and amendment of some other acts of 28 April 2000 as: "transfer of the goods for the first time in the country to its user, consumer or seller by the producer, his representative or the importer" is too narrow in its scope to be used in the product liability context (2002: 290).

liability would commence (ibid.), although to be more precise one ought to stress that the concept of introduction into circulation does not simply indicate the first time, but rather each time, the product has been introduced into the market (in order to include importers, further distributors, or sellers within the circle of possible defendants). Czachórski points out that the 'introduction into circulation' happens when the product actually "enters the market", and not when the "legal act upon which such entry is dependent" is conducted (2002: 284). These two views are only superficially contradictory. Further on in her analysis Łętowska made it clear that the moment when the producer lost control over the product ought to mark the commencement of the possibility for product liability (1999: 85). Hence, the mere 'legal act' does not suffice, because the act must have been actually executed (ibid.). Łętowska's point that this moment is when the manufacturer loses control over the product (1999: 85) could be accepted provided one acknowledges that what is lost is the direct, physical control. A certain level of indirect control over products always remains in the hands of the manufacturers.[147] This contention can also be adopted as relevant to other possible defendants, such as the importers or sellers. Czachórski merely develops further the thought that when the product enters the market, the producer begins to gain profit. The latter fact determines the stricter than ordinary liability – product liability, based upon the *cuius commodum eius periculum* rule (2002: 284).

For the needs of the present analysis it is essential to point out that liability is excluded if in certain circumstances the product has been taken outside the control of the defendant (manufacturer, importer, seller, or any other distributor) with no intention of his own. For instance a product might have been stolen from a warehouse or a factory. Although the issue has not been in any depth examined in the literature or case law of Central Europe, it is rather taken as obvious that if the defendant proves he did not introduce the product into the market he will be exempted from product liability (Mohmand 2002: 291).[148] Once it is established that product liability does not protect those injured by products not yet in circulation, such as the employees of the manufacturer or some third parties, can it be said that they remain deprived of a remedy? Łętowska is certain that those injured can use Article 435 of the Polish Civil Code in order to recover damages. This provision, analysed below, establishes strict liability of a person conducting an undertaking or an enterprise moved by the forces of nature. It is not clear from the writings of Hungarian and Czech academics what remedy their laws provide in such situations. It is possible, however, that Section 238 and the new Section 420a of the Czech Civil Code as well as Article 345 of the Hungarian Civil Code

147 Certain duties concerned with observation and monitoring were established by courts – see p. 234 above.

148 This is also the approach of the Product Liability Directive – see Chapter 3 (and the recent ECJ judgement in case C-127/04 *Declan O'Byrne v Sanofi Pasteur MSD Ltd, Sanofi Pasteur SA* 9 February 2006).

(which are counterparts of Article 435 of the Polish Civil Code) could provide a similar remedy.[149]

Apart from this exclusion, however, the notion of 'introduction into circulation' seems to have been very accommodating. For instance, nothing in the interpretation and in other provisions of the civil codes excluded products used for business purposes or privileged those used for private, consumer purposes (Mohmand 2002: 291) in the scope of application of the product liability regimes. Further, the notion has also been capable of embracing within it all persons 'actively participating' in the chain leading to the ultimate consumer (Łętowska 1999: 90). Looking at the case law of Central Europe one can notice the focus upon manufacturers and importers, although the liability of sellers cannot be excluded as a still existing possibility. Taking into account the fact that according to the Product Liability Directive the sellers' liability ought to be merely subsidiary, one can see a significant difference between the tortious regimes in Central Europe and the regime required by the Directive. Again, the Czech system distinguishes itself here, as the seller's liability is normally established only in contract.

Defect existing at the time the product is introduced into the market

The last aspect of the 'tort' analysed here, one which joins the two previously examined matters, is the requirement that the defect must have physically existed at the time the product was placed on the market by the person concerned. Łętowska argues that the defect may have appeared after the product was manufactured and supplied for the first time, due to certain actions or omissions (lack of supervision or monitoring) of further participants in the chain of distribution (1999: 92). This contention has more significance in jurisdictions such as Poland, Czechoslovakia and Hungary, where liability was based, at least initially, upon the 'fault' of the defendant. The Product Liability Directive also introduces this requirement – indeed it is one of the defences to establish that it is "probable" that the defect did not exist at the time the product was put into circulation (Article 7(b)). Specific problems with this defence (concerning the necessary enquiry into the defendant's conduct, and the differences in the standard of proof required in Central Europe) were mentioned in Chapter 3 of Part I, and will be mentioned again below (Chapter 6).

Concluding remarks: contemporary tendencies

Contemporary Central European product liability systems are obviously heavily influenced by the Product Liability Directive and its emphasis on defect as lack of safety which "a person is entitled to expect" (Article 6). The analysis above shows that elements of this approach would be familiar to Central European courts. The manner in which the notion was incorporated into the written laws is presented in Chapter 6 below, but lack of case law so far leaves its practical application in the sphere of hypotheses.

149 It is also likely that other provisions could provide a remedy in these situations – for instance the rules of employer's liability. These remain outside the scope of the book.

What is clear from the practice of product liability throughout the European Union, however, is that the definition of 'defect' provided by the Directive does not offer a universal solution to all practical problems. Thus, it is likely that some problems with which Central European courts have been faced would not be easily unpacked with the use of the Directive. As in other systems which utilized the 'boxing' of defect types, courts (even the Hungarian courts) may struggle with a general definition based entirely on the criterion of expectations in difficult design or warnings cases. The 'boxing' may still to some extent remain relevant in the academic discourse and in the practice of product liability.

Damage

The existence of damage is a crucial requisite of product liability. Here Central European courts apply the general principles of ordinary civil liability,[150] subject to the already explored focus on damage outside the defective product itself (Łętowska 1999: 103).

On the one hand, the scope of tortious damages recoverable in Central Europe has to some extent been wider than the scope prescribed by the Product Liability Directive. No limitations of the kind which the Directive introduces (the 500 Euro threshold, or a cap on damages) have been in operation. Further, because the general civil liability principles have been used, the consumer-focused limitations introduced by the Directive have not applied. For instance, even damage to property used for purposes related to business could be recovered. Such a wide scope still remains and will undoubtedly be of use even after the implementation of the Directive in cases where the latter does not apply. On the other hand, the specific practices governing assessment of damages during socialism (mentioned in Chapter 3 of Part I) contributed to the fact that on many occasions the damages awarded to victims of defective products were trivial. The damages awarded in Poland were, in the words of Gnela, of moderate amount (2000: 194). In Hungary, Harmathy stressed that, particularly in the period of socialism, awards were limited (1998: 118). Also the scope of recoverable damage in general tort law was much narrower, with a very inconsistent approach to recovery of non-pecuniary damage (mostly Hungary and Poland) and of lost profits (mostly Czechoslovakia). As mentioned in Part I, this situation is now gradually changing – the transformations are described below. The analysis observes the evolution of the relevant provisions of Central European civil codes concerning damage, and the developments in their interpretation by courts in product liability cases.

150 Similar principles, and indeed often the same provisions of the Civil Codes, normally apply to contractual and tortious damages. Thus, the analysis below is also relevant to contractual liability, with the reservations (peculiarities of contractual damage) specified in Chapter 4. The Polish Code also contains some specific provisions on tortious damage – analysed below.

In contrast to the provisions of the Hungarian Civil Code (examined below), the Czechoslovak and then Czech Code always unequivocally ensured recovery of both pecuniary and non-pecuniary damage. However, in practice it has often been difficult to recover non-pecuniary damage (both in contract and in tort), because courts applied quite stringent causation tests. Further, the former version of the Czechoslovak Civil Code, in Section 442 referring both to tortious and contractual liability, generally only allowed for recovery of *damnum emergens*.[151] Greater emphasis was placed by the Section upon *restitutio in integrum* or *restitutio in natura* (a more ideologically proper and cheaper solution, always to be given priority unless "impossible" or "inefficient" – Section 442.1) than on compensation,[152] although in practice most cases did see compensation paid to the victim (Vondracek 1988: 395).[153] *Lucrum cessans* (lost profits), which Vondracek refers to as an "ideologically tinted notion", were not usually recoverable (1988: 395). However, the Code introduced an exception to this rule: Section 422.2 provided the notion of "other damage" (recoverable on the court's discretion determined by the principles of 'socialist community life'[154] if damage was caused deliberately). Vondracek pointed out that it was unlikely for loss of earnings to be compensated (1988: 396), although it was still possible under exceptional circumstances. The Code was amended in 1991, and now Section 442 puts greater emphasis upon compensation than *restitutio in integrum*, and the compensation includes "the real damages as well as what the damaged party lost (lost profit)".[155] The Civil Code allows for recovery of personal injury and property damage, but it separates regulation of personal injuries from other kinds of damage. The former are regulated in the part of the Civil Code concerning "protection of personhood" (Sections 11–17).[156] Apart from demanding that the violation of the particular right be stopped, its "consequences be removed and that adequate satisfaction be given to him or her", the victim is also entitled to "pecuniary satisfaction of the immaterial

151 Section 442.1 reads: "Only real damage is compensated …" (Vondracek 1988: 394).

152 Also some representatives of the doctrine of law were in favour of this solution: Vondracek (1988: 395).

153 For example cases: R 1971, No. 55 c.c., 339 et seq.; R 1977, No. 27 c.c., 312. Vondracek, however, mentions the case where the Provincial Court in Bratislava held that the builder who caused damage to the neighbouring house by explosives used in his work ought to repair the building himself instead of paying the compensation (R 1984, No. 21 c.c., 175 et seq.; Vondracek 1988: 395).

154 The principles of socialist community life in the Czechoslovak Civil Code were a general clause which resembled the Polish "principles of socialist cooperation" (introduced on pp.28,29 and 61 of Part I).

155 The translation of the Code provided by Dobiasova.

156 By virtue of Section 11 "An individual shall have the right to protection of his or her personhood, in particular of his or her life or health, civic honour and human dignity as well as of the privacy, name and expressions of personal nature" (Translation provided by Dobiasova).

detriment" in case of a "considerable reduction of dignity or honour" (Section 13). Section 13, referring to the "protection of personhood", prescribes the possibility of receiving "pecuniary satisfaction" for any violation of the values included in the concept of "personhood" (life and health, honour and dignity, privacy or name). This provision applies to contractual relationships as well as to situations where a tort has been committed outside such relationships. The rules of recovery of damages in case of a violation of personhood are similar to the rules governing the recovery of other damages (Section 16). These are regulated in Sections 442–50 of the Code (concerning assessment of damages). At present, Section 444 suggests that a separate decree ought to regulate the exact levels of compensation of pain and "aggravated position in society" (Decree of 2001, amended in 2003, Hradek 2003: 89).

According to Article 318 of the Hungarian Civil Code, the same rules concerning damage are applicable both to tort and to contract liability. Damage to person and to property is recoverable (Harmathy 1998: 117). It was, however, initially stated in the Code that in case of personal injuries caused by a tortious act (and, by analogy, also by a breach of contract) only pecuniary damage was to be compensated (ibid.). Hence, although courts were willing to award compensation for non-pecuniary damage caused by injury to a person, they were unable to do so (ibid.). After the amendment of the Civil Code in 1977 an exception was inserted into the chapter of the Code concerning civil liability: in cases of serious injuries or serious infringements of personal rights it has since been possible to compensate non-pecuniary damage (Article 355 of the Code). Jurisprudence followed this amendment, but according to Harmathy there remained a lack of "clear principles of the obligation to pay non-pecuniary damages" in the Hungarian legal system (1998: 117). This situation continues until today. The suggested changes of damage rules (Draft Civil Code) were already mentioned in Chapter 3 of Part I. The draft proposes replacing non-pecuniary damages with special indemnity compensation. Initially it was suggested that no proof of 'fault' would be required, but in later versions of the draft this suggestion disappeared. Importantly, there would be no need to document the exact scope of actual harm. This has always been a significant obstacle to claiming compensation of non-pecuniary damage in Hungary[157] (Menyhárd 2004: 241). Articles 355 to 360 of the Civil Code give general guidelines with regard to assessment of damages. They specify that compensation can be awarded as a lump sum or as an 'annuity'. The latter is to be awarded if the aim of the compensation is to "assist" the victim or his family (Article 355.3).

In Poland, general rules of damage, applicable to obligations in general, are contained in Articles 361–3 of the Civil Code. Article 361 is particularly relevant here. It stipulates:

157 See for example the judgement of a Hungarian court No. 357 of 2003 – the judgement concerned an incorrect press report concerning a person involved in a pending criminal case (Menyhárd 2004: 241).

> §1 A person obliged to compensate is liable only for normal consequences of his actions or omissions which caused the damage.
>
> §2 Within these limitations, unless a legal provision or a contract specify otherwise, compensation should include damage suffered by the victim as well as profits which he would have gained if the damage did not occur.[158]

The provision encapsulates the principle of full compensation, subject to the requirements of causation which are further examined below. The more detailed rules concerning assessment of damages in tort law are contained in Articles 444–8 of the Civil Code. Personal injuries are governed mainly by Article 444 of the Code. The provision stipulates that in cases of injury to a person (damage to body and health) the victim can recover all the costs, such as the cost of treatment, and if the damage involves permanent incapability to perform the existing profession, also the cost of preparing to a different profession. In cases where the victim is not, or is to a lesser extent capable of working, his needs have increased, or his prospects for the future have decreased, the person liable may also be required to pay an allowance (paid in instalments). In special circumstances the court can, instead of the allowance of a part of it, require the defendant to pay a lump sum (Article 447). Non-pecuniary damage can be compensated, and this has normally been considered as the key benefit of tortious liability over contractual liability.[159] The recovery of non-pecuniary damages has quite a long tradition in Polish civil law, reaching the Code of Obligations of 1933 (Wałachowska 2007: 21). During the time of socialism, and indeed until 1996, compensation of non-pecuniary damage was, however, quite limited, both in the Civil Code and in the practice of Polish courts. In 1996 a significant amendment of the Civil Code was enacted,[160] and at present there are a number of provisions concerning non-pecuniary damage in the Code. Article 24 prescribes the possibility of claiming damages for breaches of "personality rights" (*dobra osobiste*) (such as privacy or dignity) and refers to Articles 445 and 448 which further specify conditions for assessing and awarding non-pecuniary damages. Such damages are awarded in cases of personal injury (Article 445) or a breach of a "personality right" (Article 448). In the former case, damages should be "moderate", reflect the compensatory aim of the award (Rozwadowska-Herrmann 2007: 429) and, according to the judgement of the Supreme Court of 10 March 2006, reflect the current standard of living in Polish society.[161] If a "personality right" has been breached, the court may award

158 Translated by the author.

159 Although certain representatives of the doctrine of law have considered that non-pecuniary damage should also be compensated in contract (Nesterowicz 2007, Gnela 2000: 194).

160 Act of 23 August 1996.

161 Here the Supreme Court increased the non-pecuniary damage award because it took into account the improved standard of living in Polish society.

compensation of non-pecuniary damage or may allocate a sum of money to a good cause specified by the victim.

Causal link

Causal issues appear in every area of civil liability, but they seem to be the focus of particular interest and controversy in tortious liability literature and practice (Hart and Honoré 1985: 84). Central European legal systems – both as regards practice and doctrine of law – universally refrained from making distinctions between causal considerations in contractual and tortious liability. Thus, the remarks below ought to be taken as relevant in contractual liability as well. They are, however, of particular importance in the context of tortious product liability, especially taking into account the fact that the Product Liability Directive leaves this issue to national law.

Causation has been subject to an extensive doctrinal analysis throughout the civil and common law legal systems, and Central Europe is no exception in this respect. Causal considerations are very complex and their detailed analysis extends beyond the scope of this book. The area of causal link exceeds the boundaries of law (Czachórski 2002: 209), to involve science and technology. Scientific analysis assists the legal assessment of what exactly has been the cause of a specific phenomenon. Although the role of science in product liability litigation cannot be underestimated, this dimension will not be examined in the book.[162] The focus remains on the legal aspect of causality, which in terms of the product liability area does not differ from the general tortious liability rules.

Some fundamental principles concerning causation and its practical application in Central Europe have been explored in Chapter 3 of Part I. It was mentioned that, especially in 'fault' liability systems, causation does not play a significant part in the courts' arguments. Most effort goes into analysing the defendant's conduct and finding fault, and once this has been done the courts often refer to causation as a matter of course. On the other hand, causation does play a part in determination of the amount of awarded damages. Because of this phenomenon of causation being 'taken over' by other requisites of liability, it is often very difficult to establish the courts' view of causal issues in a particular case. Observing the writings of scholars to ascertain the general principles governing causation in Central Europe is therefore more instructive. On the other hand, with a greater use of 'strict liability' comes a greater need to consider causation carefully. Also, developments in modern markets, legal and procedural systems, and the technological progress, mentioned above, challenge the existing principles and force courts to devote

162 This point introduces a new aspect into the product liability discourse – the use of science in product liability cases entails the use of experts. The role, quality and price of experts as well as their appointment are crucial in product liability litigation. These issues concern aspects of civil procedure and access to justice which are not analysed in the book.

much more time and effort to causal considerations. These developments can be seen throughout Central Europe.

The Polish Civil Code specifies how causation ought to be understood in civil obligations. Article 361, quoted above in the section concerning 'damage', provides for a test to be applied in establishing causation. It specifies that only 'normal' consequences of actions or omissions are covered by civil liability. As mentioned above and as confirmed by the Supreme Court on numerous occasions, the manner in which causal link is defined by Article 361 entails that causal link determines the incidence of liability as well as limits its scope.[163] This link between causation and the scope of damages is also present in other Central European legal systems (see below). Article 361 followed the Code of Obligations of 1933, in spite of the criticism that the theory of adequate causal connection, which did not comply with Marxist theory, had been used there (Wagner 1974: 159). In the jurisprudence of Polish courts, some problems with deciding upon the 'normal' consequences of a particular phenomenon have been noticed (Czachórski 2002: 213), although product liability jurisprudence does not offer any good examples of such problems.

The Czech and Hungarian civil codes do not contain any provisions directly relating to causal link. The Czechoslovak doctrine of law initially agreed that the Western European causation rules, usually based on Kantian philosophies, were irreconcilable with Marx's teachings (Vondracek 1988: 377). In the majority of cases the issue of causation did not raise any significant problems, and even if difficulties arose the courts applied the 'theory of the proximate cause' "if the damage (was) such that it could have been a natural consequence of the tortious act" (Vondracek 1988: 377). It can be noticed that, similarly with Poland, although the Western theories of causation were criticized, no important alternatives were offered by the Czechoslovak writers, and the theory of 'adequate causal connection' was followed. According to Krčmář, damage must be "due to general nature, or to the usual course of events and experiences with an appropriate result, of the wrongful act or wrongful event" (1998: 352, translated by Hradek 2004: 95). At present, the 'adequate causal connection' theory is widely accepted by courts and doctrine. In Hungary the decisions of courts did not analyse the issue of causal connection in detail (Harmathy 1998: 118). The courts were, however, said to have been choosing "from the great number of the causes of damage in order to find a legally relevant cause" (ibid.). Whenever courts did mention the issue of causation, they focused on the acts which *usually* cause certain results (ibid.). Again, the adequate causal connection theory served as a model here.

Although causation did not feature very strongly in the jurisprudence of Central European courts, causal considerations did serve an important role of limiting the scope of recoverable damages, especially non-pecuniary damage. A good example is a relatively recent judgement of the Czech Highest Court of 22 October 2003,

163 The latest judgement confirming this stance: Judgement of the Supreme Court (Civil Chamber) of 14 January 2005, OSN 7 – 8/06.

where the court denied compensation of non-pecuniary losses to a person whose close family member died in a car accident. The view of the Court was that the pain and suffering of the claimant was not 'caused' by the defendant's action (Hradek 2004: 95).[164]

Causal considerations also involved cases where a number of defendants contributed to the damage, where the Civil Codes prescribed the general rules of joint and several liability. They were also relevant in cases involving contributory negligence by the claimant, where damages were reduced accordingly by Central European courts. These are examined below.

Joint and several liability of a number of defendants

Article 441, para. 1 of the Polish Civil Code introduces joint and several liability in tort. Czechoslovak and Hungarian Civil Codes contain similar provisions (Section 438 of the Czech Civil Code,[165] and Article 344 of the Hungarian Civil Code). The accepted view with regard to product liability cases is that, in terms of any recourse claims, the level of responsibility of each person needs to remain commensurate with the level of her control over the safety of the product (Łętowska 1999: 91).

Cases where a number of defendants are involved present difficult causal issues, some of which have not yet been considered in Central Europe. Central European law has not envisaged the answer to a situation where a number of persons introduced into the market products of the same kind as the one which caused loss and it was not clear who exactly caused the damage, or indeed a situation where a number of persons might have contributed to the risk of damage (market-share liability). There is simply no legal basis for this kind of a legal construct (Łętowska 1999: 92). Łętowska suggested that in such situations Polish law could merely offer liability of those producers whom the plaintiff was able to pinpoint (1999: 92), but she did not explain how exactly this could be done.

164 The judgement should be contrasted with two other judgements given in the 1990s – the judgement of the regional court of Ostrava and of the Higher Court of Prague, where it was held that if there exist "social, moral, emotional and cultural relationships among individuals, then the breach of right to life of one of them might cause an interference with the personal rights of another individual" (Hradek 2004: 96).

165 As amended by the Act No. 131/1982 Sb. Before the amendment the courts could, as a rule, decide that those who caused the damage were liable according to their share in causing it (para. 2 of the Section). At the moment such a power of the courts constitutes an exception ('in justified circumstances' – Section 438 para. 2) and the liability is indeed joint and several (Vondracek 1988: 392, 393). This provision, similarly with Section 420, relates to liability in tort and contract.

Contributory negligence

All the Central European civil codes specify the possibility of limitation or even a complete extinction of damages in a particular case where the victim has contributed to the damage (Section 441 of the Czech Civil Code, Article 340 of the Hungarian Civil Code, and Article 362 of the Polish Civil Code). Although the concept is referred to as the 'contributory negligence', it has not always been entirely clear what kind of conduct is in fact required for the victim to be said to have contributed to the damage – in particular whether fault is required. Normally, however, especially in 'fault-based' liability, courts required the presence of 'fault' in a victim's conduct. As products liability systems developed using more objective liability standards, courts became even more reluctant to declare contributory negligence. As pointed out in Chapter 3 of Part I, the position of victims was seen as weak: especially as regards knowledge about products and the risks they carried. The victims were not required to know or enquire about the risks unless these were obvious – in any other case the manufacturers were required to provide appropriate information and warnings.

Time limits for bringing claims

The Polish Civil Code provides for different time limits in contractual and tortious liability cases. The Hungarian and the Czech Codes, both their contemporary versions and the drafts, do not make such a distinction in general, although as explored in Chapter 4 there are some distinct rules for some consumer contracts.[166] Central European courts and doctrine of law are generally in agreement regarding the nature and aims of time limits for civil claims – they stress the need to protect the interests of defendants and to ensure legal certainty and finality (Klimek 2006: 639–40, Zrałek 2005).

Some Central European scholarly writers distinguish two types of limitation periods – these are referred to as 'subjective' (*a tempore scientiae*) and 'objective' (*a tempore facti*) periods (Józefiak 2006: 670). The dichotomy is related to the time when the limitation period starts running – with the start of the subjective period contingent upon the victim's awareness of the damage, and the objective period running from the event which caused the damage. The dichotomy is recognized in the Polish and the Czech Civil Code. The Hungarian Code does not establish this distinction in general rules of civil liability, and indeed the position is quite ambiguous, with courts rather focusing on the time when the damage occurred but also stressing the importance of the awareness of the victim (for instance in personal injury cases – the moment when income was lost for the first time – see

166 The implementation of certain European consumer protection directives (regulating various contractual arrangements) led to the introduction of specified time periods for claims arising under these instruments – see Consumer Law Compendium.

below). The dichotomy is also clearly present in the Product Liability Directive.[167] While it seems a relatively well established principle across Central Europe that claims ought to be limited in time, the courts and academic writers seem very uncomfortable with the idea of claims being barred before they actually arise – which could happen in Poland and the Czech Republic under the two-element structure of the limitation period rules (and indeed under the regime introduced by the Directive). The objective limitation period may expire before the claimant learns about the damage and the person liable to repair it. The Czech courts and academic writers have been quite determined not to allow such a situation to happen, and Czech courts in fact allowed claims brought after the objective limitation period had expired.[168] According to Hradek, a different outcome would "of course be unacceptable" (2003: 132). This approach has been reinforced by Section 106 of the Civil Code (quoted below), which stipulates that the objective period 'time-barring' claims does not apply to personal injury cases. The Polish legal system headed in the same direction, and, following the Constitutional Tribunal declaring the provision regulating limitation periods to be unconstitutional (denying access to legal redress), the Civil Code was amended in 2007 and the objective ten-year period was effectively disapplied in personal injury cases (see below).

The Polish rules on limitation periods have another peculiar feature. These periods merely serve as defence against the claimant's action. They are not therefore 'bars' to litigation *per se*. As specified in Article 117, para. 1 of the Civil Code, all pecuniary claims are limited in time and this means that after the limitation period has expired the person against whom such claims could be brought can defend herself against them unless she revokes her right to do so. Obviously the ten-year long-stop introduced by Article 11 of the Directive has been contemplated as a bar to litigation. Interestingly, as it will be explored below, the Polish implementation of the Directive seems to have retained the traditional understanding of the limitation period even for the purposes of product liability cases.

As mentioned above, the Polish time limits for bringing claims in tort have experienced a crucial overhaul recently. They are established by Article 442 of the Civil Code, which is a *lex specialis* to the general provisions on limitation periods contained in Articles 117–25 of the Code (a ten-year period for all claims, starting from the time when the actual claim arose). Article 442, para. 1 provided that "claims for reparation of damage caused by a tortious act" were limited in time by a period of "three years since the victim learnt of the damage and the person who is liable to repair it". The second sentence of the same provision specified that "in any case", the claim was limited in time by a period of "ten years since the day when the event which caused the damage occurred".[169] The expression 'limited in time' has been chosen here because, as mentioned above, neither of these periods results in a true expiry of claims. The ten-year limitation period and its interplay with

167 Article 11.

168 Judgements 33 Odo 477/2001 and R 2/1992 – Hradek (2003: 132).

169 Translated by the author.

the three-year period have been the subject of doctrinal controversy and judicial uncertainty. Because the wording of Article 442 indicated that the limitation period could expire for claims which did not yet arise (before damage occurs or before the victim actually becomes aware of the damage), courts and academics attempted to rectify what was widely seen as an unjust rule (Radwański 2007). Two strands of thought appeared within doctrinal writings and court judgements: one in favour of literal interpretation of the provision confirming such position, and one suggesting a more dynamic and contextual interpretation of the Article to provide that the beginning of the limitation period is the day when the damage occurred. The Supreme Court recently provided an answer to this debate in a decision of 17 February 2006.[170] Although it held that focusing on the literal meaning of a provision may sometimes lead to unjust consequences and thus systemic and functional methods of interpretation must also be used, it found it impossible to interpret Article 442 in any other way than what it expressly indicated. Thus, the proper interpretation of Article 442 was that the ten-year limitation period started running on the day when the event which caused the damage took place, irrespective of whether the damage had already occurred or not. This judgement was given prior to the decision of the Constitutional Tribunal which declared that Article 442 was contrary to Articles 2 and 77 of the Polish Constitution of 1997.[171] The Tribunal held in the judgement of 1 September 2006 that Article 442 had the potential of limiting the claimants' right to redress and compensation. While the general aim of limitation periods – legal certainty and ensuring finality – was acknowledged by the Tribunal, it was emphasized that Article 442 went too far in ensuring such finality. The Tribunal stressed that claims could be limited in time before they even arise. The Tribunal also requested that the Civil Code be amended and the unconstitutional provision eliminated. The Parliament has duly enacted an amendment of the Civil Code on 16 February 2007, in force since 10 August 2007.[172] Article 442 has been repealed and a new Article 442[1] inserted. The new provision reads:

> 1. Claims for reparation of damage caused by tortious acts are subject to a limitation period of three years from the day when the victim learnt of the damage and the person liable for it. However, this period cannot be longer than ten years from the day when the event causing the damage occurred.

---

170 Decision of the Plenary Session of the Civil Chamber of 17 February 2006, III CZP 84/05.

171 Decision SK 14/05 of the Constitutional Tribunal of 1 September 2006. Article 2 of the Constitution describes Poland as a democratic state governed by the rule of law and realizing postulates of social justice, and Article 77 of the Constitution specifies that no legal instrument can deprive citizens of access to courts in order to protect their freedoms and rights.

172 Act of 16 February 2007 *on the amendment of the Civil Code.*

2. …

3. In cases of personal injury the limitation period cannot expire earlier than three years from the day when the victim learnt of the damage and the person liable for it."

Clearly, the previously existing ten-year limitation period was disapplied in personal injury cases. The decision of the Constitutional Tribunal and the amendment of the Civil Code met with varied responses from the judiciary, legal profession, academics, and representatives of businesses and insurance firms (Jaraszek and Makosz 2007). While the judiciary and some members of the legal profession welcomed the change, the insurance industry as well as businesses expressed concerns over possible increases in insurance premiums (ibid.). The concerns of Polish hospitals are particularly striking – they already find it very difficult to obtain insurance coverage, because their activity is considered particularly risky (ibid.).

As mentioned above, the Czech Civil Code provides for two limitation periods – the subjective one of two years from the day "when the damaged person learnt of the damage and of the liable person", and an objective one indicating that claims become "statute-barred" "three years and, as for damages caused by intention, ten years from the day when it came to the event from that the damage arose; this rule shall not apply to damages to health" (Section 106). While this is quite a clear position, Czech courts do not shy away from applying Section 106 in accordance with their sense of fairness and justice. This entails disapplying the objective period if applying it would mean that the claim expired before it arose (Hradek 2003: 132).[173]

Reiterating the concerns expressed in Part I, one may note that such a principled, fairness-focused approach to limitation periods in Poland and the Czech Republic can have an unsettling effect on product liability litigation under the new provisions of the implemented Directive.

The Hungarian Civil Code's approach to limitation periods is quite complex and requires clarification – as confirmed by 'the Conception' to the Draft Code. The limitation period is normally five years from the "due date of the claim" (Rein and Kohegyi 2006). While according to Article 308.1 of the Civil Code[174] the time limits start running from "performance", no further clarification is provided as regards non-contractual claims. Here the Supreme Court Resolutions Nos 51 and 52 explained that the limitation period shall start "at the time when income was lost the first time due to the incapacity resulting from the accident".[175]

173 Judgements 33 Odo 477/2001 and R 2/1992.

174 Version provided online and verified through the author's academic consultations: <http://www.angelfire.com/mn2/reformclub/hunc1.html>.

175 Quoted by 'the Conception' at p. 181.

Non-cumul principle

Central European civil codes do not contain a *non-cumul* principle. Thus, in theory a tort claim can be brought even if some existing contractual arrangement has been broken. On the other hand, in the jurisprudence of Central European courts the picture is much more complex.

Hungarian courts have been clear in their intention to provide a system of liability where a plaintiff can freely choose whom and according to which regime to sue for his damage. In product liability cases this means that even if there is a possibility of suing the retailer or the manufacturer in contract, the victim is entitled to directly sue the manufacturer in tort. Such a line of thinking was confirmed in the 'slippers' case.[176] Here the judicial proceedings reached the Supreme Court, although the first and second instance courts were of the same opinion with regard to the issue of freedom of choice of defendant. The case concerned a pair of slippers with a very slippery sole, which caused an injury to the plaintiff. In the first and second instance the courts held that "damages on a tort basis could be claimed only if the damage was not a consequence of a breach of contract" (Maczonkai 1996: 114). In other words, once there is a contractual relation from which the plaintiff can benefit, tort rules were held to have no application. The courts excluded the possibility of the plaintiff using the tort rules to claim compensation from the manufacturer. Nevertheless, the Supreme Court held:

> … as regards liability for damages caused by an unlawful conduct, the application of the general liability rules of private law is inevitable, even when the defendant is a producer and the product causes damage to the consumer. That principle cannot be altered by the close (contractual) relation between the producer and the person who suffered damage, and cannot be altered by that fact if the person who has suffered damage could have sued a third person for damages on the basis of a contractual relation, or would have had another legal claim (for instance warranty). Referring to the absence of a legal relation is erroneous because the injurious act in itself establishes a legal relation between the tortfeasor and the injured party. … The person who has suffered damage cannot be excluded from being able to assert her claim directly against the person who caused the damage …[177]

In Poland, the buyer could sue the seller in tort in spite of the existing contract between them. Article 443 of the Civil Code clearly allows a tortious action in the existence of a contract between the parties. Similar rationale as in Hungary: the benificial effect for victims of defective products, was used.

176 Bírósági Határozatok (Court Decisions) 1986/12 No 501. Quoted by Maczonkai (1996: 114).

177 Quoted by Maczonkai (1996: 114).

The particular situation within the Czech product liability regime was explained above. Although there was nothing within the Civil Code inducing such an approach, the courts generally allowed a tort action only if there was no contract between the victim and the responsible person. The effects of such a tendency were not, however, detrimental for the victims of defective products, as no significant divergences between these two regimes of liability existed in the Czech product liability litigation.

CONCLUDING REMARKS

The necessity for such a thorough, systematic analysis of the Central European product liability regimes demonstrates the level of their progress. The development of these regimes was ultimately very dynamic and resembled the Western European developments in the area. Even within the Czech legal system, where the very peculiar conditions led to the lack of a comprehensive and coherent legal doctrine, the ideas which did occur in the existing writings and case law were not very far indeed from the ideas represented by the Western European courts.

II. SPECIFIC TORTIOUS LIABILITY PROVISIONS OF THE CIVIL CODES AND THEIR USE IN PRODUCT LIABILITY CASES

Analysed above are provisions of civil codes concerning liability in tort at its widest and their application in product liability cases. Below is a brief analysis of provisions envisaging specific types of tortious liability, which played or at least had a potential to be playing some part in cases involving damages caused by dangerous products.

Section 245 of the Czechoslovak Civil Code of 1964 stipulated that if the use of a product was subject to special technical standard rules, unless these rules were common knowledge, it was the obligation of the 'trade organization' (seller) to inform the buyer of any such rules. If the duty has not been fulfilled, the organization must compensate the "citizen for damage so occasioned"[178] (this creates objective "information – instruction liability" – Svestka 1989: 98). The provision implies that "(T)he retailer must inform the customer how to use the thing properly, unless the use is known to the public at large" (Vondracek 1988: 134). Some cases involving defective products were based on Section 245. How the seller was supposed to fulfil his obligation under this provision was held to depend upon the kind of product and the circumstances. Generally the obligation was more extensive if the product was new or, if it was not, if its contents or intended use had been amended. According to Svestka, it should be sufficient for the seller ('trade organization') to place directions on the product or attach them

178 From the commentary to the Civil Code by Vondracek (1988: 234).

to the product in another way (1989: 99). The directions should normally clearly explain the properties of the product, its proper use and any consequences of improper use. The provision did not stipulate the standard of the sellers' liability, and hence there has been a long dispute in the Czechoslovak jurisprudence as to whether to use 'fault-based' liability or 'strict liability' here. In 1969 the Supreme Court of the Czechoslovak Socialist Republic[179] confirmed the 'strict liability' standard, but later case law has not always followed this judgement (Svestka 1989: 99). After the amendment of the Civil Code Section 245 became Section 617, but the substantive content of the provision has not changed. This provision has not recently been used in product liability litigation.

Another provision of the Czechoslovak Civil Code which was used in some product liability cases was Section 238. It gave the courts the basis for establishing strict liability of those who caused damage "by circumstances having their origin in the character of an apparatus or other things used for the service rendered" (Svestka 1989: 100). This provision has now been repealed and partly replaced by Section 420a,[180] providing for strict liability of persons who caused damage by "operational activities or "activities of an operational nature". The damage may be caused by the activity itself, by a thing used during the activity, or by "physical, biological and chemical influences of the operation upon the surroundings". Exonerating circumstances are: an "inevitable event not originating in the operation", or damage caused by own conduct of the victim.[181] Although the provisions of the former Section 238 and the new Section 420a differ, it must be acknowledged that they seem to have been meant to realize similar functions. The fact that they were used on several occasions in product liability cases shows some level of determination to render product liability strict, but this determination has not been strong enough to make these provisions the formal legal basis of the regime. Similarly with the Hungarian regime and the Polish regime, the courts largely refused to use those provisions in product liability litigation (Svestka 1989: 100).

Article 345 of the Hungarian Civil Code refers to strict liability in tort. It imposes such liability upon anyone who carries out an activity involving significant danger. Such an activity was not defined and courts apply this general provision to cases before them on an *ad hoc* basis (Harmathy 1998: 119). This provision contains two possibilities of exoneration: *force majeure* and the exclusive fault of the claimant. Although, as Harmathy admits, there was nothing preventing the courts from interpreting this provision to apply in the product liability context (1998: 119), Article 345 was not used in product liability cases. In fact, liability for defective products developed by Hungarian courts on the basis of general tortuous liability provisions reaches further than Article 345, as it does not envisage these

179 R 63/1968, as quoted by Svestka (1989: 99).

180 Inserted by the Act No. 509/1991 Coll.

181 From the translation of the Civil Code provided by Dobiasova.

exceptions (Harmathy 1998: 119, Maczonkai 1996: 113). The 'siphon'[182] and 'bee'[183] cases firmly established the 'social expectations' test which was more beneficial for claimants than the strict liability rule in Article 345 (Maczonkai 1996: 113).

The Polish jurisprudence and doctrine of law made attempts to base certain product liability cases on Article 435 of the Civil Code, but these efforts were usually abandoned and criticized as unsuitable for the needs of the regime. The provision, resembling the Czech Sections 238 and 420a and the Hungarian Article 345, establishes strict liability of those holding undertakings or enterprises set into motion by the forces of nature (vapour, gas, electricity, liquid fuels, etc.) for losses and damages caused by the functioning (or, in literal translation, 'movement') of the undertakings.[184] The liability is strict, as the only exonerating circumstances envisaged by the Article are the exclusive fault of the victim or a third person for whom the defendant is not responsible. The rationale for the introduction of this provision into the Civil Code was the contention that the cost of certain risky activities, very advantageous for the community and hence impossible to be outlawed, should not be borne by their victims (Wagner 1974: 236, 237). In cases of undertakings moved by the forces of nature it was understood that the persons running the dangerous enterprises could easily calculate the costs of the risk of causing damage within the overall costs, and, as being generally wealthier, were in a better position to bear the risk (ibid.). The rationale could have been extended to cover cases of liability for defective products, but the Polish courts have failed to use this possibility. The most determined advocate of using Article 435 in product liability litigation has been Gnela, who claimed that developing an entirely objective liability for defective products (2000: 187)[185] was a small step in the already commenced evolution.[186] However, Gnela's approach failed to reveal certain significant problems involved in using the provision, the problems clearly seen by many other representatives of the doctrine of law: Szpunar (1985b: 7) and Łętowska (1999: 88). The Polish Supreme Court in the judgement of 9 April 1952[187] involving damages caused by an explosion in the plaintiff's stove of a piece of coal containing dynamite did relate the dangerous defect of the coal to the functioning of the coal mine. This construction allowed the Supreme Court

182 1988/12 No. 911. Quoted by Maczonkai (1996: 113).

183 1991/6 No. 428. Quoted by Maczonkai (1996: 113).

184 The provision derived from Article 9 of the 1922 Statute on Electric Power, and subsequently developed in Article 152 of the Code of Obligations 1933 (Wagner 1974: 236).

185 Please refer to Gnela for further representatives of the Polish doctrine of law in favour of using this provision in product liability litigation.

186 Article 435 was suggested by Gnela as the most suitable legal basis for the establishment of a strict product liability regime. She pointed out the opportunity of the Polish legal system to introduce such a regime even before the implementation of the Product Liability Directive.

187 Judgement of the Supreme Court of 9 April 1952, C 962/51.

to base the judgement upon Article 435. The judgement, however, stands alone among the many judgements which failed to see such kind of a connection. One of the most evident examples of the unwillingness of the Polish higher instance courts to follow the 'dynamite in coal' case was the judgement in the already analysed case of the Pepsi Cola bottle.[188] The district court based its judgement on Article 435, but the Court of Appeal of Katowice overturned the judgement. It held that if strict liability under Article 435 was applied here, every producer of knives, cars, etc. would bear liability for all the accidents occurring with the use of these products, as the forces of nature were also used in their manufacture.[189] The scholarly writings generally followed the view of the Court of Appeal (Wasiak 1979).[190]

Although some evidence of use of those specific liability provisions in cases of product liability can be found, there is no doubt that they were marginal instances. The essence of tortious liability regimes was built around the general liability provisions.

188 Judgement of the Court of Appeal of Katowice of 10 October 1996, I Acr 500/96.

189 Ibid, at p. 40. As it was not clearly elaborated by the Court where such a conclusion came from, it is indeed difficult to understand the rationale for this judgement. The only indication of this rationale is the statement that Article 435 ought to deal with damages caused by the functioning of the undertaking, and not somehow related to this functioning. The functioning of the undertaking has been understood by the Court of Appeal as being in a very close conceptual relationship with the forces of nature, and hence the conclusion that the event of the cap falling off has not been caused by this functioning.

190 However, Gnela (2000: 195–8) suggested that the damages caused by dangerous products were indeed related to the functioning of undertakings. According to her it is the manner in which production is being organized in the present times, its automatization, mass character, mechanization, which is the source of defects: "the roots of the accident are in the functioning of the undertaking" (2000: 197). In order to come to this conclusion one needs to understand the 'functioning' of the contemporary undertakings as not only their operation, but also the way they manifest their existence (Gnela 2000: 195). It is very rare indeed for contemporary undertakings (industry) not to be set in motion by the forces of nature (Gnela 2000: 195).

Chapter 6
Implementation and Application of the Product Liability Directive

INTRODUCTION

Because of the very limited time during which the Directive has been in force across Central Europe, this chapter focuses on the 'implementation' rather than the 'application' element. It contains an elaboration of the manner in which Central European states have implemented the Product Liability Directive, an assessment of any remaining discrepancies with the text of the Directive, and an examination of the scope for further changes.

The analysis of the implemented provisions of the Directive is not very comprehensive in those instances where the provisions of the Central European Product Liability Acts merely translate it. More attention is devoted to those provisions which differ from the Directive, and to highlighting problems peculiar to the Central European jurisdictions. These problems derive from their general principles of civil liability, from the product liability regimes which developed there before the Directive was implemented, and from the general approach to consumer issues, all presented above.

Central European product liability legislation does not always faithfully follow the provisions of the Directive, yet, the inconsistencies are rare and it is unlikely that they would be considered serious enough to warrant an action taken by the European Commission under Article 226 of the EC Treaty. Some may be the result of misunderstandings of the motives of the Directive, and others of retained compliance with the previously existing liability systems.

The rules in force before the implementation will remain applicable to the claims which arose before the Acts came into effect, as well as to cases to which the Directive does not apply.[1]

IMPLEMENTATION OF THE DIRECTIVE – THE PROCESS

Hungary implemented the Product Liability Directive the earliest of all the Central and Eastern European Countries. Act X *on Product Liability* of 1993 was adopted by the Hungarian Parliament in anticipation of the obligations arising out of the

1 See Chapter 3 of Part I for an explanation of the binding force and scope of the Directive.

Association Agreement with the European Union. It was later amended by Act XXXVI of 2002.[2] Normally the legislative process in Hungary commences with an initiative originating in one of the ministries. Nevertheless, in the case of product liability reform two members of the Hungarian Parliament (one from the governing party and one from the opposition) prompted the Ministry of Justice to act (Tercsák 1993: 224). The initiative of the MPs reached very far, into the regulation of the whole body of consumer protection laws in one act. However, the Ministry of Justice concluded that the Hungarian legal system as it was then was not prepared for such an innovation (Kecskés 1994: 5). The codification of consumer protection laws in general necessarily involved amendments of many provisions of the Civil Code and other acts, which was envisaged by the Ministry as possible some time in the future, but not then (ibid.). Hence, only the product liability area was reformed at the time, followed later by a plethora of other regulations covering various areas of consumer protection laws, in accordance with the requirements of the European Community.[3] Although there were several voices in favour of inclusion of the implementing legislation into the Civil Code, the decision was reached to adopt an entirely separate piece of legislation. The draft Civil Code does include the provisions of the implemented Directive.

The regime of product liability has been supplemented in Hungary by the Act XXV of 1998 *on medicinal products for human use*, later amended by the Act XXXVI of 2002.[4] With regard to medicinal products, the Act on Product Liability was amended by Act XCV of 2005 (in effect from 30 October 2005), where the development risk defence was excluded in cases of damage caused "by the appropriate use of pharmaceutical products" (paragraph 14.3 of the Act). This issue is further examined below.

The Czech Republic implemented the Directive by Act No. 59/1998 Coll. *on liability for damage caused by a defective product* adopted on 5 March 1998. The Act came into effect on 1 June 1998. The Act is a *lex specialis* with regard to the Civil Code, and the provisions of the latter are still to be applied "on a subsidiary basis".[5] The Act was later amended in pursuance with the amendment of the Directive in 1999 by the Act No. 209/2000 Coll. (in effect since 1 September 2000). The amendment reflected the changes introduced by the Directive, but also used the opportunity to correct some discrepancies which still existed between the Czech text and the text of the Directive. The Draft Civil Code incorporates the provisions of the Act in Sections 2438 to 2443.

Poland seemed to have experienced some delays in implementation of the Directive. These were caused by political and academic debates as to the role and

2 Act *amending Act IV of 1959 on the Civil Code of the Republic of Hungary and other acts for the harmonization of consumer protection*, passed by the Parliament on 5 November 2002. Source: Judit Bartfai, Hungarian Ministry of Justice.

3 See Chapter 3 of Part I for a more detailed analysis of this process.

4 Source: Judit Bartfai, Hungarian Ministry of Justice.

5 See the Czech part of the Product Liability Database (BIICL).

place of product liability law in the new market structure and in the new legal system. As was explained in Part I, Polish industry was in a very economically fragile position during the 1990s (Gnela 2000: 207),[6] and there were political concerns whether it could in fact withstand the introduction of a new strict liability regime. Polish academic writers and practitioners had for some time before the implementation of the Directive remained in disagreement as to the substantive content of the new legislation, and as to its form and place in the Polish legal system. Some claimed that, although harmonization of Polish law with the European Union standards was necessary, the reform of the law ought to be conducted with the specificity of the Polish law and legal culture, as well as the position of the Polish consumers and manufacturers, in the mind of the reformers (Jagielska 1999: 196). Another view, more in line with the expectations of the European Union, was that the said specificity could only be taken into account when the provisions of the Directive allowed this (Gnela 1998: 146–7). Upon assessing the Polish implementation of the Product Liability Directive, it is clear that the latter approach prevailed in most areas. No consensus could also be seen initially as regards the form of regulation of product liability: some argued that the new regime ought to be included within the Civil Code;[7] others postulated separate regulation (Gnela 1998: 152). There were also those for whom establishment of a consumer protection act was a necessity, and the best place for product liability provisions was in this act (Suliński 1995: 21). The draft Act on Product Liability of 1992[8] contained a very laconic version of implementation of the Directive, envisaging the necessity of a further amendment (Gnela 2000: 207). Such an idea was widely criticized by Polish legal scholars (Nesterowicz 1993: 485, Skąpski 1995: 80–81). Several draft acts implementing the Directive appeared after the 1992 draft, some of which were to be part of the Civil Code, and others, independent acts. The complex amendment of the Civil Code of 1996 did not, however, include product liability law, as it was considered at the time that a separate act on product liability would be necessary.[9] On the other hand, the suggestion to establish a consumer protection act was also criticized by the representatives of doctrine of law (Gnela 2000: 219, Skąpski 1995: 592).[10] The existing drafts of consumer

6 This contrary to their Hungarian counterparts.

7 Draft acts of 1992 and 1997 – Gnela 2000: 206–7, 226–30.

8 Kwartalnik Prawa Prywatnego, R.I.: 1992, z. 1–4, pp. 190–206. See in particular the rationale for the draft: at p. 197.

9 Gnela mentions the statement of the Deputy Minister of Justice A. Marcinkowski in 1994, justifying this stance of the authorities (2000: 218).

10 The Polish legal profession, certain ministries and the Consumer Federation unsuccessfully argued in favour of consumer protection acts. This is contrary to the situation in other post-socialist states such as the Czech Republic and Hungary, but also Albania, Estonia, Latvia, Lithuania, Romania and Slovakia, where consumer protection acts were adopted (Gnela 2000: 219). Consumer law, it was submitted, involved regulation of issues remaining within various branches of law, and hence it was impossible to contain them all in one act (Skąpski 1995: 592). Even if such an act were established, some writers argued,

protection acts were criticized for their incompleteness, and the idea of a consumer protection act was not accepted: it was regarded as unable to constitute a stable piece of legislation (Gnela 2000: 219). The final decision was made by the Polish authorities to insert the act implementing the Product Liability Directive into the Civil Code. Poland adopted the Act *on the protection of certain rights of consumers and liability for damage caused by a dangerous product* on 2 March 2000.[11] The Act inserted Articles 449.1 to 449.11 into the Code (title VI.1 introduced into Book III 'Obligations' of the Code). The Act came into force on 1 January 2001. An interesting fact is that the place in which the new regulation is situated in the Code does not indicate tortious liability (the latter is covered by Title VII). This has already raised questions of some prominent representatives of the doctrine of law as to the true nature of this new category of liability.[12]

SUBSTANTIVE PROVISIONS OF THE DIRECTIVE – THEIR IMPLEMENTATION BY THE CENTRAL EUROPEAN PRODUCT LIABILITY ACTS

INTRODUCTORY REMARKS

The requisites of tortious product liability before the implementation of the Directive were: introduction into circulation of a defective product, damage, and the causal link between the two. A further requirement was the existence of 'fault', although gradually a more objective (the Czech Republic and Poland) or even an entirely 'strict liability' (Hungary) standard was introduced by courts. The liability system introduced by the Directive seems on the one hand somewhat more restricted in scope, and on the other hand much more complex in application and interpretation, than the pre-existing tortious liability rules. Obviously, these pre-existing rules remain relevant in many aspects which the Directive does not regulate, or whenever it deals with a notion or a concept in a general manner (as explored in Part I).

---

product liability law implementing the Directive ought not to be contained there. Skąpski contended that the Product Liability Directive concerned a wider category of persons than mere 'consumers' (whom he understood to be buyers of products for individual, non-professional use), and including the implementation of this Act in the consumer protection act could exclude bystanders and professional buyers from the scope of applicability of the product liability regime (1995: 593). A consumer protection act has not been adopted in Poland, and it remains an interesting question whether it was needed. Considering the fact that most of the other post-socialist states did enact such acts, one must wonder about the rationale of such initiatives and reasons why they did not influence the Polish legislators sufficiently.

11 Dziennik Ustaw (Journal of Laws) No. 22 poz. 271.

12 This is a revised version of the Introductory Part on Poland in the Product Liability Database by Sengayen (BIICL).

'PRODUCER' – IMPLEMENTATION OF ARTICLE 3

With its definition of 'producer', the Directive ought to introduce some stability and consistency, if no far-reaching change, into the Central European product liability systems. Maczonkai pointed out that one of the benefits of the Directive is precise definitions,[13] and most of all the definition of 'producer' – in contrast to the Hungarian case law (1996: 116).

The Directive places liability on the widest possible circle of persons, wider indeed than had ever been contemplated by the Central European legal scholars and courts. The definition of 'producer' provided by Article 3 of the Directive is very comprehensive and includes the manufacturers of finished products, raw materials, and component parts, quasi producers, and importers. The suppliers are to be "treated as" producers subject to certain conditions. In contrast to this very transparent regulation, Hungarian and Polish Product Liability Acts adopt the approach of distinguishing the actual 'producer' and any other persons who are not the 'producer' (importers in particular) but are liable *like* the latter. In consequence, their provisions concerning, for instance, exonerating circumstances seem quite unconvincing (Mohmand 2002: 174). The Czech act follows the wording of the Directive as regards the definition of 'producer'.

The English translation of the Hungarian Act on Product Liability provided by the Hungarian Ministry of Justice uses the notion 'manufacturer' with regard to the main category of persons liable. The 'manufacturer' is defined by Section 1 of the Act as "a producer of a finished or semi-finished product, or raw material, furthermore the person who indicates himself as the manufacturer of the product by the indication of his name, trademark or some other distinguishing mark on the product".[14] Further, in accordance with the Directive, Section 3.2 of the Hungarian Act specifies that liability for imported products rests with the importer,[15] to whom the "provisions of this Act pertaining to manufacturers shall also duly apply". The liability of other participants in the distribution chain ("distributors") is, following the intentions of the Directive, of subsidiary character, being set in motion only if the manufacturer cannot be identified by the distributor within 30 days from

13 The precision of these definitions was undermined in the writings of Western European legal scholars, and indeed also by the manner in which national courts of the Member States interpret them (differences in interpretation and application of the Directive were mentioned in Part I). Although the precision may indeed seem impressive for the Central European legal profession, for the first time faced with a written product liability regime, it is clear that very soon doubts are likely to appear even among the initially positive Central Europeans.

14 All the quotations of the Act provided hereafter have been taken from the English translation of the Hungarian Act on Product Liability provided by the Hungarian Ministry of Justice (Judit Bartfai).

15 Defined as "a foreign trader or, in respect of a foreign trade consignment contract, a consignor" (Section 1.3). Although the definition in the Directive is more detailed, the two regulations do not seem to differ in effect.

the day of the "written request of the injured party" (Section 4). The distributor can also avoid liability having revealed the identity of another distributor from whom the product was obtained, within the same time period (Section 4.1). The Hungarian Act clearly attempted introducing an element of certainty in the notion of 'reasonable time' contained in Article 3.3 of the Directive. The certainty is undoubtedly valuable for consumers who are not left waiting for some indeterminate amount of time. It may also benefit suppliers, creating a specific timeframe for them to act.

The provision concerning possible defendants in the Hungarian Act was the subject of a judgement of the Hungarian Supreme Court (2000/350).[16] The case revealed the inadequacies in the Hungarian Act. The initial version of the Act did not contain the unequivocal possibility of the defendant escaping liability upon the identification of the importer (in case of imported products).[17] Thus, it seemed possible to hold the supplier liable even if he identified the importer, as long as he did not identify the manufacturer of the defective product. The case involved a defective angle grinder imported from Germany. The claimant – an insurance company with whom the victim of the product had an insurance contract, brought proceedings against two vendors. The first vendor purchased the angle grinder from the second vendor, and the claimant demanded their joint and several liability. Neither of the defendants indicated the manufacturer or the importer, and thus their liability was declared, pursuant to the Hungarian Product Liability Act 1993. Following the judgement in this case the Act was amended in 2002,[18] and at present Section 4.1 "shall also apply to imported products where the manufacturer is indicated but the importer cannot be identified".

The Czech product liability system is likely to experience significant changes as regards the possible defendants. Under the pre-existing rules, sellers were not normally held liable in tort but rather in contract, if indeed there was one between them and the victim. Further, the liability of importers was not common; in fact, none of the reported cases involved liability of an importer in Czechoslovakia (Dobiasova). Section 2 of the Czech Act follows the wording of the Directive quite faithfully. Nevertheless, the time for the supplier to avoid liability by indicating the identity of a person who supplied the product to him was similarly with Hungary made more precise. On the other hand, the manner in which the Act specifies the beginning of the one month period – "from the date on which damages were claimed"[19] – may confuse. It does not seem to be the intended effect of the Directive for 'damages to be claimed' (assuming that this means the moment of bringing a claim) before the period lapses. The clear stance of the European Court of Justice

16 The details of the judgement provided by Kalman, Lelkes and Domokos (2003: 7).

17 This earlier version of the Act was translated by Judit Fazekas of the University of Miscoltz, also mentioned by Kalman, Lelkes and Domokos (2003: 5).

18 Act XXXVI of 2002.

19 Translation by the Czech Ministry of Trade and Industry – Dobiasova.

concerning avoiding multiplicity of proceedings (developed for instance in the case C-52/00 *Commission v France*) confirms the position.

Article 449.5 of the Polish Civil Code deals with the issue of possible defendants under the new liability regime.[20] The provision covers manufacturers of finished products, manufacturers of spare parts, and those who by placing on the product their name, trade mark or other distinguishing mark hold themselves out to be producers. Importers, defined as those who introduced a product of a foreign origin into the domestic market in the course of their business, are to be liable "like producers". The liability of suppliers is subsidiary, and by virtue of Article 449.5 it is only possible if *it is not known* who the producer, and another person who supplied the product to the supplier, is (this is not entirely consistent with the Directive, thus the italicized words – see below). The liability arises unless within one month from the day a supplier was informed of the damage he indicates the person mentioned above and his address, or, if the latter is impossible, the person from whom he himself received the product.

Central European Acts followed the wording of the Directive relatively closely in the area of possible defendants, and some of the remaining divergences have been rectified. Primary defendants are the producers, and the liability of importers or those who hold themselves out to be producers is equal to the liability of the producers. The liability of those holding themselves out as producers is a novelty, for none of the Central European states had any experience with these types of cases.

On the one hand, the subsidiary liability of suppliers has been accepted in all Central European Acts, and no discrepancies such as those noted in France or Denmark occurred. The latest judgements of the European Court of Justice[21] seem to have clarified the approach, and thus it is clear that the strict court-based liability system which has so far been applied in Hungary cannot cover supplier liability. However, the commentators of the Polish Act noted that with regard to the subsidiary liability of suppliers the position of a victim is facilitated in comparison with the Directive: while the latter refers to the liability of suppliers as arising "where the producer of the product cannot be identified", the Polish act only requires the producer "not to be known". According to Żuławska this approach relieves the victim of a possible burden to also try and identify the producer, the burden which seems to exist under the Directive (1997: 477).

VICTIMS – POSSIBLE CLAIMANTS

Although the Directive does not define the category of the possible claimants, its focus on consumers is clear from the Preamble as well as from the delimitation of the limits of recoverable damage (Article 9b). It is also apparent that the scope

20 The translation of the provisions of the Polish Act on Product Liability has been conducted by the author.

21 In particular – C-402/03 *Skov AEg v Bilka*.

of application of the Central European tortious regimes was wider than the scope of the Directive. Apart from the professional victims being able to recover their personal injuries, damage to commercial property was recoverable.

Another matter arises with the introduction of the Directive into Central European law, and it is crucial to observe whether it indeed entails any true change in future. The requirement of a product having been introduced into circulation suggests that victims of products not yet introduced into circulation (such as employees of the manufacturer or his family) would be unable to use the regime of the Directive in order to recover compensation for their injuries (Łętowska 1999: 95). From the analysis of this matter in Chapter 5 it is apparent that this approach has not been unfamiliar to the Central European jurisdictions, where the courts clearly delimited the scope of applicability of the product liability systems using the moment of introduction of a product into circulation. Now that this notion has been formalized, it remains to be seen how it is interpreted in judicial practice and whether this interpretation differs from the approach adopted before the implementation of the Directive.[22]

'PRODUCTS' IN THE IMPLEMENTING LEGISLATION

'Products' in general

The purpose of the analysis below is to determine what changes the Central European jurisdictions needed to introduce into their legal systems to formally render[23] product liability – liability for 'products' and not 'things'. It is necessary to assess whether any substantial changes in the scope of applicability of 'product' regimes are likely to occur.

The traditional civil law concept of 'things' used in product liability cases did not distinguish between immovables and movables.[24] It was, however, commonly understood that product liability was possible only in cases of defective movables (Łętowska 1999: 94). The concept also did not make a difference between processed and unprocessed goods. Thus it seems that the implemented regime of the Product Liability Directive would have a similar scope to the previously existing tortious liability regimes. Both the Hungarian and the Czech Product Liability Acts initially excluded the primary agricultural products and game from the scope of their applicability. The Polish Act was adopted after the amendment of the Directive

22 See p. 266 below for a further elaboration of 'introduction into circulation' and its implications in the new liability systems.

23 The book uses the notion 'formally', because although Central European tortious product liability before the implementation of the Directive officially functioned on the basis of the general concept of 'things', courts and scholars widely used the notion 'products' in the product liability context.

24 Although there did exist separate regimes of liability for damages caused by immovable property (see pp. 208-210 above).

and hence included the new version of the definition of 'products'. The Hungarian and Czech Acts were amended[25] following the amendment of the Directive,[26] and at present a 'product' includes: in Hungary, "any movable property, even if it subsequently becomes a component or part of another movable or real property, as well as electrical energy";[27] in the Czech Republic, "any movable goods which were produced, extracted or otherwise gained irrespective of the degree of their processing and which are intended for placing on the market" as well as "parts and accessories to movable goods and fixtures and fittings to immovable goods";[28] and in Poland, "a movable thing, even if it has been connected with another thing" as well as "animals and electrical energy".[29] More or less comprehensive, these provisions follow the spirit of the amended Directive by including the widest possible group of goods into the scope of applicability of the new regime. It also appears that although the concept has changed its legal name from 'things' to 'products', the substantive content remains the same.

The Directive is likely to introduce some confusion into the concept of subjects of product liability laws, and even perhaps into the traditional concept of 'things' in Central Europe. First of all, a change of approach to the traditionally clear distinction between movables and immovables seems inevitable. Article 2 of the Directive implies that movables attached to immovables remain independent products. Chapter 5 showed that component parts did not retain their independent nature within the concept of 'things' in Central Europe. Thus, movables which were parts of immovables normally were not subjects of product liability litigation. On the other hand, independent liability of component producers was indeed known to Central European product liability jurisprudence even under the traditional concept of 'things', and it will no doubt be reinforced by the implementation of the Directive.

Specific systems of liability for specific products

The Directive provides that its provisions should not prejudice the application of any specific liability regimes existing at the moment when it is notified (Article 13). Among the Member States of the European Union, Germany in particular can be distinguished as an example of a jurisdiction using such a regime – the German Pharmaceuticals Act (*Arzneimittelgesetz*) applies to liability of producers of pharmaceuticals "intended for human use and supplied to the consumer" (Hoffman and Hill-Arning 1994: 29).

---

25 In Hungary – Act XXXVI of 2002, in the Czech Republic – Act No. 209/2000.

26 Directive 99/34 of 10 May 1999, OJ L 14/20.

27 Section 1.1 of the Act on Product Liability amended by the Act XXXVI of 2002 *amending Act IV of 1959 on the Civil Code of the Republic of Hungary*.

28 Section 3 of the Act 59/1998.

29 Article 449.1, para. 2 of the Civil Code.

No doubt, the Hungarian Act XXV of 1998 *on Medicines for Human Use* is another example of such special legislation (Kalman, Lelkes and Domonkos 2003). The Act introduced significant changes within the scope of application of the Hungarian Product Liability Act. Until 1998 damage caused by medicines was not covered by the Product Liability Act, and the manufacturers of medicines were liable according to the general rules of liability based on the requirement of fault (Kalman, Lelkes and Domonkos 2003: 6). However, the state would cover the damages and losses of those who died or suffered a lasting health injury if the manufacturer was not at fault (ibid.). The Act on Medicines for Human Use included damages caused by medicines into the scope of application of the Product Liability Act. However, in cases where the development risk defence exonerated the defendant, the state was still required to recuperate the claimant's losses. Considering the freedom to opt out from the development risk defence under Article 15b of the Directive, it appeared that the Act remained in compliance with it. According to Kalman, Lelkes and Domonkos, "with this step the liability for damages caused by medicine became objective" (2003: 6). The Act XCV of 2005 changed this approach slightly. By virtue of the Act, which came into force on 30 October 2005, the development risk defence is not available to producers where damage was caused by "the appropriate use of pharmaceutical products".[30] Thus, the state no longer will compensate victims and their families for damages caused by pharmaceuticals in such cases. The liability was passed on to the manufacturers. This issue is further examined below, in the section exploring the developments risk defence.

STANDARD OF LIABILITY AND THE DEFENCES

Introduction

The Product Liability Directive aims to harmonize the laws of product liability by introducing what it refers to as 'strict liability', and what some more realistic observers such as Jane Stapleton refer to as a 'stricter' liability, 'hindsight cost-benefit strict liability', or even, considering the available defences, 'super-negligence' liability (1994a: 228). Is any significant change likely to occur in the Central European product liability systems as a result of the introduction of this liability standard? Based on the analysis conducted in Chapter 5 one may conclude that some major changes in approach are indeed required. While in the Czech Republic and Poland the implementation of the Directive entails formally making the liability standard stricter, in Hungary it means the opposite. It was shown above that in Hungary the standard of liability was stricter than the standard prescribed by the Directive. Taking into account the 'complete harmonization' which the Directive introduced, the liability standard there will be reduced to the disadvantage of consumers. Hungary will be unable to use the rules established

30 Product Liability Database, BIICL.

before the implementation of the Directive. The recent judgement of the European Court of Justice in *Bilka*[31] seems to have ascertained that the 'maximum harmonization' effect also extends upon court-made 'strict liability' systems.

Following the Directive, Central European product liability legislation requires the claimant in product liability cases to prove the defect, the damage and the causal link between the two. These issues are analysed in detail below. Before this, however, in order to portray the changes in the standard of liability in Central Europe introduced by the Directive, defences available to the 'producer' are introduced.

Development risk defence

Hungary, the Czech Republic and Poland have all taken up the option provided by the Directive[32] and introduced the defence into their product liability legislation. Thus, in Poland the defendant can prove that "it was impossible to foresee the existence of the dangerous qualities of the product, taking into account the state of knowledge and science at the time of introduction of the product into circulation" (Article 449.3.2 of the Civil Code). The Hungarian Product Liability Act contains Section 7d, according to which the producer can avoid liability if he provides proof that "at the time the product was placed on the market the defect could not have been discovered according to the current state of scientific and technological achievements". In the Czech Product Liability Act, Section 5.1.e stipulates that the "producer shall be exempted from his responsibility if the producer is able to prove that … the state of scientific and technical knowledge at the time at which the product was launched did not allow to identify the defect of the product". In systems previously based upon 'fault', specified standards of care required of the defendants should not be a novelty; nevertheless it must be submitted that, at least in Hungary, the existence of the development risk defence introduces a standard of liability less stringent than the one which the courts so boldly put forward. On the other hand, in Hungary the use of the development risk defence is subject to further limitations. As mentioned above (p. 264), before 2005 the existence of the development risk defence was supplemented by the provisions of the Act on Medicines for Human Use of 1998, which stipulated that the state would cover the damages caused by medicines where the defendant successfully employed the defence. As a result of the introduction of Act XCV of 2005, the state no longer compensates these damages, and paragraph 14 of the Product Liability Act now provides that the producer cannot use the development risk defence if damage was caused by the "appropriate use of pharmaceutical products".[33] The Report for the BIICL Product Liability Database indicates, however, that due to significant opposition from civil society organizations, the Ministry of Health is to revise this

31 Case C-402/03. See also pp. 124, 125 above.

32 Articles 7e and 15.1.b.

33 Hungarian part of Product Liability Database – BIICL.

approach again and to reaffirm state liability for injuries caused by drugs during the testing period and by vaccines.[34]

The product not having been put into circulation by the defendant

The Hungarian Act stipulates that the 'manufacturer' may avoid liability upon providing proof that "he did not place the product on the market".[35] The Czech Act provides for an exemption from liability if the producer proves that the product was not placed on the market by him.[36] The Polish Civil Code in Article 449.3 introduces a similar defence for the producer. It reads: "(T)he producer shall not be liable for damage caused by an unsafe product if he did not introduce the product into circulation ...."[37] The introduction of a product into circulation has been a notion commonly used by the Central European courts in product liability litigation, and thus no significant difference appeared with the implementation of the Directive. The notion has been understood to exclude from the scope of the regime all those situations where the damage had been caused by a product before its introduction into circulation.[38]

However, the notion 'put into circulation' may cause other problems in Central European countries, where modern business laws, company laws and new business structures only just started appearing (Radwan et al. 2007). Although this issue goes beyond the scope of the book, it is important to emphasize the importance of company laws and business practices for the practice of product liability law. Just how crucial they may be was illustrated in the recent English case of *O'Byrne*[39] where the corporate structure was material in identifying the moment of introducing a product into circulation.

Defect not existing at the time the product was put into circulation

Here is where a crucial difference exists between the Directive and the Hungarian and Polish legislation on product liability. The Directive exempts producers from liability if "having regard to the circumstances, it is probable that the defect

34 BIICL Product Liability Database.

35 Section 7.1.a.

36 Section 5.1.a.

37 The burden of proof, although not expressly determined in this provision, rests upon the producer according to the general rule contained in Article 6 of the Civil Code: "the burden of proof of a fact rests upon the person who draws legal consequences from the fact."

38 Although the Central European courts, similarly with the Directive, rather avoided explaining the exact meaning of the concept, the Polish scholars were more specific and defined it as "the first transaction with the product as its subject", or "the moment when the product passes onto another person, when the producer loses control over it" (Łętowska 2001: 128).

39 Case C-127/04.

which caused the damage did not exist at the time when the product was put into circulation … or that this defect came into being afterwards".[40] Both the Hungarian and Polish Acts require absolute certainty, and do not seem to be satisfied with the probability of non-existence of the defect.

This provision of the Directive is an excellent example of difficulties in pinpointing the exact boundary between substantive law and procedural law, which remains necessary in the light of the general 'procedural autonomy' of Member States to which the Directive no doubt subscribes.[41] While it is likely that this inconsistency has been conditioned by the divergences in the rules and requirements of procedure, and in particular the burden of proof and the necessity to prove a fact without doubt and not on the balance of probabilities, its impact is difficult to discern (Clermont and Shervin 2002).[42] At the very least it contributes to an even greater impression of lack of true consistency in the implementation and application of the Directive by the Member States. It is therefore unclear how a case similar to the English *Piper v JRI (Manufacturing) Limited* [2006] would be concluded in Poland or Hungary. The English Court of Appeal found that the manufacturer of a hip prosthesis was not liable under the Consumer Protection Act 1987 Part I (implementing the Product Liability Directive) because the defect did not exist at the time the prosthesis was introduced into circulation. Interestingly, there was no particular documentation evidencing the inspection of the prosthesis in question, but the Court remained satisfied that overall the system of quality and safety control at JRI was satisfactory and would be capable of detecting a defect of the kind which caused damage to the claimant.

Although the position seems different in the Czech Republic, where, again, the Product Liability Act repeats the wording of the Directive, the Czech rules on standard of proof generally resemble those of other Central European states. It is uncertain therefore whether product liability cases will receive a specific approach here, or whether courts will simply follow the general rule.

Product not introduced into circulation for business purposes

Again, the issue of business activity appears. The focus on business liability is one of the key distinguishing marks of mature product liability systems (see Part I), and the Directive follows this approach. It limits its ambit to liability of persons who introduced a product into circulation for business purposes. Central European product liability systems also developed in this direction. The emphasis on business liability was at the roots of the growing preference of tort over contract law, and of objective liability over subjective, 'fault' liability.

40 Article 7b.

41 See Chapter 3 of Part I.

42 Clermont and Shervin highlight the gap which exists in the standards of proof between the common law systems, where the "standard of proof is probabilistic" and civil law systems where a much higher level of certainty is required (2002).

On the other hand, as already pointed out, Central Europe in common with other post-socialist states only recently commenced understanding the concepts of 'business' and 'business activity' in the manner in which these concepts are understood in the 'West' (Sengayen 2002). Lack of experience with the concept can lead to problems with interpretation of the Product Liability Acts, the provisions of which are far from clear.[43] Has the defence of lack of business purpose been properly implemented by the Central European states? In Hungary, Section 7b of the Product Liability Act stipulates that it is a defence for the 'manufacturer' to show that "the product was not produced for retail purposes, or was not produced or distributed within the framework of regular business activities". Although it is very unclear what a 'regular' business activity may mean, no significant discrepancy can be noticed here. The Czech Act contains a similar defence, and the Act seems to repeat the wording of the Directive. It reads that the producer should be exempted from liability if he proves that the product was not made by him for the purpose of sale or for any other business purposes, nor was made or distributed by him within his business activities (Section 5.1c). The Polish Civil Code seems to have enforced the defence twice, but only when read together the two provisions contain a defence truly complying with the Directive. Article 449.1 reads: "whoever, in the course of his business activity (the producer) manufactures an unsafe product, shall be liable for the damage caused by the product to anyone".[44] Article 449.3 stipulates that the producer shall avoid liability if the introduction of the product into circulation took place outside the scope of his business activity.

Specific defence for manufacturers of component parts

The situation regarding component parts of 'things' in Central European civil codes was depicted above. The defence for manufacturers of these component parts is not entirely inconsistent with the traditional approach based on the concept of 'things' and requiring the presence of 'fault'. It was duly implemented by the Central European states. In Hungary "[T]he producer of raw material or a component shall be exempt from liability upon providing proof that: a) the defect was caused by the structure or composition of the final product, or b) the defect was the consequence of instructions given by the producer of the final product"; the Czech Act (Section 5.2) stipulates that "[T]he producer of any constituent part of the product shall be exempted from his responsibility if such a producer is able to prove that the defect was caused by the construction of the product in which the constituent part was incorporated or that the defect was caused by the instructions for the use of the product"; and the Polish Civil Code (Article 449.5) stipulates that the producer of a raw material or a spare part should be free of liability if the

43 *O'Byrne* case (C-127/04) demonstrated the need for more clarity in this respect (Sengayen 2007).

44 Translated by the author.

sole cause of damage was defective construction of the product or the instructions provided by the producer of the final product.

Compliance with mandatory legal provisions

This is not a regulatory compliance defence, and indeed it has been debated for some time in academic circles whether such a defence needed to be introduced. The Directive merely specifies that liability will be avoided if the defect was due to compliance with safety regulation. Curiously, this defence did not exist in the Central European tortious product regimes, even those based upon the requirement of fault (see p. 223 above). Could one, however, conclude that since the defence exists the producers of defective products have more opportunities to avoid liability? Although during the times of socialism the manufacturer could not escape liability by pointing to the mandatory legal provisions which the product complied with, the number of such provisions was not significant, and neither was their scope. In spite of the existence of centrally planned markets, surprisingly, the state did not establish an effective regulatory framework for ensuring safety of products. Thus, even compliance with all the established rules did not guarantee the safety of any product. With the transformation into market economies, the post-socialist states slowly commenced building the requested regulatory framework, significantly affected by the necessity to comply with the European Community product safety measures. Apart from having implemented the General Product Safety Directive, various vertical directives are also being implemented by the Central European states. At present it may be more confidently acknowledged that compliance with the mandatory provisions ensures safety of products.

Conclusions – standard of liability

Although in Poland and the Czech Republic the regime introduced by the Directive does indeed mean the shift to strict, or at least stricter, liability, in Hungary the standard is lower than the one developed by the case law. Maczonkai very clearly confirmed what transpires from the analysis in Chapter 5 in this book – "considering the doctrines and assuming the coherence of doctrine … only the defences of the producer who had never supplied the product and the product was not delivered with a view to profit could have prevailed" in the traditional, tortious liability regime established by the Hungarian courts (1996: 117).

DEFECT

Part I of this book explored the importance of this element of product liability systms, and observed the effect of the elusiveness of the description provided by the Product Liability Directive on the practice of product liability in Europe. The notion remains a significant challenge for those attempting to apply it. It is indeed very unfortunate that the very concept upon which the existence of the entire regime has been based should be so ambiguous (Stapleton 1994a: 235, 236).

The definition of 'defect' provided by the Directive (Article 6) is not likely to provide significant assistance to Central European courts in the application of the new liability system. The ordinary tortious liability regimes rather utilized the 'boxes' system with regard to defects,[45] and it is clear that the drafters of the Directive did not intend for such a classification to be applied. Regarding the interpretation of the 'defect' by Central European courts after the implementation of the Directive, the 'circumstances' indicated by Article 6 will be crucial, but the existing jurisprudence of Western European courts is likely to offer more insight into the desired approach to the concept. One may, however, also venture a prediction which already found its factual basis in the practice of some national courts of the Western European Member States of the European Union: the approach to the notion of 'defect' applied before the implementation of the Directive will also be relevant to some extent.

Section 2 of the Hungarian Act on Product Liability reads: "A product shall be regarded as defective if it fails to provide a level of safety generally expected, with special regard to the purpose of the product and the way in which it can reasonably be expected to be used, the information provided in connection with the product, the date of the sale of the product, and the current state of scientific and technological achievements." Section 4 of the Czech Act defines a defective product as a product which "in terms of safety of its use … fails to guarantee the properties as may rightly be expected to pertain to the product, particularly with reference to: a) the presentation of the product, including the information provided, or b) the purpose which the product is expected to serve, or c) the time as at which the product was placed on the market." Interestingly, the Polish regulation replaced the notion of 'defect' required by the Directive, with the the notion of 'lack of safety' (thus a 'defective product' is referred to as an 'unsafe product' – *produkt niebezpieczny*). The rationale behind this approach was the perceived need to distinguish defects of quality (governed by the contractual rules of legal guarantees – Sengayen 2002) from lack of safety (Łętowska 2001: 135). Łętowska's writings (she is the key consumer law scholar, and a senior member of the Polish judiciary), are symptomatic of this thinking. According to her, a very popular expression 'liability for defective products' is inadequate unless one understands a 'defect' in a way that necessarily involves an element of danger (1999: 83), and this certainly is not the common understanding of the term. Although in many cases poor quality and lack of safety do coexist, Łętowska (1999) points out that not every unsafe product must necessarily be defective.[46] Her statement can be reversed to claim that not every defective product must

45 Chapter 5, pp. 214-38 of Part II described how in Poland and in the Czech Republic this classification related to the types of fault rather than types of defects (fault in manufacture, fault in design/construction, fault in warnings, fault in observation).

46 For example certain inherently dangerous products like knifes or poisons.

necessarily be unsafe (Tenreiro 1997: 57).[47] Łętowska suggests that the notion 'defective product' should thus be changed to 'unsafe product' or 'product with dangerous features'.[48] The Polish Act implementing the Product Liability Directive indeed followed these suggestions: it distinctively refers to 'unsafe products' instead of 'defective products'. It is a truly unique approach within Europe. Can the Polish Act indeed be confirmed as in any way more precise? It is not easy to determine which notion better suits the nature of product liability, and Stapleton rather favours 'defect' as more inclusive than any other notion (1994a: 236–49). Whether one thinks that Stapleton's view should be followed or not, 'defect' is the notion required by the Directive and in the light of its 'maximum harmonization' nature, departing from it may be seen as going beyond the level of protection provided by the Directive and likely to upset the delicate balancing of interests within the regime. Article 449.1.3 of the Polish Civil Code stipulates that a product shall be considered "unsafe" if it does not provide the safety which can be expected taking into account normal use of the product. Circumstances existing at the time of its introduction into circulation, and in particular the presentation on the market and the information about the qualities of the product provided to consumers, are relevant. Thus, while the Code indeed uses a different notion, its further explanation follows the wording of the Directive.

All the Central European regulations on product liability contain the state-of-the-art element stating that the product cannot be deemed defective ('unsafe') merely because a safer product has later been put into circulation.

RECOVERABLE DAMAGE

As explored above, 'damage' recoverable under the Directive has been limited to pecuniary damage to persons, and to property other than the defective product.[49] The damaged property must exceed the threshold of 500 Euros, and be of a type ordinarily intended and actually used by the victim for private use or consumption. A further limitation imposed by the Directive is the potential for the maximum threshold of liability for personal injury of at least 70 million Euros.[50] Compensation of non-pecuniary damage was left to national law. While the 500 Euro threshold (which is in fact a threshold and not a deductable as specified by the implementing laws of some Member States) was introduced in all Central European states, none of them adopted the maximum limit of liability. Acts implementing the Directive in Poland and the Czech Republic do not regulate compensation of non-pecuniary

47 Such as a pair of shoes of a slightly different colour.

48 This has been confirmed by another Polish scholar – Gnela. Her book (2000) is entitled *Liability for Damage Caused by an Unsafe Product (The So-called Product Liability)* (translated by the author).

49 Article 9.

50 Article 16.

damage, and thus those damages will be recoverable under the general rules of tort law explored in Chapter 5.

Overall, the general rules of damage recovery in Central European product liability regimes before the implementation of the Directive were wider in scope than the Directive. Although normally only the property other than the defective product could be recovered in tort, there was no lower threshold, no maximum limit, and also property used for business purposes could be compensated. The Central European Product Liability Acts include all the limitations contained in the Directive. In Hungary, 'damage' is deemed to be "any pecuniary or non-pecuniary damage incurred by death, bodily injury or any impairment in the health of a person" and "damage exceeding at the time of incurring it the Forint equivalent of five hundred Euros at the Hungarian National Bank's official foreign exchange mid-rate, caused by a defective product in another thing, if the normal purpose of the other thing is to be object of private use or private consumption and if the injured party used it usually for such a purpose".[51] Considering the uncertainty regarding recovery of non-pecuniary damage in Hungarian law,[52] the express addition of non-pecuniary damage in the new regime seems to provide a guarantee that such damage would be recoverable at all. Otherwise the Act follows the wording of the Directive. The Czech Act provides that damage include "damage to health, or death, or any damage to any goods other than the defective product, which other goods are primarily used for purposes other than business".[53] It also provided that the lower threshold of recoverable property damage ought to be CZK 5000, with this provision expiring upon the entry into force of the Treaty of Accession of the Czech Republic to the EU, and afterwards the threshold being the equivalent of 500 Euros.[54] A considerable difference seems to exist in the manner in which the Czechs approached property damage and its limitations. The sole distinguishing criterion is the use for which the product is *primarily* put by the victim. Such an approach renders the scope of recoverable property damage wider. The Polish Civil Code stipulates that 'damage' ought not to include damage to property the intended purpose of which is personal use and if the victim mainly used the property for such purpose.[55] Also damage to the defective product itself, as well as damage not exceeding the equivalent of 500 Euros, have been excluded.[56] Thus, the Polish Civil Code does not regulate the issue of damage in a comprehensive

51 Section 1.4 of the Hungarian Product Liability Act 1993, as amended by Article 11 of the Act XXXVI of 5 November 2002 *amending Act IV of 1959 on the Civil Code of the Republic of Hungary and other acts for the harmonization of consumer protection* (as provided by the Hungarian Ministry of Justice). Before the amendment the lower threshold was 10.000 Forint.

52 See Chapter 5 (pp. 238-42) of Part II.

53 Section 1 of the Czech Product Liability Act.

54 Section 6a.

55 Article 449.2 of the Polish Civil Code.

56 Article 449.7.

manner. Such a comprehensive regulation seems, however, unnecessary because of the presence of the new product liability system within the Code, and the use of the concepts defined elsewhere in the Code. The understanding of 'damage' within the Polish tortious liability system was explored in Chapter 5, and no divergences from this understanding, apart from the restrictions introduced by the Directive and duly implemented by Poland, are envisaged. Both pecuniary and non-pecuniary damage can be recovered, including damage to persons and property.[57]

It appears that the scope of recoverable damage to some extent becomes narrower in the Central European product liability systems with the implementation of the Directive. Nevertheless, in the light of the observations above concerning the role of damages in Central European civil liability, it must be emphasized that the implementation of the Directive, and indeed the participation in this new liability system the main aim of which is compensation of damage, is bound to increase the importance and the amounts of damages awarded in product liability cases across Central Europe.

TIME LIMITS FOR BRINGING CLAIMS

The Directive introduces changes into the Central European limitation provisions, which are analysed extensively in Chapter 5.[58] All the Central European states implemented the three- and ten-year periods, although the regulation is more beneficial for the victims as regards the time limits for bringing claims in Poland: both the three- and the ten-year periods required by the Directive are not extinguishing periods, but limitation periods. The consequences of this discrepancy were elaborated in Chapter 5.

JOINT AND SEVERAL LIABILITY

The Directive prescribes the possibility of joint and several liability of a number of defendants, which undoubtedly is beneficial for victims of defective products.[59] Such a possibility was also envisaged by the traditional Central European product liability regimes, hence no significant change may be noticed here.

57 Articles 444–7, and in particular 445 of the Civil Code.

58 See in particular pp. 245-248 above. The relevant legal provisions are: Article 449.8 of the Polish Civil Code, Sections 9 and 9a of the Czech Product Liability Act, and Section 10 of the Hungarian Act.

59 Article 5 of the Directive.

CONCLUSIONS: IMPLEMENTATION OF THE DIRECTIVE – POSSIBLE PROBLEMS AND INCONSISTENCIES

The Acts implementing the Directive do not comply with it entirely. Some provisions of the Directive have not been translated literally, often for a better compliance with the spirit of the pre-existing laws and with the legal practice.

The Directive leaves certain issues to national law, and hence the traditional tortious liability rules should still apply with regard to matters such as causal link or non-pecuniary damage. The Directive also excludes certain cases from its application, through the notions of 'defect', the delimitation of the recoverable property damage, and other requirements including the time limits. These conclusions only add to the impression of incompleteness of harmonization of European product liability law, the impression of a system where national laws, procedures and legal cultures of the Member States continue to a play part in shaping the practice of product liability law.

Conclusions to Part II

The book has elucidated the extensive scope of 'transition' taking place in product liability laws of the Czech Republic, Hungary and Poland. Part II depicted the developments in substantive rules and practice of product liability of the Central European states. It portrayed the quite impressive efforts of courts and scholarly writers to fine-tune the general civil liability provisions of the Civil Codes to the needs of this new liability regime, and to build its doctrinal, political and economic foundations to accompany the wide-ranging changes in markets and market regulation explored in Part I. Ultimately, Central European product liability law is the product of this jurisprudential and scholarly discourse, although the discourse has now become to some extent contained by the instruments implementing the Product Liability Directive.

Chapter 7

Central European Product Liability Law in Transition – Conclusions and Prognosis

The evolution of product liability law in Central Europe exhibited some very idiosyncratic traits. The emergence of product liability systems, the transformation of their substance, and their role in socialist and subsequently post-socialist legal systems have been portrayed here with a view to assess the position at present.

It is clear that the 'transition' which the law of product liability is undergoing in Central Europe reaches beyond the law itself and beyond its role in the system of law of obligations: into market laws and consumer laws, and into the political, legal and socio-economic context in which it operates. The political environment, the legislative and regulatory framework of markets, the policies and rules of consumer protection, and the economic and social environment are under review. Product liability law and practice are placed in a transformed legislative and regulatory setting, in a different socio-economic context. They are surrounded by new policies, laws, regulations and other mechanisms fulfilling similar aims of compensation and deterrence. Their role and importance in this new setting are as yet unsettled, and there is no doubt that the practice of product liability will reflect this for some time. Central European systems are bringing this specific 'baggage' into the 'European product liability system'.

The Product Liability Directive is currently unable to settle such idiosyncrasies existing on the national level of European states. This is for a number of reasons. The book showed a case study of the wider issues involved in regulation of product liability. It alerted the reader to the complexity of product liability as a civil liability system rooted in the law of obligations, linked with consumer law, market law and an entire regulatory framework surrounding markets. It mentioned how crucial the procedural and legal-cultural matters are in the practice of product liability. Another reason for the uncertainty of the process of harmonizing European product liability laws lies in the Directive itself, and indeed in the nature of the European Union legal system and the harmonization of laws it entails. The Directive, although heralding 'maximum harmonization', does not completely cover all aspects of product liability systems. It is also often unable to effectively compel the desired approach to its provisions in the national jurisprudence on product liability. National laws, regulations, procedures and legal cultures remain decisive in the operation of this so far incompletely harmonized system. One only needs to observe some of the key components of the liability system established by the Directive to see the consequences of this complexity. First and foremost, in spite of its clear focus on liability for 'defective' products, the Directive does not entice a unified approach to what indeed makes products 'defective'. The approach to the notion of 'defect' on the national level is therefore often the continuation of the approach under the general tortious liability rules. In Central Europe the situation was as follows: Hungarian courts sought to ascertain broken social expectations, and Polish and Czech courts conducted a more detailed enquiry into the defendant's conduct and the condition of the product. Of course this specific position is not exclusive to Central Europe, as discrepancies in the understanding of defect are also visible across Western Europe and seem to result from deeper systemic gaps between legal systems. The Central European idiosyncrasies may also involve the understanding and the scope of causal issues, the scope of recoverable damage (especially non-pecuniary damage), or the amounts of awarded damages. Although Central European laws of obligations, market laws, and of course also product liability laws, are converging with the laws of other European states, certain idiosyncrasies will no doubt remain and will continue being material in product liability cases.

On the other hand, Central European product liability systems are in a position where they could be affected by European-level developments, policies, and laws at a much deeper level, much quicker and more comprehensively than the product liability systems of some of the Western European states. Central European product liability laws, similarly with other relatively recent legal mechanisms deriving from the presence of market economy, are still not very well settled within the jurisprudence and scholarly writings. It is therefore relatively easier to adapt them to the new approach, especially as the Central European legal profession is already 'in the mood for change'.

The problem is, however, that this 'new approach' to market regulation, to consumer protection, to product liability, and to harmonization of European law in general, is also transforming on the European Union level. The position of European product liability law within these new arrangements has not yet been firmly settled. The process of harmonization of European product liability law appears to have become much more complex. It is clear that European product liability law reaches beyond the provisions of the Product Liability Directive.

What prognosis can one offer for the European product liability law? The future of the European product liability 'project' is far from set in stone. Especially now, when harmonization of laws in Europe proves to be a much more multi-level (pan-European – national, legislative – administrative – judicial, regulatory – self-regulatory, substantive – procedural, legal – economic – social) endeavour. It seems no longer feasible to envisage harmonization of product liability law in Europe by solely focusing on substantive law of product liability. The Product Liability Directive is increasingly seen as merely opening "the way towards greater harmonization" of European law. This process of convergence of policies, laws, procedures and legal cultures includes the Central European, 'transition-style', post-socialist systems. On a more positive note, one may say that product liability law is a very instructive example for the discourse of legal harmonization conducted by the European Union. Lessons could be drawn from the experience with the Directive-driven harmonization for the future of European consumer law, and even wider – for the future of European law in general. The changes in European consumer law and policy transformed the role of product liability law, and they no doubt have prompted greater emphasis on 'maximum harmonization', utilized in case of the Directive. In fact, because of the realization of complexity of the harmonization process, 'complete/full harmonization' may well become what it should realistically be: instead of some steady future goal, a process where goalposts are moved gradually – towards deeper and wider harmonization of law and procedure (Sengayen 2007).

Bibliography

Academic Literature

Ajani, G. (1995) 'By Chance and Prestige: Legal Transplants in Russia and Eastern Europe', 43(1) *American Journal of International and Comparative Law* 93–117.

Albanese, F. (1986) 'Legal Harmonisation in Europe, Product Liability: A Comparison between the Directive of the European Communities and the Council of Europe Convention' in Miller, C.J. (ed.) *Comparative Product Liability*, London: The United Kingdom National Committee of Comparative Law, pp. 15–30.

Allen, D.K., Hartshorne, J.T. and Martin, R.M. (2000) *Damages in Tort*, London: Sweet & Maxwell.

Armstrong, K., Bulmer, S. (1998) *The Governance of the Single European Market*, Manchester and New York: Manchester University Press.

Armstrong, K. (1999) 'Governance and the Single European Market' in Craig, P. and de Búrca, G. (eds) *The Evolution of EU Law*, Oxford: Oxford University Press.

Artis, M. and Nixson, F. (2001) *The Economics of the European Union*, Oxford: Oxford University Press.

Askham, T. and Stoneham, A. (1994) *EC Consumer Safety*, London: Butterworths.

Atiyah, P.S. (1979) *The Rise and Fall of Freedom of Contract*, Oxford: Clarendon Press.

Atiyah, P.S. (1995) *An Introduction to the Law of Contract*, 5th edition, Oxford: Clarendon Press.

Atiyah, P.S. and Adams, J.N. (1995) *The Sale of Goods*, 9th edition, London: Pitman Publishing.

Ayres, I. and Braithwaite, J. (1992) *Responsive Regulation: Transcending the Deregulation Debate*, New York and Oxford: Oxford University Press.

Bagińska, E. (2000) *Odpowiedzialność za produkt w USA. Odpowiedzialność za szkody wyrządzone przez rzeczy niebezpieczne z wadami* [Product Liability in the USA: Liability for Damages Caused by Unsafe Products with Defects], Toruń: TNOiK.

Bagińska, E. (2002) 'Poland' in Koziol, H. and Steininger, B. (eds) *European Tort Law 2001*, Vienna and New York: Springer, pp. 378–99.

Bagińska, E. (2003) 'Poland' in Koziol, H. and Steininger, B. (eds) *European Tort Law 2002*, Vienna and New York: Springer, pp. 329–44.

Bagińska, E. (2004) 'Poland' in Koziol, H. and Steininger, B. (eds) *European Tort Law 2003*, Vienna and New York: Springer, pp. 317–32.

Bagińska, E. (2005) 'Poland' in Koziol, H. and Steininger, B. (eds) *European Tort Law 2004*, Vienna and New York: Springer, pp. 462–78.

Bagińska, E. (2006) 'Poland' in Koziol, H. and Steininger, B. (eds) *European Tort Law 2005*, Vienna and New York: Springer, pp. 457–82.

Bakardjieva Engelbrekt, A. (2006) 'Grey Zones, Legitimacy Deficits and Boomerang Effects: On the Implications of Extending the Acquis to Central and Eastern Europe' in Wahl, N. and Cramér, P. (eds) *Swedish Studies of European Law*, Oxford: Hart, pp. 1–36.

Baker, T. (2005) 'Liability Insurance as Tort Regulation: Six Ways that Liability Insurance Shapes Tort Law in Action', 12(1) *Connecticut Insurance Law Journal* 1–16.

Barettini, C., 'The Legal Framework as an Incentive for Strengthening Competitiveness of Small and Medium Enterprise in Central and Eastern European Countries: The Case of European Consumer Law', *L'Europa cresce*, <http://www.arsability.it/europacresce/documenti.htm>.

Benedek-Világhy (1965) *A polgári Törvénykönyv a gyakorlatban* [Civil Code in Practice], Budapest.

Benson, P. (ed.) (2001) *The Theory of Contract Law: New Essays*, Cambridge: Cambridge University Press.

Berkowitz, D., Pistor, K. and Richard, J-F. (2003) 'The Transplant Effect', 51 *The American Journal of Comparative Law* 163–203.

Bernstein, A. (1992) 'Looking at Europe for Difference Between Strict and Fault-Based Liability', 14 *Products Liability* 207.

Betlem, G. (2005) 'Torts: A European Ius Commune and the Private Enforcement of Community Law', 64(1) *Cambridge Law Journal* 126–48.

Biltoft-Knudsen, H. and Knudsen, M. (1993) 'Product Liability' in Folsom, R. (ed.) *European Community Law after 1992: A Practical Guide for Lawyers Outside the Common Market*, Deventer and Boston, MA: Kluwer.

Blackie, J. (1985) 'The Problem of Economic Loss and Products Liability' in Campbell, D. and Rohwer, C. (eds) *Legal Aspects of International Transactions*, Amsterdam, New York and Oxford: North Holland.

Blanpain, R. (ed.) (1997) *International Encyclopaedia of Laws*, The Hague: Kluwer.

Bokor-Szego, H. (1986) (ed.) *Questions of International Law: Hungarian Perspectives*, Vols 1–5, Dordrecht: Martinus Nijhoff, Budapest: Akademiai Kiado.

Boom (van), W.H. (2004) 'A Comparative Perspective' in van Boom, W.H., Koziol, H. and Witting, C.A. (eds) *Pure Economic Loss*, Tort and Insurance Law Vol. 9, Vienna and New York: Springer.

Borrie, G. (1984) *The Development of Consumer Law and Policy: Bold Spirits and Timorous Souls*, London: Stevens.

Borrie, G. and Diamond, A.L. (1981) *The Consumer, Society and the Law*, 4th edition, Harmondsworth: Penguin Books.

Bourgoignie, T., Trubek, D., Trubek L. and Stingl, D. (1987) *Consumer Law, Common Markets and Federalism in Europe and the United States*, Vol. 3 of Integration Through Law, Europe and American Federal Experience, A Series under the General Editorship of Cappelletti, M., Seccombe, M. and Weiler, J., Berlin: Walter de Gruiter.

Braithwaite, J. (2002) *Restorative Justice and Responsive Regulation*, Oxford: Oxford University Press.

Brouwer, B. and Haage, J. (2007) 'Basic Concepts of European Private Law', 1 *European Review of Private Law* 3–26.

Brownswood, R., Howells, G. and Wilhelmsson, T. (1996) 'Between Market and Welfare: Some Reflections on Article 3 of the EC Directive on Unfair Terms in Consumer Contracts' in Willett C. (ed.) *Aspects of Fairness in Contract*, London: Blackstone Press, pp. 25–59.

Brus, W. (1973) *The Economics and Politics of Socialism, Collected Essays*, London and Boston, MA: Routledge and Kegan Paul.

Brzozowski, A. (1998) in Pietrzykowski, K. (ed.) *Kodeks Cywilny. Komentarz*, Vol. II, Warszawa: C.H. Beck.

Buczkowski, S. (1972) *Kodeks Cywilny. Komentarz* [The Civil Code: Commentary], Vol. II, Warszawa: Wydawnictwo Prawnicze.

Burrows, P. (1994) 'Products Liability and the Control of Product Risk in the European Community', 10 *Oxford Review of Economic Policy* 68–83.

Bussani, M. and Palmer, V.V. (eds) (2003) *Pure Economic Loss in Europe*, Cambridge: Cambridge University Press.

Cain, M. and Hunt, A. (1979) *Marx and Engels on Law*, London, New York and San Francisco, CA: Academic Press.

Calabresi, G. (1970) *The Costs of Accidents: A Legal and Economic Analysis*, New Haven, CT: Yale University Press.

Campbell, C. (1993) (ed.) *International Product Liability*, London, New York, Hamburg and Hong Kong: Lloyd's of London Press.

Cane, P. (1986) 'Economic Loss and Products Liability' in Miller, C.J. (ed.) *Comparative Product Liability*, London: The United Kingdom National Committee of Comparative Law, pp. 45–72.

Cane, P. (1999) *Atiyah's Accidents, Compensation and the Law*, 6th edition, London, Edinburgh and Dublin: Butterworths.

Cane, P. (2002) 'Tort Law as Regulation', 31 *Comm. L. World Rev.* 305–31.

Cane, P. (2006) *Atiyah's Accidents, Compensation and the Law*, 7th edition, Cambridge: Cambridge University Press.

Cappelletti, M. and Garth, B. (eds) (1978) *Access to Justice: A World Survey*, Vol. 1, Milan: Sitjoff and Noordhoff.

Caporaso, J.A. (1996) 'The European Union and Forms of State: Westphalian, Regulatory or Post-Modern?', 34(1) *Journal of Common Market Studies* 29–52.

Carbonnier, J. (1974) 'Authorities in Civil Law: France' in Dainow J. (ed.) *The Role of Judicial Decisions and Doctrine in Civil Law and Mixed Jurisdictions*, Baton Rouge, LA: Louisiana State University Press, pp. 91–118.

Cavinet, G., Andenas, M. and Fairgrieve, D. (2004) (eds) *Comparative Law before the Courts*, London: British Institute of International and Comparative Law.

Chloros, A.G. (1992) 'Common Law, Civil Law and Socialist Law: Three Leading Systems of the World, Three Kinds of Legal Thought' in Varga C. (ed.) *Comparative Legal Cultures*, Aldershot, Hong Kong, Singapore and Sydney: Dartmouth, pp. 83–98.

Cincio-Podbiera, B. (1988) 'Orzecznictwo Arbitrażowe w sprawach majątkowej odpowiedzialności producenta za szkody spowodowane złą jakością produktu' unpublished, cited in Gnela 2000: 137.

Clermont, K.M. and Shervin, E. (2002) 'A Comparative View of Standards of Proof', 10(2) *American Journal of Comparative Law* 243–76.

Coase, R. (1960) 'The Problem of Social Cost', 3(1) *JLE* 1–44.

Coe, J. (1987) 'Products Liability in the European Community: An Introduction to the 1985 Council Directive', 10 *JPL* 197–202.

Coleman, J.L. (1982) 'Moral Theories of Torts: Their Scope and Limits. Part One', 1 *Law and Philosophy* 371–90.

Cooter, R.C. (1991) 'Economic Theories of Legal Liability', 5(3) *Journal of Economic Perspectives* 11–30.

Cotter, B. (1996) *Defective and Unsafe Products: Law and Practice*, London, Dublin and Edinburgh: Butterworths.

Cotterrell, R. (1992) *The Sociology of Law: An Introduction*, 2nd edition, London, Dublin and Edinburgh: Butterworths.

Cotterrell, R. (1997) 'The Concept of Legal Culture' in Nelken, D. (ed.) *Comparing Legal Cultures*, Aldershot, Brookfield, VT, Singapore and Sydney: Dartmouth.

Courreges (de), M. (1997) 'France' in Kelly, P. and Attree, R. (eds) *European Product Liabilities*, 2nd edition, London, Butterworths.

Cousy, H. (2002) 'Tort Liability and Liability Insurance: A Difficult Relationship' in Koziol, H. and Steininger, B. (eds) *European Tort Law 2001*, Vienna and New York: Springer, pp. 18–55.

Cox, K. (1987) 'Use of State of the Art Evidence: Confusion, Inconsistency, and Absolute Liability', 10(93) *JPL* 91–110.

Craig, P. (1999) 'The Nature of the Community: Integration, Democracy and Legitimacy' in Craig, P. and de Búrca, G. (eds) (1999) *The Evolution of EU Law*, Oxford and New York: Oxford University Press.

Craig, P. and de Búrca, G. (1998) *EU Law: Text, Cases and Materials*, 2nd edition, Oxford: Oxford University Press.

Craig, P. and de Búrca, G. (2000) *EU Law: Text, Cases and Materials*, 3rd edition, Oxford: Oxford University Press.

Cranston, R. and Goode, R. (1993) (eds) *Commercial and Consumer Law: National and International Dimensions*, Oxford: Oxford University Press.

Cseres, K. (2004) 'The Hungarian Cocktail of Competition Law and Consumer Protection: Should it be Dissolved?', 27 *Journal of Consumer Policy* 43–74.

Cunningham, R. (1982) 'Apportionment between Partmakers and Assemblers in Strict Liability', 49 *UChiLR* 544.

Curzon Price, V., Landau, A. and Whitman, R.G. (eds) (1999) *The Enlargement of the European Union: Issues and Strategies*, Routledge Studies in European Economy, London and New York: Routlege.

Czachórski, W. (1962) *Zarys prawa zobowiazań, część ogólna* [The Framework of the Law of Obligations, General Part] Warszawa.

Czachórski, W. (2002) *Zobowiązania. Zarys wykładu* [Obligations: The Framework of Study], Warszawa: Wydawnictwo Prawnicze Lexis Nexis.

Dąbrowa, J. (1968) *Wina jako przesłanka odpowiedzialności cywilnej*, Wrocław.

Dadomo, Ch. (1997) *French Substantive Law: Key Elements*, London: Sweet & Maxwell.

Dahl, B. (1975) 'Product Liability in Scandinavian Law', 75 *Scandinavian Studies in Law*.

Dainow, J. (ed.) (1974) *The Role of Judicial Decisions and Doctrine in Civil Law and in Mixed Jurisdictions*, Baton Rouge, LA: Louisiana State University Press.

Dannemann, G. (2006) 'Comparative Law: Study of Similarities or Differences?' in Reimann, M. and Zimmermann, R. *The Oxford Handbook of Comparative Law*, Oxford: Oxford University Press, pp. 383–419.

David, R. (1980) *English Law and French Law: A Comparison in Substance*, Calcutta: Eastern Law House, London: Stevens.

David, R. and Brierley, J.E.C. (1985) *Major Legal Systems in the World Today: An Introduction to the Comparative Study of Law*, 3rd edition, London: Stevens.

Dawson, A.H. (1993) *A Geography of European Integration*, London and New York: Belhaven Press.

de Cruz, P. (1993) *Modern Approach to Comparative Law*, Deventer and Boston, MA: Kluwer.

de Cruz, P. (1999) *Comparative Law in a Changing World*, 2nd edition, London and Sydney: Cavendish Publishing.

Delicostopoulos, J.S. (2003) 'Towards European Procedural Primacy in National Legal Systems', 9(5) *European Law Journal* 599–613.

Denyer, S., Wilson, P. and Solc, M. (1993) *Legal Aspects of Doing Business in the Czech and Slovac Republics*, London: Longman.

Deubner, C. (1999) 'The Enlargement: Transforming Western Europe' in Curzon Price, V., Landau, A. and Whitman, R.G. (eds) *The Enlargement of the European Union: Issues and Strategies*, Routledge Studies in European Economy, London and New York: Routlege, pp. 118–28.

Diamond, A.L. (1986) 'Product Liability: Compensation for Death and Personal Injury in English Law' in Miller, C.J. (ed.) *Comparative Product Liability*, London: The United Kingdom National Committee of Comparative Law.

Dinan, D. (1999) *Ever Closer Union: An Introduction to European Integration*, 2nd edition, European Union Series under the editorship of Nugent, N., Paterson, W. and Wright, V., Basingstoke: Macmillan.

Donovan, J. and Britton, G. (1994) 'USA v the Rest of the World: Product Liability Law Differences and the Effect on Industry', 16 *PLI*.

Douglas, M. and Isherwood, B. (1996) *The World of Goods: Towards an Anthropology of Consumption*, London: Routledge.

Dupré, C. (2003a) *Importing the Law in Post-Communist Transitions: The Hungarian Constitutional Court and the Right to Human Dignity*, Oxford and Portland OR: Hart.

Dupré, C. (2003b) Draft Version Anticipating EU Membership: Importing the Law of the West Workshop: Implications of Enlargement for the Rule of Law and Constitutionalism in Post-Communist Legal Orders, EUI, 28–29 November 2003, pp. 10–16.

Dybowski, T. (1981) *System prawa cywilnego* [The System of Civil Law], Vol. 3, Part 1, Warszawa.

Eatwell, J., Milgate, M. and Newman, P. (eds) (1990) *The New Palgrave: Marxian Economics*, London and Basingstoke: Macmillan.

Ecolivet-Herzog, B. (1983) 'The French Law of Products Liability: A Creature of the Courts' in Herzog, P.E. (ed.) *Harmonisation of Laws in the European Communities: Products Liability, Conflict of Laws, and Corporation Law*, Charlottesville, VA: University Press of Virginia.

El-Agraa, A. (2001) *The European Union: Economics and Policies*, 6th edition, Harlow: Prentice-Hall.

Eörsi, G. (1970) *Fundamental Problems of Socialist Civil Law*, Budapest: Akadémiai Kiadó.

Eörsi, G. (1977) 'Convergence in Civil Law?' in Szabó, I. and Péteri Z. (eds) *A Socialist Approach to Comparative Law*, Leyden: A.W.Sijhoff, Budapest: Akadémiai Kiadó, pp. 45–94.

Eörsi, G. (1979a) 'Contractual Remedies in Socialist Legal Systems' in Treitel, G.H. (ed.) *International Encyclopaedia of Comparative Law, Volume VII – Contracts in General*, The Hague: Mouton, Tübingen: J.C.B. Mohr (Paul Siebeck).

Eörsi, G. (1979b) *Comparative Civil (Private) Law: Law Types, Law Groups, the Roads of Legal Development*, Budapest: Akadémiai Kiadó.

Fairgrieve, D. and Howells, G. (2007) 'Rethinking Product Liability: A Missing Element in the European Commision's Third Review of the European Product Liability Directive', 70(6) *The Modern Law Review* 962–78.

Fairgrieve, D. and Vaqué, L.G. (2005) 'Introduction' in Fairgrieve D. (ed.) *Product Liability in Comparative Perspective*, Cambridge: Cambridge University Press.

Farnsworth, E.A. (2006) 'Comparative Contract Law' in Reimann, M. and Zimmermann, R. *The Oxford Handbook of Comparative Law*, Oxford: Oxford University Press, pp. 899–935.

Faure, M. (2000a) 'Product Liability and Product Safety in Europe: Harmonisation or Differentiation?', 53 *Kyklos* 467.

Faure, M. (2000b) 'Compensation of Non-Pecuniary Loss: An Economic Perspective' in Magnus, U. and Spier, J. (eds) *European Tort Law: Liber Amicorum for Helmut Koziol*, Frankfurt am Main, Berlin, Bern, Bruxelles, New York, Oxford and Vienna: Peter Lang, pp. 143–59.

Faure, M. (2005) 'Economic Analysis of Fault' in Widmer P. (ed.) *Unification of Tort Law: Fault*, European Centre for Tort and Insurance Law, The Hague: Kluwer, pp. 311–30.

Faure, M. and Hartlief, T. (1989) 'Remedies for Expanding Liability', 18 *Oxford Journal of Legal Studies* 681.

Feger, H. (2001) 'Classification: Conceptions in the Social Sciences' in Smelser, N. and Baltes, P. (eds) *International Encyclopaedia on the Social and Behavioral Sciences* Vol. III, pp. 1966–73.

Fiala, J. and Kindl, M. (2007) *Občanské právo hmotné*, 1st edition, Plzeň: Aleš Čeněk.

Fischer, D. (1995) 'Causation in Fact in Product Liability Failure to Warn Cases', 17 *JPTL*.

Flour, J., Albert, J-L. and Savaux, E. (2003) *Les Obligations*, 10th edition, Paris: Armand Colin .

Fluhr, M.J. (2007) *Unraveled: The Failure of Products Liability Markets*, Harvard Law School Student Scholarship Series, Paper 9, Berkeley Economic Press, <http://lsr.nellco.org/harvard/students/papers/9>.

Forman, J.D. (1973) *Capitalism: Economic Individualism to Today's Welfare State*, New York: New Viewpoints.

Freeman, R. (2003) 'Overview', September 2003 *EPLR*.

French, Jr., J.R.P. and Raven, B. (1959) 'The Bases of Social Power' in Cartwright, D. (ed.) *Studies in Social Power*, Ann Arbor, MI: University of Michigan, Institute for Social Research, pp. 150–67.

Frey, B. and Eichenberger, R. (1996) 'To Harmonise or to Compete? That's Not the Question', 60 *Journal of Public Economics* 335.

Friedman, L.M. (1975) *The Legal System: A Social Science Perspective*, New York: Russell Sage Foundation.

Friedman, L.M. (1977) *Law and Society: An Introduction*, Englewood Cliffs, NJ and New York: Prentice-Hall.

Friedman, L.M. (1978) 'Access to Justice: Social and Historical Context' in Cappelletti, M. and Weisner, J. (eds) *Access to Justice, Vol. II Promising Institutions*, Book 1, Milan: Sijthoff and Nordhoff, Alphenaandenrijn, Dott. A. Giuffrè Editore.

Friedman, L.M. (1986) 'Legal Culture and the Welfare State' in Teubner G. (ed.) *Dilemmas of Law in the Welfare State*, Berlin and New York: Walter de Gruyter.

Friedman, L.M. (1990) *The Republic of Choice: Law, Authority and Culture*, Cambridge, MA: Harvard University Press.

Friedman, L.M. (1996) 'Borders: On the Emerging Sociology of Transnational Law', 32 *Stanford Journal of International Law* 65–90.

Friedman, L.M. (1997) 'The Concept of Legal Culture: A Reply' in Nelken, D. (ed.) *Comparing Legal Cultures*, Aldershot, Brookfield, VT, Singapore and Sydney: Dartmouth, pp. 33–9.

Friedman M. (1999) *Consumer Boycotts: Effecting Change through the Marketplace and Media*, London: Routledge.

Galbraith, J.K. (1985) *The New Industrial State*, Boston, MA: Houghton Mifflin.

Galligan, D. and Kurchiyan, M. (eds) (2003) *Law and Informal Practices: The Post-Communist Experience*, Oxford: Oxford University Press.

Galligan, D. and Matczak, M. (2006) *Strategies of Judicial Review: Exercising Judicial Discretion in Administrative Cases Involving Business Entities*, Business in Poland Policy Brief 1, The Foundation for Law, Justice and Society, <http://www.fljs.org/images/pdf/Poland%20brief%202[1].pdf>.

Gárdos, P. (2007) 'Recodification of the Hungarian Civil Law', 5 *European Review of Private Law* 707–22.

Geddes, A. (1992) *Product and Service Liability in the EEC: The New Strict Liability Regime*, London: Sweet & Maxwell.

Geistfeld, M.A. (2004) *Economic Analysis of a Unified Conception of Tort Law*, American Law and Economics Association Annual Meetings, Paper 29, Draft of 2/16/04, Hosted by the Berkeley Electronic Press, <http://law.bepress.com/alea/14th/art29>.

Geistfeld, M.A. (2006) *Efficiency and Fairness in Tort Law*, New York University School of Law, New York University Law and Economics Working Papers, Paper 48, Draft of 3/23/06, Hosted by Berkeley Electronic Press <http://lsr.nellco.org/nyu/lewp/papers48>.

Gerven (van), W., Lever, J. and Larouche, P. (2000) *Tort Law*, Oxford: Hart.

Gilmore, O. (1970) 'Product Liability: A Commentary', 38 *UChiLR* 103.

Glenn, H.P. (2000) *Legal Traditions of the World*, Oxford: Oxford University Press.

Glenn, H.P. (2004) *Legal Traditions of the World*, 2nd edition Oxford: Oxford University Press.

Glenn, H.P. (2006) 'Comparative Legal Families and Comparative Legal Traditions' in Reimann, M. and Zimmermann, R. *The Oxford Handbook of Comparative Law*, Oxford: Oxford University Press, pp. 421–40.

Gnela, B. (1988) *Polski system odpowiedzialności za produkt* [The Polish System of Product Liability], Zeszyty Naukowe Akademii Ekonomicznej w Krakowie, nr 279.

Gnela, B. (1998) *Odpowiedzialność za produkt* [Product Liability], Akademia Ekonomiczna w Krakowie, Zeszyty Naukowe, Seria Specjalna: Monografie nr 134, Kraków.

Gnela, B. (2000) *Odpowiedzialność za szkodę wyrządzoną przez produkt niebezpieczny (tzw. odpowiedzialność za product)* [Liability for Damage

Caused by an Unsafe Product (The So-called Product Liability)], Kraków: Zakamycze.

Goławska, J. (1965) 'Zasady współżycia spolecznego a nowy kodeks cywilny' [The Principles of Community Life and the New Civil Code], 13/1965 *PiŻ* 3.

Goldberg, J.C.P. (2003) 'Tort' in Cane P. and Tushnet M. (eds) *The Oxford Handbook of Legal Studies*, Oxford: Oxford University Press, pp. 21–47.

Goldberg, J.C.P. and Zipursky, B.C. (2006) 'Seeing Tort Law from the Internal Point of View: Holmes and Hart on Legal Duties', 75 *Fordham Law Review* 1563.

Góralczyk, P. (1997) 'Moralne i prawne wątpliwości w dziedzinie transplantologii' [The Moral and Legal Controversies in the Area of Transplantology], 1997/1 *Communio* 86.

Gordley, J. (1991) *The Philosophical Origins of Modern Contract Doctrine*, Oxford: Clarendon Press.

Gordley, J. (2003) 'Contract' in Cane P. and Tushnet M. (eds) *The Oxford Handbook of Legal Studies*, Oxford: Oxford University Press, pp. 3–20.

Gower, J. (1999) 'EU Policy to Central and Eastern Europe' in Henderson, K. (ed.) *Back to Europe: Central and Eastern Europe and the European Union*, London and Philadelphia, PA: UCL Press, Taylor & Francis, pp. 3–20.

Goyens, M. (1992) 'Consumer Protection in a Single European Market: What Challenge for the EC Agenda?', 90 *CMLR* 164.

Grabbe, H. and Hughes, K. (1998) *Enlarging the EU Eastwards*, The Royal Institute of International Affairs, Chatham House Papers.

Grady, M.F. (1983) 'A New Positive Economic Theory of Negligence', 92(5) *The Yale Law Journal* 799–829.

Graebner, N.A. (ed.) (1976) *The Cold War: A Conflict of Ideology and Power*, 2nd edition, Lexington, MA and Toronto: D.C. Heath and Company.

Graves, D. (2001) 'Tobacco Claims Fail in Finland and France', 4 *EPLR* 17.

Green, M.D. (1997) 'Negligence = Economic Efficiency: Doubts', 75 *Texas Law Review* 1605–44.

Griffith, D. (1989) 'Product Liability – Negligence Presumed: An Evolution', 12 *JPTL* 75.

Grodecki (1968) 'State Economic Arbitration in Poland' 9 *ICLQ* 177.

Grønmo, S. and Ölander, F. (1991) 'Consumer Power: Enabling and Limiting Factors', 14(2) *Journal of Consumer Policy* 141–69.

Grzybowski, A. (ed.) (1985) *System Prawa Cywilnego* [The System of Civil Law] Wrocław, Warszawa, Kraków, Gdańsk and Lódź.

Grzybowski, K. (1961) 'Reform of Civil Law in Hungary, Poland and the Soviet Union', 10(3) *American Journal of Comparative Law* 253–65.

Hamada, K. (1976) 'Liability Rules and Income Distribution in Product Liability', 66 *American Economic Review* 228.

Handler, J.F. (1979) 'Public Interest Law Firms in the United States' in Cappelletti, M. and Garth, B. (eds) *Access to Justice: Emerging Issues and Perspectives*,

Leyden, London, Boston and Milan: Sijthoff/Giuffrè, Florence: Access to Justice Project Series, Vol. 3, pp. 421–42.

Hannes M. (2003) 'Stressing Consumers' Responsibility: Higher Regional Court of Düsseldorf Dismisses Appeal Claim for Damages against Masterfood', 10 *EPLR* 31–3.

Harmathy, A. (1998) *Introduction to Hungarian Law*, The Hague and Boston, MA: Kluwer.

Harris, D. and Tallon, D. (eds) (1989) *Contract Law Today: Anglo-French Comparison*, Oxford: Clarendon Press.

Hart, H.L.A. (1997) *The Concept of Law*, 2nd edition, Oxford: Clarendon Press.

Hart, H.L.A. and Honoré, A.M. (1985) *Causation in the Law*, Oxford: Clarendon Press.

Harvey, B.W. and Parry, D.L. (1996) *The Law of Consumer Protection and Fair Trading*, 5th edition, London, Dublin and Edinburgh: Butterworths.

Hass, D. (2001) 'Limitation of Actions against Producers and Their Directors, Officers or Employees', 5 *EPLR* 28–30.

Helmholz, R. (1990) 'Continental Law and Common Law: Historical Strangers or Companions', *Duke Law Journal* 1207.

Henderson, J. and Eisenberg, T. (1990) 'The Quiet Revolution in Products Liability: An Empirical Study of Legal Change', 37 *UCLA* 479.

Henderson, K. (ed.) (1999) *Back to Europe: Central and Eastern Europe and the European Union*, London and Philadelphia: UCL Press, Taylor & Francis.

Herz, M.F. (1966) *Beginnings of the Cold War*, New York, St. Louis, San Francisco, Toronto, London and Sydney: McGraw-Hill.

Hibbert, M. (2007) 'New EU Choice of Law Rules for Tort and Product Liability Claims Finalized', 28 *EPLR* 12–14.

Hill, J. (1989) 'Comparative Law, Law Reform and Legal Theory', 9(1) *Oxford Journal of Legal Studies* 101–15.

Hodges, C. (1993) 'Looking at EC Product Liability Law', 15 *PLI* 21.

Hodges, C. (2001) *Multi-Party Actions*, Oxford: Oxford University Press.

Hodges, C. (2006) 'Nordic Compensation Schemes for Drug Injuries', 29(2) *The Journal of Consumer Policy* 143–75.

Hodges, C. (2007a) 'Europeanization of Civil Justice: Trends and Issues', 26 *Civil Justice Quarterly* 96–123.

Hodges, C. (2007b) 'Encouraging Enterprise and Rebalancing Risk: Implications of Economic Policy for Regulation, Enforcement and Compensation', *European Business Law Review* 1231–66.

Hoffman, C.W. and Hill-Arning, S. (1994) *Guide to Product Liability in Europe: The New Strict Product Liability Laws, Pre-existing Remedies, Procedure and Costs in the European Union and the European Free Trade Association*, Deventer: Kluwer.

Holmes, O.W. (1881) *The Common Law* (Reprint of the 1st edition) Boston, MA: Little Brown.

Holmes, O.W. (1897) 'The Path of the Law', 10 *Harvard Law Review* 457–78.

Hondius, E. (2004) 'The Protection of the Weak Party in a Harmonized European Contract Law: A Synthesis', 27 *Journal of Consumer Policy* 245–51.

Honoré, A.M. (1971) 'Causation and Remoteness of Damage' in Tunc A. (ed.) *International Encyclopaedia of Comparative Law* Vol. XI, Chapter 7, Tübingen: Mohr.

Howells, G. (1993) *Comparative Product Liability*, Aldershot: Dartmouth.

Howells, G. (1994) 'Product Liability in the United Kingdom', 2 *ERPL*.

Howells, G. (2001) 'Product Liability: A Maximum Harmonisation Directive?', *EPLR* 10.

Howells, G. (2005a) 'Defect in English Law: Lessons for the Harmonisation of European Product Liability' in Fairgrieve D. (ed.) *Product Liability in Comparative Perspective*, Cambridge: Cambridge University Press, pp. 138–52.

Howells, G. (2005b) 'Product Liability: A History of Harmonisation' in Fairgrieve D. (ed.) *Product Liability in Comparative Perspective*, Cambridge: Cambridge University Press, pp. 202–17.

Howells G. and Weatherill S. (2005) *Consumer Protection Law*, 2nd edition, Aldershot and Burlington, VT: Ashgate.

Howells, G. and Wilhelmsson, T. (1997) 'EC and US Approaches to Consumer Protection: Should the Gap be Bridged?', 17 *Yearbook of European Law* 207–68.

Hrádek, J. (2003) 'Czech Republic' in Koziol, H. and Steininger, B. (eds) *European Tort Law 2002*, Vienna and New York: Springer, pp. 119–35.

Hrádek, J. (2004) 'Czech Republic' in Koziol, H. and Steininger, B. (eds) *European Tort Law 2003*, Vienna and New York: Springer, pp. 85–104.

Hrádek, J. (2005) 'Czech Republic' in Koziol, H. and Steininger, B. (eds) *European Tort Law 2004*, Vienna and New York: Springer, pp. 195–217.

Hrádek, J. (2006) 'Czech Republic' in Koziol, H. and Steininger, B. (eds) *European Tort Law 2005*, Vienna and New York: Springer, pp. 186–210.

Huleatt-James, M. (2003) 'Proposal for a Regulation on the Law Applicable to Non-contractual Obligations' 12 *EPLR* 22.

Hutt, G. and Hass, D. (2001) 'Tobacco Litigation in Germany' 4 *EPLR* 15.

Ibbetson, D. (2003) 'Historical Research in Law' in Cane, P. and Tushnet M. (eds) *Oxford Handbook of Legal Studies*, Oxford: Oxford University Press, pp. 863–79.

Izdebski, H. (1991) 'Existe-t-il une tradition juridique commune à l'Europe centrale? L'Europe centrale. Réalité, mythe, enjeu. XVIIe-Xxe siècles (G. Beauprêtre)', 22 *Les Cahiers de Varsovie* 243–51.

Izdebski, H. (1996) 'General Survey of Developments in Eastern Europe in the Field of Civil Law' in Ginsburgs, G., Barry, D.B. and Simons W.B. (eds) *The Revival of Private Law in Central and Eastern Europe: Essays in Honor of F.J.M. Feldbrugge*, A series of publications issued by the Institute of East European Law and Russian Studies. Leiden University Faculty of Law, No.

46, The Hague, London and Boston, MA: Martinus Nijhoff Publishers and Kluwer, pp. 3–14.

Jagielska, M. (1995) 'Odpowiedzialność za produkt w prawie polskim – uwagi de lege ferenda' [Product Liability in Polish Law: de lege ferenda Commentary], 9 *Rejent*.

Jagielska, M. (1999) *Odpowiedzialność za produkt* [Product Liability], Kantor Wydawniczy Zakamycze.

Jagielska, M. and Wagner, P. (1997) *Sprzedaż, wada, reklamacja* [Sale, Defect, Complaint], Katowice.

Janowski, M., Iordachi, C. and Trencsényi, B. (2005) 'Why Bother about Historical Regions? Debates over Central Europe in Hungary, Poland and Romania', *East-Central Europe/L'Europe du Centre-Est: Eine wissenschaftliche Zeitschrift* Vol. 32, 2005/1–2.

Jansen, N. (2006) 'Comparative Law and Comparative Knowledge' in Reimann, M. and Zimmermann, R. *The Oxford Handbook of Comparative Law*, Oxford: Oxford University Press, pp. 305–38.

Jaraszek, A. and Makosz, A. (2007) *Szkody bez przedawnienia – zyskają poszkodowani* [Damages without Limitation Periods: Victims Will Benefit] <http://prawo.money.pl/aktualnosci/wiadomosci/artykul/szkody;bez;przedawnienia;-;zyskaja;poszkodowani,147,0,221843.html>.

Jarvis, M.A. (1996) *The Application of EC Law by National Courts: The Free Movement of Goods*, Oxford: Oxford University Press.

Joerges, C. (1993) 'Product Safety in the European Community: Market Integration, Social Regulation and Legal Structures' in Snyder, F. (ed.) *European Community Law*, Aldershot: Dartmouth.

Joerges, C. and Trubek, D.M. (eds) (1989) *Critical Legal Thought: An American-German Debate*, Baden-Baden: Nomos.

Józefiak, A. (2006) 'Przedawnienie roszczeń o naprawienie szkody wyrządzonej czynem niedozwolonym w świetle konstytucji' [Limitation of Claims for Compensation of Damage Caused by an Illicit Act in the Light of the Constitution], 3 *Kwartalnik Prawa Prywatnego* 669–97.

Kagan, R.A. (2003) *Adversarial Legalism: The American Way of the Law*, Cambridge, MA: Harvard University Press.

Kahn-Freund, O. (1974) 'On Uses and Misuses of Comparative Law', 37 *MLR* 1.

Katner, W.J. (1985) *Rozważania nad pojęciem rzeczy ruchomej* [Analysis of the Notion of a Movable Thing], Studia Prawno-Ekonomiczne, Vol. XXXIV.

Kaukonen, K. (ed.) (1991) *Market and Plan in the Regulation of Economy: Proceedings of the Estonian-Czech-Finnish Seminar, October 1990*, Helsinki: University of Helsinki.

Kaye, P. (1991) *Private International Law of Tort and Product Liability*, Aldershot: Dartmouth.

Kecskés, L. (1994) *Termékfelelõsség a Magyar Jogban* [Product Liability in Hungarian Law], Budapest: Pécs.

Kelemen, D.R. and Sibbitt, E. (2004) 'The Globalization of American Law', 58(3) *International Organization* 103–36.

Kelly, P. and Attree, R. (1992) *European Product Liability*, London: Butterworths.

Kelly, P. and Attree, R. (eds) (1997) *European Product Liabilities*, 2nd edition, London: Butterworths.

Kendall, V. (1994) *EC Consumer Law*, London: Wiley Chancery.

Kępinski, M. (1995) 'Deliktowa odpowiedzialność producenta za wady wyrobów w prawie europejskim ze szczególnym uwzględnieniem odpowiedzialności za produkt' [Tortious Liability of Manufacturers for Defects in Products in European Law, with Particular Emphasis on Product Liability], *Biuletyn Rady Legislacyjnej* Nr 5.

Kerameus, K.D. (1995) 'Procedural Harmonisation in Europe', 43 *American Journal of Comparative Law* 401–16.

Klimek, R. (2006) 'Dyskusyjne problemy przedawnienia roszczeń' [Limitation of Claims: Issues for Discussion], 3 *Kwartalnik Prawa Prywatnego* [Private Law Quarterly] 633–67.

Knapp, V. (1962) 'Kotazce predmetu socialistickeho obcanskeho prava', *Pravnik* 202.

Knappowa, M. and Wilhelmsson, T. (1989) in Wilhelmsson, T. and Svestka, J. (eds) *Consumer Protection in Czechoslovakia and Finland*, Helsinki: Helsingin Yliopisto.

Knox, P. and Agnew, J. (1994) *The Geography of the World Economy: An Introduction to Economic Geography*, 2nd edition, London, New York, Melbourne and Auckland: Edward Arnold.

Koch, B.A. (2003) 'Comparative Remarks' in Koziol, H. and Steininger, B. (eds) (2003) *The European Tort Law 2002* Vienna and New York: Springer, pp. 512–28.

Koch, B.A. and Koziol, H. (2002) 'Comparative Conclusions' in Koch, B.A. and Koziol, H. (eds) *Unification of Tort Law: Strict Liability*, European Centre of Tort and Insurance Law, The Hague, London and New York: Kluwer, p. 395.

Komárek, J. (2006) *Creating a Quasi-Federal Judicial System of the European Communities*, Stockholm: Institute for European Law at Stockholm University.

Koopmans, T. (2003) *Courts and Political Institutions: A Comparative View*, Cambridge: Cambridge University Press.

Kornai, J. (2001) *The Role of the State in a Post-Socialist Economy*, Leon Koźmiński Academy of Entrepreneurship and Management (WSPiZ) and TIGER Distinguished Lectures Series n. 6, Warsaw, 16 November 2001, <http://www.tiger.edu.pl/publikacje/dist/kornai.pdf>.

Kosztolanyi, G. (1999) 'Consumerism: Shop till You Drop', 1(8) *Central Europe Review*, <www.ce-review.org>.

Kovács, E. (2003) 'A hepatitis C vírussal fertőzöttek állami kártalanítása iránti perekről' [About the Cases of Compensation for Infection with Hepatitis C Virus], 10 *Magyar Jog* 600–606.

Koziol, H. (ed.) (1998) *Unification of Tort Law: Wrongfulness*, Principles of European Tort Law Vol. 3, The Hague, London and Boston, MA: Kluwer.

Koziol, H. (2001) 'Austria' in Magnus, U. (ed.) *Unification of Tort Law: Damages*, European Centre of Tort and Insurance Law, The Hague, London and Boston, MA: Kluwer.

Koziol, H. (2005) 'Fault under Austrian Law' in Widmer P. (ed.) *Unification of Tort Law: Fault*, European Centre for Tort and Insurance Law Research Unit for European Tort Law, The Hague: Kluwer, pp. 11–26.

Koziol, H. and Steininger, B.C. (eds) (2002) *European Tort Law 2001*, Vienna and New York: Springer.

Koziol, H. and Steininger, B.C. (eds) (2003) *European Tort Law 2002*, Vienna and New York: Springer.

Koziol, H. and Steininger, B.C. (eds) (2004) *European Tort Law 2003*, Vienna and New York: Springer.

Koziol, H. and Steininger, B.C. (eds) (2005) *European Tort Law 2004*, Vienna and New York: Springer.

Koziol, H. and Steininger, B.C. (eds) (2006) *European Tort Law 2005*, Vienna and New York: Springer.

Koziol, H. and Steininger, B.C. (eds) (2007) *European Tort Law 2006*, Vienna and New York: Springer.

Kozminski, A. (1992) 'Consumers in Transition From the Centrally Planned Economy to the Market Economy', 14 *Journal of Consumer Policy* 351–69.

Kramer, L. (1986) *EEC Consumer Law*, Brussels: Droit et Consommation.

Krčmář, J. (1932) *Právo občanské, Právo obligační*, 2nd edition, Praha.

Krčmář, J. (1998) *Občanské právo hmotné II*, 2nd edition, Praha: CH Beck.

Kronman, A.T. (1980) 'Contract Law and Distributive Justice', 89(3) *The Yale Law Journal* 472–511.

Kühn, Z. (2004) 'Worlds Apart: Western and Central European Judicial Culture at the Onset of the European Enlargement', 52 *American Journal of Comparative Law* 531–67.

Kühn, Z. (2006a) 'Development of Comparative Law in Central and Eastern Europe' in Reimann, M. and Zimmermann, R. *The Oxford Handbook of Comparative Law*, Oxford: Oxford University Press, pp. 215–36.

Kühn, Z. (2006b) 'The Application of European Law in the New Member States: Several (Early) Predictions', 3 *German Law Journal* 565–82.

Kulcsár, K. (1983) 'Social Aspects of Litigation in Civil Courts' in Cain, P. and Kulcsár, K. (eds) *Disputes and the Law*, Budapest: Akademiai Kiado, pp. 85–90.

Kulcsár, K. (1984) 'Politics and Law Making in Central-East Europe' in Péteri Z. (ed.) *Legal Theory: Comparative Law. Studies in Honour of Professor Imre Szabó*, Budapest: Akademiai Kiado, pp. 179–209.

Lamm, V. (ed.) (1988) *Parliamentarism and Government in a One-Party System*, translated by Kocsis, M. and Simon, S., Budapest: Akademiai Kiado, Series: Studies of Hungarian State and Law.

Landes, W.M. and Posner, R.A. (1983) 'Causation in Tort Law: An Economic Approach', 12 *Journal of Legal Studies* 109.

Landes, W.M. and Posner, R.A. (1984) 'Tort Law as a Regulatory Regime for Catastrophic Personal Injuries', 13 *Journal of Legal Studies* 417.

Lasok, D. (ed.) (1973) 'Polish Civil Law' in Szirmai, Z. *Law in Eastern Europe*, Leiden: A.W. Sijthoff.

Lavigne, M. (1974) *The Socialist Economies of the Soviet Union and Europe*, London: Martin Robertson.

Lawson, F.H., Anton, A.E. and Neville Brown, L. (1967) *Amos and Walton's Introduction to French Law*, 3rd edition, Oxford: Clarendon Press.

Lee, P-W. (2007) 'Contract Damages, Corrective Justice and Punishment', 70(6) *Modern Law Review* 887–907.

Legrand, P. (1996) 'European Systems Are Not Converging', 45 *ICLQ* 52.

Legrand, P. (1997) 'The Impossibility of Legal Transplants', 4 *Maastricht Journal of European and Comparative Law* 111.

Lenze, S. (2003a) 'Strict Liability for Manufacturing Defects: What Proof is Needed?', 11 *EPLR* 37.

Lenze, S. (2003b) 'The European Product Liability Directive: A Global Bestseller', 12 *EPLR* 4.

Lenze, S. (2005) 'German Product Liability Law: Between European Directives, American Restatements and Common Sense' in Fairgrieve D. (ed.) *Product Liability in Comparative Perspective*, Cambridge: Cambridge University Press, pp. 100–125.

Łętowska, E. (1983) 'Kształtowanie się odrębności obrotu mieszanego' in Łętowska, E. (ed.) *Tendencje rozwoju prawa cywilnego*, Wrocław: Ossolineum, p. 374.

Łętowska, E. (1999) *Prawo umów konsumenckich* [The Law of Consumer Contracts], Warszawa: C.H. Beck.

Łętowska, E. (2001) *Ochrona Niektórych Praw Konsumentów. Komentarz*, 3rd edition, Warszawa: Wydawnictwo C.H. Beck.

Łętowska, E., Jagielska, M., Lis, K., Mikłaszkiewicz, P. and Wiewiórowska-Domagalska, A. (2007) 'Implementation of Consumer Law in Poland', 6 *European Review of Private Law* 873–89.

Levitsky, S.L. (1979) *Copyright, Defamation, and Privacy in Soviet Civil Law*, Law in Eastern Europe Series No. 22(I), Alphen aan den Rijn, Germantown, MD: Sijthoff & Noordhoff.

Lewaszkiewicz-Petrykowska, E. (1996) 'Prawo konsumenta do bezpieczeństwa osobistego' in Rokicka, G. (ed.) *Model prawnej ochrony konsumenta*, Warszawa: Urzad Antymonopolowy.

Lewis, P.G. (1994) *Central Europe since 1945*, London and New York: Longman.

Link, K.U. and Sambuc, T. (1997) 'Federal Republic of Germany' in Kelly, P. and Attree, R. (eds) *European Product Liabilities*, 2nd edition, London: Butterworths.

Lipsey, R.G. and Chrystal, K.A. (1995) *Positive Economics*, 8th edition, Oxford: Oxford University Press.

Llewellyn, K. (1940) 'The Normative, the Legal and the Law Jobs', 49 *Yale LJ* 1355.

Lloyd, D. (1985) *The Idea of Law*, Harmondsworth: Penguin.

Löfstedt, R.E. (2004) *The Swing of the Regulatory Pendulum in Europe: From Precautionary Principle to (Regulatory) Impact Analysisi*, Working Paper 04-07, March 2004, Joint Center, AEI-Brookings Joint Center for Regulatory Studies <www.aei-brookings.org>.

Lonbay, J. (ed.) (1996) *Enhancing the Legal Position of the European Consumer*, London: British Institute of International and Comparative Law.

Loofkofsky, J. (1993) 'The State of the Union … in Contract and Tort', 41 *AJCL* 89–102.

Lowe, R. and Woodroffe, G. (1999) *Consumer Law and Practice*, 5th edition, London: Sweet & Maxwell.

Macleod, I., Henry, I.D. and Hyett, S. (1996) *The External Relations of the European Communities*, Oxford: Clarendon Press.

Maczonkai, M. (1996) 'Hungarian Product Liability Case Law under Civil Code and the New Product Liability Regime' in Madl F. and Muller-Graff P-C. (eds) *Hungary: From Europe Agreement to a Member Status in the European Union*, ECSA Europe, Baden-Baden: Nomos.

Madden, M. (1988) 'The Duty to Warn in Products Liability: Contours and Criticism', 11 *JPTL*.

Madden, M.S. (ed.) (2005) *Exploring Tort Law*, Cambridge: Cambridge University Press.

Madl, F. and Muller-Graff, P-C. (eds) (1996) *Hungary: From Europe Agreement to a Member Status in the European Union*, ECSA Europe, Baden-Baden: Nomos.

Magnus, U. (1990) 'Damages for Non-Economic Loss: German Developments in a Comparative Perspective', 39(3) *The International and Comparative Law Quarterly* 675–83.

Magnus, U. (ed.) (2001a) *Unification of Tort Law: Damages*, European Centre of Tort and Insurance Law, The Hague: Kluwer.

Magnus, U. (2001b) 'Comparative Report on the Law of Damages' in Magnus, U. (ed.) *Unification of Tort Law: Damages*, European Centre of Tort and Insurance Law, The Hague: Kluwer, pp. 185–217.

Magnus, U. (2001c) 'Germany' in Magnus, U. (ed.) *Unification of Tort Law: Damages*, European Centre of Tort and Insurance Law, The Hague: Kluwer.

Magnus, U. (ed.) (2003) *The Impact of Social Security Law on Tort Law*, Vienna and New York: Springer.

Magnus, U. and Casals, M-M. (eds) (2004) *Unification of Tort Law: Contributory Negligence*, European Centre of Tort and Insurance Law, The Hague: Kluwer.

Maher, I. (1994) 'National Courts as European Community Courts', 14(2) *Legal Studies* 226–43.

Majone, G. (2005) *Dilemmas of European Integration: The Ambiguities and Pitfalls of Integration by Stealth*, Oxford: Oxford University Press.

Mańko, R. (2005) 'The Culture of Private Law in Central Europe after Enlargement: A Polish Perspective', 11 *European Law Journal* 527–48.

Mańko, R. (2007) 'Is the Socialist Legal Tradition "Dead and Buried"? The Continuity of Certain Elements of Socialist Legal Culture in Polish Civil Procedure' in Wilhelmsson, T., Paunio, E. and Pohjolainen, A. (eds) *Private Law and the Many Cultures of Europe*, The Hague: Kluwer, pp. 83–103.

Maresceau, M. (ed.) (1997) *Enlarging the European Union: Relations between the EU and Central and Eastern Europe*, London and New York: Longman.

Markesinis, B. (1990) 'Litigation-Mania in England, Germany and the USA: Are We So Very Different?', 49(2) *Cambridge Law Journal* 233–76.

Markesinis, B. (1993) 'Bridging Legal Cultures', 27(3) *Israel Law Review* 363–83.

Markesinis, B. (1994) 'Learning from Europe and Learning in Europe' in Markesinis, B. (ed.) *The Gradual Convergence: Foreign Ideas, Foreign Influences, and English Law on the Eve of the 21st Century*, Oxford: Clarendon Press.

Markesinis, B. (1997) *Foreign Law and Comparative Methodology: A Subject and a Thesis*, Oxford: Oxford University Press.

Markesinis, B. (2001a) 'Unity and Division: The Search for Similarities in Contemporary European Law', *Current Legal Problems* 591–617.

Markesinis, B. (2001b) *Always on the Same Path: Essays on Foreign Law and Comparative Methodology*, Oxford: Oxford University Press.

Markovits, I. (1986) 'Pursuing One's Rights Under Socialism', 38 *Stan. L. Rev.* 689.

Marshall, W. (1988) 'Z zagadnień odpowiedzialności za produkt', *PiP* Nr 3.

Mattheussens, L. and Oosting, B. (2001) 'The Danish Kidney Case', June *EPLR* 20–21.

Mayhew, A. (1998) *Recreating Europe: The European Union's Policy towards Central and Eastern Europe*, Cambridge: Cambridge University Press.

McCrudden, C. (2006) 'Legal Research and the Social Sciences', 122(Oct.) *L. Q. R.* 632–50.

McDonald, F. and Dearden, S. (eds) (1999) *European Economic Integration*, 3rd edition, London: Longman.

McGuire, P. (1988) 'Product-Use Instructions: How to Evaluate Them in Manufacturers' Negligence', 11 *PLI* 203–7.

McKendrick, E. (1994) *Contract Law*, 2nd edition, London: Macmillan.

Meltzer, J., Freeman, R. and Thomson, S. (2003) 'Report on Product Liability in the European Union', 12 *EPLR* 4.

Menyhárd, A. (2003) 'Hungary' in Koziol, H. and Steininger, B. (eds) *European Tort Law 2002*, Vienna and New York: Springer, pp. 152–62.

Menyhárd, A. (2004) 'Hungary' in Koziol, H. and Steininger, B. (eds) *European Tort Law 2003*, Vienna and New York: Springer, pp. 231–44.

Menyhárd, A. (2005) 'Hungary' in Koziol, H. and Steininger, B. (eds) *European Tort Law 2004*, Vienna and New York: Springer, pp. 349–62.

Menyhárd, A. (2006) 'Hungary' in Koziol, H. and Steininger, B. (eds) *European Tort Law 2005*, Vienna and New York: Springer, pp. 332–47.

Merryman, J.H. (1969) *The Civil Law Tradition: An Introduction to the Legal Systems of Western Europe and Latin America*, Stanford, CA: Stanford University Press.

Merryman, J.H. (1985) *The Civil Law Tradition: An Introduction to the Legal Systems of Western Europe and Latin America*, 2nd edition, Stanford, CA: Stanford University Press.

Michaels, R. (2006) 'The Functional Method of Comparative Law' in Reimann, M. and Zimmermann, R., *The Oxford Handbook of Comparative Law*, Oxford: Oxford University Press, pp. 339–82.

Micklitz, H.W. (1997) 'EC Product Safety Regulation: A Still Uncompleted Project', 48 *Consumer Law Journal*.

Micklitz, H.W. (2003) 'The Necessity of a New Concept for the Further Development of the Consumer Law in the EU', 4(10) *German Law Journal* 1043–64.

Micklitz, H.W. (2007) 'The Relationship Between National and European Consumer Policy: Challenges and Perspectives' in Twigg-Flesner, C., Parry, D., Howells, G. and Nordhausen A. (eds) *The Yearbook of Consumer Law 2008*, Aldershot: Ashgate, pp. 35–65.

Mildred, M. (2007) 'Pharmaceutical Products: The Relationship between Regulatory Approval and the Existence of a Defect', *European Business Law Review* 1267–82.

Millar, J.R. and Wolchik, S.L. (eds) (1994) *The Social Legacy of Communism*, Cambridge, New York and Melbourne: Woodrow Wilson Center Press and Cambridge University Press.

Millard, F. (1994) *The Anatomy of the New Poland: Post-Communist Politics in its First Phase*, Studies of Communism in Transition series, edited by Ronald Hill, Aldershot and Brookfield, Vermont: Edward Elgar.

Miller, C.J. (ed.) (1986) *Comparative Product Liability*, United Kingdom Comparative Law Series, Vol. 6, London: The United Kingdom National Committee of Comparative Law.

Miller, C.J. (1991) *Product Liability and Safety Encyclopaedia*, London: Butterworths.

Miller, C.J. and Goldberg, R.S. (2004) *Product Liability*, 2nd edition, Oxford: Oxford University Press.

Mills, J., Roach, D. and Rowbotham, I. (1994) *Business Law Guide to the Czech Republic*, Bicester: CCH Europe.

Mohmand, F. (2002) 'Odpowiedzialność za produkt według przepisów kodeksu cywilnego' [Product Liability according to the Provisions of the Civil Code], unpublished PhD thesis, Łódź.

Montgomery, D. and Owen, W. (1976) 'Reflections on the Theory and Administration of Strict Tort Liability for Defective Products', 27 *Santa Clara Law Review*.

Morris, D. (ed.) (1980) *Economics of Consumer Protection*, London: Heinemann.

Mortelmans, K. and Watson, S. (1996) 'The Notion of Consumer in Community Law: A Lottery?' in Lonbay J., *Enhancing the Legal Position of the European Consumer*, London: British Institute of International and Comparative Law.

Nash, J. (1998) *Recent Development in Contract Law*, text of a lecture to the London Solicitors Litigation Association <http://www.3vb.com/pgs-articles/jn-recent-devs-contract.shtml>.

Nelken, D. (ed.) (1997) *Comparing Legal Cultures*, Aldershot, Brookfield, VT, Singapore and Sydney: Dartmouth.

Nelken, D. (2004) 'Using the Concept of Legal Culture', 29 *Australian Journal of Legal Philosophy* 1.

Nelsen, B.F. and Stubb, A.C-G. (eds) (1994) *The European Union. Readings of the Theory and Practice of the European Integration*, London and Boulder, CO: Lynne Rienner.

Nesterowicz, M. (1979) 'Odpowiedzialność za szkody wyrządzone wprowadzeniem do obrotu rzeczy niebezpiecznych z wadami' [Liability for Damages Caused by the Introduction of Dangerously Defective Products into Circulation], *Pal* Nr 11.

Nesterowicz, M. (1981) *Glosa do wyroku SN* [Commentary to the Judgement of the Supreme Court] z 6 VIII 1981 (I CR 219/81), OSPiKA 1983/2, poz. 23.

Nesterowicz, M. (1983) *Glosa do wyroku SN* [Commentary to the Judgement of the Supreme Court] z 6 VIII 1981, I CR 219/81, OSPiKA 1983, z. 2, s. 67.

Nesterowicz, M. (1988) *Ochroną prawa nabywcy pojazdu mechanicznego z wadami* [Protection of Rights of Buyers of Defective Automobiles], Warszawa.

Nesterowicz, M. (1993) 'Odpowiedzialność za produkt' [Product Liability], *KPP* Nr 4.

Nesterowicz, M. (1997) 'Odpowiedzialność cywilna za szkody wyrządzone wirusem HIV na skutek transfuzji krwi w prawie francuskim' [Civil Liability for Damages Caused by the HIV Virus as a Result of a Blood Transfusion in the French Law] in *Studia z prawa prywatnego. Księga pamiątkowa ku czci Profesor Biruty Lewaszkiewicz-Petrykowskiej*, Łódź.

Nesterowicz, M. (2001) *Prawo medyczne* [Medical Law], 5th edition, Toruń: TNOiK.

Nesterowicz, M. (2007) 'Zadośćuczynienie pieniężne ex contractu i przy zbiegu z odpowiedzialnością ex delicto' [Compensation of Non-pecuniary Damage ex contractu and in Accumulation with Delictual Liability], 1 *Państwo i Prawo*.

Newdick, C. (1987) 'The Future of Negligence in Product Liability', 103 *LQR*.

Newdick, C. (1988) 'The Development Risk Defence of the Consumer Protection Act 1987', 47 *CLJ* 454.
Nicolas, B. (1992) *The French Law of Contract*, 2nd edition, Oxford: Clarendon Press.
Nowakowski, L. (2004) *Ubezpieczenia odpowiedzialności cywilnej* [Civil Liability Insurance], Warszawa: Poltext.
Oates, W. and Schwab, R. (1988) 'Economic Competition among Jurisdictions: Efficiency Enhancing or Distortion Inducing?', 35 *Journal of Public Economics* 333.
Ogus, A. (1994) *Regulation, Legal Form and Economic Theory*, Oxford: Clarendon Press.
Ogus, A. (1999) 'Competition between National Legal Systems: A Contribution of Economic Analysis to Comparative Law', 48 *The International and Comparative Law Quarterly* 405.
Ohanowicz, P. (1958) *Zobowiązania, część ogólna* [Obligations, General Part], Warszawa.
Oliver, J.M. (1979) *Law and Economics*, Economics and Society, No. 7, London, Boston, MA and Sydney: George Allen & Unwin.
Oliver, J.M. (1988) *Free Movement of Goods in the EEC*, London: European Law Centre.
Opalski, W. (1978) 'Odpowiedzialność deliktowa producenta (sprzedawcy) za wady towaru' [Tortious Liability of Producers (Sellers) for Product Defects], *PUG* No. 3.
Oppenhaim, K. and Power, J. (1990) *Hungarian Business Law*, Deventer and Boston, MA: Kluwer.
Oppenhaim, K. and Power, J. (1998) *Hungarian Business Law*, 2nd edition, The Hague and Boston, MA: Kluwer.
Örücü, E. (1987) 'Internal Logic of Legal Cultures', 7 *Legal Studies* 310.
Örücü, E. (2002a) 'Law as Transposition', 51 *ICLQ* 205.
Örücü, E. (2002b) *Critical Comparative Law: Considering Paradoxes for Legal Systems in Transition*, EJCL (Netherlands Comparative Law Association), Vol. 4, 1 June 2000 <http://www.ejcl.org/41/art41-1.html>.
Owen, D.G. (1985) 'The Intellectual Development of Modern Products Liability Law: A Comment on Priest's View of the Cathedral's Foundations', 14(3) *Journal of Legal Studies* (Critical Issues in Tort Law Reform: A Search for Principles) 529–33.
Owen, D.G. (1993) 'The Moral Foundations of Products Liability Law: Toward First Principles', 68 *Notre Dame L. Rev.* 427–506.
Owen, D.G. (2005) *Products Liability Law*, St Paul, MN: Hornbook Series, Thomson West.
Ozimek, I. *Ochrona Konkurencji. Co polscy konsumenci wiedzą o swoich prawach?* [Protection of Competition: What do Polish Consumers Know about Their Rights?], <www.uokik.gov.pl/auto/biul23/biul2.htm>.

Pajor, M. (1989) 'Problematyka odpowiedzialności majątkowej producenta za szkody spowodowane złą jakością towarów w orzecznictwie Sądu Wojewódzkiego w Krakowie za lata 1985–1988' [Pecuniary Liability of Manufacturers for Damages Caused by Poor Quality Products in the Jurisprudence of the District Court in Kraków from 1985 to 1988) unpublished, cited in Gnela 2000: 137.

Pajor, T. (1982) *Odpowiedzialność dłużnika za niewykonanie zobowiązania* [Liability of the Debtor for not Fulfilling an Obligation], Warszawa.

Palmer, V. (1989) 'A General Theory of the Inner Structure of Strict Liability: Common Law, Civil Law and Comparative Law', 12 *JPTL* 158.

Palmer, V.V. (2005) 'From Lerotholi to Lando: Some Examples of Comparative Law Methodology', 53 *Am. J. Comp. L.* 261–90.

Pasa, B. and Benacchio, G.A. (2005) *The Harmonization of Civil and Commercial Law in Europe*, Budapest: CEU Press.

Paterson, T.G. (1992) *On Every Front: The Making and Unmaking of the Cold War*, revised edition, New York and London: W.W. Norton.

Patten, K. (2006) 'Limitation Periods in Personal Injury Claims: Justice Obstracted?', 25 *Civil Justice Quarterly* 349–66.

Perram, N. (1992) 'The Law of Torts in Eastern Europe and the Vital Role of Liability Insurance in an Emerging Market Economy', 18(3) *Review of Central and East European Law* 253.

Pescara, *Droit hongrois – droit compare: etudes pour le VIIIe Congres international de droit compare*, Budapest: Akademiai Kiado.

Pescatore, P. (1983) 'The Doctrine of "Direct Effect": An Infant Disease of Community Law', 8 *ELR* 155.

Petr, T. (2004) '"I didn't kill him! The doctor did!" Causation and the Novus Actus Interveniens in Czech and English Criminal Cases involving Medical Care', 5 *Common Law Review* (Medical Law) 14, <http://review.society.cz/index.php?option=com_content&task=view&id=87&Itemid=2>.

Petrik, F. (2003) 'A nem vagyoni kár megtérítése védelmében' [In Defense of Non-Pecuniary Damages], 2 *Polgári Jogi Kodifikácio* 6–8.

Phinnemore, D. (1999) 'The Challenge of EU Enlargement: EU and CEE Perspectives' in Henderson, K. (ed.) *Back to Europe: Central and Eastern Europe and the European Union*, London and Philadelphia, PA: UCL Press and Taylor & Francis, pp. 79–88.

Piirainem, T. (ed.) (1994) *Change and Continuity in Eastern Europe*, Aldershot, Brookfield, VT, Singapore and Sidney: Dartmouth.

Pistor, K. (2002) 'The Evolving Legal Framework in the Former Socialist Countries', *Columbia International Affairs Online* (CIAO), <www.ciaonet.org>.

Poiares Maduro, M. (1998) *We the Court: The European Court of Justice and European Economic Constitution*, Oxford and Portland, OR: Hart.

Polack-Nelson, C. (1994) 'The Effect of Warning Label Language on Behavioural Intent', 16 *JPTL*.

Pontin, B. (2000) 'Tort Interacting with Regulatory Law', 51 *N. Ir. Legal Q.* 597–618.

Posner, R. (1972) 'A Theory of Negligence', 1 *Journal of Legal Studies* 29.

Pound, R. (1910) 'Law in Books and Law in Action', 44 *Am. L. Rev.* 12.

Pound, R. (1921) *The Spirit of the Common Law*, Francestown, NH: Marshall Jones.

Pound, R. (1968) *Social Control Through Law*, Hamden, CT: Archon Books.

Prechal S. (1995) *Directives in European Community Law: A Study on EC Directives and their Enforcement by National Courts*, Oxford: Oxford University Press.

Preston, Ch. (1997) *Enlargement and Integration in the European Union*, The Routledge/University Association for Contemporary European Studies, Series editor: Church, C., London and New York: Routlege.

Priest, G. (1989) 'Strict Product Liability: The Original Intent', 10 *Cardozo LR* 2301.

Prohazka, A. (1971) *Komentar k hospodarskemu zakoniku a ka zakonu o hospodarske arbitrazi* [Commentary to the Commercial Code and to the Act on Economic Arbitrage], Praha.

Prosser, W. (1960) 'The Assault Upon the Citadel (Strict Liability to the Consumer)', 69 *Yale Law Journal* 1099.

Prosser, W. (1966) 'The Fall of the Citadel (Strict Liability to the Consumer)', 50 *Minnesota Law Review* 791–848.

Puchalska-Tych, B. and Salter, M. (1996) 'Comparing Legal Cultures of Eastern Europe: The Need for a Dialectical Analysis', 16(2) *Legal Studies* 157–84.

Pyrzyńska, A. (1996) 'Odpowiedzialność za produkt w orzecznictwie sądów polskich' [Product Liability in the Jurisprudence of Polish Courts], *Monitor Prawniczy* z. 8.

Quigley J. (1989) 'Socialist Law and the Civil Law Tradition', 37 *Am J Comp L* 781.

Radé, C. and Bloch, L. (2004) 'Compensation for Pure Economic Loss Under French Law' in van Boom, W.H., Koziol, H. and Witting, C.A. (eds) *Pure Economic Loss*, Tort and Insurance Law Vol. 9, Vienna and New York: Springer; pp. 41–7.

Radwan, A. et al. (2007) 'European Private Company: A View from the New Europe. Position of the "Expert Group 10+"', 18(4) *European Business Law Review* 772–9.

Radwański, Z. (1986) *Prawo zobowiązań* [The Law of Obligations], Warszawa.

Radwański, Z. (2007) 'Przedawnienie roszczeń z czynów niedozwolonych w świetle znowelizowanego Art. 442 KC' [Limitation Periods for Tortious Claims in the Light of the Amended Art. 442 of the Civil Code], 11 *Monitor Prawniczy*, <http://www.monitorprawniczy.pl/index.php?mod=m_artykuly&cid=20&id=1929>.

Reich, N. (1986) 'Product Safety and Product Liability', *Journal of Consumer Policy* 137.

Reich, N. and Leahy, D. (1990) *Internal Market and Diffuse Interests*, Brussels, Deventer, Paris: Story Scientia.

Reich, N. and Micklitz, H-W. (1980) *Consumer Legislation in the European Community Countries: A Comparative Analysis*, Wokingham: Van Nost. Reinhold.

Reimann, M. (2002) 'The Progress and Failure of Comparative Law in the Second Half of the 20th Century', 50 *American Journal of Comparative Law* 671.

Reimann, M. and Zimmermann, R. (2006) *The Oxford Handbook of Comparative Law*, Oxford: Oxford University Press.

Rein, U. and Kohegyi, D. (2006) 'Hungary' in *The International Comparative Legal Guide to: Product Liability 2006. A practical insight to cross-border Product Liability work*, London: Global Legal Group, pp. 160–65.

Rembielinski, A. and Pryca, C. (1983) 'Odpowiedzialność deliktowa za wady towaru na tle innych środków ochrony nabywcy' [Tortious Liability for Defects in Products in the Context of Other Means of Protection for Buyers], *Studia Prawno-Economiczne*, z. XXX, p. 99.

Rémy, P. (2003) 'Private International Aspects: Conflict of Jurisdiction', Paper presented at the Academy of European Law/Lovells Conference, Product Safety and Product Liability: Recent Developments in Community Law, on 1–2 May 2003, London.

Rezabakhsh, B., Bornemann, D., Hansen, U. and Schrader, U. (2006) 'Consumer Power: A Comparison of the Old Economy and the Internet Economy', 29 *Journal of Consumer Policy* 3–36.

Rhee (van), C.H. (2000) 'Civil Procedure: A European Ius Commune?', *European Review of Private Law* 589–611.

Rhodes, C. and Mazey, S. (eds). (1995) *The State of the European Union. Vol. 3. Building a European Polity?* Boulder, CO: Lynne Rienner, London: Longman, pp. 569–83.

Rinderknecht, S. (1993) 'European Community' in Campbell, C. (ed.) *International Product Liability*, London, New York, Hamburg, Hong-Kong: Lloyd's of London Press.

Ritchie, D.G. (1894) 'Aristotle's Subdivisions of "Particular Justice", 8(5) *The Classical Review* 185–92.

Roach Anleu, S.L. (2000) *Law and Social Change*, London, Thousand Oaks, CA and New Delhi: Sage.

Roberts, J.M. (1996) *A History of Europe*, Oxford: Helicon.

Rogers, H. (ed.) (2004) *Unification of Tort Law: Multiple Tortfeasors*, European Centre for Tort and Insurance Law, The Hague: Kluwer.

Ronovska, K. (2008) 'Civil Law in the Czech Republic: Tendencies of Development (Some Notes on the Proposal of the New Civil Code)', 1 *European Review of Private Law* 111–20.

Roper, B. and Snowdon, B. (eds) (1987) *Markets, Intervention and Planning*, London and New York: Longman.

Rosamond, B. (2000) *Theories of European Integration*, Basingstoke and New York: Macmillan and St. Martin's Press.
Rozwadowska-Herrmann, M. (2007) *Kodeks Cywilny z komentarzem* [Civil Code with a Commentary], 2nd edition, Warszawa: C.H. Beck.
Rubeš, J. (1970) *Obcansky soudni rad, komentar*, Praha.
Rupp, M.A. (1999) 'The Pre-accession Strategy and the Governmental Structures of the Visegrad Countries' in Henderson, K. (ed.) *Back to Europe: Central and Eastern Europe and the European Union*, London and Philadelphia, PA: UCL Press and Taylor & Francis.
Sadurski, W. (1984) 'Marxism and Legal Positivism' in Galligan, D.J. (ed.) *Essays in Legal Theory*, Melbourne: Melbourne University Press, pp. 187–221.
Safjan, M. (1992) 'O metodach rozwiązywania problemów bioetyki' [On the Methods of Solving Bioethical Problems], *Państwo i Prawo* 1992/5, p. 51.
Safjan, M. (1994) 'Odpowiedzialność deliktowa osób prawnych. Stan obecny i kilka uwag de lege ferenda' [Tortious Liability of Legal Persons: Current Position and a Number of Suggestions de lege ferenda], *Studia Iuridica*, Vol. 21, Uniwersytet Warszawski.
Salewski, S. (2005) 'Is the Abolishment of Privity Necessary in Modern Warranty Law? A Comparative Analysis of the System in the US, the CISG, the European Union, and Germany', 7(3/4) *European Journal of Law Reform* 367–427.
Sandholtz, W. and Stone Sweet, A. (1998) *European Integration and Supranational Governance*, Oxford: Oxford University Press.
Schwartz, G.T. (1997) 'Mixed Theories of Tort Law: Affirming Both Deterrence and Corrective Justice', 75 *Texas Law Review* 1801–34.
Sedláček, J. (1932) *Komentář k čsl. Obecnému zákoníku občanskému* [Commentary to the present Civil Code], Praha.
Sengayen, M. (2002) 'Consumer Sales Law in Poland: Changing the Law, Changing Attitudes', 25(3/4) *Journal of Consumer Policy* (Special Issue on Law, Information and Product Quality) 403.
Sengayen, M. (2005) 'Product Liability: The Perspective of New Member Countries' in Fairgrieve D. (ed.) *Product Liability in Comparative Perspective*, Cambridge: Cambridge University Press, pp. 244–94.
Sengayen, M. (2007) 'Recent Judgements of the European Court of Justice and the Elusive Goal of Harmonization of Product Liability Law in Europe' in Twigg-Flesner, C., Parry, D., Howells, G. and Nordhausen, A. (eds) *The Yearbook of Consumer Law 2008*, Aldershot and Burlington, VT: Ashgate.
Shavell, S. (1987) *An Economic Analysis of Accident Law*, Cambridge, MA: Harvard University Press.
Silva, F. and Cavaliere, A. (2000) 'The Economic Impact of Product Liability: Lessons from the US and the EU Experience' in Galli, G. and Pelkmans, J. (eds) *Regulatory Reform and Competitiveness in Europe*, 1, *Horizontal Issues*, Cheltenham: Edward Elgar, pp. 292–323.

Simitis, S. (1986) 'Products Liability: The West-German Approach' in Miller, C.J. (ed.) *Comparative Product Liability*, London: The United Kingdom National Committee of Comparative Law, pp. 99–125.

Skąpski, J. (1976) *System Prawa Cywilnego* [The System of Civil Law] Vol. 3, part. 2 *Prawo Zobowiązań. Część szczegółowa* [The Law of Obligations: General Part] Warszawa: Ossolineum.

Skąpski, J. (1995) 'Odpowiedzialność za wadliwe produkty. Wprowadzenie' [Liability for Defective Products: Introduction], *KPP*, R. IV: 1995, z. 4.

Smith, R. (1997) *Justice: Redressing the Balance*, London: Legal Action Group.

Snyder, F. (ed.) (1993) *European Community Law*, Aldershot, Hong Kong, Singapore and Sydney: Dartmouth.

Solente, A. and Claret, K. (1994) 'French Product Liability Law: Recent Developments through Court Action', 16 *PLI*.

Sołtysiński, S. (1970) 'Odpowiedzialność producenta wobec konsumenta za szkody wyrządzone wprowadzeniem do obrotu rzeczy z wadami' [Liability of Producers to Consumers for Damages Caused by the Introduction into Circulation of Defective Things], *Studia Cywilistyczne*, t. XV, Kraków, 172.

Spier, J. (ed.) (1996) *The Limits of Liability: Keeping the Floodgates Shut*, The Hague, London and New York: Kluwer.

Spier, J. (ed.) (1998), *The Limits of Expanding Liability*, The Hague, London and New York: Kluwer.

Spier, J. (ed.) (2000) *Unification of European Law: Causation*, The Hague, London and New York: Kluwer.

Spier, J. (ed.) (2003) *Unification of Tort Law: Liability for Damage Caused by Others*, The Hague, London and New York: Kluwer.

Stapleton, J. (1991) 'Duty of Care and Economic Loss: A Wider Agenda', 107 *LQR* 249.

Stapleton, J. (1994a) *Product Liability*, London: Butterworths.

Stapleton, J. (1994b) 'Minimum Directives: Do Not Be Misled', 110 *LQR* 213.

Stapleton, J. (2002) 'Bugs in Anglo-American Products Liability', 53 *South Carolina Law Review* 1225.

Stapleton, J. (2003a) 'The Golden Thread at the Heart of Tort Law: Protection of the Vulnerable', *ABR* 29.

Stapleton, J. (2003b) 'Cause in Fact and the Scope of Liability for Consequences', 119 *LQR* 388.

Stapleton, J. (2005) 'Bugs in Anglo-American Products Liability' in Fairgrieve D. (ed.) *Product Liability in Comparative Perspective*, Cambridge: Cambridge University Press, pp. 295–333.

Stapleton, J. (2007) 'Benefits of Comparative Tort Reasoning: Lost in Translation', 1(3) *Journal of Tort Law* Article 6.

Steiner, J.M. (1982) 'Putting Fault Back into Products Liability: A Modest Reconstruction of Tort Theory', 1(3) *Law and Philosophy* 419–49.

Stelmachowski, A. (1984) *Wstęp do teorii prawa cywilnego* [Introducing the Theory of Civil Law], Warszawa.

Stelmachowski, A. (1986) 'Znaczenie klauzuli generalnej zawartej w art. 386 k.c. w obrocie uspołecznionym' [The Interpretation of the General Clause in Art. 386 of the Civil Code in Business Transactions], 185(7) *PUG* 186.

Streeck, W. and Schmitter, P. (1991) 'From National Corporatism to Transnational Pluralism: Organized Interests in the Single European Market', 19 *Politics and Society* 133–64.

Suchańska, E.A. (1979) 'The Current State of Law Enactment in Poland', 5(1) *Review of Socialist Law* 47.

Suliński, A. (1995) 'Harmonizacja przepisów prawnych i wymagań dotyczących wyrobów, ze szczególnym uwzględnieniem dyrektyw ogólnego bezpieczeństwa wyrobów i odpowiedzialności za wadliwe wyroby' [Harmonization of Laws and Regulations Concerning Goods, with Particular Emphasis on General Product Safety and Product Liability Directives], *ABC Jakości. Akredytacja. Badania. Certyfikacja. Quality Review*, no. 4.

Svestka, J. (1989) 'Damage Caused by the Sale of a Defective Product by a Trading Corporation to a Citizen as Buyer under the Czechoslovak Civil Code' in Wilhelmsson, T. and Svestka, J. (eds) *Consumer Protection in Czechoslovakia and Finland*, Helsinki: Helsingin Yliopisto, pp. 90–107.

Svestka, J. and Knappová, M. (eds) (2002) *Občanské právo hmotné* Vol. 2, 3rd edition, Praha: ASPI Publishing.

Szalma, J. (2003) 'Alanyi és tárgyi felelősség' [Subjective and Objective Liability], 3 *Jogtudományi Közlöny* 117–29.

Szostak, R. (1995) 'O konieczności dostosowania polskich przepisów o ochronie konsumenta do europejskich rozwiązań prawnych' [On the Requirement to Harmonize the Polish Consumer Protection Law with the European Law], *Przegląd Sądowy* 2/53.

Szpunar, A. (1970) 'Czyny niedozwolone w Kodeksie Cywilnym' [Torts in the Civil Code], *Studia Cywilistyczne*, t. XV.

Szpunar, A. (1985a) *Glosa do wyroku SN* [Commentary to the Supreme Court Judgement] z 26 III 1984 (II CR 57/84), OSPiKA 1985/3, poz. 58.

Szpunar, A. (1985b) *Odpowiedzialność Skarbu Państwa za Funkcjonariuszy* [Liability of the State for Civil Servants], Warszawa.

Szpunar, A. (1985c) *Odpowiedzialność za szkody wyrządzone przez zwierzęta i rzeczy* [Liability for Damages Caused by Animals and Things], Warszawa.

Szpunar, A. and Łętowska, E. (1984) *Glosa do wyroku SN* [Commentary to the Supreme Court Judgement] z 26 III 1984, II CR 57/84; OSN 1984/186.

Taschner, H.C. (1986a) 'European Initiatives: The European Communities' in Miller, C.J. (ed.) *Comparative Product Liability*, London: The United Kingdom National Committee of Comparative Law, pp. 1–14.

Taschner, H.C. (1986b) *Produkthaftung*, München: C.H. Beck.

Taschner, H.C. (2003) *Basic Problems of Product Liability in a Comparative Perspective*, Conference Paper given at the British Institute of International and Comparative Law.

Tatham, A. (1995) 'The Development of Product Liability in Hungary: The Effect of the EC Directive Implementation, 17 *PLI*.

Tenreiro, M. (1997) 'Product Liability and Consumer Guarantees in the European Union: A Brief Comparison between an Old Directive and a New Proposal', *Consumer Law Journal* 56.

Tercsák, T. (1993) 'A termékfelelõsség jogintézményének alakulása az Európai Közösség irányelvének nyomán – különös tekintettel a küszöbönálló hazai szabályozásra' [The Development of Product Liability Due to the Directive of European Communities: With Special Attention to Hungarian Regulation in Progress], in *Polgári jogi dolgozatok* [Papers on Civil Law] MTA Államés Jogtudományi Intézet, ELTE Állam- és Jogtudományi Kar, Budapest.

Teubner, G. (1986a) 'The Transformations of Law in the Welfare State' in Teubner G. (ed.) *Dilemmas of Law in the Welfare State*, Berlin and New York: Walter de Gruyter, pp. 3–10.

Teubner, G. (1986b) (ed.) *Dilemmas of Law in the Welfare State*, Berlin and New York: Walter de Gruyter.

Teubner, G. (1988) 'Evolution of Autopoietic Law' in Teubner G. (ed.) *Autopoietic Law: A New Approach to Law and Society*, New York: Walter de Gruyter; pp. 217–41.

Teubner, G. (1997) (ed.) *Global Law Without the State*, Aldershot: Dartmouth Gower.

Teubner, G. (1998a) 'Legal Irritants: Good Faith in British Law or How Unifying Law Ends Up in New Divergences', 61 *MLR* 11.

Teubner, G. (1998b) 'After Privatization? The Many Autonomies of Private Law', 51 *Current Legal Problems* 393.

Teubner, G. (2000) 'Global Private Regimes: Neo-spontaneous Law and Dual Constitution of Autonomous Sectors in World Society?' in Ladeur, K-H. (ed.), *Globalisation and Public Governance*, Cambridge: Cambridge University Press, pp. 71–87.

Tichy, L. (2002a) 'Czech Republic: Development of Czech Law of Tort' in Koziol, H. and Steininger, B.C. (eds) *European Tort Law 2001*, Tort and Insurance Law Yearbook, Vienna and New York: Springer, pp. 105–23.

Tichy, L. (2002b) 'Czech Republic' in Koch, B.A. and Koziol H. (eds) *Unification of Tort Law: Strict Liability*, European Centre for Tort and Insurance Law, The Hague, London and New York: Kluwer, pp. 75–99.

Tichy, L. (2005) 'Fault under Czech Law' in Widmer, P. (ed.) *Unification of Tort Law: Fault*, European Centre for Tort and Insurance Law, The Hague: Kluwer, pp. 53–64.

Treitel, G. (1976) 'Remedies for Breach of Contract (Courses of Action Open to a Party Aggrieved)' in von Mehren, A. (ed.) *International Encyclopaedia of Comparative Law*, Mouton, The Hague and Paris: J.C.B. Mohr (Paul Siebeck).

Treitel, G.H. (ed.) (1979) *International Encyclopaedia of Comparative Law, Volume VII: Contracts in General*, Mouton, The Hague and Tübingen: J.C.B. Mohr (Paul Siebeck).

Tugendhat, Ch. (1986) *Making Sense of Europe*, Harmondsworth: Viking, Penguin Books.

Van Dam, C. (2006) *European Tort Law*, Oxford: Oxford University Press.

Van der Bergh, R. (1999) 'Economics in a Legal Straight-Jacket: The Difficult Reception of Economic Analysis in European Law', Paper presented at the workshop 'Empirical Research and Legal Realism: Setting the Agenda', Haifa, 6–9 June 1999.

Várady, T. (1999) 'The Emergence of Competition Law in (Former) Socialist Countries', 47 *American Journal of Comparative Law* 229–75.

Varga, C. (2001) 'Legal Scholarship at the Threshold of a New Millennium', 42 *Acta Juridica Hungarica* 181–201.

Vervaele, J.A. (1999) *Compliance and Enforcement of European Community Law*, The Hague: Kluwer.

Viney, G. (1986) 'The Civil Liability of Manufacturers in French Law' in Miller, C.J. (ed.) *Comparative Product Liability*, London: The United Kingdom National Committee of Comparative Law, pp. 73–98.

Visser, D. (2006) 'Unjustified Enrichment in Comparative Perspective' in Reimann, M. and Zimmermann, R. *The Oxford Handbook of Comparative Law*, Oxford: Oxford University Press, pp. 969–1002.

Vogel, H-J. (1979) 'Zur Diskussion um die Normenflut', 34 *Juristenzeitung* 321.

Vogenauer, S. (2006) 'Sources of Law and Legal Method in Comparative Law' in Reimann, M. and Zimmermann, R. *The Oxford Handbook of Comparative Law*, Oxford: Oxford University Press, pp. 869–98.

Vogenauer, S. and Weatherill, S. (2005) 'The European Community Competence for a Comprehensive Harmonisation of Contract Law: An Empirical Analysis', 30(Dec.) *E.L.Rev.* 821–37.

Vondracek, T.J. (1988) *Commentary on the Czechoslovak Civil Code*, Dordrecht, Boston, MA and Lancaster: Martinus Nijhoff Publishers.

Vries (de), H.P., Galston, N.M. and Bermann, G.A. (1981) *French Law: Constitution and Selective Legislation*, New York: M. Bender.

Wade, J. (1973) 'On the Nature of Strict Tort Liability for Products', 44 *Mississippi Law Journal*.

Wagner, G. (2005) 'The Project of Harmonising European Tort Law', 42 *Common Market Law Review* 1269–312.

Wagner, G. (2006) 'Comparative Tort Law' in Reimann, M. and Zimmermann, R. *The Oxford Handbook of Comparative Law*, Oxford: Oxford University Press, pp. 1003–41.

Wagner, W.J. (1974) 'Polish Civil Law. Volume II: Obligations in Polish Law' in Szirmai, Z., *Law in Eastern Europe*, Leiden: A.W. Sijthoff.

Wałachowska, M. (2007) *Zadośćuczynienie pieniężne za doznaną krzywdę* [Compensation of Non-pecuniary Loss], Toruń: TNOiK.

Ward, I. (1996) *The Margins of European Law*, Basingstoke: Macmillan and New York: St. Martin's Press.

Warkałło, W. (1983) 'Przemiany odszkodowawczej odpowiedzialności cywilnej' [Transformations in Civil Liability] in Łętowska, E. (ed.) *Tendencje rozwoju prawa cywilnego* [The Trends in the Development of Civil Law] Wrocław: Ossolineum.

Wasiak, W. (1985) *Determinanty i podstawy prawne ochrony interesów konsumenta w Polsce* [Main Features and Legal Bases of Consumer Protection in Poland], Prace Naukowe Akademii Ekonomicznej, Wrocław, No. 298.

Wasiak, Z. (1979) 'Odpowiedzialność za szkodę wyrządzoną przez rzecz niebezpieczną – zakres obowiązków producenta' [Liability for Damages Caused by a Dangerous Thing: The Scope of Producers' Duties], *Studia Prawno – Ekonomiczne*, t. 17, s. 53.

Wasilkowski, J. (1963) *Zarys Prawa Rzeczowego* [The Features of Civil Law Concerning Things], Warszawa.

Wasilkowski, J. (1964) 'Metoda Opracowania i Założenia Kodeksu Cywilnego' [The Formation and Premises of the Civil Code], 5/6 *Państwo i Prawo* 737.

Wassenaer, O. van (1986) 'Products Liability in Europe', 34 *AJCL*.

Watkin, T.G. (ed.) (1998) *The Europeanisation of Law*, London: The United Kingdom National Committee of Comparative Law.

Watson, A. (1974) *Legal Transplants*, Edinburgh: Scottish Academic Press and Charlottesville, VA: University Press of Virginia.

Watson, A. (1976) 'Legal Transplants and Law Reform', 92 *LQR* 79.

Watson, A. (1993) *Legal Transplants*, 2nd edition, Athens, GA: University of Georgia.

Watson, A. (2004) 'Legal Culture v Legal Tradition' in Van Hoecke M. (ed.) *Epistemology and Methodology of Comparative Law*, Oxford and Portland, OR: Hart.

Weatherill, S. (1995) *Law and Integration in the European Union*, Oxford: Clarendon Press.

Weatherill, S. (1999) 'Consumer Policy' in Craig, P. and de Búrca, G. *The Evolution of EU Law*, Oxford and New York: Oxford University Press, p. 692.

Weatherill, S. (2000) *Cases and Materials on EC Law*, 5th edition, London: Blackstone.

Weatherill, S. (2002) 'Pre-emption, Harmonisation and the Distribution of Competence to Regulate the Internal Market' in Scott J. and Barnard C. (eds) *The Legal Foundations of the Internal Market*, Oxford: Hart, ch. 2.

Weatherill, S. (2003a) *Cases and Materials on EU Law*, 6th edition, Oxford: Oxford University Press.

Weatherill, S. (2003b) 'Product Safety and Product Liability in a Community Context', Paper presented at the Academy of European Law/Lovells Conference Product Safety and Product Liability: Recent Developments in Community Law, of 1–2 May 2003, in London.

Weatherill, S. and Beaumont, P. (1999) *EU Law: The Essential Guide to the Legal Workings of the European Union*, 3rd edition, London: Penguin.
Weick, G. (1993) *National and European Law on the Threshold to the Single Market*, Frankfurt am Main: Peter Lang.
Weir, T. (1983) in Tunc, A. *International Encyclopaedia of Comparative Law, Volume XI: Torts*, Tübingen: J.C.B. Mohr (Paul Siebeck) and The Hague, Boston, London: Martinus Nijhoff Publishers.
West, A. (1998) *The French Legal System*, 2nd edition, London: Butterworths.
Whitehead, G.M. (1989) 'Product Liability and European Integration in Light of the EEC Strict Liability Directive' in *EEC Strict Liability in 1992*, PLI Litigation & Administrative Practice Course Handbook Series No. 371.
Whittaker, S. (1985) 'The EEC Directive on Product Liability', 5 *Yearbook of European Law* 242.
Whittaker, S. (1989) 'European Product Liability and Intellectual Products', 105 *LQR* 125.
Whittaker, S. (2005) *Liability for Products: English Law, French Law, and European Harmonisation*, Oxford: Oxford University Press.
Widmer, P. (2005a) *Unification of Tort Law: Fault*, European Centre for Tort and Insurance Law, The Hague: Kluwer.
Widmer P. (2005b) 'Comparative Report on Fault as a Basis of Liability and Criterion of Imputation (Attribution)' in Widmer P. (ed.) *Unification of Tort Law: Fault*, European Centre for Tort and Insurance Law, The Hague: Kluwer, pp. 331–67.
Wilhelmsson, T. (1996) 'Consumer Images in East and West' in Micklitz H.W. (ed.) *Legal Unity or Legal Diversity*, Baden-Baden: Nomos, ch. 3.
Wilhelmsson, T. (2000) *Is There a European Consumer Law – and Should There Be One?* Centro di studi e ricerche di diritto comparator e straniero, Saggi, Conferenze e Seminari 41, Roma.
Willett, C. (1996) 'Introduction: The Scope of the Collection' in Willett, C. (ed.) *Aspects of Fairness in Contract*, London: Blackstone Press.
Winiger, B. (2002) 'Strict Liability: What About Fault?' in Koziol, H. and Steininger, B.C. (eds) *European Tort Law 2001*, Vienna and New York: Springer, pp. 2–17.
Wiszniewski, A. (1964) *Prawo Cywilne*, 3rd edition, Warszawa.
Wittman, D. (1977) 'Prior Regulation versus Post Liability: The Choice between Input and Output Monitoring', 6 *J. Legal Studies* 193.
Wojtasiewicz, O.A. (2000) *The Polish Civil Code*, ed. by Joanna Miler, Warszawa: TEPIS Publishing House of the Polish Society of Economic, Legal and Court Translators.
Woodroffe, G. (1984) *Consumer Law in the EEC*, London: Sweet & Maxwell.
Worley, D. (1986) 'Remedies for Breach of Contract in Common Law Jurisdictions' in Yelpaala, K. (ed.) *Drafting and Enforcing Contracts in Civil and Common Law Jurisdictions*, Deventer, Antwerp, London, Frankfurt, Boston and New York: Kluwer.

Yiannopoulos, A.N. (1974) 'Jurisprudence and Doctrine as Sources of Law in Louisiana and France' in Dainow J. (ed.) *The Role of Judicial Decisions and Doctrine in Civil Law and Mixed Jurisdictions*, Baton Rouge, LA: Louisiana State University Press.

Youngs, R. (1998) *English, French and German Comparative Law*, London: Cavendish.

Żabczynski, A. (1996) *Prawa Konsumentów* [Consumer Rights] Publication of the Polish Office for the Protection of Competition and Consumers, POL/1998/0001.

Zekoll, J. (1989) 'German Product Liability Act', 4 *AJCL*.

Zemans, F.H. and Thomas, A. (1999) 'Can Community Clinics Survive? A Comparative Study of Law Centres in Australia, Ontario and England' in Regan, F., Paterson, A., Goriely, T. and Fleming, D. (eds) *The Transformation of Legal Aid: Comparative and Historical Studies*, Oxford: Oxford University Press.

Zimmermann, R. (1998) 'Savigny's Legacy: Legal History, Comparative Law, and the Emergence of a European Legal Science' in Watkin, T.G. (ed.) *The Europeanisation of Law*, London: The United Kingdom National Committee of Comparative Law.

Zimmermann, R. and Whittaker, S. (2000) *Good Faith in European Contract Law*, Cambridge: Cambridge University Press.

Zivnostensky zakon English [Trade Act, in English], The Trade Licensing Act, No. 455/1991 coll. including *amendments of 1 November 1995*, translated by Trade Links, Prague: Trade Links, 1995.

Zoll, F. (1997) 'Potrzeba i kierunki nowelizacji kodeksowego ujęcia problematyki wzorców umownych' [The Need and Direction in the Amendments of the Civil Code Concerning Contractual Clauses], 1 *Biuletyn Rady Legislacyjnej* 68–9.

Zollers, F. (1991) 'Labels, Tables and Fables: User's Guide to Product Liability Studies', 13 *JPTL*.

Zrałek, I. (2005) 'Przedawnienie roszczeń w polskim prawie cywilnym – szkic prawnoporównawczy' [Limitation of Claims in Polish Civil Law: Comparative Analysis] in *Rozprawy Prawnicze. Księgu Pamiątkowa Profesora Maksymiliana Pazdana*, Kraków, p. 1565.

Żuławska, Cz. (1973) *Gwarancja przy sprzedaży* [Warranties], Warszawa: Wydawnictwo Prawnicze.

Żuławska, Cz. (1983a) 'Ewolucja odpowiedzialności za jakość świadczenia' [Liability for Services] in Łętowska E. (ed.) *Tendencje rozwoju prawa cywilnego. Zbiór studiów* [The Tendencies in the Development of Civil Law: The Collection of Studies], Wrocław.

Żuławska, Cz. (1983b) *Glosa do orzeczenia GKA* [Commentary to the Judgement of the Arbitrazh Collegium] of 24 June 1981, IP-3478/81, OSPiKA 1983, z.2.

Żuławska, Cz. (1983c) *Glosa do orzeczenia Sądu Najwyższego* [Commentary to the Judgement of the Supreme Court] of 4 December 1981, OSPiKA 1983, poz. 55, p. 142.

Żuławska, Cz. (1985) 'Ochrona konsumenta w reformowanej gospodarce' [Consumer Protection in the Reformed Economy], 3 *Spółdzielczy Kwartalnik Naukowy* 41.
Żuławska, Cz. (1987) *Obrót z udziałem konsumenta – ochrona prawna* [Consumer Transactions: Legal Protection], Wrocław.
Żuławska, Cz. (1997) *Komentarz do Kodeksu Cywilnego. Księga Trzecia. Zobowiązania* [Commentary to the Civil Code. Book Three. Obligations], Vol. II, Warszawa: Wydawnictwo Prawnicze.
Zweigert, K. and Kotz, H. (1992) *An Introduction to Comparative Law*, Oxford: Clarendon Press.
Zweigert, K. and Kotz, H. (1995) *An Introduction to Comparative Law*, 3rd edition, Oxford, Clarendon Press.
Zweigert, K. and Kotz, H. (1998) *An Introduction to Comparative Law*, 3rd revised edition, Oxford: Clarendon Press.

EU Policy Documents, Reports and Action Programmes (in chronological order)

Preliminary Programme of the European Economic Community for a Consumer Protection and Information Policy, O.J, C 92/1 (25 April 1975).
Economic and Social Committee Report on Proposal for a Council Directive on Liability for Defective Products, COM(76)372 final at 41–5.
Report of the Legal Affairs Committee of the European Parliament EUR. PARL. DOC. (COM 246)26–27 (1978); EUR.PARL.DOC. (COM 71) 16–17 (1979).
Commission of the European Communities, Consumer Redress, COM(84) 692, 12 December 1984.
Supplementary Communication from the Commission on Consumer Redress COM(87) 210, 7 May 1987.
Council Resolution of 25 June 1987 on consumer redress [1987] O.J. C 176/2.
Cecchini Report, *Europe 1992: The Overall Challenge* [Report for the European Commission]. SEC (88) 524 final, 13 April 1988.
Commission of the European Communities, DG Information, Communication and Culture (1990) The European Community and its Eastern Neighbours Luxembourg: Office for Official Publications of the European Communities ('The European Community and its Eastern Neighbours Study 1990').
Commission of the European Communities, Association Agreements with Poland, Czechoslovakia and Hungary, Background Brief (Brussels, February 1992).
Commission of the European Communities, Europe and the Challenge of Enlargement, Bulletin of the European Communities, Supplement 3/92, 9.
Commission of the European Communities, Green Paper: Access of consumers to Justice and the settlement of consumer disputes in the single market COM(93) 576, 16 November 1993 (not published in the Official Journal).

Council of the European Union Presidency, Conclusions: Copenhagen European Council (Brussels: 1993).

Commission of the European Communities (1993), Green Paper on Guarantees for Consumer Goods and After-Sales Services COM (93) 509 final.

Commission of the European Communities, The Europe Agreements and beyond: a strategy to prepare the countries of Central and Eastern Europe for accession COM (94) 320 final, and Follow up to Commission Communication COM (94) 361 final, 1994.

Commission of the European Communities, First Report on the application of Council Directive on the approximation of laws, regulations and administrative provisions of the Member States concerning liability for defective products, O.J. C 617 (1995); 13.12.1995, COM (95) 617 final ('First Report on Product Liability Directive').

Commission of the European Communities, White Paper: preparation of the associated countries of Central and Eastern Europe for integration into the internal market of the Union COM (95) 163 final.

Commission of the European Communities, The Impact and Effectiveness of the Single Market (1996) <http://europa.eu.int/comm/dg15/en/update/impact/smsumen.htm>.

Commission Communication Action plan on consumer access to justice and the settlement of consumer disputes in the internal market COM(96) 13 final, 14 February 1996.

von Freyhold, H., Gessner, V., Vial, E.L. and Wagner, H. (eds) (1996) *The Costs of Judicial Barriers for Consumers in the Single Market*, A Report for the European Commission DG XXIV, <http://www.freyvial.de/Publications/egi-2.pdf>.

Communication from the Commission of 30 March 1998 *on the out-of-court settlement of consumer disputes* (COM(1998) 198 final – not published in the Official Journal).

Commission Recommendation of 30 March 1998 *on the principles applicable to the bodies responsible for out-of-court settlement of consumer disputes* (COM(1998) 198 final – OJ L 115 of 17.04.1998).

Feldtman, B., von Freyhold, H. and Vial, E.L. (1998) *The Costs of Legal Obstacles to the Disadvantage of Consumers in the Single Market*, Report for the European Commission DG XXIV, <http://www.freyvial.de/Publications/egii-42.pdf>.

Action Plan of the Council and the Commission on how best to implement the provisions of the Treaty of Amsterdam on an area of freedom, security and justice – Text adopted by the Justice and Home Affairs Council of 3 December 1998, OJ C 019, 23.1.1999.

Tampere European Council, 15, 16 October 1999 – Presidency Conclusions <http://www.europarl.europa.eu/summits/tam_en.htm#top>.

Commission of the European Communities, Green Paper on liability for defective products, of 28 July 1999 (COM (1999) 396 final).

European Commission, The Commission adopts a Green Paper on producer liability (1999) <www.europa.eu.int/comm/internal_market/en/update/consumer/99-580.htm>.

Commission of the European Communities, Report on the Application of Directive 85/374 on Liability for Defective Products 31.1.2001, COM (2000) 893 final ('Second Report on Product Liability Directive').

Lisbon European Council Presidency Conclusions (2000) <http://www.europarl.europa.eu/summits/lis1_en.htm>.

Communication from the Commission of 4 April 2001 *on widening consumer access to alternative dispute resolution* COM(2001) 161 – not published in the Official Journal.

Commission Recommendation of 4 April 2001 *on the principles for out-of-court bodies involved in the consensual resolution of consumer disputes not covered by Recommendation* 98/257/EC, COM(2001) 1016 – OJ L 109 of 19.04.2001.

Communication from the Commission to the European Parliament, the Council, the Economic and Social Committee and the Committee of the Regions: Consumer Policy Strategy 2002–2006 2002/C 137/02, COM (2002) 208 final.

Report from the Commission of 31 January 2001 on the Application of Directive 85/374 on Liability for Defective Products (COM (2000) 893 final) ('Second Commission Report on Product Liability Directive').

Commission of the European Communities, The Macroeconomic Effects of the Single Market Programme after Ten Years (2002) <http://europa.eu.int/internal_market/10years/background_en.htm>.

Communication from the Commission to the European Parliament and the Council: A More Coherent European Contract Law: An Action Plan COM(2003) 68, 12 February 2003.

European Commission Report on the safety of services for consumers COM (2003) 313 final.

Commission of the European Communities Internal Market Strategy – Priorities 2003–2006 COM(2003) 238 final – not published in the Official Journal.

Extracts from Presidency Conclusions on The Lisbon Strategy by Theme. European Councils: Lisbon (March 2000) to Brussels (June 2004): <http://ec.europa.eu/growthandjobs/pdf/thematic_lisbon_conclusions_0604_en.pdf>.

Communication from the Commission: European contract law and the revision of the acquis: the way forward COM(2004) 651, 11 October 2004.

Communication from the Commission to the Council and the European Parliament Common Actions for Growth and Employment: the Community Lisbon Programme SEC[2005] 981, Brussels 20.07.2005, COM (2005) 330 final, pp. 7–9.

Special Eurobarometer No. 215 Lisbon European Commission 2005 <http://www.ec.europa.eu/public_opinion/archives/ebs/ebs_215_en.pdf>.

European Commission, Green Paper: Damages actions for breach of the EC antitrust Rules of 19.12.2005, COM(2005) 672 final.

Commission of the European Communities, Green Paper on the Review of the Consumer Acquis COM(2006) 744 final.

DG Sanco, Eurobarometer 252 Consumer Protection in the Internal Market of September 2006 <http://ec.europa.eu/consumers/topics/eurobarometer_09-2006_en.pdf>.

Report from the Commission to the Council, the European Parliament and the European Economic and Social Committee, Third report on the application of Council Directive on the approximation of laws, regulations and administrative provisions of the Member States concerning liability for defective products (85/374/EEC of 25 July 1985, amended by Directive 1999/34/EC of the European Parliament and of the Council of 10 May 1999). Brussels, 14 September 2006 COM(2006) 496 final ('Third Report on Product Liability Directive').

Commission Green Paper on the Review of the Consumer Acquis of 8 February 2007, COM(2006) 744 final.

A Single Market for Citizens, Interim Report to the 2007 Spring European Council Brussels, COM(2007) 60, 21.2.2007 ('A Single Market for Citizens Interim Report 2007').

Communication from the Commission to the Council, The European Parliament and the European Economic and Social Committee EU Consumer Policy Strategy 2007–2013 Empowering Consumers, enhancing their welfare, effectively protecting them, Brussels, 13.3.2007, COM(2007) 99 final ('EU Consumer Policy Strategy 2007–2013').

Report from the Commission, Second Progress Report on the Common Frame of Reference, Brussels 25.07.2007, COM (2007) 447 final – <http://ec.europa.eu/consumers/cons_int/safe_shop/fair_bus_pract/cont_law/COMM_PDF_COM_2007_0447_F_EN_ACTE.pdf>.

Communication from the Commission to the Council, the European Parliament and the European Economic and Social Committee EU Consumer Policy Strategy 2007–2013. Empowering consumers, enhancing their welfare, effectively protecting them, Brussels 13 March 2007, COM(2007) 99 final.

Presidency Conclusions of the Brussels European Council (21–22 June 2007) (11177/07): <http://www.consilium.europa.eu/ueDocs/cms_Data/docs/pressData/en/ec/94932.pdf>.

Communication from the Commission to the European Parliament, the Council, the European Economic and Social Committee and the Committee of the Regions, Second strategic review of Better Regulation in the European Union 30 January 2008, COM(2008) 32 final.

Communication from the Commission, Monitoring consumer outcomes in the single market: the Consumer Markets Scoreboard 29 January 2008, COM(2008) 31 final.

Other Policy Papers, Research Reports, Databases and Collections of Principles (in chronological order)

United Kingdom Royal Commission on Civil Liability and Compensation for Personal Injury Cmnd 7054 (1978) Chapter 22 (vol. 1).

Calais-Auloy, J. (1981) 'Consumer Legislation in France, A study prepared for the EEC Commission' in *Consumer legislation in the EC Countries*, Reich/Micklitz, 'Verbraucherschutz in den EG-Staaten', 1979; Fontaine/Bourgoignie, 'Consumer legislation in Denmark', 1981; Calais-Auloy et. al., 'Consumer legislation in France', 1981; Reich/Micklitz, 'Consumer legislation in Germany', 1980; Ghidini, 'Consumer legislation in Italy', 1980; Hondius, 'Consumer legislation in the Netherlands', 1980; Whincup, 'Consumer legislation in the United Kingdom and the Republic of Ireland', 1980.

Czech Republic 1996: hints to businessmen: Czech constitution, compiled by Trade Links, Prague, 1996.

von Freyhold, H. (1998) 'Access to Justice in Europe: A Single Market for Litigants?' in Feldtmann, B., von Freyhold, H. and Vial, E.L., Report for the European Commission DG XXIV – Consumer Policy and Consumer Health Protection – The Cost of Legal Obstacles to the Disadvantage of Consumers in the Single Market; <http://ec.europa.eu/dgs/health_consumer/library/pub/pub03.pdf>.

Commission on European Contract Law ('Lando Commission') *Principles of European Contract Law* (Parts I and II – published in 1999, Part III – published in 2002) <http://frontpage.cbs.dk/law/commission_on_european_contract_law/.

Urząd Ochrony Konkurencji i Konsumentów [The Office for the Protection of Competition and Consumers] (2000) *Ochrona Konsumentów* [Consumer Protection], vols 1 and 2, Warszawa.

Bojarski, Ł., Polish Helsinki Foundation for Human Rights, Access to Justice Country Report: Poland, Project on Promoting Access to Justice in Central and Eastern Europe, Access to Justice Forum in Budapest, 2002, <http://www.pili.org/2005r/dmdocuments/CR_Poland.pdf>.

Bukovská, B., Counseling Center for Citizenship, Civil and Human Rights, Access to Justice Country Report: Czech Republic, Project on Promoting Access to Justice in Central and Eastern Europe, Access to Justice Forum in Budapest, 2002 <http://www.pili.org/2005r/dmdocuments/CR_CzechRepublic.pdf>.

Kádár, A., Pardavi, M. and Zádori, Z., Hungarian Helsinki Committee, Access to Justice Country Report: Hungary, Project on Promoting Access to Justice in Central and Eastern Europe, Access to Justice Forum in Budapest, 2002 <http://www.pili.org/2005r/dmdocuments/CR_Hungary.pdf>.

von Bar, C. and Drobnig, U. (2002) Study on Property Law and Non-contractual Liability Law as they relate to Contract Law Submitted to the European Commission – Health and Consumer Protection Directorate General SANCO B5–1000/02/000574.

Lovells (2003) Product Liability in the European Union. A Report for the European Commission, February 2003 MARKT 2001/11/D ('Lovells Report').

European Commission for the Efficiency of Justice (CEPEJ), European Judicial Systems 2002, Facts and figures on the basis of a survey conducted in 40 Council of Europe Member States Strasbourg 2004 <http://www.coe.int/T/E/Legal_Affairs/Legal_co-operation/Operation_of_justice/Efficiency_of_justice/systeme%20judiciaire%20A.pdf>.

Fondazione Rosselli (2004) Analysis of the Economic Impact of the Development Risk Clause as provided by Directive 85/374/EEC on Liability for Defective Products Study for the European Commission ('Fondazione Rosselli Report'), <http://ec.europa.eu/enterprise/regulation/goods/docs/liability/2004-06-dev-risk-clause-study_en.pdf>.

European Group on Tort Law (2005) Principles of European Tort Law. Text and Commentary Vienna and New York: Springer.

Éless, T. (Freshfields Bruckhaus Deringer), Németh, Á. (Kovács Réti Szegheő) Hungary Response to the Commission's Green Paper Damages Actions for breach of the EC antitrust rules (presented by the Commission) COM (2005) 672 final, 19 December 2005, SEC {2005} 1732.

British Institute of International and Comparative Law Product Liability Database – only available to members of the Product Liability Forum at the Institute <www.biicl.org>; (several reports written for the database were used in this book, with the permission of the authors).

EU Law Consumer Acquis Database: <http://www.eu-consumer-law.org/index.html>.

Consumer Law Compendium – 2006 – <http://ec.europa.eu/consumers/cons_int/safe_shop/acquis/comp_analysis_en.pdf>.

Baker & McKenzie General Product Safety Directive (GPSD) – Comparative Inventory of 2006, Service Contract 17.020100/04/391471, <http://ec.europa.eu/consumers/cons_safe/keydocs/gpsd comp_inv_a_en.pdf>

Study Group on a European Civil Code and the Research Group on EC Private Law (Acquis Group); von Bar, C., Clive, E. and Schulte-Nölke, H. (eds) (2008) *Principles, Definitions and Model Rules of European Private Law.* Draft Common Frame of Reference (DCFR) Interim Outline Edition, Munich: Sellier ('Draft Common Frame of Reference 2008').

Legislation, Including Drafts (in chronological order)

European Union

Convention of 27 September 1968 *on jurisdiction and the enforcement of judgements in civil and commercial matters* < http://curia.europa.eu/common/recdoc/convention/en/c-textes/brux-idx.htm>.

Commission of the European Communities (1976) Proposal for a Council Directive on the approximation of laws, regulations and administrative provisions of the Member States concerning liability for defective products, OJ C 241, 14 October 1976.

EEC Directive on Liability for Defective Products, Explanatory Memorandum of September 1976; COM (76) 372 final.

Commission of the European Communities (1979) Revised proposal for a Council Directive on the approximation of laws, regulations and administrative provisions of the Member States concerning liability for defective products, OJ C 271, 26.10.1979.

Rome Convention *on the law applicable to contractual obligations* 80/934/EEC, OJ L 266, 09.10.1980; <http://www.rome-convention.org/instruments/i_conv_orig_en.htm>.

Council Directive 84/450/EEC of 10 September 1984 relating to the approximation of the laws, regulations and administrative provisions of the Member States concerning misleading advertising OJ L 250, 19.09.1984, pp. 17–20.

Council Directive 85/374/EEC of 25 July 1985 on the approximation of laws, regulations and administrative provisions of the Member States concerning liability for defective products OJ L 210, 7.8.1985, p. 21 ('Product Liability Directive').

Council Directive 85/577/EEC of 20 December 1985 to protect the consumer in respect of contracts negotiated away from business premises OJ L 372, 31.12.1985, pp. 31–3.

European Commission Notes of the E.C. Commission on the individual articles of the draft Directive Commercial Laws of Europe 1986, part 96, pp. 82–3.

Convention of 27 September 1968 *on jurisdiction and the enforcement of judgements in civil and commercial matters* <http://curia.europa.eu/common/recdoc/convention/en/c-textes/brux-idx.htm>.

Council Directive on the approximation of laws, regulations and administrative provisions of the Member States concerning liability for defective products, 85/374/EEC, OJ L 210, 7 August 1985.

Council Directive 90/314/EEC of 13 June 1990 *on package travel, package holidays and package tours* OJ L 158, 23.6.1990, pp. 59–64.

Association Agreement between the European Union and the Czech Republic of 16 December 1991, OJ L 360, 31/12/1994 pp. 2–210.

Association Agreement between the European Union and Hungary of 16 December 1991, OJ L 347, 31/12/1993 pp. 2–266.

Association Agreement between the European Union and Poland of 16 December 1991, OJ L 348, 31/12/1993 pp. 2–180.

Council Directive 92/59/EEC of 29 June 1992 *on general product safety* OJ L 228 of 11.08.1992.

Council Directive 93/13/EEC of 5 April 1993 *on Unfair Terms in Consumer Contracts* OJ L 095, 21 April 1993, pp. 29–34.

Directive 94/47/EC of the European Parliament and the Council of 26 October 1994 on the protection of purchasers in respect of certain aspects of contracts relating to the purchase of the right to use immovable properties on a timeshare basis OJ L 280, 29. 10.1994, pp. 83–7.

Directive 97/7/EC of the European Parliament and of the Council of 20 May 1997 *on the protection of consumers in respect of distance contracts* OJ L 144, 4.6.1997, pp. 19–27.

Directive 97/55/EC of the European Parliament and of the Council of 6 October 1997 *amending Directive 84/450/EEC concerning misleading advertising so as to include comparative advertising*, OJ L 290, 23.10.1997, pp. 18–23.

Directive 98/6/EC of the European Parliament and of the Council of 16 February 1998 *on consumer protection in the indication of the prices of products offered to consumer*s OJ L 80, 18.3.1998, pp. 27–31.

Directive 98/27/EC of the European Parliament and of the Council of 19 May 1998 *on injunctions for the protection of consumers' interests* OJ L 166/51, 11.6.98.

Directive 1999/44/EC of the European Parliament and of the Council of 15 May 1999 *on certain aspects of the sale of consumer goods and associated guarantees*, Official Journal L 171, 07.07.1999, P. 0012–0016.

Council Regulation (EC) No. 44/2001 of 22 December 2000 (Brussels I) *on jurisdiction and the recognition and enforcement of judgements in civil and commercial matters* OJ L 12/1, 16.01.2001, amended by Regulation (EC) No. 1496/2002 29.8.2002 – OJ L 225, 22.8.2002 Regulation (EC) No. 1937/2004 17.11.2004 – OJ L 334, 10.11.2004 Regulation (EC) No. 2245/2004 4.1.2005 – OJ L 381, 28.12.2004 and the Act concerning the conditions of accession of the Czech Republic, the Republic of Estonia, the Republic of Cyprus, the Republic of Latvia, the Republic of Lithuania, the Republic of Hungary, the Republic of Malta, the Republic of Poland, the Republic of Slovenia and the Slovak Republic and the adjustments to the treaties on which the European Union is founded (OJ L 236, 23.9.2003).

Council Decision of 28 May 2001 establishing a European Judicial Network in civil and commercial matters, OJ L 174/25, 27.6.2001.

Directive 2001/95/EC of the European Parliament and of the Council of 3 December 2001 *on general product safety* Official Journal L 011, 15/01/2002 pp. 4–17.

Directive 2002/8/EC of 27 January 2003 of the European Parliament and of the Council to improve access to justice in cross-border disputes by establishing minimum common rules relating to legal aid for such disputes OJ L 026, 31.1.2003.

Council Regulation No. 743/2002 of 25 April 2002 establishing a Community framework of activities to facilitate the implementation of judicial cooperation in civil matters OJ L 115/1, 1.5.2002.

European Parliament and Council Regulation 805/2004 *creating a European Enforcement Order for uncontested claims* OJ L 143 of 30.04.2004.

Regulation (EC) No. 2006/2004 of the European Parliament and of the Council of 27 October 2004 *on cooperation between national authorities responsible for the enforcement of consumer protection laws* (Consumer Protection Cooperation Regulation) OJ L 364, 9.12.2004, pp. 1–11.

Directive 2005/29/EC of the European Parliament and of the Council of 11 May 2005 concerning unfair business-to-consumer commercial practices in the internal market and amending Council Directive 84/450/EEC, Directives 97/7/EC, 98/27/EC and 2002/65/EC of the European Parliament and of the Council and Regulation (EC) No. 2006/2004 of the European Parliament and of the Council ('Unfair Commercial Practices Directive') OJ L 149, 11.6.2005, pp. 22–39.

Proposal for a Regulation of the European Parliament and the Council *on the law applicable to contractual obligations (Rome I)* COM (2005) 650 final, 15.12.2005, 2005/0261 (COD), <http://europa.eu.int/eur-lex/lex/LexUriserv/site/en/com/2005/com2005_0650en01.pdf>.

Communication from the Commission to the European Parliament, the Council, the European Economic and Social Committee and the Committee of the Regions *Healthier, safer, more confident citizens: a Health and Consumer Protection Strategy* Proposal for a Decision of the European Parliament and of the Council establishing a Programme of Community Action in the field of Health and Consumer Protection 2007–2013, of 6 April 2005, COM (2005) 115 final. <http://ec.europa.eu/health/ph_overview/Documents/com_2005_0115_en.pdf>.

Amended Proposal for a Regulation of the European Parliament and the Council creating a European order for payment procedure COM (2006) 57 final, CEC 7.2.2006 <http://europa.eu.int/eur-lex/lex/LexUriserv/site/en/com/2006/com2006_0057en01.pdf>.

Regulation (EC) No. 1896/2006 of the European Parliament and the Council of 12 December 2006 *creating a European Order for Payment Procedure* OJ L 399, 30.12.2006.

Regulation (EC) No. 861/2007 of the European Parliament and of the Council of 11 July 2007 *establishing a European Small Claims Procedure*, OJ L 199, 31.07.2007, pp. 1–22.

Regulation (EC) 864/2007 of the European Parliament and of the Council of 11 July 2007 *on the law applicable to non-contractual obligations (Rome II)* OJ L 199/40, 31.07.2007 <http://eur-lex.europa.eu/LexUriserv/site/en/oj/2007/l_199/l_19920070731en00400049.pdf>.

Treaty of Lisbon amending the Treaty on European Union and the Treaty establishing the European Community, 13 December 2007, OJ C 306, Vol. 50 <http://eur-lex.europa.eu/JOHtml.do?uri=OJ:C:2007:306:SOM:EN:HTML>.

Central Europe

Czechoslovakia and the Czech Republic

'Občanský zákoník' (*Civil Code*) No. 141/1950 Coll.

'Občanský zákoník' (*Civil Code*) No. 40/1964 Coll. (the book draws largely on the translation of the up-to-date version of the Code provided by Monika Dobiasova of the Czech Ministry of Trade and Industry in 2004).

Act No. 509/1991 Coll., amending the Civil Code.

The Hunting Act, No. 512/1992 Coll. (amending the Hunting Act No. 23/1962 Coll.).

Consumer Protection Act No. 634/1992 Coll., as amended by Acts No. 217/1993 Coll., No. 40/1995 Coll., No. 104/1995 Coll., and as promulgated in Act No. 34/1996 Coll. Subsequently amended by Acts No. 110/1997, No. 356/1999, No. 64/2000, <www.spotrebitele.cz/legislativa/zakochrspot000710.html>.

Constitution of the Czech Republic, Act No. 1/1993 Sb.

Občanský zákoník English. Civil Code, Criminal Code, translated by Trade Links, Prague: Trade Links, 1996.

Trade-related legislation 1996: public procurement, economic competition, consumer protection, bankrupcy, copyright, public service companies, translated by Trade Links, Prague: Trade Links, 1996.

The Act on State Liability, No. 82/1998 Coll.

Commercial Code – No. 513/1998 Coll.

Vyhláška, kterou se mění vyhláška č. 440/2001 Sb., o odškodnění bolesti a ztížení společenského uplatnění [Decree Amending the Decree on Compensation for Pain Suffered and for an Aggravated Position in Society], No. 440/2001 Coll., Vyhláška č. 50/2003 Sb.

Act on Courts and Judges, Act No. 6/2002 Sb.

Návrh občanského zákoníku (Draft Civil Code) (provided and translated by Jiri Hradek and Professor Lubos Tichy), the latest version of the Draft (of 17 December 2007) is available on the website of the Czech Ministry of Justice: <http://portal.justice.cz/ms/ms.aspx?j=33&o=23&k=381&d=125304>.

Hungary

Civil Code of the Hungarian People's Republic, Act IV of 1959; *Civil Code of the Hungarian People's Republic. Polgari Torvenykonyv English*, translated by Lamberg, P., Budapest: Corvina, 1960 (a more up-to-date English version of the Code is available on the following website: <http://www.angelfire.com/mn2/reformclub/hunc1.html>.

Act IV of 1977 (amending the Civil Code of 1959).

Act IV of 31 October 1984 on Prohibition of Unfair Economic Activity.

Act X on Product Liability, 1993.

Act LV of 1996 on the Protection of Wild Animals, the Wild Economy and Hunting.

Act CLIV of 1997 on Public Health.

Act No. 66 of 1997 on the Organization and Administration of Courts <http://www.birosag.hu/engine.aspx?page=birosag_english_01_act>.

Act of 1998 on the Protection of Health and Consumers.

Hungarian Ministry of Justice, *The Conception and Regulatory Syllabus of the New Civil Code*. Version approved for the preparation of the draft of the standard text at the 18 November 2002 meeting of the Codification Committee, <http://www.im.hu/?mi=1&katid=44&id=75&cikkid=2312>; established by the Government resolution 1009/2002. (I.31.) Korm., published in the *Official Hungarian Gazette (Magyar Közlöny)* ('Conception').

Act XXXVI of 5 November 2002 amending Act IV of 1959 on the Civil Code of the Republic of Hungary and other acts for the harmonization of consumer protection (version in English provided by the Hungarian Ministry of Justice for the purposes of the Product Liability Database).

Act No. XCV/2005 on clinical testing, production, registration, distribution, marketing, labelling and state control of medical products for human use.

Poland

Kodeks Zobowiązań (*Code of Obligations*) of 27 October 1933, Dziennik Ustaw (Journal of Laws) of 1933, No. 82, item 598.

Kodeks Handlowy (*Commercial Code*) of 27 June 1934, Dziennik Ustaw No. 57, item 502.

Ustawa o Normalizacji (*Act on Normalization*) of 27 November 1961, Dziennik Ustaw No. 53, item 298.

Kodeks Cywilny (*Civil Code*) of 23 IV 1964, Dziennik Ustaw 1964 No. 16, item 93.

Ustawa o Jakości Dóbr, Usług i Budynków (*Act on the Quality of Goods, Services and Buildings*) of 8 February 1979, Dziennik Ustaw No. 2, item 7.

Rozporządzenie Nr 119 Rady Ministrów o organizacji kontroli jakości dóbr, usług i budynków Act No. 119 of the Council of Ministers of 3 August 1979 *on the organization of quality control for goods, services, works and buildings* Monitor Prawniczy (Lawyers' Monitor) No. 20, item 117.

Ustawa o przeciwdziałaniu praktykom monopolistycznym w gospodarce narodowej (*act on countering monopolistic practices in national economy*) of 28 January 1987, Dziennik Ustaw No. 43, item 18.

Ustawa o zmianie Kodeksu Cywilnego (*Act amending the Civil Code*) of 28 July 1990 Dziennik Ustaw No. 55, item 321.

Ustawa o Normalizacji (*Act on Normalization*) of 3 April 1993, Dziennik Ustaw No. 55, item 251.

Ustawa o zmianie Kodeksu Cywilnegp (*Act on the amendment of the Civil Code*) of 23 August 1996, Dziennik Ustaw No. 114, item 542.

Konstytucja Rzeczpospolitej Polskiej (*Constitution of the Republic of Poland*) of 2 April 1997, Dziennik Ustaw of 16 July 1997.

Ustawa o ochronie zwierząt (*Act on the protection of animals*) of 21 August 1997, Dziennik Ustaw No. 111, item 724.

Ustawa o ochronie niektórych praw konsumentów i odpowiedzialności za szkodę wyrządzoną przez produkt niebezpieczny (*Act on the protection of some consumer rights and liability for damage caused by an unsafe product*), of 2 March 2000 <www.rzeczpospolita.pl/Pl-iso/pub/doc/kon0415.html>.

Ustawa o systemie oceny zgodności, akredytacji i zmianie niektórych ustaw (*Act on the Assessment of Compliance, Accreditation, and amendment of some other acts*) of 28 April 2000, Dziennik Ustaw No. 43, item 489.

Ustawa o warunkach zdrowotnych żywności i żywienia (*Act on the Health Conditions of Food and Nutrition*) of 11 May 2001, Dziennik Ustaw No. 63, item 634.

Ustawa o szczególnych warunkach sprzedaży konsumenckiej oraz o zmianie Kodeksu Cywilnego (*Act on specific conditions of consumer sales and amendments of the Civil Code*) of 27 July 2002, Dziennik Ustaw No. 141, item 1176 ('Consumer Sales Act').

Ustawa o Sądzie Najwyższym (*Act on the Supreme Court*) of 23 November 2002 Dziennik Ustaw of 2002 No. 240, item 2052.

Komisja Kodyfikacyjna Prawa Cywilnego (Civil Law Codification Commission), Ministerstwo Sprawiedliwości (Ministry of Justice) 'Zielona Księga. Optymalna Wizja Kodeksu cywilnego w Rzeczypospolitej Polskiej' (Green Book. Optimal vision of the Civil Code in the Republic of Poland) pod redakcją Zbigniewa Radwańskiego (edited by Zbigniew Radwański), Oficyna Wydawnicza Ministerstwa Sprawiedliwości, Warszawa 2006 ('The Green Book').

Ustawa o zmianie Kodeksu Cywilnego (*Act on the amendment of the Civil Code*) of 16 February 2006, Dziennik Ustaw No. 80, item 538.

Western Europe

Austria

ABGB – Austrian General Civil Code – *Allgemeines Bürgerliches Gesetzbuch* of 1811, <http://www.ibiblio.org/ais/abgb1.htm>.

Denmark

Law No. 371 of June 7 1989 on product liability, amended by Law No. 1041 of 28 November 2000 (Order No. 261 of 20 March 2007 promulgating the Law on product liability. (Lovtidende, 2007, Part A, 30 March 2007, No. 48, pp. 1643–5).

France

Law No. 98-389 of 19 May 1998 on liability for defective products, JORF of 21 May 1998, p. 7744.

Loi No. 2004-1343 de simplification du droit – Law of 9 December 2004, JORF of 10 December 2004, p. 20857.

Greece

Law No. 2251/94 *on consumer protection*, Official Journal of the Hellenic Republic 191/A/16.11.1994.

Switzerland

ZGB – Swiss Civil Code – *Zivilgesetzbuch* of 1907.

United Kingdom

Consumer Protection Act 1987, Part I, C. 43.

United States of America

Class Actions Fairness Act of 2005 –<http://fl1.findlaw.com/news.findlaw.com/hdocs/docs/clssactns/cafa05.pdf>.

The Sarbanes-Oxley Act of 2002 Pub. L. No. 107-204, 116 Stat. 745, also known as the Public Company Accounting Reform and Investor Protection Act of 2002.

Restatement (Third) of Torts: Products Liability 1998.

Other International Law Instruments

Council of Europe, *European Convention on products liability in regard to personal injury and death* of 27 January 1977, E.T.S. No. 91, <http://conventions.coe.int/treaty/en/Treaties/Html/091.htm>.

United Nations Convention on Contracts for the International Sale of Goods, 1980, *Lex Mercatoria*, <http://www.jus.uio.no/lm/un.contracts.international.sale.of.goods.convention.1980/>.

Unpublished Documents and Individual Reports

Dobiasova, M. (2003) Introductory part on the Czech product liability law prepared for the Product Liability Database established by the British Institute of International and Comparative Law.

Kalman, E., Lelkes, V. and Domonkos, M. (2003) Database report on the Hungarian Product Liability Law, BIICL.

Case Law (in chronological order)

European Union

European Court of Justice

26/62 NV Algemene Transporten Expeditie Onderneming van Gend en Loos v Nederlandse Administratie der Belastingen [1963] ECR 1, [1963] CMLR 105.
6/64 Flaminio Costa v ENEL [1964] ECR 585, [1964] CMLR 425.
4/69 Alfons Lütticke GmbH v Commission of the European Communities [1971] ECR – 00325.
11/70 Internationale Handelsgesellscheft GmbH v. Einfuhr-und Vorratsstelle für Getreide und Futtermittel [1970] ECR 1125, [1972] CMLR 225.
41/74 Van Duyn v Home Office [1974] ECR 1337, [1975] 1 CMLR 1.
120/78 Rewe-Zentrale AG v Bundesmonopolverwaltung fur Branntwein [1979] ECR 649 (Cassis de Dijon).
148/78 Pubblico Ministero v Tullio Ratti [1979] ECR 1629, [1980] 1 CMLR 96.
C-106/89 Marleasing SA v La Comercial Internacional de Alimentacion SA [1990] ECR I-04135.
C-213/89 R. v Secretary of State for Transport, ex parte Factortame Ltd. and Others [1990] ECR I-2433, [1990] 3 CMLR 1.
C-339/89 Alsthom Atlantique v Sulzer [1991] ECR I-107.
C-6/90 and C-9/90 Francovich and Others v Italian State [1991] ECR I-5357.
C-46/93 and C-49/93 Brasserrie du Pecheur SA v Germany and R v Secretary of State for Transport, ex parte Factortame and others [1996] ECR I-1029.
C-48/93 R v Secretary of State for Transport, ex parte Factortame (Factortame III) [1996] ECR I-1029.
C-233/94 Germany v European Parliament and Council of the European Union Judgement of 13 May 1997, ECR 1997 I-02405.
C-352/98 Laboratoires Pharmaceutique Bergaderm SA and Gouplin v Commission, ECR 2000, I-5291.
C-376/98 Federal Republic of Germany v European Parliament and Council of the European Union Judgement of 5 October 2000, ECR 2000 I-08419.
C-456/98 Centrosteel Srl v Adipol GmbH [2000] ECR I-6007.
C-203/99 Heening Veedfald v Århus Amtskommune, [2001] ECR I-3569.
C-52/00 Commission of the European Communities v French Republic 25 April 2002, ECR 2002 I-03827.
C-154/00 Commission of the European Communities v Hellenic Republic, ECR 2002 I-03879.
C-168/00 Simone Leitner v TUI Deutschland GmbH & Co., ECR 2002, I-2631.
C-183/00 Gonzalez Sanchez v Medicina Asturiana, ECR 2002 I-03901.
C-491/01 R v Secretary of State for Health, ex parte British American Tobacco (Investments) Ltd and Imperial Tobacco Ltd Judgement of 10 December 2002, OJ C 31/3, 08.02.2003.

C-173/03 Traghetti del Mediterraneo SpA v Repubblica Italiana OJ C 190, 12 August 2006.

C-402/03 Skov AEg v Bilka LavprisvarehuscA/S and Bilka Lavprisvarehus A/S v Jette Mikkelsen, Michael Due Nielsen OJ C 48/4, 10 January 2006.

C-127/04 Declan O'Byrne v Sanofi Pasteur MSD Ltd, Sanofi Pasteur SA OJ C 86/09, 9 February 2006.

C-177/04 Commission of the European Communties v French Republic 14 March 2006, ECR 2006 I-02461.

C-234/04 Rosmarie Kapferer v Schlank & Schick GmbH OJ C 131, 3 June 2006.

Central Europe

Central European judgements are referred to using their numbers, dates and other required symbols, and sometimes the issuing court (whenever this is the standard manner of referring to judgements). The descriptions of facts are added for easier recognition in the text of the book. Central European judgements never mention the names of the parties, so some academic writers use such descriptions for easier referencing.

Czechoslovakia and the Czech Republic

Statement of the Czechoslovak Supreme Court of November 23, 1967, Prz 36/67, Published in: Nejvyšši soud o občanském soudnìm řizeni a řizeni před státnìm notářstwim. Sbornik směrnic, usneseni, rozboru a zhodnoceni soudni praxe pléna a presidia Nejvyššìho soudu 1965–1967 [The Supreme Court on Civil Proceedings and Proceedings before the State Notary. Collection of Directives, Resolutions, Analysis and Evaluation of the Case Law issued by the Supreme Court in 1965–1967], Praha 1974, 92, at 143.

Judgement of the Regional Court of Ostrava, No. 23 c 52/1996.

Judgement of the Higher Court of Prague, No. 2 Co 96/1999.

Judgement of the Highest Court: NS ČR 22 October 2003, 25 Cdo 1455/2003 (Causation).

Hungary

Supreme Court – the 'paint case' – cited and analysed in Bedenek-Világhy (1965) *A Polgári Torvénykönyv a gyakorlatban* [Civil Code in Practice], Budapest, pp. 301–6.

Supreme Court – the 'motorcycle accident case' – Birósági Határozatok (Court Decisions) 1973/1 no. 19.

Supreme Court – the 'chickens case' – cited and analysed in Tamás Tercsák (1993) 'A termékfelelősség jogintézményének alakulása az Európai Közösség irányelvének nyomá – különös tekintettel a küszöbönálló hazai szábalyozásra' [The Development of Product Liability Due to Directive of European Communities: With Special Attention to Hungarian Regulation in Progress] in *Polgári jogi dolgozatok* [Papers on Civil Law] MTA Allamés Jogtudományi Intézet ELTE Allám-és Jogtudományi Kar, Budapest, p. 224.

Supreme Court – the 'turnip cabbage seed case' – cited and analysed in Tamás Tercsák (1993) 'A termékfelelősség jogintézményének alakulása az Európai Közösség irányelvének nyomá – különös tekintettel a küszöbönálló hazai szábalyozásra' [The Development of Product Liability Due to Directive of European Communities: With Special Attention to Hungarian Regulation in Progress] in *Polgári jogi dolgozatok* [Papers on Civil Law] MTA Allamés Jogtudományi Intézet ELTE Allám-és Jogtudományi Kar, Budapest, p. 224.

Supreme Court – the 'chemical spray case' – Birósági Határozatok (Court Decisions) 1977/1 No. 31.

Supreme Court – the 'exploding television sets case' – Legfelsõbb Biróság Gf. III. (Supreme Court. Economic Affairs College) 31. 208/1984.

Supreme Court – the 'defective slippers case' – Supreme Court Decision No. 1986/12/501.

Supreme Court – the 'whipped cream maker case' – No. 1988/12/446.

Supreme Court – the angle grinder case – No. 2000/350.

Judgement of the Highest Court: NS ČR 22 October 2003, 25 Cdo 1455/2003.

Supreme Court – judgement No. 357 of 2003 (non-pecuniary damages for incorrect press information concerning a pending criminal case).

Poland

Sąd Najwyższy (Supreme Court) – judgement No. II CR 96/62, OSN 1964/95 ('Fiat Multipla case').

Sąd Najwyższy – judgement No. II CR 540/63, OSN 1965/32 ('P 70 car case').

Kolegium Arbitrażu Gospodarczego (Collegium of Economic Arbitrage) GKA – decision of 4 November 1963, Przegląd Ustawodawstwa Gospodarczego (*Economic Laws Monitor*) 1964, No. 11, item 407.

Sąd Najwyższy – judgement of 6 July 1966, OSPiKA (Orzecznictwo Sądów Polskich i Komisji Arbitrażowych – *Jurisprudence of Polish Courts and Arbitration Committees*) 1967/7-8, item 183 (non-pecuniary damage recoverable in contractual liability).

Sąd Najwyższy – judgement of 7 August 1967, II PR 268/67 Informacja Prawnicza (*Lawyers' Informator*) 1967 No. 11, poz. 4).

Sąd Najwyższy – judgement of 24 February 1969, I CR 438/69 (non-pecuniary damages).

Sąd Najwyższy – judgement of 28 June 1972, II CR 218/72, OSN 1972/228 ('chemical spray case').

Sąd Najwyższy (Supreme Court) – judgement of 28 VI 1972, II CR 218/72, OSN 1972/228 ('farm rental case').

Wytyczne (*Guidelines*) Uchwała of the National Economic Arbitrazh (PAG) No. 1/77 of 25.04.1977, PUG No. 6/1977, poz. 1264.

Sąd Najwyższy – judgement of 21 November 1980, III CZP 50/80, OSN 1981/205 ('Fiat 125p case').

Sąd Najwyższy – judgement of 6 August 1981, I CR 219/81, OSPiKA 1982/7-8, s. 144 ('pin in the cake case') with the commentaries of Nesterowicz (1983) and Szpunar (1982).

Sąd Najwyższy – judgement of 24 July 1981, IV CR 252/81, OSN 1982/84 ('exploding television sets case').

Sąd Najwyższy – judgement of 4 December 1981, IV CR 433/81, OSPiKA 1983, z. 2, item 55, with the commentary of Żuławska.

Sąd Najwyższy – judgement of 26 March 1984, II CR 57/84; OSN 1984/186 ('Wartburg case').

Sąd Najwyższy – judgement of 21 June 1985, I CR 127/85 – unpublished, Gnela 2000: 182 ('sugar beetroot plantation case').

Sąd Najwyższy – judgement of 3 June 1986, II CR 131/86 – unpublished, Gnela 2000: 182 ('poultry farm case').

Sąd Najwyższy – judgement of 26 May 1986, II CR 127/86 – unpublished, Gnela 2000: 182 ('Chemical used on a sugar beetroot farm case').

Sąd Najwyższy – judgement of 1 December 1986, II CR 362/86, Państwo i Prawo 1989/2 (death caused by poisonous substances in an apartment).

Sąd Najwyższy – judgement of 11 December 1987, I CR 257/87, unpublished, with the commentary of C. Żuławska, Nowe Prawo 4/1989 ('defective poultry feeding stuff').

Sąd Najwyższy, *Wytyczne w zakresie wykladni prawa i praktyki sądowej w sprawach rekojmi i gwarancji* (Guidelines on interpretation of law and jurisprudence concerning legal and commercial guarantees) of 30 December 1988, III CZP 48/88, OSNCP 1989/3 poz. 36.

Judgement of the Appeal Court of Katowice of 10 October 1996, I ACr 500/96, Wokanda 2/1998 ('Pepsi Cola bottle cap case').

Judgement of the Court of Appeal of Bialystok of 30 November 2000, I ACa 340/00, OSA 6/01/33 ('chemical spray triggering explosion case').

Judgement of the District Court of Rzeszów of 18 April 2001, Rzeczpospolita 19 April 2001 ('exploding airbag case').

Sąd Najwyższy Izba Cywilna (Civil Chamber) of 14 January 2005, III CK 193/04, *Orzecznictwo Sądu Najwyższego* (Jurisprudence of the Supreme Court) 7 – 8/06 ('causal link – bank debts case').

Uchwała Pełnego Składu Izby Cywilnej (Decision of the Plenary Session of the Civil Chamber) of 17 February 2006, Orzecznictwo Sądu Najwyższego, Izba Cywilna (Jurisprudence of the Supreme Court, Civil Chamber) 2006, No. 7 – 8, I 114, III CZP 84/05 (beginning of the period of limitation for claims).

Sąd Najwyższy – judgement of 10 March 2006, IV CSK 80/05, OSNC Nr 10/2006, poz. 13 ('non-pecuniary damages in the wrong diagnosis case').

Trybunał Konstytucyjny (Constitutional Tribunal) – Decision SK 14/05 of 1 September 2006 (Article 442 on limitation periods for tortious claims unconstitutional); commentary by Bagińska, W. <http://www.legeartis.wpia.uw.edu.pl/glosa2.pdf>.

Western Europe

Austria

Judgement *OGH-Urteil*: 406 94/04h, reported in Lovells' *European Product Liability Review*, Issue 19, June 2005, p. 32.

United Kingdom

Barnett v Chelsea and Kensington Hospital Management Committee [1969] 1 QB 428.

McGee v National Coal Board [1972] 3 All ER 1008.

Galoo v. Bright Grahame Murray [1995] 1 All ER 16.

Foster v Biosil [2000] 59 BMLR 178.

Worsley v Tambrands Limited [2000] PIQR P95.

A v. National Blood Authority [2001] 3All ER 289.

XYZ & Others v Schering Health Care Limited, Organon Laboratories Limited, John Wyeth & Brother Limited [2002] EWHC 1420 (QB).

Fairchild v Glenhaven Funeral Services Ltd and others Fox v Spousal (Midlands) Ltd Matthews v Associated Portland Cement Manufacturers (1978) Ltd and others [2002] All ER (D) 139 (Jun).

Chester v Afshar [2004] UKHL 41 (pt. 2).

Gregg (FC) v Scott [2005] UKHL 2.

Barker v Corus (UK) plc (formerly Saint Gobain Pipelines plc) Murray v British Shipbuilders (Hydrodynamics) Ltd Patterson v Smiths Dock Ltd and others [2006] All ER (D) 23 (May).

Piper v JRI (Manufacturing) Limited [2006] EWCA Civ 1344.

United States of America

Mazetti v. Armour & Co (1913) 135 P 633.

Baxter v. Ford Motor Co (1934) 12 P 2d 409.

Press Releases and Press Interviews

Interview with Andrzej Wróbel, judge of the Polish Supreme Court, 'Sądy odmawiają stosowania prawa wspólnotowego' [Courts Refuse to Apply Community Law] 246 *Gazeta Prawna* (1864) 19 December 2006.

Personal Interviews Conducted by the Author

Interviews with Monika Dobiasova (Czech Ministry of Trade and Industry) conducted via email and telephone in June and September 2003.

Interview with Troy Weeks (Clifford Chance, Budapest) by telephone in September 2003.

Index